Language and the Nuclear Arms Debate: Nukespeak Today

Edited by
Paul Chilton

Frances Pinter (Publishers)
London and Dover, N.H.

© Paul Chilton 1985

First published in Great Britain in 1985 by
Frances Pinter (Publishers) Limited
25 Floral Street, London WC2E 9DS

Published in the United States of America in 1985 by
Frances Pinter (Publishers), 51 Washington Street,
Dover, New Hampshire

All rights reserved. No part of this publication may be
reproduced, stored in a retrieval system, or transmitted in any form,
by any means, electronic, mechanical, photocopying, recording
or otherwise, without the prior permission of the publisher.

British Library Cataloguing in Publication Data
Language and the nuclear arms debate.
    1. Nuclear weapons   2. Propaganda   3. Linguistics
    I. Chilton, Paul
    358'.39   U264
    ISBN 0-86187-524-9

Library of Congress Cataloging-in-Publication Data
Main entry under title:

Language and the nuclear arms debate.

    1. Languages—Political aspects.   2. Discourse
analysis.   3. Mass media and language—United States.
4. Nuclear arms control—United States.   I. Chilton,
Paul A. (Paul Anthony)
P119.3.L32   401'.41   85-9579
ISBN 0-86187-464-1

Typeset by Joshua Associates Ltd, Oxford
Printed and bound in Great Britain by
Biddles Ltd, Guildford and King's Lynn

Language and the Nuclear Arms Debate: Nukespeak Today

Open Linguistics Series

The *Open Linguistics Series*, to which this book makes a welcome contribution, is 'open' in two senses. First, it provides an open forum for works associated with any school of linguistics or with none. Linguistics has now emerged from a period in which many (but never all) of the most lively minds in the subject seemed to assume that transformational-generative grammar—or at least something fairly closely derived from it—would provide the main theoretical framework for linguistics for the foreseeable future. In Kuhn's terms, linguistics had appeared to some to have reached the 'paradigm' stage. Reality today is very different. More and more scholars are examining approaches to language that were formerly scorned for not accepting as central the particular set of concerns highlighted in the Chomskyan approach—such as Halliday's systemic theory, Lamb's stratificational model and Pike's tagememics—while others are developing new or partly new theories. The series is open to all approaches, then—including work in the generativist–formalist tradition.

The second sense in which the series is 'open' is that it encourages works that open out 'core' linguistics in various ways: to encompass discourse and the description of natural texts; to explore the relationships between linguistics and its neighbouring disciplines such as psychology, sociology, philosophy, artificial intelligence, and cultural and literary studies; and to apply it in fields such as education and language pathology.

This book makes a particularly welcome addition to the series, in that it is the first to focus squarely on the relationship of language and discourse to cultural studies: it brings a 'critical linguistics' to bear on texts in order to illuminate what they are doing to us.

Open Linguistics Series Editor
Robin P. Fawcett, The Polytechnic of Wales

Modal Expressions in English, Michael R. Perkins
Text and Tagmeme, Kenneth L. Pike and Evelyn G. Pike
The Semiotics of Culture and Language, eds: Robin P. Fawcett, M. A. K. Halliday, Sydney M. Lamb and Adam Makkai
Functional Approaches to Writing, Barbara Couture
Into the Mother Tongue: A Case Study in Early Language Development, Clare Painter

Contents

List of contributors	viii
Foreword	ix
Introduction Paul Chilton	xiii

Part I	*Language, text, discourse*	1
1	The war against peacemongering: language and ideology Roger Fowler and Tim Marshall	3
1.1	Context	3
1.2	A paradigm: priests, politics and morality	8
1.3	A paradigm: women, reason and passion	14
1.4	Conclusion	20
2	Pragmatics of speeches against the peace movement in Britain: a case study Kay Richardson	23
2.1	Introduction	23
2.2	A toolkit for the inspection of political discourse	24
2.3	Marginalizing dissenters	27
2.4	Margaret Thatcher	27
2.5	Michael Heseltine	39
2.6	John Nott	42
2.7	Conclusions	44
3	Rhetoric of defence in the United States: language, myth and ideology Peter Moss	45
3.1	Introduction	45
3.2	'I' and 'we' in a presidential speech	46
3.3	Popular culture and the discourse of the military	51
3.4	Events and obligation in the world view of Defense Department Reports	57
3.5	Conclusion	62
4	Discourses, texts, readers and the pro-nuclear arguments Gunther Kress	65
4.1	The questions	65

4.2	Institutions, meanings and discourses	67
4.3	Texts and the motivations of texts	73
4.4	Difference and texts	74
4.5	Leaders, discourses and texts	77
4.6	Kinds of text: genre	81
4.7	Strategies	84

Part II *The discourse of deterrence* 89

5 The logic of deterrence: a semiotic and psychoanalytic approach
William Van Belle and Paul Claes 91

5.1	The discourse of deterrence	91
5.2	How to deter?	93
5.3	Why deterrence?	95
5.4	The semiotics of the strategy of deterrence	97
5.5	Deterrence as a narrative (without a happy ending)	98
5.6	The 'imaginary' character of the strategy of deterrence	100

6 Words, discourse and metaphors: the meanings of *deter*, *deterrent* and *deterrence*
Paul Chilton 103

6.1	Deterrence as an object of linguistic inquiry	103
6.2	The verb *deter*	104
6.3	Causes and conditions	111
6.4	Deter, deterrent, deterrence and discourse	113
6.5	Metaphors and morphisms	121

Part III *Aspects of media discourse* 129

7 Getting the message across: a systemic analysis of media coverage of a CND march
Bob Hodge 131

7.1	Introduction	131
7.2	The coverage syntagm and network of influences	132
7.3	War and peace	135
7.4	Class, gender, age and race network	137
7.5	Analysis from text to systems	141

8 Cultural silence: nukespeak in radio discourse: a case study
Peter Moss 147

8.1	Background and political context	147
8.2	Mass media and knowledge	148
8.3	The definition of events in news reports	149
8.4	Control of topic in interviews and discussions	152

9 Disintegrating narrative: an analysis of the television film *The Day After*
Peter Jeffery and Michael O'Toole 167

| 9.1 | Introduction | 167 |

CONTENTS

9.2	Visual syntagms and collapsing paradigms	169
9.3	Semiotics of holocaust	175
9.4	Semiotics of the nuclear family	176
9.5	Conclusion	181

10 Disarming criticism
   Michael O'Toole — 183
   10.1 The rhetoric of balance — 183
   10.2 *The Day After* according to *Newsweek* — 184
   10.3 Editorial rhetoric: *The Australian* — 189
   10.4 Why? — 191

11 'Nothing left to laugh at . . .': humour as a tactic of resistance
   Bob Hodge and Alan Mansfield — 197
   11.1 The role of humour and carnival — 197
   11.2 Semiotics of humour — 199
   11.3 Analysis of anti-nuclear humour — 203

Part IV *Towards a critical linguistics* — 213
12 The concept of context and the theory of action
   Erich Steiner — 215
   12.1 'Critical linguistics' — 215
   12.2 Rhetoric — 215
   12.3 Linguistics — 216
   12.4 Context and action: sociological models — 217
   12.5 Context and action: psychological models — 220
   12.6 A linguistics of context and action — 225
   12.7 The role of theory — 227

Bibliography — 231

Index — 239

List of contributors

Paul Chilton	Department of French Studies, University of Warwick, UK
Paul Claes	Department of Linguistiek, Katholieke Universiteit, Leuven, Belgium
Roger Fowler	School of English and American Studies, University of East Anglia, UK
Bob Hodge	School of Human Communication, Murdoch University, Australia
Peter Jeffery	School of Human Communication, Murdoch University, Australia
Gunther Kress	Faculty of Humanities and Social Sciences, New South Wales Institute of Technology, Australia
Alan Mansfield	School of Human Communication, Murdoch University, Australia
Tim Marshall	School of English and European Studies, University of East Anglia, UK
Peter Moss	Education Department, University of Adelaide, Australia
Michael O'Toole	School of Human Communcation, Murdoch University, Australia
Kay Richardson	The Centre for Communication Studies, University of Liverpool, UK
Erich Steiner	Fachrichtung Anglistik, Universität des Saarlandes, W. Germany
William Van Belle	Department Linguistiek, Katholieke Universiteit, Leuven, Belgium

Foreword

Often we do not recognize the existence of a phenomenon until it has a name. It was Paul Chilton who found the name for one of the most important linguistic phenomena of our time: 'Nukespeak'. It is perhaps significant that it was the NAME that came first, with the study and in turn the writings that so persausively demonstrated its existence following after. Paul Chilton simply mentioned the new word in a letter to a friend, but in due course he found himself being invited to speak on the topic at the Institute of Contemporary Arts in London—on Hiroshima Day, 1981. This, to the best of our knowledge, was the word's public début. It first appeared in print in the autumn of that year (Chilton 1981), then twice in 1982 (Chilton 1982a and b).

It seems, however, that an American writer may have independently hit upon the same name for the same phenomenon at about the same time, because a book with 'Nukespeak' in the title also appeared in 1982 in the USA (Hilgartner et al. 1982). If this was an independent coinage it is a powerful corroboration of both the aptness of the label and our need for it.

What is Nukespeak? The name is, of course, a punning invocation of Orwell's 'Newspeak'. Chilton (1981) reminds us that in his novel *Nineteen Eighty-Four* Orwell describes a centralized, repressive and militarized state in which the rulers attempt to control thought itself by controlling language, by creating new words and grammatical rules:

> The purpose of Newspeak was not only to provide a medium of expression of the world-view and mental habits proper to the devotees [of the dominant ideology], but *to make all other modes of thought impossible* [my emphasis].

Chilton echoes Whorf in suggesting that 'the words and grammar of a language can codify a view of the world (including a view of nuclear arms) and that when people use "their" language, the language itself confirms, reinforces, or even directs people's attitudes and beliefs'. And he goes on to point out that 'if this is so, we are not all that far from Orwell's world of *Nineteen Eighty-Four*, and language does indeed play a subtle role in the direction of thought'.

There is a danger, however, of seeing Nukespeak simply as a matter of vocabulary. It is true that Chilton's writings of 1981–2 gave most space to the significance of the choice of names for weapons of terrible destruction, such as Fat Boy and Trident. But Chilton himself has always been aware of the role of syntax and other aspects of language in the way that Nukespeak does its insidious work. Indeed, the whole of the complex nature of language and its use is brought into play: the non-realization of agency (and so the avoidance of assigning responsibility) when the process is one of killing; the use of modality; everyday words with unnoticed affective connotations; the clever use of negativity to imply that, while some fool might believe the proposition being denied, you, the sensible addressee, will of course not; euphemisms (e.g. *collateral damage* for killing hundreds of thousands of civilian people when a missile aimed at a military installation lands a little off target); *non-sequiturs* linked by logical connectors; various aspects of discourse structure and argument construction (including the 'straw-man' technique), humour that serves to create a knowing in-group, and so forth. This book illustrates something of the immense range and cunning of the way that we are daily subjected to Nukespeak, and it does more than any other that I know of to awaken us to the insidious manner in which it is still being used on us today.

How can we protect ourselves against the effects of Nukespeak? It is not easy. As Chilton points out (1982b):

> Nukespeak is not the product of a concerted propaganda effort to rewrite dictionaries. It is more subtle, more pervasive, and probably unconscious, though none the less effective for that. It would be rash to think that a critical awareness of Nukespeak alone could change anything about the processes that give rise to the military industrial complex and nuclear politics. But it can contribute to change by increasing our awareness of the extent to which Western culture is intertwined with notions of nuclear violence; it can provide a means whereby people can begin to retake control of their own language and exchange their own meanings and values . . . There is certainly no substitute for facts and arguments based on them, but what must be recognized is that there are no 'facts' or 'arguments' in public discussion that are not selected, defined or dressed up by the devious devices of human language.

Paul Chilton, in his introduction, acknowledges that the book has a clear bias against nuclear weapons. How could one correct for this bias? Let me tell you about one attempt to do this—and the lesson it involved. One of my students was planning a practical linguistics project which was to consist of a systemic functional analysis of a particularly significant and dangerous Nukespeak text: Gray and Payne's 'Victory is possible' (1980). I suggested that, in order to counter any possible accusation of bias in the study, it should be matched with a passage of similar register (subject matter, purpose, technicality, mode and tenor) that reflected an ANTI-nuclear position, so that we could compare and evaluate the methods of the pro- and anti-nuclear lobbies. This we did. But to our surprise we found that even the writings of the well-known and deeply committed anti-nuclear writer whose text we had chosen was permeated with the syntax and vocabulary—and so the semantics—of Nukespeak. This is a measure of the extent to which the 'devotees of the dominant ideology' have made all 'other modes of thought', if not 'impossible', at least difficult—so that they require a special and conscious effort. It is thus probable that even the contributors to this book will have used SOME Nukespeak. In such circumstances, where the semiotic system itself is 'biased' against the anti-nuclear writer, a compensatory 'bias' or 'commitment' becomes almost inevitable.[1]

Although all the contributors are opposed to nuclear weapons, they do not necessarily all occupy the same political position. What is of general significance, however, is that they have all chosen to express their positions in the framework of a CRITICAL LINGUISTICS, rather than assume the supposed 'neutrality' of a 'scientific' linguistics. It is a pity, perhaps, that it has not been possible to include the analysis of a text of Soviet Nukespeak, but this should not be taken to imply that the contributors are 'on the Soviet side', and still less that they consider that there is no equivalent phenomenon in Soviet society. Finally, I should point out that there are a number of places in the book where the discourse of the peace movement is indeed examined, and where suggestions are made for more effective practices.

But the essence of the book is the explication of texts. The many rich and varied approaches demonstrated here are not only persuasive in their own right; they will inspire other scholars—including, I hope, undergraduate students—to apply similar methods to other texts, whether from the nuclear arms debate or some other area of equal significance.

Rosedale
April 1985

Robin P. Fawcett

NOTE

1. It may be of interest to say what line of approach was followed in the study of 'Victory is possible' when we found that the original idea for a comparison was not feasible. Instead, a comparison was made with an artificially constructed 'unravelled' version of it—one in which all the covert agents and affected entities were made overt, all processes that involved a euphemism for *kill* were re-expressed to bring in *kill*, all nuances of modality were made explicit, and so on. This was a demanding but highly instructive task. The technique proved very insightful, and I would be interested to hear from others who have tried anything similar.

Introduction

Paul Chilton

For around two thousand years the study of language in Western culture meant not merely, or primarily, the study of grammar, but the study of speech in particular institutionalized settings: courts of law, political assemblies and, later, religious contexts. Rhetoric up till relatively recent times was regarded as a political science. The natural place for the study of speaking was the agora or forum —the public place of assembly used for political debate, trials, elections, buying and selling. The rise of rhetoric in classical Greece was integral with the emergence of democratic forms of social organization, whatever its later restrictions and ossifications. In the late twentieth century, when the electronic media have the potential to reconstitute the agora, it is arguable that a revived practical and critical rhetoric is needed if genuinely democratic forms of participation are to stand a chance.

Consider the following quotation, which is from the *Rhetorica ad Herennium*, one of the most influential handbooks in the rhetorical education of the classical and medieval world. The author's concern is to link standard oratorical arguments and themes ('topics') with types of political purpose and situation.

> Advantage in political deliberation has two aspects: Security and Honour.
>
> To consider Security is to provide some plan or other for ensuring the avoidance of a present or imminent danger. Subheads under Security are Might and Craft. . . Might is determined by armies, fleets, arms, engines of war, recruiting of man power, and the like. Craft is exercised by means of money, promises, dissimulation, accelerated speed, deception, and the other means. . . The Honourable is divided into the Right and the Praiseworthy. . .
>
> . . . If it happens that in a deliberation the counsel of one side is based on the consideration of Security and that of the other on Honour, as in the case of those who, surrounded by Carthaginians, deliberate on a course of action, then the speaker who advocates Security will use the following topics: nothing is more useful than safety; no one can make use of his virtues if he has not based his plans upon safety; not even the gods help those who thoughtlessly commit themselves to danger; nothing ought to be deemed honourable which does not produce safety. One who prefers the considerations of Honour to Security will use the following topics: Virtue ought never to be renounced; either pain, if that is feared, or death, if that is dreaded, is more tolerable than disgrace and infamy; one must consider the shame which will ensue . . . virtue finds it noble to go even beyond death . . . [*Ad Herennium*, III, ii, iii.]

In the rhetoric of the new cold war of the 1970s and 1980s there is indubitably more at stake for humankind. But the structural similarities, the political purposes, the patterns of thought are strikingly and disturbingly familiar. Einstein once said, 'The power set free from the atom has changed everything, except our ways of thought'. And our ways of public discourse. What we have in the passage above is a partial list of the recurrent arguments, which, *mutatis mutandis*, any state, empire, alliance or bloc might be expected to deploy when seeking to preserve, define, and consolidate its boundaries or sphere of influence. Surrounded by Carthaginians, shall we use the topics of Peace through strength, Security is the first duty of the state, Better dead than red? The point about rhetorical analysis is that it makes it clear that these slogans are indeed selected from a stock of topics.

Modern linguistics, even in its sociolinguistic forms, has generally suffered from agoraphobia—fear of the agora. Yet in order to give an account of language in use, with which linguistics is increasingly concerned, the political context has to be confronted, if only because of the volume of politically motivated public discourse. The contributions to this present book are in various ways all prompted by this consideration, and all are the product of a peculiar historical moment. In the late 1970s government agencies and their ramifications used the electronic and print media to assert more and more stridently that the Carthaginians were coming. Some salient aspects of this complex period are worth recalling. World recession, the post-Vietnam resurgence of America, the ever-increasing technological sophistication of the military-industrial complex, confrontation and even war by proxy in the Third World: this was the back-cloth. Particular events signalled the frightening acceleration of the nuclear arms race and East–West confrontation: NATO's 1979 'modernization' decision, the Soviet invasion of Afghanistan, the repression of Solidarity in Poland, the Falklands/Malvinas episode with its militarist and nationalistic rhetoric, American interventions in Latin America, the Soviet attack on a Korean airliner in 1983—an event that led to new depths of 'evil empire' rhetoric. Most significant and symbolic of all were the 'deployment' of Soviet SS20s and of American cruise and Pershing missiles, the research and development of Trident, the MX missile system (later dubbed 'Peacekeeper') and space-based 'Star Wars' systems: all these have led to widespread anxiety, with linguistic reflexes in intensified hegemonic and counter-hegemonic discourse.

These, then, are the broad historical circumstances in which the studies included in this book were conceived. It would be idle to pretend that this was not a biased volume. All contributors, whatever their finer political differences, are opponents of nuclear arms and the arms race, and stand as dissidents with respect to the official discourses that have legitimated nuclear arms. Those who would wish to hear the other side need only read, view or listen to voluminous output from both the relevant government departments and predominantly, though not exclusively, from the media. To many linguists, however, the very admission of political involvement will imply an abandonment of objective scientific standards. A full reply to such a charge would have to be long and complex. But it would for a start have to challenge at least the relevance of notions derived from the physical (or 'natural') sciences to the whole of language study. Even if Chomsky is correct, and there are natural, genetically innate universals of language which are susceptible of objective, scientific study, there still remain socio-political questions to be asked about historically contingent usage and text production—questions frequently raised by Chomsky himself in his political writings. A reply of a different kind would argue that irrespective of the status of our 'science', at a time when natural, social and cognitive scientists are massively implicated in armaments research and development, linguists who oppose such developments have an obligation to speak on the concerns of their discipline—in the same way as concerned physicists, lawyers, architects, medical workers, and other professional groups have done.

A project based on historical circumstances runs risks. There is for example in this book a diversity of approach that tends inevitably towards inconsistency and incompleteness. This is not the place to seek definitive definitions of discourse, language, ideology, or the elusive boundaries between competence and performance, semantics and pragmatics, or any other theoretical issue. Yet there are certain serious and far-reaching assumptions common to the contributors to this book. The first is that humans are more than talking heads: rather, the capacity for speech is interconnected with the life of individuals in social formations. The second is the recognition that the text is the crucial unit in such a perspective. The third, that the production and reception of text-meanings is dependent on the distribution of power in industrial and post-industrial societies. Fourthly, it is recognized that an interdisciplinary approach is required to grasp the interaction of language behaviour with other semiotic systems.

There is another risk to which a historically based critical linguistics or discourse analysis will resign itself: it might itself become redundant. Pro-nuclear discourse is not, however, likely to disappear at the behest of linguists and discourse analysts. It is likely to disappear when the threat of extermination disappears along with nuclear weapons themselves. However, such a circumstance will come about only through human action, and it is not the least of the roles of the linguist to point out that speech itself is a form of action.

This book, then, is concerned in varied ways with the relationship between specimen texts, be they spoken or written, and the historical circumstances of their production. There is here a general question for anyone occupied with the phenomenon of language, although it is particularized in the present collection to those historical circumstances in which humans have witnessed and participated in the unprecedented creation of the means of their own destruction. That such a disturbing tendency should result in a large quantity of texts related in content and perhaps communicative function is not surprising. We tend to talk most about what most concerns us. But in all the texts that surround the nuclear phenomena are there systematic regularities? And if so, how do we describe and explain them? To pose such questions is to propose the existence of regularities that in some sense and to some degree determine the meanings of texts.

In general terms one might imagine two ways of accounting for the regular occurrence of similar textual meanings, including those one might judge erroneous or delusive. On the one hand, one could blame 'language'—either human language in general or some particular language. Such a view should perhaps not be too promptly written off as a logophobia in thrall to the myth of Babel. It is not in itself irrational to speculate that some components of a language, or even language itself, could become dysfunctional at certain historical conjunctures, for some purposes, for some groups. . . . After all, few would find it odd that natural language does not work well for the calculus or quantum theory or propositional logic, or that hierarchically differentiated pronoun systems should become irrelevant to a changed social structure. The crucial point is that the semiotic capacities of humans make it possible to create alternative, supplementary and modified systems. On the other hand, one could explain the recurrence of textual meanings by assuming the existence of more general patterns of behaviour governing selections of meaning from a language, which would then be seen as neutral. Between these two extremes, however, one need not necessarily exclude all communication. It would be compatible with the second view, for instance, to think of a culture's patterns of behaviour—values, beliefs, common-sense 'knowledge', and descriptions—being to some extent stabilized (at least in the lexicon), while still maintaining that textual meanings can in principle (general regulatory patterns of behaviour aside, that is) be freely created.

These are abstract and speculative matters which it is inappropriate to pursue further here. But one further point arises from such questions that is relevant to the contributions in this volume. If one attempts to comprehend regularities in text meanings in terms of general constraints on behaviour, it is necessary to take account of historical conditions. And this in turn implies a consideration of the practices, linguistic and otherwise, by which specific ways of talking and writing, or specific unavoidable features of a language, come to be established in relative stasis. This brings us to the term 'discourse', which is used by the contributors to this volume in two broad (individually varying) ways.

In the first sense the term 'discourse' designates representations of the social and physical universe that are ideological in nature. These can perhaps be thought of as abstract structures postulated in order to account for regularities across a range of semiotic behaviours. They can usefully be termed 'macro-discourses'. In the second sense 'discourse' designates not only the local organization of talk and writing to achieve local referential coherence, but also (a) the local organization of lexis and syntax in such a way as to highlight certain meanings and obfuscate others, and (b) the organization of the talking/listening, writing/reading roles of interactants in such a way that those roles endorse the distribution of power and status. This we can call 'micro-discourse', and expect it to involve many and various practices that correspond to such distinctions as 'register', 'genre', 'institution', 'situation', 'activity', etc. That the term has these two senses is not necessarily unfortunate; indeed, it is no coincidence. For the implicit assumption is that macro- and micro-discourses are reciprocally related: macro-discourses are required, for instance, for the understanding processes, and micro-discourse practices are in part responsible (and note the moral force of the word) for the selection and promotion of macro-discourses. It is also possible to see an analogy—let us for the moment say it is no more than that—between macro-discourses and Halliday's 'ideational function', and between his 'interpersonal' function and micro-discourse practices. Finally, in this connection, debate over terminology is symptomatic of the early days of conceptual reorientations: category distinctions should emerge from inquiry, not predetermine it.

The papers included in Part I of the present book reflect this rather complex and relatively unresearched conception of language in use. They are concerned with the interaction of texts with their particular historical moment, and at the same time with more stable patterns of thought. Roger Fowler and Tim Marshall, in the first chapter, raise the question of whether there exists a unitary set of linguistic practices centering on the nuclear arms issue—is there a 'register', say, that we might term 'Nukespeak'? They conclude, however, that discourse about nuclear matters has implicated several distinguishable sets of 'propositions' which they term 'paradigms'. An important part of their argument is that such 'paradigms' do not necessarily refer explicitly to nuclear-related referents, but are implicitly linked to them. Hence, when the nuclear issue is in crisis there are ideological ripples that require management of discourse in those channels which government has the power to control (pamphlets and propaganda) or to influence (mass media). These and other points are examined by Fowler and Marshall by means of an examination of public texts produced in the period April–May 1983—a pre-election period in which the installation of American-operated cruise missiles was a sensitive issue and simultaneously led to discourse about the boundaries of religion, morality, war, peace, gender and rationality.

In Chapter 2 Kay Richardson examines texts from approximately the same critical phase of British politics, but while Fowler and Marshall point to general normative principles (akin to what I term above 'macro-discourses'), Richardson's aim is to examine the pragmatics of particular speeches, using a framework of analysis derived from the work of Goffman and Grice. Interestingly, however, broader sets of assumptions (in particular assumptions about morality and war, as discussed in Chapter 1) play an interacting role in the micro-level processes of text understanding. This chapter makes it clear that ideological discourse is far from being a straightforward conceptual transplant. The diversity of audiences and the selectivity of the media ensure complications and even rejections. This means that, for instance, the marginalizing of nuclear dissenters in prime-ministerial speeches is a crucial but hazardous rhetorical task, in which ambiguity, irony and chains of potential inference are essential. Certain speeches of the present Minister of Defence and his predecessor are compared with those of their leader, and significant pragmatic differences discovered within an overall ideological concern to establish the ethical bounds that define the antinuclear lobby as the unrighteous.

One method by which governments legitimate themselves and their policies is to create, through language and also through other semiotic means, a compatibility between policies and relatively stable stereotypes and narrative syntagms already present (probably with an existing ideological function) in traditional and popular culture. Peter Moss, in Chapter 3, investigates such 'myths' and their various mediations in several specific situations. The use of pronouns in American presidential speeches, together with invocations of American urban and rural culture, thus play a role in the marginalizing of dissent—a parallel with some of the findings expressed in Chapters 1 and 2. In the more circumscribed context of magazines designed for the armed forces readership, traditional pioneering frontier 'myths' combine with more recent popular culture (the massively marketed 'Star Wars' lore), with the apparent purpose of familiarizing and assimilating technically incomprehensible weapons systems. In the naming of weapons themselves 'mythical' patterns are discernible. Further, these constructions of American national identity correspond to a 'myth' of America's world role. While the 'myths' expressed in the speeches, magazines and weapons inventories depend largely (though not exclusively) on lexical choices and metaphorical processes combining different areas of cultural 'knowledge', Moss's account indicates that the world view of the Defense Department is also (and perhaps predominantly) implied in the syntax of its official reports, which he analyses by utilizing an adapted version of the systemic-functional description of English clauses.

Chapter 4 concludes Part I with a return to two key issues that emerge during the course of the preceding chapters. One concerns the notion of large-scale ('macro-') ideological structures, the other whether and to what degree the texts mediating them are accepted or resisted by hearers and readers. With respect to the second, it is central to the view of language developed here by Gunther Kress that language is itself a form of social action, not merely of expression and exchange, and, furthermore, that the 'reading' or 'consuming' of text is as active as 'producing' it. The kind of potential for resistant interpretations demonstrated minutely by Richardson in Chapter 2 is thus placed by Kress in a theoretical statement on the nature of language in use. This should not be taken to imply that resistance to nuclear arms can be effectively linguistic: but an understanding of the interrelationships between linguistic, social, political and economic actions is relevant to such resistance. With respect to the first question, Kress, like Fowler and Hodge, adopts the notion of 'systematically organized modes of talking' about aspects of reality, but, following Foucault, terms these simply 'discourses'. They have two major properties, illustrated already in Chapter 1, and now stated in general terms. First, they stipulate what it is possible and not possible to say and do—a formulation, incidentally, that one might confront with Halliday's notion of the meaning potential of language, and the way in which it may be strongly determined by a given type of social context. And secondly, they tend to 'colonize' other areas of social life in competition with differing discourses. Kress illustrates the multiple occurrence of often conflicting discourse in texts of different 'genres' (a category Kress distinguishes from 'discourse') and from different sides of the argument: a propaganda pamphlet issued by the Campaign for Defence and Multilateral Disarmament; a Socialist Workers Party handbill; a diocesan news-sheet; a rally speech by a peace movement 'leader'; a local peace group newsletter; and a pro-Conservative press report. The point, however, is not just to demonstrate the operation of (macro-) discourses, but to show how dominant discourses can be 'interrupted' in resistant 'readings', and to give indications as to how such a goal might be pursued. Kress's conclusion in this respect is important (and of course contestable): it is, essentially, that the discourses that bear on the nuclear issue cohere around a cold-war representation of the Soviet Union which requires special analytical attention.

Part II, then, begins some of the work of dismantling this particular ideological construct, but it should in no way be construed, any more than the rest of this book, as an apologia for corresponding Soviet constructs. We focus in this part of the book on what is the most rationalized and most mystified area of cold-war discourse: the 'theory' of deterrence. This is a notion elaborated by military planners in the West (the Soviet strategic philosophy being the object of much debate) following the realization that atomic weapons had no military use in the sense in which military action was then conceived. The notion of deterrence is, and has long been, under strain, partly in consequence of technological developments, partly perhaps in consequence of an inherent culture-based difficulty concerning the concept of a weapon that is neither use nor ornament. The interpretation broadly adopted by the contributors to Part II—which is an interpretation currently being explored by some workers in several peace research institutes—is this. 'Deterrence doctrine' is not, as professional strategists would have us believe, an objective, even scientific description of and prediction about things as they are. Rather it is indeed a 'doctrine'—a teaching or, rather, a dogma, with ideological, psychological and cultural underpinnings.

In order to pursue this line, one needs to consider not only linguistic semiosis, but also other sign systems that operate in conjunction with language. In Chapter 5 William Van Belle and Paul Claes argue that the documents and declarations of official NATO doctrine are grounded not, as their originators would claim, on a rational, neutral logic, but on 'a way of reasoning that has a more or less narrative character'. They go further. After describing the literal surface and the claims of the orthodoxy (which depend on the magical modal trio, capability, intention and credibility), they analyse its psycho-logic in terms of closed systems of inference in which axioms are unquestioned, in terms of culturally entrenched stereotypes and stories, and finally in terms of psychopathological relations between persons. According to this unusual and intellectually provocative interpretation, not only is deterrence doctrine related to (legitimated by, or even generated by) stereotypical story patterns that can be elucidated through the narrative theory of A. J. Greimas, but also, and more provocatively, the destructive spiral into which the superpowers have been locked can be elucidated through Lacan's psychoanalytic notion of the paradoxical 'mirror relationship'. Whether one regards this as an explanation or as an illuminating analogy, Van Belle and Claes provide a perspective on 'deterrence' which sees it as a semiotic behaviour—and one for which both sides in the cold war are responsible. Their general conclusion is that the 'theory' itself is an intrinsic part of the superpower behaviour that it claims to interpret and control, from which it follows (in their argument) that any resolution of the bloc conflict must include also the discourse of deterrence in its purview.

As Van Belle and Claes point out, the word *deterrence*, with its complex of causative, intentional and instrumental associations, is itself central to the discourse. Chapter 6, therefore, undertakes a semantic investigation of the verb *deter* and its derived forms in English. This raises an issue that is of major importance for the interrelations between 'language' and sociopolitical processes. And this in turn has important implications for the way in which certain branches of semantic theory are presently conducted within linguistics. What is at issue is the extent to which word meanings can be specified truth-conditionally, in terms of necessarily analytic entailments, and independently of stored knowledge of other kinds. The position assumed is that no clear distinction can easily be made between semantic and pragmatic factors—although it may APPEAR to speakers that words have inherent meaning independently of systems of belief and knowledge of various kinds. This is not necessarily to imply that ALL word meanings are ideologically determined in any significantly specific way; but it is to claim that SOME are, and that *deter, deterrent* and *deterrence* currently mean what they do mean in virtue of ideologically conditioned 'knowledge' that constitutes political realities. It is implicit in this that it is insufficient merely to speak of 'background knowledge'. Some semantic properties of the words in question are shared with others in the same lexical field and express our culture's conceptualizations at a very general level (actions, causation, mental states, for example). Other semantic properties, however, appear to depend on more specific knowledge bases that are concerned primarily with social and political realities, or rather the constitution of such realities. While the latter are perhaps comparable with Fowler's and Marshall's 'belief systems' and 'paradigms' and the 'discourses' of Kress and other contributors, I have interpreted them broadly in terms of the concept of 'frame' (and its congeners 'script', 'schema', etc.), which has its origins in cognitive science. This also makes it possible to elucidate further an aspect of the use of *deter* in texts: namely, the fact that not only is the word a 'trigger' for a frame of meanings about cold-war power relations, but that this frame frequently co-occurs with other frames —those to do with the law, education and social roles, for example. It is argued that the relationship between such frames can be thought of as metaphoric, and the important role of metaphor in deterrence thinking and cold-war reasoning in general is considered. If there is anything in this, then one implication is that deterrence discourse has deep conceptual and cultural roots that give it, to put it at its lowest, considerable stability in the population at large. Strictly speaking this does not necessarily mean that deterrence does not work. But, and this is the essential point of Chapters 5 and 6 taken together, it does not necessarily either guarantee its functional adequacy in managing a material situation in which two military powers reciprocally provoke one another's potential for unimaginable destruction. Russell, Einstein and other scientists put it thus in their 1955 Manifesto: 'We have to learn to think in a new way'.

The basic theoretical argument of the volume thus far—if one may attribute a collective convergence to a number of chapters contributed by concerned individuals—has been (a) that samples of text indicate ideologically structured (and sometimes competing) meanings, whether we call them 'paradigms', 'frames', 'discourses' or 'macro-discourses', and (b) that also the language resource itself is conceivably ideologically affected. To investigate fully such a view of language one would have to explicate the social and political processes by which (a) speakers and readers come to establish and acquire systematic text-meaning tendencies, and (b) the ways in which lexical items, for example, are promoted to a commonly learned lexicon. It is possible to take an idealistically pluralist view of this process—language and utterances are a vast semiotic free market in which all interests have an equally free opportunity and the semiotic outcome is somehow in natural equilibrium for society as a whole. To some extent such a picture is true for the media-dominated capitalist democracies; but it contains distortions also. Power differentials exist in access to media, in what meanings are favoured by them, in the degree of dialogue permitted. This is not surprising, for power differentials clearly exist in person-to-person exchanges also, differentials which regulate speaking turns, rights of and obligations to reply, and so forth—although the role of status and power in such matters is usually naturalized out of existence in standard ethnographic accounts of 'discourse'. It is, however, at this level of discourse ('micro-discourse') that ideological (macro-)discourses compete and come to dominate; and it is with the practices of discourse management in this sense that Part III is in general concerned.

The reciprocal relationship between macro- and micro-discourse is evident in Chapter 7, where Bob Hodge writes of both 'discourse strategies' (in general terms these would include rhetorical devices, lexical and syntactic choices, turn-taking options and tactics), and of 'different discourses from a range of social positions' (the abstract ideological schemata of assumptions and values). Hodge's aim is in fact to show how general ideological patterns are realized in the talking and writing practices of the mass media in such a way as to construct a preferred picture of events. The events in question are the London CND rally of 1981. Using the informal study of these events by the Birmingham Centre for Contemporary Cultural Studies, Hodge explicates and generalizes their findings in order to outline a model for the way such events are at the moment typically mediated. The model itself is an idiosyncratic adaptation of Hallidayan system-network and macro-function theory. Like Kress's account, it allows in principle for variable 'readings' dependent on class, race, gender, etc., and gives the notion of 'meaning potential' an explanation in terms of ideology. It is by thus mapping out the structured options in media communication that Hodge points to the possibilities for resisting dominant discourses (in both the 'macro' and the 'micro' sense) that seek to promote specific meanings for such domains as 'war', 'peace', 'protester', etc., in interaction with specific representations of class, gender and race.

In an ideal totalitarian state, control of the media will involve the exclusion and inclusion of information by external fiat, and there will be little evidence of competing and competitive discourses. In Western democratic societies, on the other hand, where 'freedom of the press' is an ideological given, control probably operates through a greater exploitation of the micro-discourse potential peculiar to each medium. If this occurs to the advantage of government and the required (macro-)discourses become predominant, then there is simply no need for censorship. Peter Moss in Chapter 8 shows that radio discourse constructs approved versions of reality in the Australian context, where commercial and public radio networks flourish and give all the appearance of freely mediated dialogue. Two theoretical frameworks are drawn upon by Moss in his analysis of one particular media event (a demonstration against a uranium-mining installation). In one approach, adapting concepts and methods from systemic-functional grammar, Moss indicates how lexical and grammatical choices in news reports favour a particular interpretation of events. The other approach is sensitive to the discourse structure of programmes, and in particular to the potential limitations of talk-back programmes, where one would expect in principle that alternative views of the world could be formulated.

As the revealing transcripts show, programme hosts often have the power to attempt to neutralize alternative interpretations, to control topics, and indeed to silence dissenting voices. Moss makes clear, however, as do other contributors, that there is always risk in such attempts: they may none the less fail to prevent 'wrong' interpretations from being disseminated.

The interpretative control of media performances may of course be more diffuse. In the case of television the potential for radio-type talk-back is limited for various reasons, not all of them technological. This means that press review and commentary can in theory play an ideological corrective role. It also helps to explain the sensitivity of television companies in the matter of 'balance' within and between programmes: images do not lend themselves to talk-back, and thus to control by hosts, interviewers or question-masters (though it is true that camera work can comment ideologically even on discussion programmes). While the anti-nuclear lobby has sometimes succeeded in screening important documentary and other programmes, there have been revealing cases of censorship or near-censorship. The most notorious are the BBC's early refusal to show Peter Watkins' *War Game*, the long delay over John Pilger's *Truth Game*, the confusion over Edward Thompson's invitation to give the Dimbleby Lecture, and the fact that Nicholas Humphrey's Bronowski Lecture apparently happened as a result of an embarrassing oversight. It is quite possible that genre is a factor here, and it is of interest that the American drama-documentary *The Day After* was shown with rather less fuss, as was the British film *Threads*.

Chapters 9 and 10 deal with different aspects of *The Day After* as a mass communicative event. Peter Jeffery and Michael O'Toole show that the film adapted the documentation of nuclear disaster not just to the soap-opera genre, but also thereby to American cultural 'myths', which are related to the patterns of popular culture examined in an earlier chapter. Perhaps that was the price of its acceptability, but the authors of Chapter 9 argue in their analysis of both the visual and the verbal semiotics of the film that the 'myths' are in the process 'deconstructed' and 'disintegrated'. This is clearly open to debate, and is perhaps another instance of the ambiguity and indeterminacy of mass messages. If so, then the ideological role of press reviews debunking anti-nuclear films is obvious: they produce 'balance' in the wider communicative situation. In Chapter 10 Michael O'Toole describes the linguistic devices by means of which, in one review, *The Day After* was, as he puts it, 'disarmed'. But it is also the claim of this chapter that this is not an isolated instance of an isolated, freely expressed opinion: O'Toole compares the 'balanced' review style with similar, 'balanced' stylistic peculiarities in other instances of commentary on the anti-nuclear movement, and proposes that they are characteristic of a generalized ideological stance.

A case can surely be made for the joke as a genre in its own right, and one that is transmitted not only by all the electronic and print media but also, and with extraordinary rapidity, in face-to-face interaction. Irish jokes, black jokes, women jokes . . . all show us this. Soviet and nuclear jokes also spread, as comedians Everett, Reagan and Hope have shown with their variants of the 'Let's bomb Russia' joke. But the function of humour is complex, and can be used by the opposition also, as Bob Hodge and Alan Mansfield demonstrate in Chapter 11. In so doing they relate this linguistically neglected topic to certain major themes of this book. First, the interaction of language with other systems of meaning: Hodge and Mansfield not only take into account the visual signs of cartoons, but develop a psychoanalytical framework, based on a reinterpretation of Freud that makes jokes social as well as psychological. Second, the plurality of competing discourses in various genres: it is argued in this chapter that knowledge of established discourses (others might term them frames, etc.) has to be postulated for a linguistic account of humour, although modality, the importance of which has been seen also in Part III, is also deeply implicated. Third, the element of interpretative risk: the anti-nuke jokes analysed by Hodge and Mansfield are often complex and ambiguous, serving devious psychological purposes. There is, finally, a broader connection between the concept of humour and the anti-nuclear movement. Like Fowler and Marshall in Chapter 1, Hodge and Mansfield refer to the work of Mikhail Bakhtin, for whom humour is the form of the popular carnival tradition (feasts of fools, saturnalia . . .), a form of potential subversion, and a form of solidarity amongst the members of marginal groups. One interesting aspect of the peace movement is the way that its diversity has fostered, along with libertarian, pacifist and anarchist attitudes and modes of organization, corresponding modes of exchanging and creating meanings which official discourse has found either nasty or naïve or both. There is a conflict here, not only between macro-discourses (values, beliefs, interpretations), but also between the actual ways in which micro-discourses are conducted: both have to do with the way people relate and combine.

It is, however, the purpose of this book to point to such themes—not to exhaust them. Its major task is to illustrate a way of dealing with language in an academic context that does not occlude its conditions of use. It is therefore with Erich Steiner's wide-ranging theoretical paper that the book concludes— a paper in which the main question addressed is precisely that of relating linguistic description to linguistic situation in such a way that it will make sense to criticize language practices just as one criticizes social and political practices. There are numerous ways in which a critical linguistics might be formulated, and much remains to be done. Steiner indicates one point of origin, and pursues one possible line of development. The major European tradition of rhetorical analysis certainly favours a situational and ultimately critical linguistics. How can such an orientation be allied with the dominant traditions of recent linguistics with their roots in philosophy and philosophical logic? Language, situation and action are the crucial concepts requiring definition and linkage, and Steiner reviews work in the fields not only of lingustics, but also of sociology and cognitive psychology.

Whether linguists like it or not, they are increasingly involved in the 'information explosion', as their increasing role in the research and development of information technology testifies. It is not the explosion of information that will cause the destruction that has become so much a source of anxiety in our time. But conflicts begin in words and the means of destruction can be legitimized by words. Information cannot kill, but a naïve neglect of the ideological determination of what may be called 'information' can do us no good.

Part I
Language, text, discourse

1 The war against peacemongering: language and ideology

Roger Fowler and Tim Marshall
University of East Anglia, UK

1.1 CONTEXT

One aspect of nuclear discourse has been fittingly labelled 'Nukespeak'—an allusion to Orwell's 'Newspeak' in *Nineteen Eighty-Four* and to his general views on political language, including those expressed in 'Politics and the English Language' and those embodied in his concept of 'Duckspeak'.[1] Nukespeak in a restricted sense is not our main concern here, but we will sketch it as an introduction to other kinds of linguistic practice.

One characteristic of Nukespeak is EUPHEMISM. The 'cruise' of 'cruise missiles' connotes smooth, comfortable travel; more generally, the word belongs to the world of holiday-making. 'Modernize' is used to refer to provisions of the latest 'generation' of nuclear weapons: 'Cruise missiles simply modernise a capability NATO already has.'[2] Since these euphemistic processes seek to assign pleasant associations to horrific concepts, in extreme cases they bring reversal of meaning. The American MX missile is called 'Peacekeeper'—not only a false description, but also an instance of doublethink. The rulers of NATO in 1984, like the rulers of Ingsoc in *Nineteen Eighty-Four*, can tolerate the contradiction that war is peace and peace is war.

A second characteristic of Nukespeak is JARGON, including bureaucratic gobbledegook (cf. Duckspeak):

> The main point that should be understood is that both sides now have, and will continue to have, invulnerable second-strike forces, and that with those invulnerable second-strike forces it is inevitable, or virtually inevitable, that the employment by one side of its forces against the cities of the other side in an all-out strike will immediately bring a counter-strike against its own cities.[3]

Then there is a quasi-technical jargon in which phrases are reduced to acronyms. The military policy of 'mutual assured destruction' becomes 'MAD'; 'Strategic Arms Limitation Talks' are 'SALT'; 'confidence and security building measures' are 'CSBMs'. Missiles, their parts and their accessories attract this jargon: 'The GLCM shelter concept divides each structure into three cells which each hold two TELs or LCCs'.[4] Such jargon is common to technical registers, not peculiar to Nukespeak; its function is to give an air of technical or scientific authority while making the concepts referred to inaccessible to non-specialists: it is thus mystificatory in aim and power-building in effect.

In sociolinguistic terms, Nukespeak is a REGISTER: a specialized variety of usage with its own range of meanings and of contexts for use.[5] It is a salient mode of discourse, for one of its principal functions is to adorn its users with the badge of expertise. We now intend to examine some linguistic practices which are less easy to spot. Like Orwell, we believe that linguistic practices shape and alter ideology or consciousness; for these purposes, invisibility of the practice is an asset.

A dominant group manages its own maintenance and reproduction by a variety of means. The government of a state can wage wars; or pass legislation and cause its agents to administer it; or manipulate the economy or the workforce or the education system, and so on. Hand-in-hand with these direct exercises of power go some very complex ideological practices. It is in the interests of a government that the governed population should represent reality in terms of favourable belief-systems, that is to say, systems of ideas which tend to legitimate the direct actions of the government. These beliefs are not necessarily formulated consciously and then promulgated in the population in a conspiratorial manner; indeed, the ruling group may not be aware of the structure of its ideology (or it may be different from what is asserted). What we try to do in this paper is bring to the surface certain official belief-systems (which we call PARADIGMS) and suggest how language operates in mediating these paradigms.

The nuclear issue, and the language it gives rise to, is a major instance of such processes. We will hypothesize various parts of the paradigm through which the British Government conceptualizes its relationship with nuclear armaments (e.g. the proposition that 'nuclear deterrence' is an exclusively political and technical, nor moral, matter). This paradigm, we argue, produces crises of relationship with other groups. We shall illustrate how discourse—particularly in government publications and in the newspapers—is used in attempts to manage these crises.

An important point is that the propositions concerned are very abstract, so they underlie language which is not necessarily about nuclear issues. Thus people can experience attitudes within many ordinary branches of their everyday lives which implicitly relate to nuclear issues but appear to involve quite other topics. An instance of this process is the new £1 coin which bears on its rim an arcane Latin inscription: *Decus et tutamen*. This legend is in fact an incomplete quotation from the poet Virgil: '*Decus et tutamen in armis*' ('a glory and defence in war'); the military reference has been deleted. Without a knowledge of Latin (or indeed of Virgil, since we need to complete the quotation) people are unlikely to realize that we carry daily on our persons a little bit of the Bomb. We suggest, then, that attitudes towards good housekeeping in everyday life intersect with our attitudes towards defence expenditure or even military considerations. The link is symbolized by the fact that the official defence policy (and some of its consequences in the Falklands) is literally inscribed on the coin of the realm. When the coin was introduced its durability was put at thirty years by the Treasury: thus it is not only the Bomb, as politicians say, that 'has kept the peace for thirty years'—it will also be our present and future attitudes towards producing and distributing wealth.

Discourse analysis is essentially historical: language cannot be interpreted without understanding what is going on in a particular social and political context. We studied official and party-political statements on nuclear arms in the period April–May 1983, and within that period we made a detailed study of all British daily newspapers for the last two weeks of April. Our central interest was the management of the nuclear issue by the Conservative Government, and the role of the Press in mediating the paradigms which the Government and the Conservative Party were working with. Two longer-term features of this situation were significant for the discourse of this period: the Government's commitment to what they called 'deploying' (i.e. receiving and installing) cruise missiles by the end of 1983; and the imminent General Election in Britain (which returned the Conservatives overwhelmingly on 9 June 1983, a date not yet announced in April). It is relevant that the Government's popularity owed a great deal to aggressively nationalistic foreign policies and to their practical military enactment in the Falklands conflict twelve months earlier. Meanwhile, 'cruise' had provoked a high level of public resistance to the Government's nuclear policies. The women's peace camp was well established outside RAF Greenham Common, the intended site for cruise missiles. The Campaign for Nuclear Disarmament was in its most active phase since the late 1950s. The Labour Party was going to fight the election with unilateral disarmament as one plank of its platform—an ineffective stance as it turned out, but in April one of the apparent threats to the Government.

The fortnight we studied turned out to be an extremely busy phase in nuclear activity and nuclear discourse. Apart from preparations for the development of cruise, and the protest at Greenham, there was also an intense war of words between the Government and CND; still at home the Sizewell nuclear power station enquiry reopened; abroad, President Reagan was having difficulty getting his MX missile budget approved; but France committed itself to increased expenditure on nuclear weapons. We decided to concentrate on certain clusters of British domestic events, and the following diary summarizes what seemed significant from our perspective. We concentrated on the period Monday 18 April–Saturday 30 April 1983, but have noted one or two relevant events which occurred just before and after our chosen period.

The difficulties of 'drawing the line' may be instructive for further studies of this kind. We have not mentioned scores of 'small' incidents—'demos', court cases, speeches—because we have concentrated on some central themes. Thus we perhaps under-represent the proliferation of activities. We also could not study the paradigms, themes and images in non-nuclear discourse; that is a significant limitation and in a fuller study we would have wanted to look at least at the discourse of leisure, of home-building, of finance. Finally, we would have liked to study the Government's anti-CND activities in the context of their repressive policies towards the professions, education, trade unions, young people, the unemployed, etc. We feel sure that a constant system of paradigms could be shown to underlie all these practices; but such a study would be on a vast scale.

Calendar of events and reports

April

1–2—Large-scale Easter demonstrations by CND at Burghfield nuclear weapons factory, Greenham Common and Aldermaston.

12 —Row broke over threat by Dr Gerald Vaughan, Consumer Affairs Minister, to withhold £3m. of the £6m. annual grant to the National Association of Citizens' Advice Bureaux, pending inquiry into political bias and into financial accountability. (Vaughan was MP for Reading South; Joan Ruddock, Chairperson of CND, worked in Reading CAB.)

17 —CND national council resolved to canvass in marginal constituencies.

18 —Announcement that Michael Heseltine, Defence Secretary, had persuaded US Defense Secretary Caspar Weinberger to withdraw from Oxford Union debate with E. P. Thompson.

19 —Reconvention of public inquiry into proposed Sizewell B nuclear power station.

20 —Demonstration in public gallery of House of Commons by nine women during debate on a proposed referendum about the siting of cruise missiles.
—TV screening of film on the effect of nuclear strike on London, 'A Guide to Armageddon'.

21 —Home Office minister Patrick Mayhew confirmed that Home Secretary was considering making demonstrators pay for their own policing.
—Leeds City Council published a booklet, 'Leeds and the Bomb', forecasting massive casualties.
—£1 coin went into circulation.
—TV programme, 'The War about Peace' (Max Hastings).

22 —British nuclear test in Nevada: 'Britain's baby A-blast' (*Sun*, 23 April).
—Heseltine sent a letter to Conservative candidates in marginal constituencies alleging that CND leaders were extreme socialists or communists.
—Vaughan retracted comments on Joan Ruddock and CAB; full grant still in doubt.

23 —Ruddock accused Heseltine of smear.
—'Rent-the-police plan to curb demos dropped' (*Guardian*).
—Kissinger and Heseltine in TV 'debate' proposing deployment of cruise and Pershing missiles in Europe.
—TV programme, 'Nuclear France'.

24 —Test of Pershing missile in New Mexico.
—*The Sunday Times* reported American study claiming that early atomic tests in New Mexico and Nevada had affected the IQ of children.
—*The Observer* reviewed Raymond Briggs's anti-nuclear play, *When the Wind Blows*.

25 —Heseltine's letter main topic in newspapers.
—Reports and complaints about Women's Institute's plan to 'modernize'.
—Alternative Defence Commission published its report, *Defence without the Bomb*.
—Announcement in House of Lords that policing of Easter demonstrations cost £252,000.

—Dr Vaughan gave an assurance that CAB funds 'would not dry up' pending review.
—CND officials complained about phone-tapping.
—Reports in Tory press of ILEA plan to ensure political education in schools.

26 —Cardinal Hume, Archbishop of Westminster, made public his 'concern' over Monsignor Kent's involvement with CND.
—Duke of Edinburgh delivered a speech to the Institution of Civil Engineers advocating nuclear weapons.
—CND offered to mail out Ministry of Defence leaflets on cruise and Trident with their own literature.
—News in the *Guardian* of Government's suppression of pamphlet, *Home Defence and the Farmer*, despite protests from 'Farmers for a Nuclear-Free Future'.

27 —Announcement that European Court of Human Rights had accepted a case from Portskewett Action Group against Government's refusal to fund objectors at Sizewell Inquiry.
—Professor Leonard Hamilton, addressing Sizewell Inquiry on behalf of pro-nucear group, 'Power for Good', alleged that people have 'irrational fears' about nuclear power.
—Anti-CND organization 'British Atlantic Committee' re-formed as 'Peace through NATO' and lost charitable status.

28 —Civil Defence orders announced in Commons to force the 155 'nuclear-free' local authorities to make civil defence plans. Cf. *The Daily Telegraph* (28 April): MPs seek curbs on 'misuse of power' by Left councils, thus relating the Defence orders move to the Government's long-term attack on Labour councils such as the GLC, Sheffield, etc.

29 —Reports that Greenham Peace women have £19,000 in bank accounts; speculation on how local authority might sequester this.
—CND mail offer (26 April) refused.
—Mgr. Kent alleged spying and smearing by 'Coalition for Peace through Security' (a group linked to Winston Churchill's 'Campaign for Defence and Multilateral Disarmament').
—Anti-CND speeches by Heseltine, Churchill and Parkinson.

30 —Letter in *The Times* from E. P. Thompson: Heseltine's persuasion of Weinberger to withdraw from Oxford Union debate was 'an improper intervention by a minister of Government in the affairs of a private society —and also, since the debate was to be televised, in the affairs of the media'.

May

1 —Trafalgar Square rally of Lady Olga Maitland's 'Women and Families for Defence'.

4 —Publication of British Medical Association's report, *The Medical Effects of Nuclear War*. Nuclear attack 'would cause the medical services . . . to collapse'.

1.2 A PARADIGM: PRIEST, POLITICS AND MORALITY

A notable feature of this period was a series of personal and general attacks against opponents of the Government's 'defence' policies: Dr Vaughan against Mrs Ruddock, Mr Heseltine against CND, the Home Office against demonstrators, Cardinal Hume against Mgr. Kent, Berkshire County Council against the Greenham women, and so on. A precipitating event was the letter sent on 22 April by Mr Heseltine to Conservative candidates in marginal constituencies. CND had announced that, though it would not field candidates in the General Election, it would canvass opinion on the nuclear issue in such constituencies. Heseltine's response was to claim that CND was 'an organization led and dominated by left-wing activists ranging through the Labour Party to the Communist Party'. In support of this allegation he published brief notes about the (largely past) political affiliations of eighteen officers, members of National Council, and regional delegates. CND was a 'front organization' for the Labour Party, whose 'purpose is the advance of the socialist and communist cause'. As the *Daily Mail* gleefully reported, 'Heseltine brands CND a Red Tool!' A tool of the Kremlin: in Heseltine's words, 'At its most extreme it is to argue the cause of the Soviet Union at the expense of the free societies of the West'. What is remarkable is not only the substance of this accusation but the identity of the person who delivered it: since the smear was delivered in an electioneering context, it might have come more appropriately from the Chairman of the Conservative Party than from the Defence Secretary. That it was Heseltine who made the allegation gave it an apparent authority, as if CND were a threat to national security rather than just to the election chances of the Conservatives.[6]

Five days later, a similar attack came to light. Cardinal Basil Hume, Archbishop of Westminster, had written to Mgr. Bruce Kent, who for three years had been seconded from his parish to work full-time for CND, expressing concern about his involvement in a movement which was 'increasingly political and controversial'. Cardinal Hume's intervention sparked off a row. Had Heseltine, or the Pope, put pressure on him? The Press, ostensibly outraged, wanted its readers to see Mgr. Kent's CND role as scandalous. If we examine the discourse used to condemn him we shall learn much about the Tory paradigm which experienced Kent as a peculiar anomaly and threat.

The major complaint against Kent was that priests should not meddle with politics; but this is expressed in a number of forms. There is neglect of pastoral duties: 'Go Back to Your Flock' (*Daily Express*, 30 April); 'rather more attention to the cares of State than to the care of souls' (*Sun*, 29 April); 'a priest who so clearly prefers such work to the normal duties of his calling, is likely to be a priest who no longer takes his calling seriously' (*Daily Telegraph*, 29 April). Again, 'how best to avoid war is political [not 'religious'] calculation' (*The Times*, 5 May); 'Politics and Priestliness Collide' (*Daily Telegraph*, 28 April). Nuclear defence is represented as an entirely political question, with no moral considerations. Another version of this division finds fault with Kent's alleged involvement with PARTY politics. Heseltine's letter provided an opportunity to accuse Kent of being involved in an election campaign, or, even worse, working for the Soviet Union: 'The Priest and the Kremlin' (*Sun*, 29 April).

Several newspapers refer to him as a 'turbulent priest', an allusion to Henry II's appeal to get rid of Becket ('Who will free me from this turbulent priest?'). Becket was murdered, so the allusion indicates a tremendous violence of sentiment against Mgr. Kent, a person presumably unknown to the majority of readers before the papers appropriated him as a symbol of menace to 'yourself, your wife, your child or your neighbour' (*Times*, 5 May). The implicit accusations of treason go with a suggestion of subversion by an alien: it is surely no accident that Kent, a priest of the ROMAN church, should be virulently attacked for interfering in British political affairs, while, for example, the Anglican Canon Paul Oestreicher, vice-president of CND, was not subject to such censure. But on the other hand Kent is criticized for political activity in disobedience of the policy of his own Church. So he is the focus of a complex set of accusations; we will see that the language of the attacks strains under complexity to the point of contradiction. Here is the first paragraph of an article which reflects that strain:

WHERE POLITICS AND PRIESTLINESS COLLIDE FOR MGR KENT
By Canon D. W. Gundry, Churches Correspondent
Monsignor Bruce Kent's activities as secretary general of CND run contrary to the official policy of the Roman Catholic Church that priests should not engage openly in partisan politics. This has been underlined in the recently revised canon law. [*Daily Telegraph*, 28 April.]

Though faulting Kent as a priest absolutely ('[his] primary duty is the service of God and the pastoral care of souls . . . [he] is considered less effective as a priest'), this writer ostensibly criticizes him primarily for going against Catholic policy. He makes it clear that such a restriction does not apply to Church of England clergymen, and indeed at the end of his article innocently reveals that Anglican clergy have been invited by Douglas Hurd (Minister of State at the Foreign Office) to a symposium 'to look at the way forward in arms control'. Double standards apply then to the issue of the involvement of priests in politics: Anglicans may join the nuclear debate, Catholics may not.

The precariousness of this as a MORAL criterion is reflected in a generalized equivocation of the language. The Anglican Canon Gundry is saying some more complicated things about his colleagues in the Catholic Church than what he asserts or literally entails. We need refer only to the first sentence of the above quotation to demonstrate that more serious accusations are latent. The presence of adverbs and adjectives in the context of a negative always allows the assumption that some opposite proposition might have been spoken. The following incriminating claims about the Catholic Church are possible if we relocate the negative:

(i) the official policy of the Roman Catholic Church that priests should engage covertly in partisan politics;
(ii) the official policy of the Roman Catholic Church that priests should engage openly in non-partisan politics.

In the first case, Kent's offence is that he is too open, and the Church is implicitly condemned for condoning undercover politicking; in the second, he ought to keep out of party politics but may engage politically at some higher level (like the Pope). So by not editing the signals of alternative presuppositions out of his language, this writer manages to attack Mgr. Kent from several angles simultaneously. We feel that this is a sign that Canon Gundry experiences Kent in a spirit of generalized crisis, not as a specifically focused problem.

In the context of this crisis it is noteworthy that on 26 April, the day on which Cardinal Hume's criticism of Mgr. Kent was published, the Duke of Edinburgh made a widely reported, and commended, intervention in the argument. The Duke of course is a national figurehead, and, as Royalty, he is purportedly non-partisan. To judge from his comments, however, he IS partisan (favouring retention of a nuclear capacity) and, what is more, on this political matter he unhesitatingly uses a moral argument. As regards the possession of nuclear bombs, an essential credential, the Duke argues, is a 'good character' and moreover:

> what matters are the scruples of the people with the ultimate power to unleash them.

It appears that the official distinction between politics and morality does not apply to this supposedly non-partisan voice. Indeed, 'unleash' is perhaps a less than scrupulous choice of verb, but it reveals the meaning behind the Duke's allusion to

> strong countries invading their weaker neighbours.

General Galtieri, in other words, is no satisfactory candidate for a 'good character'. Thus does the Duke issue a timely reminder of the Falklands victory as a victory for the right kind of scruples, the anniversary of which fell in this pre-election period.

If the timing of the Duke's speech in relation to the public condemnation of Kent was fortuitous, it nevertheless served structurally, within the system of rhetoric the Press was creating at the time, as a riposte to the kind of unilateralism advocated by Kent. This system embodies double standards. Kent, it is argued, has no authority to mix morality with politics, but the Duke can put all his royal authority behind a moralistic argument with a political conclusion.

In other respects the Duke's speech is an important instance of a case being made against CND indirectly, by the tacit employment of official paradigms. One is the implied proposition that the state is a benign protector. Again, the tell-tale evidence is in the forms of language:

> the trouble is that any weapon with the capacity of killing is dangerous the moment it gets into the hands of anyone with the intention of using it.

Although this sentence does not specify the weapon in question to be a nuclear weapon, the supposition that it is nuclear is confusing since the real intention of 'using it' is an essential premise of the deterrent argument. This argument necessarily rests upon the presumed deterrent-value of real terroristic intentions in procuring peace and protection; but the Duke's form of words muffles this implication by attributing terroristic intentions not to the State but to others. The phrase 'ANY weapon' attaches terrorism to weapon-using outlaw groups such as, perhaps, the IRA, the PLO, or the Red Brigade. The Duke's allusion to 'strong countries invading their weaker neighbours' does indeed concede that forms of government terror exist as well, but only when practised by governments of 'bad character' (Argentina? Russia?). The Duke's moral proviso enables him to deflect any idea of state-authorized terror by saying in effect that terror amounts to much the same thing as outlaw violence: the attempt to gain political goals through intimidation of our 'good' government. In other words the loaded form of the Duke's definition of terror as a mode of opposing government is made to preclude another sense of the term in which terror is also a mode of governing. The implied proposition that this State is a benign protector remains intact as a powerful assertion against CND's alternative perceptions.

Our analysis of all these materials has taught us that the different events and statements of the period are not distinct, and distinctly signifying, occurrences, but outcrops from an underlying stratum of paradigmatically organized discourse. If we stay with the attack on Kent we will be able to show this in a more systematic way. However much the papers insist that the issue with Kent is ecclesiastical or pastoral, not political, they insist on interpreting the incident in terms of current political discourse. For example, the *Daily Express*'s editorial comments on Kent (30 April) explicitly invoke Heseltine's attack on the CND leadership, though Heseltine's letter on 22 April did not mention Kent. The *Express* accuses Kent of being 'deeply involved in politics . . . denouncing Parliamentary candidates who uphold Western defence and even-handed disarmament'; of believing that his status as a priest would make him 'immune to counter-attack'; of belonging to an organization led by Communists; of an irresponsible pacifism which, like that of the 1930s, 'counselled one-sided disarmament'. The representation here is political rather than religious: CND, including Kent, 'should remain under the public spotlight' in the interests of 'national security' because they are in league with the Russians and because they advocate unilateralism which would weaken defence.

The sub-text of the *Express* editorial is in fact the leaflet propaganda[7] of the 'Campaign for Defence and Multilateral Disarmament' (one of the organizations set up by the Conservatives to counter CND and led by Winston Churchill, MP). CDMD constantly contrasts multilateral and unilateral disarmament, which it calls 'balanced' and 'one-sided' disarmament, respectively. These terminological substitutions do not simply paraphrase the more technical, Latinate, words; they also have positive and negative connotations, and their associations with debate allow them to evaluate implicitly the quality of the arguments on each side. 'One-sided' suggests 'biased' or 'partial', whereas a 'balanced' view judiciously appraises all sides of the case. The *Express*'s substitution of 'even-handed' for 'balanced' reverts to the original metaphor in the CDMD literature where a pair of scales is drawn containing unequal quantities of Soviet and NATO missiles. 'Even-handed' connotes a process of giving equally: in this case, putting more weapons into the NATO side of the balance (which is what NATO argues, and is actually doing). 'Even-handed disarmament' is, then, an unintended contradiction. At the centre is what the Tories assert is a major hypocrisy—disarmament is in fact armament, a build-up of weapons. It is no wonder that their confrontation with Mgr. Kent ('a man with special sacramental powers and peculiarly solemn duties' (*Daily Telegraph*, 29 April)) should be conducted in a spirit of crisis and in a discourse style that reveals paradoxes.

The fact is that at this time the Tories and their newspaper apologists were struggling to sustain some insupportable contradictions during an electoral crisis. Three central contradictions within the paradigms were as follows:

(i) The claim that armament and disarmament are matters which do not involve moral considerations but which are wholly political or practical. As far as we can make out, this is the premise on which a speech by John Nott, Heseltine's predecessor as Defence Secretary, rests:

> What are the realities which form the basis upon which a moral decision on our deterrent must rest?
> There are three, namely war, weapons and warlike governments.[8]

'Reality' is opposed to 'morality'. Nott asserts that, since 'wars do happen', 'nuclear weapons inescapably exist' and 'the Russian leadership will use military force when it thinks it can get away with it', these realities must be faced with a strong defence policy. He puts moral questions which might subvert this conclusion into a ridiculous rhetorical form (e.g. whether nuclear weapons are more immoral than conventional ones); pays lip-service to the moral integrity of 'the genuine pacifist' (thus logically presupposing the existence of false pacifists, e.g. CND); and concludes that HIS only responsible position, as 'a Government Minister', is quite different from what is allowed a private individual—he must ensure the 'survival of the State' by commanding nuclear weapons. Surprisingly, he cites the Bishop of London, the Archbishop of Canterbury and the Pope in support of his claim that defence ministers and their nuclear charges are beyond moral question. Actually, the whole argument, and its phraseology ('that seems to me to be a practical defence question, not a moral one') would tend to detach weaponry from morality, and thus ostensibly disqualify professionals concerned with morality (such as Mgr. Kent or the Bishop of London) from any comment, just as Kent's detractors maintained. The general argument comes through in the following muddy articulation of principle (what does the oxymoron 'moral force' mean?) by the *Sun* (29 April):

> But disarmament is a political issue. It will be solved not by moral force, but by political agreement.

(ii) A second contradiction which troubled Conservative pro-nuclear discourse at that time centres on the definition of 'political'. Nuclear arms are in the sphere of the political, and when the *Sun* censures Kent for 'playing politics', it is saying that he should keep his nose out of that sphere and stick to his pastoral profession. But elsewhere he is accused of 'partisan politics' or 'party politics' or 'practical politics', by which is meant active socialism as supposedly defined in Heseltine's letter against CND. So there is 'the political' of Government, which, as far as nuclear arms are concerned, has an unchallengable validity and authority, and the 'political' of anti-nuclear protest, which, associated with socialism, is represented as the politics of partial interest (or worse, treasonable liaison with 'the Soviets'). So Heseltine is justified in his political role as Defence Secretary, but Joan Ruddock, Chairperson of CND, is damned because she was a Labour Parliamentary candidate in 1979. We can only say that the two meanings of 'political' are hard to distinguish, and paticularly so in a period when the Conservative Government was engaging in military activities (the Falklands, cruise) designed to enhance the electoral chances of the Conservative Party.

(iii) The third contradiction which so tortures the pro-nuclear discourse of the period is the doublethink proposition that war is peace and peace is war. When Mrs Thatcher proclaims 'We are the true peace movement' (*Daily Telegraph*, 29 April, summarizing a Commons statement of the previous day), her declaration has to be interpreted in a special way because it appears to be inconsistent with the facts of the situation. She is the leader of a Government whose main 'defence' objective in 1983 was the installation of cruise missiles. However, this is supposed to serve the cause of peace by building up NATO arms to balance those of the Warsaw Pact. The argument goes on to claim that 'balance' constitutes 'effective deterrence' (because neither side could 'win', neither side will use their weapons), and that balance is the only basis for disarmament negotiations.[9] These are the basic premises of the 'true' peace movement. Now the 'false' peace movement (CND, Greenham women, etc.), in challenging these premises, is 'actually harming the cause of peace' (*Sun*, 29 April).

The paradoxical claim that war is peace and peace is war is the thematic mainspring of a virulent anti-Kent leader in *The Sunday Telegraph* (1 May). An article which sets out to be scathing and witty, it is full of semantic clashes which can only be accepted if one reverses the commonsense meanings of words. The title,

MR HESELTINE AND PEACEMONGERING

contains a cleverly ironic neologism. The few words which precede *-mongering* in compounds (war, scandal, rumour) are all decisively negative in connotations, so working for peace is presented as a bad thing. This perverse inversion of meaning is the main rhetorical feature of the text. In the first sentence we read that 'disarmament is thought, quite wrongly, to promote peace'—an astonishing judgement which requires us to reject the reasonable and deeply traditional (swords into ploughshares) view that disarmament would aid the cause of peace. The leader-writer means unilateral disarmament as advocated by CND, but the argument is not given for another two paragraphs, and then only in part. Official Conservative ideology claims, as we have seen, that multilateral disarmament would promote peace. The fact that the leader-writer's judgement, taken at its face value—disarmament does not promote peace—is in total contradiction with the official claim seems very significant. It suggests that the official position is merely hypocritical and that the real Conservative objective is exactly what appears, namely, the build-up of arms. But in the view of the editorial, the hypocrisy is all on the other side. In advocating disarmament, CND is 'a dangerous and misguided body', and hypocritical because it 'has been allowed to acquire an aura of holiness, made all the more explicit by the presence at its head of a Roman Catholic priest'. The editorial's foil to this 'peacemongering . . . in saintly hands' is the secular mind of the 'rational person'[10] who knows from history that disarmament is an 'age-old delusion'.

The doublethink paradigm is thus supposedly sanctioned by reason, but the editorial's language is not unequivocal on the subject of rationality. The writer advocates the use of 'tough language and brutal frankness' against CND; and 'peacemongering . . . should be exposed with passion'. 'Brutal' and 'passion' are endowed with positive attributes notwithstanding the fact that brutality is an attribute of non-reasoning brutes (and 'passion' is perceived as a dangerously irrational attribute of women, as we shall see). The editorial's claim, none the less, is that peace will prevail if reason will prevail over the 'dangerous and misguided body' of CND. In this image of CND as an unruly *body* with the wrong kind of *head* there is an inversion of traditional hierarchical assumptions about rule and order, knowledge and action, and the suggestion of a crisis of rule is strongly implicit; as it is in the phrase 'allowed to acquire', which suggests an over-permissive Government.

The scathing charge of hypocrisy against CND (peacemongering is warmongering) is a neat manoeuvre that enables the point to be made as to how gullible electorates can be, thus disguising what is anyway an anti-democratic assumption to this effect on the part of the editorial itself. For example, in the verb 'allowed' the assumption of a subverted relationship of command and obedience is used to deplore not CND merely but the very access as such of erroneous thinking ('quite wrongly') to the possible determination of defence policy in an election. This is the real crisis. It thus becomes important for the editorial to attack CND in violent terms which would be appropriately applied to warmongers or traitors: 'an organization which can do terrible harm; an organization which preys on people's fears to promote a cause which, if successful, would certainly endanger the peace of the world'. The hypocrisy of CND is heightened by contrasting their 'pious pretensions' with their 'murky Communist pasts' 'courageously' revealed by Heseltine: 'very far from being saintly, [they] are erstwhile supporters of, and apologists for, the aggressive Soviet tyrants'. The predicates 'prey' and 'aggressive' construct a rhetorical emphasis. 'Prey' presupposes a predator (the 'peacemongering' CND), and a predator without aggressive designs on its prey ('people's fears') is a contradiction in terms. 'Aggressive', however, transferred to CND from the tyrants they allegedly serve, resolves the contradiction in the required direction. The advocacy of peace is actually the aggression of war.

1.3 A PARADIGM: WOMEN, REASON AND PASSION

The cause of disarmament is also dismissed by the editorial we have been discussing as 'peace hysteria'—as with the title, this is another apparently anomalous conjunction of terms. Evidently, it is being said that hysteria is no state of mind in which to determine policy and guarantee peace. But no less evident is the tilt against the Greenham women, given that the dictionary defines hysteria as

> a functional disturbance of the nervous system (esp. of women) . . . usually attended with disturbance of moral and intellectual faculties.[11]

What we have so far observed to be the official elimination of moral considerations from political matters is taken to an extreme by the article's allusion to hysteria. Hysterics are unamenable to reason. In this condition the women epitomize the collapse of a rational defence policy in which, as the paradox dictates, peace hysteria is irrational since it is war that keeps the peace. The nervousness in the editorial has to do essentially with the apprehension that CND and like movements (especially Greenham) threaten the very basis of the rational defence posture, since they alert in the public precisely those fears which the posture is supposed to assuage: the fear of violent death by burning and radiation.

We move now to a second threat to the Tory paradigm: women in the peace movement. Just as Kent, by his role as priest, was a symbol of an intrinsically moral challenge, so do women's roles symbolize life confronting the nuclear threat to life.

In the pro-nuclear texts which we have surveyed, nuclear affairs are represented as national, political, practical and technical matters. This representation has the effect of excluding certain topics and perspectives from the discourse as supposedly irrelevant, and certain classes of people from commenting, as supposedly incompetent to do so. Mgr. Kent was caught under such a proscription; a related one attempts to exclude women. This prohibition was necessary because women's protest undermined an effort by the Government to treat nuclear arms as an issue which does not touch personal or family life. This effort expressed itself as an attempt to suppress consciousness of the material effects of nuclear attack: people and organizations who emphasized the inevitable huge scale and horror of death, sickness, public disorder, ecological damage, etc., were branded as irresponsible or irrational. A characteristic of the period we studied was constant attempted censorship, both of and by the media, of presentations of the physical horrors of nuclear war. When the film *The Day After* was screened on British television, Heseltine demanded a 'right to reply'.[12] A highly significant self-censorship was the withdrawal of the 'civil defence' booklet *Protect and Survive*. This notorious publication which instructs its readers on how to construct a nuclear shelter under the dining room table, what kind of curtains to hang, and what to do 'if a death occurs' and so on was originally supposed to go to every household in Britain, but was never distributed, and when we needed a copy, in April 1983, we could obtain one only from CND. It is obvious why it was suppressed: the Tories realized that by drawing attention to the domestic implications of nuclear attack they would scare people into opposition to the nuclear 'defence policy' generally. And the blatant fact that the self protection measures recommended in *Protect and Survive* would be pathetically inadequate adds fuel to the anti-nuclear argument. *Protect and Survive* had to be withdrawn because it showed the wrong side of the 'defence posture'. Along with this sort of self-censorship goes an attempt at coolness of style in official and pro-government discussions of 'defence'. Only the habitually sensationalist *Sun* mentions things like 'the nightmarish prospect of nuclear annihilation' (29 April). It is the OTHER side (the 'peacemongers') 'which preys on people's fears'.

In the nervous climate which reigned at the time of our study, the conventional images of women were particularly disturbing for this paradigm. They are supposed to be peculiarly associated with life through child-bearing, and thus offer an intrinsic critique of weapons of death. They are supposed to be impractical and irrational, and so their pronouncements on the bomb are regarded as incompetent and dangerously emotive (hysterical). Then women are supposed to be subservient to the leadership of males, and since nuclear armament has been defined as a technical and professional matter, their challenge is a serious insubordination. This problem is compounded by an alleged inability to organize 'properly' constituted groups, so women's involvement is anarchic (an image which has been actively exploited as an instrument of protest).

For such reasons, the women's peace movements have been a sharp thorn in the pro-nuclear flesh. The Greenham Common peace camp, begun in September 1981 and well established by April 1983, was under constant attack, physical and discursive, but remarkably resilient (a fairly effective eviction from the area of Greenham main gate seems to have been carried out on the day these pages were being typed, 4 April 1984). Taking up the point about lack of organization, the committee-less style of the Greenham women was an effective use of creative anarchy.[13] The police and the courts, which have regularly prosecuted them for minor offences, failed to identify 'ringleaders' and 'spokespersons', so could not interact with (or subdue) the peace campers by the normal tried judiciary mechanism of punishing scapegoats. Discourse against the women, nationally and locally, saw them as an affront to society, and hurled accusations of dirt, disease, neglect of families, and the like. Underlying this is a stock anti-feminist discourse, founded on a bourgeois detestation of unwomanly women. It is the basis of the newspaper discourse which represents the two incidents we shall now analyse. These did not involve the Greenham women, but public attitudes to the Greenham women were surely the ideological reference point for the treatment of these incidents.

The first event was an anti-cruise demonstration in the House of Commons by members of a Brighton parents' group on 20 April and the ensuing newspaper comments; the second, newspaper reactions on 25 April to news that the Women's Institute planned to modernize its image.

The Commons demonstration occurred during a debate on a motion for a referendum on cruise missiles. Nine women were expelled from the public gallery for 'singing and chanting', and were detained; meanwhile twenty-one children remained in the lobby, looked after by nine other women from the group. This incident seems to have been experienced as simultaneously shocking and entertaining. The official reaction was solemnly delivered by the Speaker of the House: 'I take a very serious view indeed of anyone trying to hold up the proceedings of Parliament. This is the heart of our democracy . . .'. The solemn, authoritarian, male world condemns an intrusion by a noisy, disorderly and childish group. The opposition of 'serious' and 'women' comes out in one headline: 'Speaker's "serious view" of missiles demo by women' (*Daily Telegraph*, 21 April). The protesters, being women, were not taken seriously. In the Press, the political substance of their protest was played down and the whole event trivialized and ridiculed. What is emphasized is their status as women and mothers, thus their disqualification from participating in serious debate.[14]

This representation is encoded in an informal and domestic lexical register: the words 'mums', 'mothers', 'toddlers', 'children', 'kids', 'babies' abound in the reports. The overall effect of this vocabulary is to trivialize and neutralize the protest. 'Protesting peace mums' (*Daily Mirror*), 'ban-the-bomb mums' (*Sun*), 'women protesters' (*Daily Mirror*) are cheerfully dismissive contradictions-in-terms. All the reports refer to the participants in the plural, blocking any identification of or statement of individual responsibility. Ridicule goes further in the *Guardian* which spells them as 'wimmin', an allusion to the linguistic politics of the women's movement. In several reports the children displace the women as the centre of attention and the agents of protest—for example:

> A-DEMO TODDLERS SHATTER THE PEACE
> Toddlers staged their own demonstration at the Commons yesterday after their mothers were locked up for an anti-nuclear protest in the public galleries. [*Daily Mail*, 21 April.]

The women's demonstration ('noisy', 'singing and chanting') is reduced to the level of children's play, that of the children 'running around' the lobby (cf. the accusation that Mgr. Kent was 'playing politics'). The women are presented as children.

But they are also presented as unwomanly women. More of an offence than disrupting Parliament was abandoning their children: ' "Peace" kids left on run' (*Star*). This irresponsible desertion is magnified by the *Star*'s vague but suggestive miscounting of the participants:

> A dozen [sc. 9] protesting peace mums were arrested at the Commons yesterday.
> Their arrest left more than 20 [sc. 21] children running around the main lobby, looked after by only a handful [sc. 9] of other women in the ban-the-bomb group.

The next stage of this representation is to put the women into a sexual relationship with MPs:

> MPs LEFT HOLDING BABIES! [*Sun*]

This headline is in no sense true, but it sums up an underlying allegation in many of the reports. The women have invaded a male's restricted territory (like his study or his club), and, worse still, they have let his children into that preserve, and left them there, distracting him from his debate on cruise missiles (which have nothing to do with children). But the headline alludes to a more personal threat. A man who is left holding the baby has been forced to take responsibility for his own offspring. He may of course be an object of sympathy in bourgeois sexual mores, in the sense that it is believed that the wife should be solely responsible for the children; and the *Sun* surely upholds this—it accuses the women of neglect. But the phrasing of the headline unconsciously acknowledges the women's point: these are your children, look after them as such and stop threatening their future by your war games. The linguistic excitement evinced by the newspapers at this time suggests awareness of the severity of this accusation.

The rise in blood pressure caused by the women's protest can be sensed in this apoplectically abusive piece of writing (*Daily Telegraph*, 21 April):

COMMONS SKETCH
ENOUGH OF THESE SQUAWS!
By Godfrey Barker
MP's have had enough

> Those women shot up like squaws in the undergrowth in another publicity grabbing TV stunt in the Commons yesterday.

> What with their babies, their quarrels, their ceaseless daily dramas and their chanting about treachery and dirty tricks, they are never off our screens. Now there is no escape in the Chamber. If only they could all be like Anna Ford.

Although the article seems to have been provoked by the Commons protest of the previous day, it is 'about' something else. 'Squaws' and 'undergrowth' are a confused metaphorical allusion to the Greenham Common campers (their 'benders', polythene tents on sticks, recoded as wigwams), representing them as savages. 'Chanting' may refer to what happened in the Commons, but it also connotes primitivism. This is a complaint against the 'irrational' elements of the female stereotype: squabbling, child-bearing, public misbehaviour. Significantly, men need to *escape* from this irrationality: to be protected from it by the media, and to hide in an inviolate male sanctum, the Chamber of the House of Commons. (There is an image of rape here.) The model woman is Anna Ford, a newsreader who sits disciplined within the frame of a TV screen, obediently reading out the official news made and written by men.[15]

This article seems to us to display a hysterical alarm at the prospect of women engaging in the public politics of the nuclear argument. Another opportunity for the newspapers to express this alarm was provided a few days later when the Women's Institute proposed to depart from its traditional domestic and unpolitical image. A headline in the *Daily Mail*, 25 April, is one instance:

WI UNFURLS £3 MILLION BANNER ON MARCH TO THE
NEW JERUSALEM
The Women's Institute is to spend £3 million on its march into the nuclear age. Part of the image-changing money will go on car stickers and Ban the Bomb debates.

Unfurling a banner is a military action, a prelude to marching into battle. The *Sun* (25 April) also represents the WI's plans in military terms:

A SAD LOSS
The Women's Institutes are said to be planning a £3 million campaign to

modernise their wonderful movement and involve their members in controversial issues such as nuclear disarmament.

'Planning . . . a campaign' alludes to strategy in war, to an election campaign, and to the Campaign for Nuclear Disarmament. The argument against CND is in the background here: that it is a warmongering movement, and that it is involved in the 1983 election campaign. Marching under a banner is not only a feature of old-fashioned warfare, it is familiarly an aspect of protest street marches. Car stickers are used by CND and by election candidates. The WI stickers were going to read 'The WI has the country at heart', but in the context of the *Daily Mail* sentence they might have said 'Ban the Bomb'. Thus in both papers the WI is appropriated as a substitute for the peace movement and is subjected to the standard attack. If this seems an unlikely appropriation, recall the evidence presented so far of an official panic at the prospect of women speaking for peace.

Both papers also highlight the £3 million to be spent by the WI: they are conscious of the connection between money and war (coded in the £1 coin, remember) and between money and the power to protest. One sensitivity in both the Reagan and the Thatcher administrations' handling of their nuclear posture with their electorates is the phenomenal cost of the weapons, and so they are impelled to defend 'the Morality of the COST of Trident', not the morality of possessing the weapon. The possession of the weapon is essential to the Conservatives' staying in power (thus, to the commercial success of the nuclear and other businesses whose interests they work for), so their major rhetorical efforts are to minimize the cost of the weapons and to attack and to silence the opposition. The latter involves spending Conservative Party money, and taxpayers' money, on anti-CND brochures, on campaigns in the Press, on pro-nuclear organizations such as CDMD, Peace through Nato, and Lady Olga Maitland's 'Women and Families for Defence' (a pro-nuclear WI?). And it involves attacks on the opposition's resources. The *Mail* headline reminds its readers of the cost of street marches, a preoccupation during that period (the cost to the taxpayer of the Easter demonstrations had been estimated at upwards of £250,000). The Home Office let it be known that it was considering a proposal that demonstrators should pay for their own police security—a blatant threat, fortunately withdrawn, to cripple CND financially. The same equation of money and power was also implicit in the Government's refusal financially to aid minority representations at the recently reconvened Sizewell inquiry. On the other hand, there were also some impertinent suggestions that women were using illicit money to gain political objectives. The *Star* reported (29 April) that the Greenham women had 'nearly £20,000 stashed in the bank', and it is surely only the criminal who are said to 'stash' money. The papers which reported this detail speculated on whether Berkshire County Council could sequester this money to defray expenses caused by the peace camp. In another extraordinary incident (see Calendar, 12 April), the Consumer Affairs Minister, Gerald Vaughan, threatened to withhold half of the National Association of Citizens' Advice Bureaux' annual grant; the chairperson of CND, Joan Ruddock, happened to work in the Reading Bureau, in Vaughan's constituency . . .

Such circumstances help to explain the newspapers' preoccupation with the WI's £3 million, though that figure is mere housekeeping compared to official estimates of, for instance, the effect of the Civil Defence orders.

In terms of this ideology, then, it is no surprise that the *Sun* threatens the WI through an economic metaphor:

> But they must remember if they enter the political arena then they will do so at a price.

Protest is expensive. The Brighton parents' group 'entered the political arena' and got off lightly; the WI will lose, if not its £3 million, at least its womanly virtue. The *Sun* continues:

> On matters affecting the home and the family, they are listened to with great respect because they represent the unbiased voice of womankind.
> It would be a sad loss to sacrifice that influence merely to be trendy.

We note in passing here the operation of two paradoxes already discussed: nuclear arms do not concern the home and family; nuclear disarmament is a biased position.

For the *Mail*, the wayward trendiness of the WI stems from a crisis of leadership. Just as the leaders of CND were attacked, so

> The leaders [of the WI] should remember before they start meddling that the virtue of the Women's Institute in the eyes of many who belong is precisely that it is always the same—a haven of sanity in a mad world.

These conspiratorial leaders, seeking trendiness (outward show without substance), threaten to destroy the WI's perennial domestic integrity, and, worse, its sanity. Given the paradigm disuniting women and nuclear affairs, we can bring more interpretation to the opposition sanity/madness. Sanity consists of making jam, not 'meddling' in the male world, and preserving a 'haven', a sanctuary (cf. comments on the 'Chamber', above). Madness is not, paradoxically, the insane world of TELs, NATO, SALT and MAD, but the carnivalistic protest of the Greenham women and of the Brighton parents.[16] The panic provoked by the WI's plans is a fear of the institutional collapse of the WI, the most stable embodiment of the official perception of reliable womanhood. In this complex of incidents spanning the brief period from the Commons demonstration to the Women's Institute proposals, one is bound to wonder who is the real hysteric.

1.4 CONCLUSION

Throughout this chapter we have of course strongly implied an answer to this question. The propaganda warfare waged against the peace movement in this period reveals a concerted effort on the part of the Tory Party and its Press to make its own panic look like reason. The peace movement alerted the Government to the fact that a growing number of people on an international scale no longer tolerate the defence posture that rests upon the contradiction that war is peace and peace is war. Needless to say, the exponents of the official form of reason never spell out this contradiction with complete candour: the legitimation of the policy seems to require a less than explicit presentation of the awkward premise. In this pre-election period the effort to legitimate the policy took the pronounced form of an adamant reassertion of what we have called paradigms, the systems of belief and perception most favourable to the direct actions of the Government. The war against peacemongering was only ostensibly a matter of a policy debate: its real form, as we have tried to show, was a diffuse ideological assault upon any development within the culture that threatened the dominant paradigms. What is at stake in defence policy during the war that seems to keep the peace is an entire system of officially sanctioned assumptions about how everyone should think and behave. Ideology is invisibly present in any utterance, and one main purpose of the analysis of language is to reveal this fact and its implications. At a time of crisis in the culture, such as this period undoubtedly was (and still is), the material for a continuing analysis is everywhere at hand.

NOTES

1. See R. Fowler, R. Hodge, G. Kress and T. Trew (1979), Ch. 1. On 'Nukespreak', cf. Chilton (1982), Hilgartner *et al.* (1982).
2. Ministry of Defence pamphlet, 'Cruise Missiles: Some Important Questions and Answers' (April 1983).
3. US Secretary of Defense James Schlesinger (10 January 1974).
4. US Air Force Fact Sheet, 'Ground-Launched Cruise Missile' (September 1981: 5). 'GLCM' is 'Ground-Launched Cruise Missile', 'TEL' means 'Transporter-Erector-Launcher', and 'LCC' is 'Launch Control Center'.
5. See M. A. K. Halliday (1978).
6. Heseltine's electoral intervention was clearly an abuse of his office of Defence Secretary. For a similar abuse, see Calendar (30 April).
7. The interaction is two-way: two of the three leaflets sent to us by CDMD reproduce anti-CND cartoons from Express Newspapers. On cartoons, cf. pp. 203 ff. below.
8. 'The Morality of the Cost of Trident' (17 November 1982), subsequently printed up as a pamphlet published and distributed by the Ministry of Defence.
9. The literature published by the Campaign for Defence and Multilateral Disarmament spells out these claims; see also 'Defence Fact Sheet', No. 1. 'Arms Control and Disarmament' and No. 3 'Deterrence', published by the Ministry of Defence (February 1983). On the semantics and semiotics of deterrence, see Chapters 5 and 6, this volume.
10. All words and phrases given in quotation marks here are literal quotations from the editorial.
11. *Concise Oxford Dictionary.* Etymologically, the word is derived from the Greek word for 'womb'.
12. However, in September 1984, a television film on the same topic, *Threads*, received little such attention. For further accounts of *The Day After* and its reception, see Chapters 9 and 10.
13. See the *Guardian* (31 March 1983), 'Peace movement without leaders that won't go away'.
14. The debate interrupted on 20 April hardly impressed by its seriousness; one Conservative opponent of the referendum spoke against it in childish and abusive limericks.
15. A comically inappropriate fantasy at the time. The papers during this period had for their other main story the downfall of the presenters of 'TV-am', including Anna Ford, who expressed her feelings by throwing a glass of wine over her ex-boss. Hardly ladylike.
16. An interpretation of the events of this period could be made using the concept of

carnivalization: see Mikhail Bakhtin (1973). In brief, the carnival world is a subversion of the dominant hierarchical forms of power and social relations; it is a public and festive 'de-crowning' of dogma, authoritarianism and narrow-minded seriousness by unorthodox and normally marginalized groups. There is a tendency towards theatricality in the carnival since the new space it creates is undefined and open to everyone. A reading of the period in these terms would obviously be relevant to the Commons demo, but also to other events, e.g. the implicitly theatrical media presentations of Bruce Kent as the 'peacemongering Monsignor': in the carnival idiom the priest with a funny title who preaches unorthodoxy is at once a clown and a usurper. The kind of anarchy fostered by the carnival can of course be seen as diabolical by those who have a strong interest in its suppression, but for the participants this energy is a release into new relationships and ideas that are normally discouraged by the prohibitions and protocols of usual life. For a development of such an approach, cf. Chapter 11.

2 Pragmatics of speeches against the peace movement in Britain: a case study

Kay Richardson
University of Liverpool, UK

2.1 INTRODUCTION

This chapter is concerned with the language of arguments employed by the British Government against opponents of nuclear weapons during February to May 1983 (cf. the calendar of events in Chapter 1). The Greenham Common women's peace camp had attained high media visibility, and the CND revival was an established fact. Although I have set the scene with past-tense references to the period of time covered by my account, I propose to use the present tense henceforward, treating it as part of an extended 'now'. This is partly for the rhetorical purpose of giving my observations contemporary relevance, and partly to avoid complications when discussing relations between speakers and hearers at the moment of utterance. The data for this study are public statements by ministers during these months, concentrating especially upon one particular speech by Margaret Thatcher. The method of analysis involves an informal but closely-argued pragmatics of discourse, referring all interpretations to an understanding of the political speech as a discourse genre. The aim was to explore the attitudes of Conservative ministers to dissenters from current government nuclear defence policy as expressed at different levels of meaning in the language which they use.

Nuclear defence is an area of national policy which is controversial. In this debate, however, the scales are unevenly balanced. Political power belongs only to one side's supporters, and the nuclear status quo in Britain is as the powerful side wants it to be. True, the powerful side has acknowledged the controversy and has allowed that the status quo is a matter for debate by responding to the challenges of those who oppose the status quo. Yet it also makes use of the fact of controversy in order (amongst other things) to marginalize dissenters. To this end, dissenters must be separated from the mainstream, circumscribed, and judged. 'The mainstream' is the speaker and his/her addressees, sharing crucial givens as far as the speaker is concerned. Dissenters (by implication or otherwise) do not share those givens. They are circumscribed in so far as speakers choose to supply versions of dissenters' arguments and address those versions critically, as often as they address versions taken from the mouths of dissenters. And they are judged in so far as speakers strengthen the ethical basis for discounting dissenting opinions: audiences are encouraged to find dissenters morally culpable, as well as (or rather than) mistaken in their estimation of political realities.[1] These claims will be given some substance in the textual studies which follow.

2.2 A TOOL KIT FOR THE INSPECTION OF POLITICAL DISCOURSE

2.2.1 Pragmatics

Pragmatics is currently a growth area in linguistic theory (construing linguistic theory broadly). From a starting-point of an interest in language and meaning, the view is taken that a theory of semantics is necessary to account for the meanings of sentences, considered as abstractions divorced from any context of utterance, whilst a pragmatic theory is needed to take account of what happens to sentence meanings when sentences become utterances. Thus pragmatic descriptions involve references to the context in which the utterance is produced.

For research in pragmatics the seminal article is Grice (1975) in which the notion of the 'co-operative principle' was first developed, with the derivative conversational maxims of QUALITY, QUANTITY, MANNER, and RELATION. Leech (1980) suggests the alternative labels of truthfulness, informativeness, clarity, relevance (pp. 11-12), which are useful glosses on Grice's proposals concerning the regulative rules for linguistic behaviour and its interpretation. For example, Gricean principles are useful to theorists trying to resolve anomalies in semantic theory and understand the relationship between sentence meaning and speaker's meaning (semantics and pragmatics).[2] The consensus now seems to be that entailment is a semantic relationship (sentences entail), implicature is a pragmatic relationship (utterances, or speakers, implicate), and presupposition is a problem case which may not be a theoretically distinct phenomenon.

In the present context the distinction between speaker meaning and sentence meaning is a somewhat irrelevant one. The present study is an exercise in applied pragmatics; it is concerned with meaning-in-context. The emphasis on speaker's meaning is not an emphasis on the theoretical category 'speaker' (i.e on potential, abstract speakers), but on real people—Margaret Thatcher, Michael Heseltine, John Nott—and on their attested utterances. Focusing upon particular speakers makes the question of speaker meaning versus sentence meaning a question about degrees of speaker commitment. A speaker is committed to the truth of entailments and presuppositions if he or she utters the entailing/presupposing sentence in an appropriate context and manner, even if these are more suitably theorized as semantic rather than pragmatic properties. The 'applied pragmatics' approach should also be relevant for identifying cases of utterances which are not intended literally and where, as a consequence, some or all of the entailments will not be speaker commitments.

Pragmatic and semantic concepts alone do not constitute an adequate toolkit for analysing the rhetorical complexities of political discourse. The pragmatic perspective is concerned with the speaker–hearer relationship, but very much in the abstract. Pragmatics idealizes away from the ethnographic details of particular speech-event types. The ethnographic facts about political speeches make for decidedly complex sets of relations between speaker, hearer, and spoken-about. It is important to bear these relationships in mind, since participants exploit any 'communicative competence' (Hymes 1971) which they have for this particular genre, in their utterances and their interpretations.

2.2.2 The ethnography of the political speech

In Goffman's terms (1981: 124–57), political speeches have a complex 'participation framework'. He observes that instead of the crude notion 'speaker', we need three concepts to analyse the production of spoken utterances: 'animator', for the person verbalizing them; 'author', for the person composing them; 'principal', for the 'person' whose views they represent. In a poltical speech the animator need not have authored the text. If the author and animator are different people, the author nevertheless writes a text which will sustain a fiction of animator as author: the first-person pronoun refers to the animator. Political speeches make the animator and the principal the same person. Although many other principals are spoken for, their voices appropriated and represented as required, the animator's principality is an organizing device, helping to underline the status of these sequenced sentences as a 'text' by giving them coherent texture (cf. Halliday and Hasan 1976).

On the reception of discourse Goffman distinguishes the 'hearer' from the 'ratified participant', in order clearly to differentiate the hearing, ratified participant from the bystander or eavesdropper who hears in spite of not being a ratified participant, and the ratified participant who fails to hear. This distinction may be applied to the political speech. As a material speech event it takes place with a particular set of ratified participants, usually an audience which is 'on the speaker's side' to begin with (Young Conservatives, Conservative Party candidates, constituency parties, etc.). Goffman makes the point (p. 138) that the ratified participants for podium talk are a 'massed but visible grouping off the stage', by contrast with broadcast talk, for which the recipients are imagined. But the ratification of the 'massed but visible' grouping in the case of podium talk also involves the imagination of the speaker, if he or she chooses to address those recipients. When Margaret Thatcher addresses the Young Conservatives at a conference, she must tailor her speech to a concept of 'Young Conservative', rather than to people that she personally knows. To 'address' ratified participants a speaker may only need to direct a gaze at them. If all ratified participants are addressed then perhaps it does not need even as much as that: they know they are addressed by the circumstances of the event. This, however, is a rather simple idea of what is involved in addressing someone. Recent work in conversational analysis and pragmatics (see e.g. Schegloff 1971; Grice 1975; Clark and Haviland 1977) demonstrates for more informal discourse the importance of building assumptions around what the addressee already knows—as a prerequisite for ensuring that they may understand what they are to get from this latest input to the conversation. This is true, in principle, for podium talk as well, though the differences in the circumstances make for different results.

A combined need to select and address, i.e. to treat only a subsection of recipients as addressees, will force a speaker into using overt signals so that the selected persons may know themselves as selected. For non-mediated events overt signals may be linguistic and paralinguistic (vocatives and names, intonation), non-linguistic (direction of gaze), or linguistic and non-linguistic (vocatives with gaze). Mediated events with remote audiences require combinations of overt signals suited to the form of the mediation. Gesture may be important for the speaker aware of a television audience whilst the signals must be linguistic if print is the medium of communication.

At a political speech-giving the massed grouping includes, alongside the identified set of people whose group name will appear in media reports of the event, the journalists. With all encouragement from the politicians, journalists make it their business to take elements of the speech, aspects of the occasion, and render these into journalistic forms for the benefit of their own mass audiences and readerships. Journalists are likely to work from a typed transcript, representing a written version of the speech and available shortly before 'the event' itself, to accommodate news deadlines. This written version persists in a 'limited edition' after the event, as its permanent and authoritative record. It is a joint effect of: the universal adult suffrage constitution; a dominant ideology which respects the egalitarianism of universal adult suffrage; the fact that mass communication is able to turn political speeches into POTENTIAL national broadcasts. The ability of a citizen to take advantage of these would-be national broadcasts depends upon what the mass media make available and how, hence the qualification POTENTIAL national broadcasts.

Texts of this kind can have a large number of overt addressee-selectors. I have argued that ALL CITIZENS are ratified partipants, even if they do not get to hear the speech. But this group is remote, massive in size, and heterogeneous, which makes it impossible to address as a group (or at least impossible simultaneously to sustain the overt address to all British citizens AND conduct a political argument through a complete speech). The major difficulty is that the group is heterogeneous in its relationships to the content of the speech. It includes people who know and believe what the speaker knows and believes, people who know what the speaker believes but are not themselves convinced that it is true, people who know what the speaker believes and think it is false, people who have not yet heard what the speaker believes (probably not for the want of telling). This level of heterogeneity makes it impossible to select the entire group as addressee, since no utterance could simultaneously take account of the hearer's belief of, scepticism about, ignorance of, opposition to, incomprehension of, the idea that the speaker wishes to have 'in play'. One solution is to keep on the move, addressing first one set, then another. A similar solution is to address the proximate audience consistently whilst allowing the distant recipients affiliation possibilities, 'if the cap fits . . .'.

It is possible for the national audience to be in a more homogeneous relationship with particular 'bits' of information contained in a political speech. When a change or development in party or government policy is announced for the first time, it is news generally, except for those who have had a hand in devising the policy and any journalists with prior knowledge. Political speeches are scanned by those who will report them to mass audiences for precisely this type of feature.

2.3 MARGINALIZING DISSENTERS

The best-known illustration of the Conservative marginalizing of dissenters is the 'communist links' argument, which makes it possible to see treachery in unilateralism. Those people are traitors who promote the interests of another nation at the expense of their own nation's interests, and in times of war, when there are 'sides', it is presumed self-evident that the interests of one side are incompatible with the interests of the other. In these circumstances either a person opposes the other side's interests or he/she is a traitor. The Soviet Union is a communist nation. Communists in the West cannot be trusted to oppose the other side's interests. Unilateralist leaders have communist links. Such unilateralists cannot be trusted to oppose the other side's interests, so they may be traitors.

In principle, a persuasive treachery charge makes the arguments of traitors irrelevant. Traitors will not say what their real goals are. They will produce persuasive lies that make their proposals sound attractive to people who would reject those real goals out of hand. In this scenario the real goal for unilateralist leaders is that there should be a communist take-over of the West. This unrighteous objective is disguised by them as the righteous pursuit of peace through an attempt to reduce the world levels of nuclear armaments.

It is not necessarily inconsistent for Conservative ministers who have helped to lay the 'communist links' charge to go on and raise objections to particular unilateralist arguments. To do so does not automatically establish their disingenuousness in claiming treachery but treating the arguments as honest and non-treacherous. In the first place the connection between communism in the CND leadership and treachery is not always spelled out. More often than not it is left up to the readers/listeners to make that connection. This is a form of equivocation and it requires a matching equivocation at the level of particular arguments. This can be achieved by identifying false propositions in the claims of unilateralists. Readers/listeners may or may not then be 'cued in' to a mendacity interpretation of the falsehoods, as the speaker prefers. But in general the mendacity interpretation requires a context in which a reason for lying is 'in the air', i.e. it presupposes the relevance and availability of the treachery schema in hearers' minds.[3]

2.4 MARGARET THATCHER

The textual study which follows is a demonstration of how, in one particular speech, Margaret Thatcher's use of language works to marginalize dissenters from Conservative government policy. The speech, under the heading of 'Defence and Disarmament', was delivered to the Young Conservatives at Bournemouth on 23 February 1983; a typed version was released by the Conservative Central Office.

Margaret Thatcher's contradictory task is to portray her Government's procurement of further weapons of mass destruction as the pursuit of a national policy of peace. Some would say that this is not a contradictory task at all.

The official rationale for deterrence as a strategy can be crudely captured in the slogan 'weapons for peace'. But, possibly, Margaret Thatcher is less than certain of the non-contradiction, for she is less than certain that belief in the non-contradiction is properly established amongst specific members of her distant audience. That uncertainty—'I know it's true, but I'm afraid THEY might not'—has to be handled carefully. Awkwardly for Margaret Thatcher, it commits her, firstly, to the belief that it is in principle possible not to know that 'weapons for peace' is non-contradictory. That awkwardness is compounded as follows. One group which is actually ignorant on this point is THEM, the unilateralists, who can be foolish or uninformed or wilful or deceitful in not knowing the truth. But there may be others. The counter-arguments put forward can scarcely be for the benefit of THEM, or for the benefit of people who already know these things (US). Therefore they must be for the benefit of a hypothetical VULNERABLE AUDIENCE. The hypothesis that there is such an audience must be a very serious one to warrant the propaganda efforts of that period.

On the one hand, devices must be found that inhibit audience members from inferring that judgements of foolishness, ignorance, stubborn perversity, etc., apply to them in not-yet-knowing-the-truth. On the other hand, the inference that not-yet-knowing-the-truth is a position which many of the good in the nation at large may be in cannot be allowed to become too prominent in the text. As a prominent meaning it can too easily be represented by others as anomalous. If scarcely a good word can be said for those who have definitely decided against the Government on the nuclear issue, to put those who have not been persuaded either way too firmly on 'our' side threatens to undermine the emphasis upon the 'compelling weight' of 'our' counter-arguments. And without that emphasis, the unilateralists don't look so bad after all. If the arguments are indeed persuasive for all right-minded people, does not this risk CREATING doubts in listeners' minds about the right-mindedness of these 'vulnerable', 'undecided' hearers, who have so far failed to recognize where truth and virtue lie? The attitude that there are people who can be persuaded to the correct view is incompatible with the attitude that the correctness of this view is self-evident to the right-minded. Sensing this risk, a speaker may feel that further arguments are called for.

2.4.1 Characterizing the dissenters

As a starting-point, I have identified most of the explicit references to the dissenters that Margaret Thatcher makes.

Who, then, are the dissenters? The dissenters are named as follows (the sentences of the printed text were numbered and these numbers are used here for cross-reference):

(13) those who seek one-sided disarmament;
(18) those who support unilateralism;
(21) those who hold these views;
(29) many in CND;
(33) the unilateralists;

(43) the one-sided disarmers;
(54) the Labour Party.

These glosses mainly define people by the policy idea of unilateralism. In two instances only is it possible to map these unilateralists on to any independently identifiable social groups. In sentences (32)–(33) Margaret Thatcher says: 'May I quote from *The Church and the Bomb*? There the unilateralists say, "The Russians do not want war . . ."'. This identifies unilateralists with the authors/principals of a particular text. In sentence (54) she turns her attention to the Labour Party, here featuring as the unilateralist party.

What do the dissenters say, think, believe? Under the heading 'Unilateralism—the Myths' we are given five numbered subheadings. The latter are propositions belonging to the unilateralists' discourse rather than to Margaret Thatcher's:

(17)—1. IF WE GIVE UP THE WEAPON WE SHALL BE SAFE.
(27)—2. THE SOVIET UNION WILL NOT SEEK TO ACHIEVE HER ENDS BY FORCE.
(42)—3. UNILATERALISM IS A MORAL GESTURE.
(74)—5. DEFENCELESSNESS PREVENTS ATTACK.

Sub-sub heading 4 (sentence (61)) reads: 'THE MYTH OF IMMUNITY', which does not have the same syntactic form as the other four.

Many other sentences characterize the sayings, beliefs, thoughts, actions and reactions of unilateralists, in various ways, as indicated in the right-hand column:

(18)	Those who support unilateralism believe that the nuclear weapon is so horrific that we should have nothing to do with it.	(belief)
(19)	Some of them counsel the West to give up its deterrent.	(illocution)
(29)	Sadly, however, there are many in CND who minimise the danger from the Soviet Union . . .	(belief/rhetoric)
	. . . and refuse to acknowledge its tyrrany . . .	(belief/rhetoric)
	. . . in order to promote . . .	(perlocution/plan)
	. . . their scheme for one-sided disarmament . . .	(plan)
(31)	By underplaying the threat from Russia . . .	(rhetoric/belief)
	. . . they convince themselves that it would be safe for the West to dismantle her defences.	(perlocution/belief)
(32)–(33)	May I quote from *The Church and the Bomb*? There the unilateralists say, 'The Russians do not want war; they recognise that war is not now a viable instrument of Soviet foreign policy.'	(locution)
(38)	They feel so fearful that they demand that something be done whatever it is and whatever the consequence.	(emotion) (illocution)
(46)	They suggest instead that Britain should make an individual moral gesture.	(illocution)

(47) They want us to disengage from what they call (belief)
the confrontation of the superpowers and set
a moral example.
(49) Evidently the nuclear bomb is too horrific for (implied belief)
the British to own but not too horrific for the
Americans to protect us with. So long as they
do it from their soil and not from ours. We are
to be protected by our allies, but contribute
nothing towards that protection.
(54) Yet that now appears to be the official policy (implied belief)
of the Labour party.
(55) They believe that we should dismantle our own (belief)
deterrent, throw out our American partners
yet still expect them to defend us.
(63) People believe that if we had no missiles of our (belief)
own, and if we had no foreign bases on our
territory, we would cease to be a target.

There is also a series of sentences implicitly answering the question 'Why do they, the dissenters, say, think, believe the things they do?':

(29) Sadly, however, there are many in CND who minimise the danger from the Soviet Union and refuse to acknowledge its tyranny in order to promote their scheme for one-sided disarmament.
(31) By underplaying the threat from Russia they convince themselves that it would be safe for the West to dismantle her defences.
(36)-(38) The trouble is that the sheer horror of modern warfare can drive people to unreason. For as Edmund Burke said, 'No passion so effectually robs the mind of all its powers of acting and reasoning as fear'.

Let us summarize. The dissenters are 'unilateralists', they believe a number of propositions which do not hold water, and they maintain untenable beliefs because they have lost their powers of reason through fear. However, this is not the full story. Less overt characterizations of the dissenters can also be found, for example through the use of rhetorical questions and denials.

2.4.2 Rhetorical questions

Margaret Thatcher asks a question to which she knows the answer, and in the knowledge that her audience will come up with the same answer:

If in the 1930s nuclear weapons had been invented and the allies had been faced by Nazi SS20s and Backfire Bombers, would it then have been morally right to have handed to Hitler total control of the most terrible weapons which man has ever made?

In this case the heavily cued correct answer is clearly that it would not have been morally right. The rhetorical strength of an 'of course' question like this is that it simultaneously makes its point and underlines the obviousness of the point. It foregrounds the fact that whilst formally there could be two possible answers to the question (*yes* or *no*), in fact there is only one answer which selects itself without further thought on the part of the hearer.

In context a further advantage of this rhetorical question is that because it is redundant and therefore violates the Quantity maxim, to use Gricean terminology, it triggers hearers into hunting for an implicature:

> Of course it wouldn't have been morally right. Fancy even asking that question. There must be a reason. There is—I can turn it into a criticism of unilateralists. If the answer to Margaret Thatcher's question was as obvious to unilateralists as it is to me, they couldn't recommend unilateralism in the 1980s any more than they (being right-minded people) would have done in the 1930s. Therefore Margaret Thatcher may be suggesting that there is some doubt about whether they have the correct answer; and therefore the question must be posed after all.

In fact, Margaret Thatcher frames the Nazi Germany analogy with a direct address to unilateralists:

> May I remind those who hold these views of the lesson but half a century old?

The significance of this is that it characterizes the dissenters as 'remindees', as people who have known but forgotten what she is about to tell them (by contrast with other knowers who do not need reminding and with non-knowers of various kinds, such as the uninformed/ignorant and sceptics/heretics). She thereby shows non-remindees that she gives unilateralists the benefit of the doubt.

Both remindees and non-remindees can recognize from this passage that remindees are in a 'marked' relationship to important cultural knowledge. This characterization is consistent with the overtly expressed attitude to unilateralists —that they are righteous people with defective mental processes (alternatively it is concerned with that kind of unilateralist, not with the unrighteous, calculating kind).

The explicit illocutionary force of 'remind' is foregrounded for any remindees or non-remindees who find it rhetorical (in the sense that it does not REALLY expect that 'those who hold these views' will readily accept the role of 'remindees'). Readers/listeners might recognize, from the foregrounding (a violation of Grice's Relevance maxim) that Margaret Thatcher has chosen a charitable interpretation of the marked relationship between unilateralists and cultural knowledge, when much less charitable interpretations would also be available. (They've only forgotten it, rather than disputing it, or ignoring it on purpose because they are on the enemy's side after all.) It is left to readers to decide whether this is intentional euphemism and, if so, what it euphemistically distorts (e.g. they ARE deliberately ignoring history for their own nefarious reasons).

At this point it is worthwhile returning to the question of the dividing-line between righteous and unrighteous elements in the peace movement. The covert distinction between those who are covered by the non-euphemistic meaning of 'remind and those who are covered by the unspoken, less benign interpretations that readers may want to provide, is an ethical matter. 'Remindees' are exempted from any moral judgement, because forgetting history can be seen as an aspect of the unreason from which they are suffering.

2.4.3 Denials

Margaret Thatcher's language in this text admits the 'myths' to be propositions serious enough to warrant her efforts at countering them. It would be relevant to investigate the 'seriousness' threshold for Conservative ministers during this period. This particular text is important because it is explicitly organized on the basis of addressing the 'other side's' arguments. Calling them 'myths' and spelling them out in her 'own' words does not in itself cancel their admission to the debate. Admission to debate of opponents' propositions is a discourse-level phenomenon, though it can have sentence-level realization. In this respect, negative sentences are of particular interest.

Consider the following sentences:

(41) It cannot be sensible for the West to disarm and abandon this most terrible weapon to a nation whose philosophy and whose actions show their total disregard for freedom and justice.
(100) We cannot take things on trust.
(133) NATO threatens no one.

These three sentences deny, or cancel, the following propositions:

> It can be sensible for the West to disarm,
> We can take things on trust,
> NATO threatens someone.

Leech (1983: 101) suggests that because in general negatives are less informative than their positive counterparts, Grice's Co-operative principle predicts that

> they tend to be used precisely in situations where they are not less informative for a given purpose than positive ones: and this will be when [the speaker] wants to deny some proposition which has been put forward or entertained by someone in the context (probably the addressee).

Who is it that has entertained these three false ideas? Possibly, in fact probably, we're supposed to realize that it is, specifically, the defence dissenters, though this is not made explicit in the text. (Recovering the 'speaker' of cancelled propositions is never a mechanical process. They may not even have real-world speakers for they may be speculative ideas entertained by the speaker and then discarded by him/her.) For socio-pragmatic reasons, the best guess here is that Margaret Thatcher is representing unilateralists as tending to say or suggest that disarmament could be sensible, that we can take things on trust, that NATO is a threat.

Denials vary in 'seriousness'. In a political speech a speaker may deny a proposition that no contributor to debate has ever proposed for consideration. It is possible to imagine Margaret Thatcher declaiming 'Russia is NOT our ally!'.

This sort of irony may be intended to make the audience develop the belief that dissenters subscribe to the cancelled proposition. If so, it wears its intentions on its sleeve, in a context where Margaret Thatcher believes that her audience will find it a redundant denial on first reading, and will therefore seek implicatures.

In this hypothetical example the speaker pretends that the hearers know that unilateralists have been saying 'Russia is our ally', knowing that they know that unilateralists have not said this and intending that listeners should recognize this as a DELIBERATE mismatching of actual and purported prior knowledge. This is less 'serious' than a denial which sets out to construct the 'prior knowledge' of the listeners so that there is a GOOD fit between the construction and the actuality, and that as a result its constructedness should go unnoticed.

But serious denials can misjudge the given knowledge of the audience and give life to the cancelled propositions that they might not have acquired otherwise. A mistake about audience knowledge can activate the same interpretative capacities as are employed when intended implicatures are being sought; but this time in pursuit of latent meanings that the speaker would wish to remain latent, unrecognized by the listener/reader ('So they think it necessary to deny THAT; how interesting . . .').

Fortunately or unfortunately, serious well-judged, serious ill-judged, and ironic denials can't be distinguished purely on the basis of the language forms used, for the differences between them relate to differences in the cultural knowledge of hearers and readers. The difficulty is compounded with a heterogeneous audience. What is for some a well-judged denial, is for others ill-judged or ironic. Politicians do not, generally speaking, tailor their speeches for politically acute audiences, as is illustrated in (41) above. On the assumption that it is a serious denial, then it is well judged for people who already know, or are ready to learn, that there is in circulation an argument to the effect that Western nuclear disarmament could be a sensible move. It is a crude, not to say irrelevant denial for people whose knowledge of unilateralist arguments is more developed. Amongst the disarmers there are people who do not think in terms of an instantaneous event but of a longer-term process. One important criterion in deciding what can be done in the short term is precisely the criterion of what is 'sensible', and being sensible will include being cautious in extending trust, to the Soviet Union and so on. Denials which were well judged for people as knowledgeable as this would be much riskier denials with the less well-informed. Such statements might, for a start, be positively educative; and, furthermore, the uninformed audience might, in hearing the speaker go on record with serious denials at a more detailed level than normal, get the impression that the speaker had accepted the prima facie case of the disarmers at the general level. Another difficulty is that an approach which looked seriously at the detail of dissenters' arguments would begin to look like an argument addressed TO dissenters. This has been avoided, presumably because Margaret Thatcher wants to concentrate upon the vulnerable audience rather than the hard-line opposition. It is possible that the speechwriter is aware of the possible 'oversimplification' charge. After (41), the text continues:

(42)—3. UNILATERALISM IS A MORAL GESTURE
(43)   But, of course, many of the one-sided disarmers don't face up to the logic of their case.

Restrospectively, this characterizes the proposition denied in (41) as 'the logic of their case'. Thus it is not even intended as a representation of what unilateralists SAY; only of what (according to the speaker) they are committed to as a matter of logical necessity.

This example again raises the question of the dividing line between righteous and unrighteous elements in the peace movement. The peace movement is characterized by a categorization into those who do and those who do not face up to the logic of their case. It is no sin to be illogical. This is consistent with the overtly expressed opinion about unilateralists' thought processes. And the unreasonableness of the 'logical' case has also been established in the previous section. But the formulation 'don't face up to' introduces other possibilities. If at some level of thought the illogicality is intentional, it would be vulnerable to ethical objection, depending upon the contribution made by the reader/ listener.

This is similar to the line taken in (29) and (31) above. Sentence (29) makes ethical condemnation of unilateralists easy. It cues readers to suppose either that CND selects its 'beliefs' not on grounds of truth but of expediency, or even that CND knows how dangerous the Soviet Union is really and lies in order to promote unilateralism. Sentence (31) emphasizes the 'goal-orientated' nature of CND arguments but claws back the invitation to see CND arguments as lies by making the observation reflexive: they misrepresent the facts in order to convince THEMSELVES, rather than other people. In retrospect, (29) could also be interpreted reflexively.

It is interesting to note when Conservative ministers take specific unilateralist arguments seriously, and to find serious (non-ironic) denials which are well judged for hearers who are quite well informed about the varieties of argument from disarmers.

(133)-(135) NATO threatens no one. Together with all the other NATO heads of Government I made a solemn pledge at our meeting in Bonn last June. That no NATO weapons—conventional or nuclear—would ever be used except in response to attack.

If (133) is a serious denial, it is well judged for people who know 'NATO threatens someone' as an opinion in circulation, which may include people who know of arguments to the effect that the Soviet Union could with reason perceive Nato as threatening. For example, they might know the argument that the Russian leaders would perceive 'theatre' weapons as a threat because theatre weapons are not ONLY usable in a European theatre distinct from the home territory of each superpower, but are also capable of inflicting damage on centres of population within the Soviet Union though not upon the United States (cf. Thompson 1980).

But (133) is not definitely serious, nor definitely ironic. As an ironic denial it would want hearers for whom (133) was so obviously true as to be redundant, generating an implicature of adverse comment upon anyone who could, counter-factually, counter-intuitively, irresponsibly, suppose that NATO is threatening to any part of the Eastern bloc. As a serious denial it would want hearers who would know that dissenters' arguments involve 'looking-at-it-from-their-point-of-view' and seeing NATO as fearful, though not necessarily persuaded to this themselves.

Even though it would be 'best' for Margaret Thatcher if the majority of her hearers were in the former rather than the latter category, it seems to me that her use of this particular denial does not 'cue' the ironic interpretation (i.e. it does not invite hearers to belong to those who 'take it for granted' that NATO is no aggressor and could disapprove of any who do not take it for granted). Margaret Thatcher's intention to speak a serious denial seems to be shown by the subsequent two sentences, which offer a kind of 'evidence' for the truth of (133), and evidence would be unnecessary if the speaker's intention was, unequivocally, to be ironic. In general, the production of evidence in discourse implies 'don't take my word for it'. The kind of evidence produced here is factual. Suspicious hearers could actually check on whether or not Margaret Thatcher had made the pledge that she claims to have made. Her critics will find this naïve because it supposes that from 'their point of view', promises made by their enemies can be taken on trust. The Conservative Government is far from ready to trust the promises of the West's enemies (cf. the issue of 'verification' in the context of arms-reduction talks between NATO and the Warsaw Pact), so they should understand the point.

But whilst the Conservative Government doubts Soviet promises, it expects the Russians to trust its own. Margaret Thatcher says in (130) that 'It is not enough for other powers to say that they will refrain from using nuclear weapons first. Such promises could never be relied upon if ever war started'. 'Such promises' does not mean enemy promises in general, for the NATO 'solemn pledge' is mentioned in the very next paragraph, pre-formulated as 'a credible assurance against starting military action at all', i.e. THEY only promise not to use nuclear weapons first; we go further and promise not to use any weapons first. This is the most favourable-to-us representation of the current NATO policy to use nuclear weapons first in response to a Soviet conventional attack (a policy rejected by the General Synod of the Church of England on ethical grounds). It partly explains the importance of playing down the moral difference between nuclear and non-nuclear forces in warfare.

Serious denials are of more interest when they are not wholly predictable. Presumably politicians try to avoid serious unpredictable denials for fear of playing into the hands of their opponents. They need to make their own subjective assessments of the current state of political debate, and say no more than (they believe) they have to, to cope with any public disquiet. Sentence (133) is by a small degree riskier in this sense, as a serious denial, than (41), where the latter is just heard as one way of stating the well-known Conservative position.

The ethical case against nuclear weapons is a strong one and presumably, for the vulnerable audience that Margaret Thatcher is interested in, a starting-point in any sympathy which they may have for the unilateralist cause. Consequently it would be hard for the Conservatives to censor themselves to the extent of not allowing some voice for this kind of thinking. The two sentences with which the speech begins (both denials) illustrate what can be done when faced with this kind of difficulty:

(2) The horror of the nuclear bomb needs no underlining from me.
(3) None of us can ignore the devastation which would result from a war waged with nuclear weapons.

In order for (2) to be a serious denial of the view that 'the horror of the nuclear bomb needs underlining from Margaret Thatcher', the speaker should be speaking from an assumption that some people subscribe to this opinion and that others who don't are nevertheless aware that the opinion is in circulation. Expressed in the positive, the opinion which (2) denies sounds rather strange and unnatural for the defence debate. However, the point behind both (2) and (3) is that they speak to hearers' feelings about the state of opinion amongst their fellow citizens. 'Need' in the positive implies a contrast between the world as it is and the world as it should be. Combined with an inanimate subject, implications that people could be responsible for the circumstances out of which 'needs' arise (cf. 'Your car needs washing' vs. 'You haven't washed your car recently') are blocked. But implications that people could be responsible for setting things to rights are not blocked, and in the case of this sentence, hearers are allowed to suppose that, if circumstances were such that 'the horror of the nuclear bomb' DID need underlining, then the speaker herself could have a responsibility for remedying the situation. Only two possible scenarios are allowed for. In one, 'the horror of the nuclear bomb' needs underlining, and Margaret Thatcher obliges. It is a scenario in which some of us have been ignoring 'the devastation which would result from a war waged with nuclear weapons'. In the other scenario, the proposition does not need underlining and she forbears. Either she knows the horror and does what's needed; or she knows and refrains from doing anything unnecessary. The real situation is the latter. She forbears to underline and the reason for her forbearance is the first thing drawn to the attention of hearers.

If 'the horror of the nuclear bomb' did need underlining, this would constitute an objective cause for any failure to take account of that proposition, on the part of actual people: 'They don't understand because they haven't been told, often enough, loudly enough'. Margaret Thatcher's denial is well judged for people with doubts about the extent to which all OTHER citizens appreciate the horror. For themselves, it is a given which they share with the speaker, signalled by the use of a definite article with a noun phrase in topic position (on the distribution of given and new information in clauses, see Chafe 1970; Halliday 1967; Jackendoff 1972; Chomsky 1971; Clark and Haviland 1977). Sentence (3) in this respect clarifies a meaning which in sentence (2) is only a possibility, by denying that anyone could 'ignore the devastation which would result from a war waged with nuclear weapons'. It makes explicit that the reason why 'the horror of the nuclear bomb' needs no underlining is indeed the SATISFACTORY state of public opinion on this point, adding to that as properly new information one thing in particular: the modality of that knowledge as either a matter of obligation or necessity (the alternative meanings of 'can').

A general principle for discourse is that speakers tell hearers what hearers don't know. Kempson (1975: 166–71), for example, builds on this principle via the conversational maxim 'Do not assert any proposition which is a member of the Pragmatic Universe of Discourse' (p. 169). Propositions known to both speaker and hearer belong to the Pragmatic Universe of Discourse. More specifically, a proposition belongs there if the speaker believes it; believes that the hearer knows it; believes the hearer knows that the speaker believes it; believes that the hearer knows that the speaker believes that the hearer knows it.

The generality of this principle is not absolute. It is not the guiding principle for phatic communion, for example. In political speeches there can be rhetorical/communicational pay-offs from speaking AS IF there were people in the audience who do not know some key propositions that the speaker wishes to have in play. Sentences (2) and (3) illustrate this. Margaret Thatcher, in choosing to speak as if some of her audience can be told that, notwithstanding anything they may have heard or thought to the contrary, the awful potential of nuclear weapons is well enough known to everyone, manages to allow for more interesting meanings to be brought out by readers/listeners whose 'take' on the proferred information is not the canonical one. Listeners who feel that they already know that there is universal understanding will hear the new information in these two sentences as redundant. They may even hear it as intentionally redundant, infringing the Quantity maxim in order to generate a conversational implicature. As with previous examples that I have discussed, the implicature is underspecified by the text and thus provides opportunities for hearers to make their own contributions. It seems to me possible for like-minded hearers to discover implicatures about 'underliners' of the horror of the nuclear bomb, because these are people who apparently do not know, or choose not to know, that there is universal understanding on this point.

On the basis of this input, like-minded hearers may find it in their hearts to condemn the underliners, because of their supposed motives for constantly emphasizing the obvious. Margaret Thatcher could deny responsibility for what hearers do with her utterances in this way. They would have moved away from 'the text itself' in employing their own beliefs about the motives for unilateralist anti-Bomb rhetoric in order to produce their condemnations. But the opportunity is there, and any hearers who did use the text for this kind of speculation would find that it goes on to offer more opportunities. This is particularly the case with sentences (29)–(31), which introduce a causal explanation of unilateralism.

It is not only the like-minded who will be able to develop this train of thought. But, as I have suggested, a precondition for doing so is to hear the denials as redundant, infringing the Quantity maxim, in the first instance. Now, on my interpretation, as far as Margaret Thatcher is concerned, one group of people especially is in theory unable to make that first move—the unilateralist 'underliners'. So if unilateralists begin to hear, in what Margaret Thatcher says, the possibility of criticism directed against them from a particular section of her audience, this would indicate their imaginative access to a universe of discourse in which 'the horror of the bomb needs no underlining' has the status of a taken-for-granted, even though they should not themselves subscribe to that universe of discourse.

On the other hand, there are people committed to the belief that there are citizens who don't know enough about the horror of the Bomb (medical and scientific groups, for example, who have tried to extend public knowledge here). On the other hand, there are people committed to the belief that the public does fully understand about the horror (Margaret Thatcher and people who can hear (2) as enunciating a taken-for-granted, the informational redundancy of which can be used to trigger an implicature of criticism for the 'underliners'). The unilateralist listener who has a sense of what it is like to belong to the latter group, has a foot in both camps, and may even feel a kind of tension in being in such a position.

Some listeners' interpretations will centre upon the given information in the theme/subject of the sentence, noticing its givenness as a key fact about THIS sentence in the mouth of THIS speaker. Since the relationship between given and new information in a sentence is a matter of background/foreground relations, the NOTICING of given information is to that extent a non-canonical readerly act: and such a noticing may or may not be cued by the speaker (intentional implicatures can involve cueing listeners to notice given information). In the case of (2) and (3) I have proposed the likelihood of listeners noticing the given information ('So Margaret Thatcher takes it for granted that the nuclear bomb is a horror; that devastation would result from a war waged with nuclear weapons'). There is nothing here to suggest that the speaker intentionally cues them to notice it. I believe that its 'noticeability' is a function of what listeners know about the state of play in the defence debate, and specifically any knowledge that they have of CND-type attacks on the nuclear ethics of the Conservative Government. If listeners know of such attacks, AND have not dismissed them out of hand (the like-minded may react to an attack on the Conservative Government's beliefs as to an attack on their own beliefs), then their live interest in the question of Margaret Thatcher's beliefs may lead them to 'misread' the sentence by mentally reorganizing the given and new information (that is, they derive true meanings from the text but with relative emphasis that is false to the 'intentions' of the speaker).

However, there are at least two ways of doing this 'misreading'. One way results in an interpretation which is favourable to Margaret Thatcher's reputation: the listener infers that 'Margaret Thatcher takes it for granted that the nuclear bomb is a horror, I needn't have worried'. Such a listener would be acting under the assumption that the formal structure of given/new information distribution in the sentence was a direct reflection of the speaker's cognitive state: Margaret Thatcher in fact believes that the nuclear bomb is a horror. A less naïve interpretation is not as favourable to Margaret Thatcher's reputation, because it assumes rhetorical intentions. It assumes in fact that, the absence of cues notwithstanding, this is a case of intentional implicature in disguise, for the benefit of listeners who, she has calculated, are likely to do this sort of misreading because of the extra-textual schema which they bring to bear upon their task of interpretation. From this point of view the 'naïve misinterpretation' is not a misinterpretation at all since Margaret Thatcher is calculating for a particular audience.

Presumably the 'sophisticated misinterpretation' remains a misinterpretation. At least, the speaker's intentions to cue the naïve misinterpretation are 'off record'. Challenged by the sophisticated misreader (if such a challenge could be expressed in more everyday terms), she could point to the formally new information in the sentence ('. . . needs no underlining from me'), claiming only that was the 'point' of her utterance. Formally there would be no gainsaying her. The case could only be made on sociopragmatic grounds: not that the 'naïve misinterpretation' was THE point of the sentence, rather than its new information, but that the sentence had different 'points' for different audiences. The naïve misinterpretation is a useful result amongst the vulnerable audience, whilst the implicatures derived from the new information are useful results amongst the like-minded.

2.5 MICHAEL HESELTINE

Margaret Thatcher's ideas about the peace movement, as expressed (not always explicitly) in the Bournemouth speech present ambiguities and indeterminacies, when the heterogeneity of the audience is taken into account, and it is recognized that elements of the discourse have different rhetorical pay-offs depending upon the inferential frameworks deployed in specific subsections of the audience. This situation makes the text ambiguous, whether or not it is empirically the case that for any and all readers only one of the possible interpretations will be in play. An adequate explanation of how the rhetoric works must transcend the limitations of single interpretations and recognize the coexistence of different meanings for different sympathies. A text which bears a more homogeneous population in mind as its audience, and speaks to a construction of that group's communicational 'needs', will be correspondingly less ambiguous.

Such is the case with Michael Heseltine. He very rarely says anything that close textual analysis could claim to be defensive. Part of what is involved in achieving a more offensive rhetorical style is a concentration upon addressing the already like-minded, i.e. eschewing provision of alternative interpretations:

> We all know what the Russians will do. They will continue to develop their nuclear capability, and they will continue to introduce new nuclear capability, and they will continue to introduce new nuclear weapons systems. [Conservative Central Office statement, 6 May 1983, following Labour's letter to Moscow concerning unilateral disarmament.]

Notice here the reference to what 'we all know', and notice the odd-sounding rhetorical questions in the following:

> And what do the men in the Kremlin see in Britain this weekend? They see the marchers, the protesters. And are they impressed? Do they see the marchers as peacekeepers? [Article by Michael Heseltine, *News of the World*, 3 March 1983.]

The next quotation shows Michael Heseltine employing another rhetorical question:

> But if we disarmed first, do you really think the Soviets would follow suit? [Party political broadcast, 23 February 1983.]

This is intended as the sort of rhetorical question which has an obvious answer. Assuming that Michael Heseltine's audience are indeed all of the same basic opinion as himself on the nature of the Soviet threat, it will work in this way. But it will work as intended for a smaller proportion of the national audience than Margaret Thatcher's hypothetical rhetorical question concerning disarmament in the 1930s. It has become possible in quite respectable areas (the Labour Party, the General Synod of the Church of England) at least to entertain the possibility that a moral gesture of the sort envisaged by unilateralists could be a contribution in developing the much-needed mutual trust between East and West; and could EVEN (though reciprocity is not asserted as a PROBABLE consequence of British nuclear disarmament by unilateralists) lead to Soviet concessions. For many people 'would the Soviets follow suit?' has become a real rather than a rhetorical question. The views of these people are not taken into account by Michael Heseltine in arguing his case. Margaret Thatcher allows the same issue to be a real rather than a rhetorical question when she deals with it in the Bournemouth speech as one of the unilateralist 'myths'.

Michael Heseltine's concentration upon the like-minded allows him to pose (and solve) as the puzzle in all this unnecessary fuss, the question of the Labour Party. CND and the rest ('extremists'), are marginal to current debate, so the extraordinary development which needs explanation is the Labour Party's defection from the consensus viewpoint. This theme is frequently used by Michael Heseltine, whilst he is also prepared to speak the taken-for-granted that nothing has changed to justify Labour's shift:

> The Labour Party now proposes to abandon those policies in a reckless gamble based upon their willingness to trust the Soviet Union.
> The fact of the matter is that the case for these policies—for deterrence—has not changed. The Soviet threat has not diminished; rather it has increased with the SS20 development. The only change is within the Labour Party itself—in opposition they are unable to keep their policies in line with the realities which they have always, thus far, recognised when they are in office. [From South Mimms speech to Conservative candidates, Saturday 16 April 1983.]

> Has public opinion changed? The evidence here is incontrovertible. There is massive support for NATO. The polls show that over two-thirds of our people reject the proposition that we should give up our nuclear weapons, while other countries keep theirs. [From an article by Michael Heseltine in the *Sunday Times*, 13 March 1983.]

It is also worth noting that Michael Heseltine's serious denials sometimes address quite specific points raised by CND:

> Some criticise Cruise missiles on the grounds that they are intended to be used to fight a limited nuclear war in Europe. But this charge ignores the fact

that it was the Europeans who asked for them to deter a threat to Europe from the SS20. [From an article by Michael Heseltine, *Sunday Times*, 13 March 1983.]

This is interesting because of the implication that the specific points are worth addressing, and that the general case ('unilateral nuclear disarmament') does rest upon detailed argument. When addressing himself to Labour-Party unilateralism, the seriousness of his attempts to tackle Labour's proposals is cancelled out by the style of the rebuttal which is generally calculated to expose the policies as ridiculous, unworkable, etc. (this is especially true of the South Mimms speech). Other serious denials, in being made emphatic, suggest that the proposition being denied itself carries some emphasis in the competing discourse:

> There is no credible explanation of our own or of our allies' forces that can be interpreted as an aggressive capability. [Article by Michael Heseltine, *Sunday Times* 13 March 1983.]

This denial is made emphatic by the use of 'credible'. Yet 'credible' may have a counter-productive effect on listeners for whom the idea of an intrinsically 'credible' or 'incredible' explanation is suspect on the grounds that 'credibility' is a subjective judgement and that others besides Michael Heseltine ought to be given the chance to make such judgements on their own account.

The existence of such specific serious denials in Michael Heseltine's rhetoric may undermine his concentration on the like-minded as expresssed in his use of rhetorical questions (see above). On the other hand, it can be argued that his denials do need to be serious if they are to be heard as compatible with his analysis of how CND is constituted. As suggested above, intendedly ironic denials are the ones which can cue 'bad faith' interpretations of why CND says what it does. The corollary of this is that intendedly serious denials do not cue bad faith interpretations. Michael Heseltine is less inclined than Margaret Thatcher to use ironic denials and thereby cue bad faith interpretations. This is inconsistent with what he tells his interviewer Susan Crosland in *The Sunday Times* (1 May 1983):

> I have two very different approaches to CND, you will see. There is the approach which I hope understands the anxiety and concern that large numbers of people—across the parties—feel for the dangers of nuclear warfare. I have another approach for those who organise CND—the successful political operators of the hard left whose motives are very different from those of the first group.

The propositions denied may be the sincere beliefs of innocent CND members at the same time as being the persuasive superficial arguments disguising the real but dishonourable goals of the leaders. Thus:

> Some people say that the Soviet threat is exaggerated and that they don't mean any harm. But look at the facts. [Article by Michael Heseltine, *News of the World*, 3 April 1983.]

Nothing in these two sentences or in the accompanying text suggests that the 'some people' in question might have their (unspoken) REASONS for saying that 'the Soviet threat is exaggerated', that 'they don't mean any harm'. To have hinted as much about 'some people' would have been a cue to a bad-faith interpretation of an argument which Heseltine would probably want to believe could as well be held in good faith. Most dissenting arguments are dealt with in this 'hands clean' way by the Defence Minsiter. Whereas Margaret Thatcher's speech has BOTH good-faith and bad-faith interpretations on offer (but without being clear as to why both SHOULD be on offer), Michael Heseltine, in this quotation and elsewhere, has NEITHER on offer (even though he could, on the basis of his theory about CND, have both).

2.6 JOHN NOTT

John Nott was Michael Heseltine's predecessor at the Ministry of Defence. If Michael Heseltine's rhetoric seems more offensive than the line taken by Margaret Thatcher, then John Nott's rhetoric seems more defensive. Margaret Thatcher, in the Bournemouth speech, takes account of themes in the language of defence-dissenters which put her side in a bad moral light (e.g. in trying to signal that she knows and accepts the horror of nuclear weapons, she tacitly acknowledges a point of view in which there is some doubt about where she really stands on this basic ethical point). John Nott, in a speech at St. Lawrence Jewry, November 1982, takes this kind of defensiveness one stage further. He acknowledges more openly than the Prime Minsiter that he/his side is a target for moral criticism.

In common with both Margaret Thatcher and Michael Heseltine, John Nott indicates that the ethics of the other side's position ought to be brought into the argument. He also, as they do, tends to formulate defence dissenters as 'the other', a group to be spoken about, rather than spoken to, even in the process of addressing their arguments. The following quotation illustrates both of these tendencies:

> I hope that the unilateral disarmers have thought through the moral responsibility which they might bear for their actions. I believe unilateral disarmament by Britain would not only reduce our security but would seriously undermine the achievement of multilateral nuclear weapons reduction on all sides.

John Nott's discourse is less tied to his construction of what the already like-minded think and believe, than that of the other two ministers, as illustrated in the following rhetorical question:

> Is it seriously suggested that if we give up our weapons, the West would remain as secure as it is today? Would not it make war more likely? I think so. If so, why should it be a morally defensible act?

This is, on the face of it, a rhetorical question with an 'obvious' answer, analogous to Margaret Thatcher's question about Nazi Germany and Michael Heseltine's question about Soviet reciprocity of hypothetical Western nuclear disarmament. But unlike the other two, John Nott does not leave the obvious answer unspoken, as is required for maximum possible taken-for-grantedness. He answers it himself (perhaps the answer is not so obvious after all) and he answers it in personal terms ('I think so, but others might come to different conclusions'). Another speaker might have chosen to carry the rhetorical questions through, thereby staying with a construction of what the like-minded believe. John Nott's personal-opinion answer opens the field of interpretation to readers beyond the like-minded by indicating that they are to think of the question as a real one. It has merited the speaker's serious consideration and by implication it merits the serious consideration of his audience also.

John Nott's openness here is consistent with his attitude as expressed in several of his denials in the St. Lawrence Jewry speech. For example:

> I have never claimed that the Soviet Union is seeking war with the West.
> Even to pose such questions means of course that some people may misrepresent the argument and accuse me of advocating the use of nuclear weapons. I do no such thing.

A less defensive speaker could well have refrained from mentioning the other side's morally weighted criticisms, especially since their deployment by the other side is merely hinted at in the first example, suggested as a possibility in the second. But they are mentioned, and denied, 'as if' the speaker felt that without the denials audiences that were not too well informed could find themselves asking whether John Nott is saying or implying that the Soviet Union wants war with the West, or advocating the use of nuclear weapons.

Aside from the evidence of rhetorical questions and denials, John Nott's speech has other features which can be taken as symptoms of defensiveness. One such feature is the simple fact that the specific case of Trident missiles is argued out over approximately 1,200 words of the speech. This, of course, takes John Nott quite deeply into serious debate with the anti-Trident cause. Another indicator of defensiveness is his use of the definite article when mentioning 'moral complexities' in the nuclear debate:

> If by the credible threat of a nuclear response we successfully deter war, then I believe that the good that comes from this must exceed the risks in spite of the moral complexities involved.

The definite article indicates that the existence of moral complexities in this issue is taken for granted. It is arguable whether either of the other two speakers would permit themselves the use of this expression, as it implies difficulties in coming to the most morally acceptable conclusion. Michael Heseltine and Margaret Thatcher use styles which depend upon having resolved any difficulties in their thinking; in a sense the difficulties no longer exist for them. John Nott has also resolved the difficulties in his mind but his style allows that they continue to exist notwithstanding the resolution.

It is important not to discount the effect of each politician's perception of his proximate audience upon the rhetorical style adopted, and to acknowledge that perhaps those at St. Lawrence Jewry were thought by John Nott to warrant a more serious and more explicitly ethical presentation of the case than other audiences that he was wont to address in his days at the Ministry of Defence. Whether or not this calculation on his part could account for all of the stylistic differences between John Nott and the other two speakers is a separate question.

2.7 CONCLUSIONS

Without wishing to overstate the differences, I think it is fairly clear from the extracts that I have presented above that there are stylistic differences between the three ministers. This range of differences indicates significant differences in the assumptions that the speakers make about the kind of national audience that they are addressing, and/or about which part of that audience they are addressing. Margaret Thatcher's rhetoric is designed to accommodate more of the national audience than Michael Heseltine's. Her approach is more ambitious than his because it tries for different pay-offs with different parts of that audience. Michael Heseltine makes fewer concessions to the heterogeneity of the audience, producing a more assured style, in spite of his willingness to consider points of detail put on to the agenda for discussion by CND (these are usually questions of strategy rather than moral issues). Finally, in John Nott's speech, the moral position of the 'like-minded', is passed over to a greater extent than in the speeches of the other two politicians; he is willing to make 'the moral case for Trident' (this is the title of his speech), rather than assume it is already made for all righteous citizens.

Although the textual studies that I have presented here have been very selective, I believe that they have resulted in a number of more specific questions about the meanings in the Conservative Government's 'defence' discourse, providing rhetorical features to monitor as the debates continue. Will there be more discourse addressed TO dissenters, and to those who have begun to hear and think about what the disarmers are saying? Or will most addressees continue to be presumed to be on the Government's side for important debatables? Will the joint efforts to marginalize dissenters introduce more grounds for moral condemnation? For example, will like-minded hearers and vulnerable audience members be more often invited to condemn unilateralists as much for speaking their views as for holding those views ('They know Russia won't agree at Geneva while they carry on protesting'). Will the more tentative style adopted by Nott decrease? Will there be any increase in the double-faceted utterance, with different advantages for different audiences, as noted in Margaret Thatcher's Bournemouth speech?

NOTES

1. On the lexis of morality used for the discourse of power, cf. Lerman (1973).
2. See e.g. Leech (1980, 1983), Kempson (1975), Gazdar (1979), Wilson (1975), Levinson (1983).
3. On the notion of 'schema' (or 'script' or 'frame') operating by default in the interpretation of discourse, cf. Chapters 6 and 12.

3 Rhetoric of defence in the United States: language, myth and ideology

Peter Moss
University of Adelaide, South Australia

3.1 INTRODUCTION

The study of myth is a study of the origin of beliefs out of historic experience. The study of ideology is a study of the moulding of beliefs by social situations. The social function of myth is to bind together social groups as wholes or, in other words, to establish a social consensus. The social function of ideology is to segregate and serve special interests within societies.[1]

The above is a useful way of beginning the task of trying to make sense of defence rhetoric. Myth and ideology are well represented in the language of the policy-makers and bureaucrats. I use this perspective as a structuring method for my argument. It is useful because it prevents one from concentrating solely upon the gross aspect of nuclear and defence rhetoric. These will be discussed later, but as part of a wider argument. It is time that the easy language targets of euphemism, jargon, distortion were placed in the context of our general language and not considered simply and solely as excrescences. My assumption is that the language of nuclear politics and its dispersion in public discourse is something more complex than can be explained by the crude mendacities of leading politicians.

Ronald Reagan is consistently presented in the world's media as 'the great communicator'. What he communicates or whether his audiences receive his messages as they were conceived are questions rarely addressed, however. It might be more revealing to call him the great magician because both he and his administration's spokespeople constantly remind Americans of a potent strain in the national psyche, the attachment to an individualist primitivism. Some, like D. H. Lawrence, would term it an atavistic primitivism: '[the American soul is] hard, isolate, stoic and a killer'.[2]

Aspects of this cultural reflex are frequently evident in the speeches of President Reagan and in those of members of his government. Reagan's skill is that he massages these traditional nerves and makes them co-terminous with policy. The question is whether these persistent underlying themes are the product of an obsessive mentality or are a public consciousness of mythic themes, emphasized in order to create social consensus on the one hand and to serve specific ideological ends on the other. There is no scope in this essay, nor is it the place, to trace the historical antecedents for the apparent need in America to stand witness to manliness, aggression and the simple directives of action and moral certainty. My intention is to indicate the tenacity of these elements in defence matters, and to show that at several levels the rhetoric of nuclear militarism is consistent in its attempts to soothe the alarmed, deflect the sceptical and to confuse the unthinking members of society. I shall examine a number of 'popular texts' to try to show that the public rhetorics of defence are not merely the products of a bellicose mentality common to a few politicians. Rather, aggressive discourses are frequent at a number of different levels of the defence establishment[3] and, in sum, they suggest strongly a revised cultural primitivism used in the service of military and political policies.

3.2 'I' AND 'WE' IN A PRESIDENTIAL SPEECH

The main themes are evident in many of Reagan's speeches and public pronouncements. The following example captures the relaxed surface style, vehicle for a more tense and active message (emphasis added):

> Today, I would like to discuss another vital aspect of our national security—OUR efforts to limit and reduce the danger of modern weaponry.
> WE live in a world in which total war would mean catastrophe. WE also live in a world torn by a great moral struggle—between Democracy and its enemies, between the spirit of freedom and those who fear freedom.
> In the last fifteen years and more the Soviet Union has engaged in a relentless military build-up, overtaking and surpassing the United States in major categories of military power, acquiring what can only be considered an offensive military capability. All the moral values which THIS COUNTRY cherishes—Freedom; Democracy; the right of peoples and nations to determine their own destiny; to speak and write and live and worship as they choose—all these basic rights are fundamentally challenged by a powerful adversary which does not wish these values to survive.
> This is OUR dilemma, and it is a profound one: WE must both defend freedom and preserve the peace. WE must stand true to our principles and our friends while preventing a holocaust.
> THE WESTERN COMMITMENT to peace through strength has given Europe its longest period of peace in a century. WE cannot conduct ourselves as if the special dangers of nuclear weapons did not exist. But WE must not allow ourselves to be paralysed by the problem—to abdicate OUR moral duty.[4]

A widely used rhetorical device in official rhetoric is to coalesce speaker, audience and theme so that the immediate impression is one of unity and common purpose. More subtly, the repeated use of the plural first-person pronoun *we* (presumably interpreted inclusively) links the individual with the state and, through insistent repetition, may weaken in some sense the individual's hold on independent thought.

Reagan begins with a tentative expression: 'I would like', as opposed to a possible choice in this context of 'I will', 'I am going', etc. (corresponding roughly with degree of tentativeness in directives: 'will you', 'would you', 'would you like to', etc.). It might even be heard as an offer, rather than a direct statement of intent. He moves immediately to an ambiguous use of the first-person plural pronoun ('our efforts'): if it is interpreted inclusively, 'efforts' are ascribed by hearers to themselves, not just to their President. Moreover, between the superficially similar 'our national security' and 'our efforts' (possessive pronoun plus noun phrase), there is a semantic movement that transforms the abstract possessive into shared activity. For the rest of this part of the speech the inclusive sense of the pronoun seems to prevail, largely perhaps because of its association with broad moral injunctions. The presidential pronoun presents him not as a private individual but as a representative symbol:

We live in a world torn by a great moral struggle.
We must defend freedom.
We must stand true to our principles.
We must not . . . . . abdicate our moral duty.

The point is that these apparent assertions are really oblique commands possessing the force of binding obligations, and serving the double purpose of suggesting firm leadership and shared commitment.

Reagan, then, creates a community of interests and concerns around a series of abstractions and obligations.[5] Normally, such a method would be seen as a sure way to narcotize the audience, but his abstract themes reach deep into primitive mental depths and are thus capable of sustaining conviction and of creating identification. The words are general enough to allow diverse groups to attach concrete meanings according to their own conscious or unconscious interpretation of private and public meanings in culture and history: 'struggle, spirit, freedom, rights, destiny'. It is a heady mixture and it is made more potent by the juxtaposition with the Soviet 'fear' of freedom, 'relentless military build-up', and 'offensive military capability'.

Having created common emotional cause, Reagan moves on to a rapid historical survey of American initiatives since 1945 in arms negotiations, followed by his attempts to fulfil his own promises to reduce nuclear weapons. At this point he moves into a species of doublethink—the elimination of contradiction:

> Today, not only the peace but also the chances of real arms control depend on restoring the military balance. We know that the ideology of the Soviet leaders does not permit them to leave any Western weakness unprobed, any vacuum of power unfilled. It would seem that to them negotiation is only another form of struggle. Yet, I believe the Soviets can be persuaded to reduce their arsenals—but only if they see it as absolutely necessary. Only if the Soviets recognize the West's determination to modernize its own military forces will they see an incentive to negotiate a verifiable agreement establishing equal, lower levels. And, very simply, that is one of the main reasons why we must rebuild our defensive strength.

The rhetorical use of pronouns is again skilfully contrived. The generalized 'we', invoked at the beginning as part of a shared knowledge of Russian intentions, and at the end as a more formal imperative which widens the connection to implicit military power and activity, is joined in the middle by the presidential judgement of Russian response. The paragraph represents a structured statement of Western political practice: it presupposes a community of shared assumption facilitating specialized individual judgement, and enabling a widening of action in the name of the national abstraction 'we'.

In establishing surface connectedness in the context of apparently open discussion, the skilful rhetorician can slip in the real theme, as a natural extension of the presumed general knowledge of Soviet duplicity. The rhetorical concealments at the end of the message get in almost unnoticed, with the consequence that Reagan's descriptions of military modernization and the rebuilding of 'defensive strength' are accepted at face value rather than as bare statements of the intention to increase military arsenals.

In the next section of his speech Reagan continues the I/we method, using a similar sequence as in the example immediately above but adopting a change in tone:

> My other national security priority on assuming office was to thoroughly re-examine the entire arms control agenda. Since then, in co-ordination with our allies, we have launched the most comprehensive program of arms control initiatives ever undertaken. Never before in history has a nation engaged in so many major simultaneous efforts to limit and reduce the instruments of war . . .
>
> Together with our allies we have offered a comprehensive new proposal for mutual and balanced reduction of conventional forces in Europe . . .
>
> We have recently proposed to the Soviet Union a series of further measures to reduce the risk of war from accident or miscalculation . . .
>
> We have joined our allies in proposing a conference on disarmament in Europe . . .
>
> We have proposed to the Soviet Union improving the verification provisions of two agreements to limit underground nuclear testing, but, so far, the response has been negative. We will continue to try.
>
> And most important, we have made far-reaching proposals . . . for deep reductions in strategic weapons and for elimination of an entire class of intermediate-range weapons.
>
> I am determined to achieve real arms control . . .

Notice that in this passage singular 'I' frames plural 'we', suggesting an active agent, in control, yet working with a larger constituency. The rhetorical development of this section in relation to the speech as a whole creates a shift in tone to a more aggressive style. The repeated declaratives ('We have') lend a sense of urgent busyness. And the verbs themselves are selected and sequenced to give the appearance of increased energy and commitment: from 'launched' and 'offered', with their sense of readiness to act, to 'proposed' and 'continue to try', with their sense of intention to act.

In the final section of his speech Reagan turns to specific consideration of nuclear weapons and summarizes his aims:

> Our allies—as important nuclear exporters—also have a very important responsibility to prevent the spread of nuclear arms. To advance this goal, we should all adopt comprehensive safeguards as a condition for nuclear supply commitments we make in the future. In the days ahead, I will be talking to other world leaders about the need for urgent movement on this and other measures against nuclear proliferation. That is the arms control

agenda we have been pursuing. Our proposals are fair, far-reaching, and comprehensive, but we still have a long way to go.
We Americans are sometimes in impatient people. I guess it's a symptom of our traditional optimism, energy and spirit. Often this is a source of strength. However, impatience can be a real handicap. Any of you who have been involved in labor-management negotiations, or any kind of bargaining, know that patience strengthens your bargaining position...
This is a basic fact of life we can't afford to lose sight of when dealing with the Soviet Union. Generosity in negotiation has never been a trademark of theirs; it runs counter to the basic militancy of Marxist–Leninist ideology.
So, it is vital that we show patience, determination, and, above all, national unity. If we appear to be divided—if the Soviets suspect that domestic, political pressure will undercut our position—they will dig in their heels. And that can only delay an agreement, and may destroy all hope for an agreement.
That is why I have been concerned about the nuclear freeze proposals...

This section is more pointed than the earlier parts of the speech but the rhetorical evocation of a collective *we* persists. The only potentially disturbing element is the chilling ambiguous reference to the allies as 'important nuclear exporters'. To the extent that this is construed as criticism of the allies, it serves to reinforce the united patriotic *we*. Yet the allies remain allies, as implied by the comment immediately following, where the generalized 'we' is extended to include Europe: 'we should all adopt comprehensive safeguards'. Since he cannot presume total inclusion in such a 'we', however, Reagan is obliged to return to a contrastive 'I', and refocus the speech on his own action ('I will be talking to other world leaders about the need for urgent movement').

There follows a pause from the possibilities of action, in which the American 'we' is linked to assumed sources of traditional strength and historical identity. The reference to the impatient national psyche is not simply a nod in the direction of themes which Reagan has consistently alluded to throughout his presidency. It is a moment of rhetorical populism which allows him to begin the attack on his opponents, the supporters of a nuclear freeze. Whilst not excluding them from mainstream American virtue (all Americans are impatient), the implication is that his opponents' impatience is the exception to the rule that 'often this is a source of strength'. What they lack is indicated later in the section: 'determination' and the willingness to be part of a unified national voice.

Reagan isolates his opponents further by using the analogy of industrial relations, implicitly assuming it can be perceived as a similar activity to international arms negotiations. It is a clever comparison to use for his general audience. Industrial affairs usually have attached to them strong opinions and beliefs in contemporary folklore and, regardless of where one's sympathies lie, the whole area creates involvement at some level. Its invocation acts as a culture-trigger to the audience and facilitates the drawing of conclusions in a more familiar frame of reference. In that frame the President can count on the accepted lore that 'strength' (in all its symbolic vagueness) is desirable. The nuclear freezers are further marginalized by quantification and a modalizing expression:

> Most of those who support the freeze, I'm sure, are well intentioned—concerned about the arms race, . . .

which seem to carry the implication that there are SOME about whom one might be not sure, which in turn implies that this minority is ill intentioned, etc.

Having dealt with his opponents' motives and credibility, Reagan's final section in his speech is devoted to specific reasons why America cannot freeze weapons production:

> Finally, the freeze would reward the Soviets for their fifteen year build-up while locking us into our existing equipment, which in many cases is obsolete and badly in need of modernization. Three-quarters of Soviet strategic warheads are on delivery systems five years old or less; three-quarters of the American strategic warheads are on delivery systems fifteen years or older. The time comes when everything wears out—the trouble is it comes a lot sooner for us than for them. And, under such a freeze, we couldn't do anything about it.
> Our B-52 strategic bombers are older than many of the pilots who fly them; if they were automobiles, they would qualify as antiques. A freeze could lock us into obsolescence. It is asking too much to expect our service men and women to risk their lives in obsolete equipment. The two million patriotic Americans in the armed services deserve the best and most modern equipment to protect them—and us.

Reagan's opponents are not merely naïve and misguided but are, by implication, traitorous: the freeze would prevent America from properly defending itself; patriotic Americans in the services would be betrayed by the rest of America.

The homely automobile analogy has a twofold point. It makes simple and graphic America's alleged missile difficulty by placing the issue at the heart of urban familiarity, no matter how false the comparison; and it makes, again, the link with the past, this time to America's industrial genius and to the development of another mass technology. Finally, it touches on the issue of age and obsolescence: old things are dangerous and have limited usefulness (a nice irony there) and must be replaced. The cultural circle is closed, then, with this reminder that America's mass-technological society is about progress and the new.

The end of his speech returns to the *I/we* coalescence, recapitulating all the themes introduced earlier:

> I call upon all Americans, of both parties and all branches of government, to join in this effort. We must not let our disagreements, or partisan politics, keep us from strengthening the peace and reducing armaments.
> I pledge to all our allies and friends in Europe and Asia: we will continue to consult closely with you. We are conscious of our responsibility when we negotiate with our adversaries on issues of concern to you, your safety and well-being . . .

> ... Let us practice restraint in our international conduct, so that the present climate of mistrust can some day give way to mutual confidence and secure peace.
> What better time to rededicate ourselves to this undertaking than in the Easter season, when millions of the world's people pay homage to the one who taught us peace on earth, goodwill toward men?
> This is the goal, my fellow Americans, of all the democratic nations—a goal that requires firmness, patience and understanding. If the Soviet Union responds in the same spirit, we are ready. And we can pass on to posterity the gift of peace—that, and freedom are the greatest gifts that one generation can bequeath to another. Thank you and God bless you.

The only new point to make about this section is the religious reference. This is not merely pietistic sentimentality. Reagan, again, is reaching deep into the heart of America, a country, as G. K. Chesterton said, 'with the soul of a church'. Often, middle America seems to believe that it has a special covenant with God. That group seems to be Reagan's natural constituency.

I have dealt at length with this speech because it represents the public face of defence language. This particular, contemporary discourse cannot function for long at the level only of doomsday rhetoric and the cataloguing of mortality rates per explosive megatonnage. The human mind just cannot assimilate such statistics in any way that could be personally real. There is no experiential basis for nuclear holocaust. Defence matters and nuclear strategy have, therefore, to be addressed through the familiar.

The Reagan speech makes the complexities of nuclear diplomacy appear to be straightforward and uncomplex. By reducing issues to the level of conventional culture and insular domesticity, the crucial issues are ignored or swept aside. This kind of language is the real evasion and distortion because it denies the existence of special problems. Reagan's cultural identifications and *I/we* representations of involved agents have the effect of appropriating to himself the area of action. In actuality, this is true since he IS the President but the structure and language of this and other speeches also claim precedence symbolically (as guardian of America's cultural continuity), metaphorically (by presenting his own attitudes and beliefs as those of all Americans) and through superior knowledge. His apparent command of facts gives him power over the rest of the nation, and that is a power based upon the way words are organized and presented.

3.3 POPULAR CULTURE AND THE DISCOURSE OF THE MILITARY

Another facet of official defence is the 'private' yet public voice of the armed services. *SSAM* (i.e. Soldier, Sailor, Airman, Marine in an acronymic allusion to America's mythic uncle) is tabloid in format, printed partly in colour and produced by the Department of Defense (Arlington, Virginia). Its role is to provide 'information and entertainment to improve the morale and welfare of U.S. Military personnel'.

Since the purpose of the paper is openly didactic the articles are designed to reassure and to confirm fondly held and optimistic beliefs. The paper is an interesting special case because of the similarity to the public face of defence discourse discussed above.

Not surprisingly, *SSAM* develops sympathetic cultural interpretations. It would scarcely be sensible to use a style suggesting a blatantly violent attitude. The surrogates it uses to present the message are therefore of some interest. In *SSAM* (No. 16, 1980), there is a full page article, with appropriate photographs, celebrating the first anniversary of the death of John Wayne:

> BIG JOHN SEEMED BIGGER THAN LIFE
> He walked tall when he wore uniform,
> and so did we.

The article describes his movie career thus (original emphasis):

> Twenty-two movie roles in various uniforms of his country. An impressive list. In a way, though, you'd have thought the list would be longer. It seemed that Big John was ALWAYS leading the charge somewhere.
> The critics didn't like him much . . . moviegoers did, though. So did military people, who identified from the very first with the way that the Duke played them on the screen . . . after watching one of those films you felt like a million bucks.
> They said it all on the medal, approved by Congress and authorized by the President to be struck just before the Duke died: JOHN WAYNE—AMERICAN.

What is evoked here are straightforward acts of courage, pride and individualism —attributes shared, it is implied, by 'military people', but not by 'critics'. It is not just that 'military people' (notice that this could be a general description of a type of person, not just a designation of those employed in the services) are opposed to a critical intelligentsia; also opposed to 'the critics' (this too could be a description of a type) are the ordinary 'moviegoers'. There is a potential inference that equates ordinary people with those who espouse military values.

The military use of popular culture is a regular feature of *SSAM*. When it is used to explain modern weaponry to the non-specialist military it makes for fascinating reading both as culture text and as propaganda text. A long feature article on laser weaponry was headlined

> LASER—MAY THE FORCE BE WITH YOU

and was illustrated by three large colour photographs. Two of these showed troops being trained with laser devices; the third showed the character Darth Vader fighting Obi Wan Kenobi in a still from the movie *Star Wars*. These illustrations were headlined and described as follows:

> FEROCIOUS!
> Darth Vader and Obi Wan (Ben) Kenobi flailing away with 'light saber' force beams in *Star Wars* may be ferocious. The troops are using Miles Laser training devices. They safely plink away at each other with harmless laser beams.

The gadgetry also simulates smoke and fire, which adds to the realism of the training.

This article might be seen as an early public (military) indication of possible future American commitments and therefore uses a cultural vehicle to make its points, albeit in an indirect way. The picture sequence is a good example of the way mass media blur the distinctions between fact and fiction, using familiar fiction as a means of grasping the unfamiliar fact. In this case, fantasy is presented as more dangerous. Indeed, reality is presented as play: the training beams are only harmless gadgetry.

The function of the accompanying article is, on one level, to convey technical information. But on another level we have a model of cultural confusion and domestic analogy-building, one of whose consequences is the relaxing of the reader for the details of destructive potential:

> Light consists of bunches of electro-magnetic waves known as photons . . . What a laser does is to line all these little rascals up in the same direction. When they're all on the same frequency, the laser bounces them back and forth within mirrors inside a tube until the light intensity is brighter than Pittsburgh after the Super Bowl. The photons come charging out of the tube as a beam of highly-focussed, incredibly pure light. If nothing unfortunate happens (and *SSAM* will get to that in a minute), the beam stays focussed over great distances—well enough, say, for a modest-sized laser to heat a pot of coffee a thousand miles away.

The references to 'rascals' (playful friends), the 'Super Bowl' (games), and 'coffee pot' (domesticity) are the main metaphoric themes in the structure of the explanation. These homely references interpret and at the same time obscure the vague unfortunate happenings, which are postponed for later in the article. Once introduced, they can be strategically alluded to in the description of the equipment in a way that creates a specific kind of discourse coherence. Thus the culinary frame and the games frame are continued in the following, as is the downgrading register of 'little rascals' ('pokes along', 'dinky'):

> A high-energy laser of the kind military scientists have in mind could easily intercept an enemy missile in flight, burn a hole through the missile and may be melt the guidance system. Or it could cook the warhead until it explodes harmlessly somewhere out in space. Moreover, there's no need to 'lead' the target. In duck-hunting, skeet-shooting and present-day missile intercepting, you have to shoot somewhere ahead of your target . . . Not so with a laser beam, which is light, remember. It travels at the speed of light . . . the enemy missile pokes along at only four times the speed of sound, a dinky 4,000 miles an hour. It will move only an inch in the time the laser beam takes to get there.

After taking a break with America's favourite coffee, the new weapon melts warheads in space using techniques of outdoor summer sports. What could be more rugged, relaxing or innocuous! Later in the article the domestic frame is briefly triggered to enable the playing-down of serious technical problems in the development of laser systems: 'When it passes through clouds of smoke, a lot of the mustard goes out of it . . . '. And the article concludes by returning to the readers' knowledge of popular culture and exploiting their attitudes towards movie heroes:

> Once you marveled at fictional space age heroes and their Amazing Ray Guns. Soon it may be turnabout—with Buck, Kirk and Luke smacking their lips at the prospect of looking at YOUR tech manuals [original emphasis].[6]

SSAM is a well-produced paper whose aim seems to be to give enough information to enable military personnel to have basic knowledge about developments without allowing any difficult moral, political or social issues to intrude. It is a sanitized publication which extols both technology and the familiar American beliefs and values. It has an important function, therefore, in defence discourse, because it provides a human face to war games.

The texts examined so far have in common the function of exclusion. They either fail to present the total case or they control the readers' and listeners' responses by various rhetorical methods and emotive cultural references. These methods tend to soothe the mind whilst giving the impression that, however difficult and complex are the realities of nuclear life, there are agencies and people who understand the issues and who have matters under control. These discourses represent a gentle, low-level censorship, whose principle is to assimilate nuclear realities into existing patterns of understanding which I referred to earlier as the American myth. There are two further areas of defence discourse where the same patterns are apparent: the discourse of post-nuclear survivalism, and the systematic pseudonyms given to nuclear weapons themselves.

There have been a large number of manuals and popular books detailing ways of protection from radiation and blast. The nature of the genre is perhaps peculiarly American; the willingness to contemplate post-nuclear-attack conditions—indeed the attractiveness of the pioneering primitivism that such conditions might be thought to offer—may be one interesting way in which American nuclear ideology is different from the European variety. Consider the following:

> The English endured the bombing of Britain.
> The French and Belgians endured the Juggernaut of two world wars.
> The Japanese endured the disastrous firebombing of their major cities, plus two nuclear attacks.
> The Jews endured genocide.
> The early Christians endured the Colosseum and catacombs.
> Our own ancestors endured the wilderness and Valley Forge.
> Yes, and the Russians endured, too—nearly 20 million dead in World War II . . .
> If you have the courage, here is what you may have to face:
> —The fireball
> —Heat
> —Air blast
> —The crater
> —Initial and residual fallout radiation

—The aftermath, with its nagging low level radiation, creating new problems to be solved, new hostile surroundings to be conquered only by courage and wit.[7]

It is an extraordinary verbal mixture with its comparison confusions (Valley Forge with the Fireball), reluctant apologetics ('Yes, and the Russians endured, too'), the invited inference that suicide, or perhaps capitulation, may be the alternative ('If you have the courage . . .'). For my argument, what matters is the stress on endurance, courage and self-reliance ('wit'), pioneer virtues, and individualism. The passage reads as an atavistic cry from the American heart.

The naming of weapons systems rests on broad cultural paradigms,[8] somewhat of the type we have seen being involed by *SSAM*. Consider the tentative classification of terms, culled from US Defense Department reports, given in Table 3.1. Without seeking too delicate a classification, what we seem to have here is the system underlying isolated uses of the terms (in reports, the Press, etc.). On a tacit knowledge of such a system depend the connotations and semiotic effects of these isolated occurrences. Notice that some descriptive names are also heroes, or associated (syntagmatically) with heroes or animals. Similarly, the traditional weapons are attributes (again the relationship is syntagmatic) of heroes or gods. The classification does of course represent a set of choices from a broader cultural classification, and depends on it. For example, the choice of code names for Russian weapons is significant with respect to such background knowledge. So also is the selection of male sky-gods (the French prefer gods of the underworld for their rockets: Pluto and Hades).

The names fall into two broad categories, those of fierce animals, birds and reptiles and those which describe attributes. Predictably, most of the terms suggest threat, violence or sinister intent (Prowler, Intruder), whilst the animals are generally either venomous or are hunting creatures, though this is not the whole story. The attributive names suggest intended function. This ranges from the Harpoon and Trident, to be used at sea, to the Rapier, a light, slender sword used for thrusting attacks. Phoenix, symbol of fiery rebirth, also possesses the meaning of uniqueness. Vulcan (the god of fire), Poseidon (sea-god and 'earth-shaker'), Trident (his three-pronged spear symbolizing control of the oceans) and Hercules (hero of mythic strength)—all these names connnote supernatural power and control. The class of traditional weapons, in particular, illustrates the symbolic and actual recourse to the American past as ways of negotiating nuclear discourse with the non-military public. Here, the names signify the individual in various guises. The Tomahawk and Hawkeye are clear references to America's frontier past, where lone strength and skill were critical attributes. Honest John echoes John Wayne and also the mythic pioneer John Henry with his Herculean feats of strength in building the railways.

Lance, Harpoon, Rapier and Trident are all, traditionally, 'personal' weapons whose utility is related to the skill and resourcefulness of the user. The use of terminology which presses cultural-historical nerves is well entrenched. In April 1983 the director of a private science and engineering company announced that it is now possible to build a complete space-borne defence system. He called this High Frontier—a name since adopted by the associated pressure-group.

Table 3.1 The nomenclature of weapons systems

Beings: animals: wild (or aggressive)	Descriptive names
Jaguar	Hawkeye
Bear (Russian)	Hellfire
Bison (Russian)	Honest John
Bushmaster	Patriot
Cobra	Quickstrike
Sidewinder	Harm
Copperhead	Seafire
Hornet	Prowler
Eagle	Intruder
Blackhawk	Sergeant
	Captor
Tomcat	Thunderbolt
Terrier	Stinger
	Redeye
Harmless	Peacekeeper
Frog (Russian)	
Badger (Russian)	
Sparrow	
Non-animals: gods	*Traditional weapons*
Titan	Trident
Poseidon	Tomahawk
Vulcan	Lance
Hercules	Rapier
Jupiter	Mace
Thor	Harpoon
Atlas	Thunderbolt
Phoenix[9]	
Heroes	
Minuteman	
Pershing	
Honest John	
Roland	
Hawkeye	

The link between the myths of the pioneering past and the myths of popular science fantasy is clear. The technology High Frontier seeks to promote is now widely known—not surprisingly in view of the discourse we saw in *SSAM*—as Star Wars technology.

The point about naming, I think, is that there seems to be a consistent form to the nomenclature, and that from it one can judge a particular 'mindset' on the part of those who select the names. In other words, there is a significant suggestion that naming 'policy' fits in with the general structures of American defence language and rhetoric. In the list of American weapons a significant proportion have no connotation of lethal violence and the classical allusions (reserved for nuclear weapons) primarily connote positive strength rather than negative destruction. Most of the names can be offered, without any labouring of the argument, to illustrate the establishment's efforts to use language either to reveal less than it might or to switch meaning from specific object and effect to more generalized, emotive conditioning.

3.4 EVENTS AND OBLIGATIONS IN THE WORLD VIEW OF DEFENSE DEPARTMENTS REPORTS

The final rhetorical style which I want to consider is probably the most significant because it belongs to the official establishment and is found in the annual reports of the United States Department of Defense. I have used the reports from the Ford and Carter presidencies.[10] Not surprisingly, the general drift of the language is not dissimilar to the other sets of texts which I have examined, though these reports are more complex and more dense in meanings.

To help with the analysis of this language style I have used a descriptive method developed by Michael Halliday. In his *Short Introduction to Functional Grammar* he shows how English clauses can be analysed as consisting of three main elements, which, when combined, produce coherent meanings. These three elements are: message, interaction and representation. I want to concentrate on this latter aspect because, as Halliday points out (p. 156),

> Usually when people talk about what a word or a sentence 'means', it is this kind of meaning they have in mind—meaning in the sense of content.

But what do we mean by 'content'? Halliday explicates the notion as follows:

> A fundamental property of language is that it enables human beings to build a mental picture of reality, to make sense of their experience of what goes on around them and inside them. Here again the clause is the most significant grammatical unit . . . because it is the clause that functions as the representation of processes. What does it mean, to say that a clause represents a process? Our most powerful conception of reality is that it consists of 'goings-on': of doing, happening, feeling, being . . .
> The basic semantic framework for the representation of processes is very simple. A process consists potentially of three components:
> 1. The process itself
> 2. participants in the process
> 3. circumstances associated with the process.

For the purposes of examining these defence reports, processes are the most important element of this analytic method, because they are concerned with the verb forms and, at the lowest level, the nature of these 'doings', in the verb types, will indicate significant things about the way the world is represented in the reports. The nature and function of participants and the circumstances in such texts make for more elaborate analyses. There are six main process types in Halliday's grammar:

Material	*Behavioural*	*Mental*
Action		Perception
Event		Reaction
		Cognition
Verbal	*Relational*	*Existential*
	Attribution	
	Identification	

I shall analyse two short sections of text from the 1980 and the 1981 reports, using the basic elements in Halliday's system. I do not intend to perform a formal analysis but shall use the above terminology in the course of a general interpretation. The point for the reader is to be aware of the source of the method.

Text 1

INTERNATIONAL TURBULENCE

Largely for economic reasons, the United States has become heavily involved outside its traditional areas of concern in Europe, Latin America and the Far East. Some of these other areas are now suffering increased turbulence from within as well as from the intervention of the Soviet Union.

Nowhere is this more the case than in the Middle East. The region has become a breeding ground for internal upheaval—as has already occurred in Iran—for war, terrorism and subversion. Temporary disruptions or a more permanent decline in the supply of oil from the Persian Gulf could easily occur as a consequence.

The Soviet invasion of Afghanistan, its footholds in South Yemen and the horn of Africa, and the Soviet naval presence in the Red Sea and the Indian Ocean, only make a volatile situation potentially even more explosive.

Africa has become a major source of oil and other minerals for our economy. The main oil routes from the Persian Gulf to Europe and America run along its coasts. Yet internal strife wracks parts of the continent, and there is a continuing danger of more to come. Existing conflicts have already been exacerbated by a Cuban expeditionary force of perhaps some 36,000 men in two principal areas, by Soviet military assistance to the more radical factions and regimes on the continent, and by the presence of Soviet and East European advisers. These conflicts may be settled short of critical damage to our economic and other ties, but we cannot count on it.

Cuba has already shown its willingness to exploit the forces of change in the Caribbean for its own ends. The grave dangers associated with further subversion should persuade Havana and Moscow that non-intervention is in order. But there is no certainty that they will see the virtues of restraint.

At the same time, we have to allow for the possibility that the tragic conflict between Communist states in South East Asia will spill over into Thailand. And we must still take precautions against the substantial expansion in the armed forces of North Korea that has been going on during the last decade.

As a result of these developments, our defense establishment could be faced with an almost unprecedented number of demands. And some of those demands could arise more or less simultaneously. To meet them we must solve a number of immediate and longer-term problems.[11]

The general purpose of this Report is to justify (by these and other arguments) the details of the defence budget and the expenditure on new and newly modified weapons and defence systems. This is part of the section of the report which deals with how the formal defence establishment sees the world. The world view that emerges is a cohesive one. The participants in it are not only America and others but 'areas of concern', '[Russian] footholds in South Yemen', 'existing conflicts', 'grave dangers', and so forth. They are thus not presented directly as collectivities of human individuals, although the participant America is referred to by means of the personal pronoun 'we'. The verbs and their processes are summarized in Table 3.2.

Table 3.2 Analysis of verbs taken from Department of Defense Annual Report, 1981

Verb group	*Process*
has become (3 occurrences)	Relational: Attribution
are suffering	Behavioural
has occurred	Material: Event
could occur	Material: Event
make	Material: Action
run	Material: Event
wracks	Material: Event or Mental: reaction
is (4 occurrences)	Relational: Attribution and existential
have been exacerbated	Material: Action
may be settled	Material: Action
count on	Mental: Cognition
has shown	Mental: Cognition
should persuade	Mental: Cognition
see	Mental: Cognition
have to allow for	Mental: Cognition
will spill	Material: Event
[we] [must] take	Material: Action
has been going on	Material: Event
could be faced with	Mental: Cognition
arise	Material: Event
meet	Material: Action
solve	Material: Action or Mental: Cognition

The choice of verbs/processes, and their distribution with respect to participants, gives the discourse a discernible ideological cohesiveness. What strikes one about the relatively coarse analysis of Table 3.2 is, first, the predominance of material and mental processes. This is probably what one should expect for the report grenre, since such texts are concerned with representing happenings of various types and with explaining them. But, secondly, the slightly more delicate classification of processes reveals that Material Event processes tend to be associated with the 'areas of concern' participants. It is as if they were naturally occurring phenomena rather than volitional actions. On the other hand, and thirdly, Material Action processes tend, in general, to be associated with the participant 'we', i.e. America. There is thus throughout the text a contrast or tension between, as it were, 'active' processes and 'passive' ones. Finally, mental processes are largely of the cognition type—emotional reactions are not selected for expression (except, and then in attenuated fashion, in 'suffering', 'wracks' and possibly 'exacerbate'). In more specific semantic terms the cognition has to do with explanation and problem solving. Generalizing, therefore, the choice and distribution of processes represents a world view in which the political actions of certain geopolitical regions are seen as eventuating, rather than being willed, creating a hostile 'environment' in which America uses its resourcefulness first to comprehend and plan, then to take action. There is an analogy to be drawn here with the pioneering spirit myth discussed earlier.

There is in this text a high degree of MODALITY, that is, modal verbs and other elements, expressing the degree of the speaker's/writer's commitment to assertions. The choice of modal expressions, too, has interesting distributions. The main examples are the following (emphasis added):

(i) [Disruptions in the supply of oil] COULD EASILY occur.
(ii) [conflicts] MAY be settled.
(iii) we CANNOT count on it.
(iv) [subversion] SHOULD persuade [Havana and Moscow]
(v) [we] HAVE to allow for
(vi) the possibility that [conflict] WILL spill over.
(vii) COULD be faced with.
(viii) MUST solve.

The distinction here is between what Halliday has called modality and MODULATION (see Kress 1976: 189 ff.), that is between the expression of possibility (probability and certainty) on the one hand, and the expression of necessity (obligation, compulsion, etc.) on the other. First, it is clear from the above list that event processes are in the realm of the possible ((i), (ii), and perhaps, indirectly, (iii)), rather than the probable or the predictable. Second, the mental processes of the Russians (iv) are uncertain, as they typically are in cold-war discourse. The 'Should' of (iv) is of course ambiguous: a modulative reading is also available, which places the Russians under an obligation to see the world in a certain fashion; both readings carry the presupposition 'the Russians do not/will not ...'. Thirdly, modulation is in general associated with 'we' in a strong form of necessity. For 'we' it is not merely the 'should' of obligation, but 'cannot' (ambiguously either 'aren't able' or 'aren't permitted'). More insistently, and unambiguously, it is 'must' and 'have to'—the compulsion of a (perhaps moral) necessity.

Clearly, underlying this passage is the sense of international duty, a call to act responsibly and firmly because of high obligation. It is a high-minded explanation and justification for what in the very next paragraph turns out to be a matter of naked power:

> there can be no doubt that [our strategic nuclear capabilities] still provide the foundation on which our security rests.

The defence reports of the Carter administration give ample evidence of this moral twitch, of a burden reluctantly but necessarily carried. Such texts as this one provide an agonized respectability to the intricacies of nuclear politics but they do not hide the essential combative and sieged mentality that underlies it. Nor does it hide the strange confusion (or even coalescence) between human will and missile characteristics.

Text 2

We can already foresee some of the difficulties that will arise for us during the next five years or so, unless we take timely countermeasures. Our strategic nuclear forces already are armed with more than 9,000 warheads, and that number will increase with the addition of Trident ballistic missiles and air-launched cruise missiles. Nevertheless, our strategic submarines and bombers are ageing; the ICBM leg of the TRIAD [i.e. air, sea, land-based missiles] is becoming vulnerable; and our command–control system is not as capable as it should be of handling a controlled nuclear response. More war-heads, throw-weight, or megatonnage will not by themselves improve our strategic posture, regardless of what they do to the static comparisons between the United States and the Soviet Union. Repairing the TRIAD—and improving our command, control and communications capabilities—will.[12]

We can usefully compare the choice of verb processes in this text with those found in Text 1:

Table 3.3 Analysis of verbs taken from Department of Defense Annual Report, 1980

Verb	Process
[we] can foresee	Mental: Cognition
[difficulties] will arise	Material: Event
[we] take [countermeasures]	Material: Action
[nuclear forces] are armed [with . . .]	Relational: Attribute
[that number] will increase	Material: Event
[submarines, etc.] are ageing	Material: Event or Relational: Attribute
[ICBM leg] is becoming vulnerable	Relational: Attribute
[command and control system] is not capable	Relational: Attribute
[it] should be [sc. capable]	Relational: Attribute
[More war-heads, etc.] will not improve	Material: Action
[they] do to	Material: Action
[Repairing the Triad] will [sc. improve]	Material: Action

If the reader has the sense that in this text nuclear arms and systems have taken on an independent existence, this feeling (not uncommon in reading or hearing such discourse) can perhaps be made sharper by noting three related aspects of the choice of verb processes and lexical terms. First, while 'we' is associated with one action verb ('take countermeasures'), 'nuclear forces' (and other noun groups from the same lexical field) are associated with action verbs also, and repeatedly so: 'improve' and 'do'. These are most usually the action and causative processes of human agents. Secondly, the lexical choices in the relational clauses are humanizing attributes ('ageing', 'vulnerable', 'capable') and the modulation in 'SHOULD be [capable]' supports this: it is most usually humans that are said to be under the obligation implied by 'should'. The continuous aspect (*is/are . . . -ing* forms) in the attributive clauses suggests natural process. It is consistent with this last point that weapons should also be represented in clause structure as participants in event processes ('increase' and, indirectly, 'arise'), as if outside the sphere of human intentionality (cf. also Text 1). Thirdly, the only other explicitly human action (apart from the negative and subordinate 'take') is the Mental cognitive process 'foresee', modalized, and in its context suggesting lack of control.

So, this section of the Report is a step along the road to a natural acceptance of weaponry. Along with attribution of human qualities to missiles, the passage posits duty and responsibility as motivations for more complex defence systems. There is the implication that the responsibility is transferred to weapons. The stressed final 'will' is significantly ambiguous. It expresses both tense (future time) and modality (likely tendency), and is thus capable of being interpreted not just as contingent probability ('if we repair. . .'), but as a prediction, statement of intent or promise. This fact, of course, depends in part on the choice of the modality-free, tense-less clause 'repairing the Triad'.

3.5 CONCLUSION

I have tried to indicate the language reflexes of aspects of some of the military establishments in the United States. It is no more than indicative of much larger political trends. To have argued, as I have, that military language is something more than insane inventories of destruction is hardly original, nor is it especially original to suggest that the style of rhetoric owes something to larger cultural styles; we are all products of our histories. But it is a useful and necessary exercise to be reminded that political action is often rooted in deeper processes than mere reaction to current crises. Certain American myths seem to be used consciously to structure public ways of thinking in the interests of ideological consensus.

The documents we have examined suggest two broad things. Firstly, that America's defence rhetoric is not only a Doctor Strangelove lexicon, but is underpinned emotionally and philosophically by abstractions such as duty, honour and obligation held in place by the assumed vitality and private aggressiveness of a flexible democratic nation. Secondly, these general cultural structures are becoming synonymous with the military or the defence cast of mind.

Furthermore, as military and culture move closer together in language, so does the generalized national perception, which is itself partly controlled by that language. In a society where military objects and attitudes are given high profile (as in presidential speeches), where custodians of national policy confusedly suggest that weapons have human traits, and where everything is said to be done as the result of a mysterious, shared effort of will and consciousness, it is time that we all looked at official words more closely and began the process of imposing alternative words on the general consciousness.

NOTES

1. Halpern (1961).
2. Quoted in Hofstadter (1970: 49).
3. i.e. all groups involved in defence activities and policies, not merely a powerful cabal.
4. From an address by President Reagan, given to the World Affairs Council, Los Angeles, 31 March 1983. Source: US Information Service.
5. This abstract assertiveness is not an isolated spasm and is not confined to presidential set pieces. Alexander Haig, as Secretary of State, made similar pronouncements, e.g.: 'We have recovered ourselves as Americans. We are confident again, our values are sound, and our institutions are worth defending. America's new confidence is founded ON OLD TRADITION [my emphasis]: respect for the irrepressible genius of the individual . . .' (Commencement Address, Syracuse University, New York, 9 May 1981. Source: Department of State *Bulletin*, June 1981). For a discussion of such attitudes in post-Vietnam foreign policy, cf. Chomsky 'Towards a new cold war' and 'Resurgent America' in Chomsky (1982).
6. To see the effect of *SSAM*'s choice of expository style, compare the discussion of the same topic (*Listener*, 8 September 1983, p. 17): 'Using current technologies, the United States has just 1800 seconds to defend itself from an initial salvo of, say, one thousand incoming international ballistic missiles. It's no use having death rays and space-based lasers unless their entire response can be co-ordinated and made operationally successful within those 1800 seconds. Missiles identified by satellites on launch would have to be attacked, and most destroyed, within 250 seconds. Those that survive (leakage) would then have to be attacked in space, probably by lasers. But each ICBM flying through space throws out a large number of decoy warheads, chaff, used fuel tanks, and so on, and something has to identify the REAL killer warhead in the middle of all this flying garbage, and hit it.'
7. *You can Survive the Bomb*, Mel Mawrence and John Clark Kimball (1961).
8. Cf. Chilton (1982).
9. Not a god, but supernatural: there is an overlap with animals, since *eagle* has a similar status. Note that SSAM No. 16 (1980) announced successful testing of Phoenix, describing it as 'a mean bird to tangle with'.
10. It should be noted that there is a run-over of reports from one administration to the next. Thus, the 1982 Fiscal Year report was produced under Harold Brown, President Carter's Secretary of Defense and was presented to the Congress on 16 January 1981, a few days before President Reagan took office.
11. Department of Defense Annual Report, Fiscal Year 1981, Washington, DC.
12. Department of Defense Annual Report, Fiscal Year 1980, Washington, DC.

4 Discourses, texts, readers and the pro-nuclear arguments

Gunther Kress
New South Wales Institute of Technology, Australia

4.1 THE QUESTIONS

There is now a significant and large body of work which enables us to see the operation of ideology in language and which provides at least a partial understanding of that operation.[1] Some, perhaps the major, problems remain. I take these to be around the question 'what now?'. Having established that texts are everywhere and inescapably ideologically structured, and that the ideological structuring of both language and texts can be related readily enough to the social structures and processes of the origins of particular texts, where do we go from here?

No doubt the initial work of description and analysis had the aim of providing the intellectual means for participating in ideological struggles and so to have political effects. And there are sufficient signs that such work has begun to have effects in specific ways and in different spheres.[2] Nevertheless, my view is that only the first steps have been taken. Writers engaged in this debate need to ask about the next steps, need to be more specific about aims, and need to think about strategies whereby their work can have further and perhaps more far-reaching effects in this area, ways in which it can be made more telling. It is my intention here to ask some questions in this area and to suggest some possible ways of proceeding.

First and foremost, analyses and descriptions of what IS can only achieve a limited amount. It is important to ask about what can be, and what can be done. Speaking of my own thinking and writing, the analysis had led me to a metaphoric hand-wringing, a resignation in the face of seemingly overwhelming and monolithic forces at work. This prevented me from going beyond description to the considering of strategies. One reason for my own paralysis lay in a fundamentally incorrect view or theory of language which I had brought with me from the discipline of linguistics and which continued to shape my understanding of linguistic, social and political processes. This theory views linguistic processes from the point of the producer alone, who is therefore privileged in the theory at the cost of the consumer. In other words, a power differential which characterises all linguistic interactions in varying ways is built into the theory as a fixed given, invisibly and 'naturally'. Such a theory naturalises the view that meanings are produced AND imposed. It takes it as a given that those on whom meanings are imposed inevitably have to accept those meanings, that is, have to read texts in the way that they have been constructed. Further, it assumes that readers see texts as ideologically/discursively 'of one piece', without internal tensions or contradictions. Nor do I consider accounts which talk of 'the negotiation of meaning' as being exceptions to my critique. The fundamental question that needs to be posed, however, is one about the nature of linguistic activity, and consequently about the status of linguistic theory. If we wish to devise strategies to alter the present ideological determinations of texts, we need to know what kinds of strategies we are talking about: are they linguistic strategies? or social strategies? or sociolinguistic strategies? And what are the political processes into which these strategies will need to be inserted?

In my discussion I wish to put forward a view of language in which the actions and effects of producers and of consumers (as reproducers) are given proper evaluation, in which the reader's role is therefore nearly as privileged as that of the writer. In my account the activities of both producers and consumers are placed in a theory that treats linguistic activity as one kind of social activity. Such a theory, and the revaluations to which it might lead, might open the path for a reassessment of current strategies for intervention in the debate around the nuclear arms race and of the issues associated with that.

Any politically motivated account of language must focus on the following central questions: how do texts arise? how do they come into being? how and why do they get produced? Why in short DO people talk and write. In addition to saying something about the producers of texts—the speakers and writers—such an account needs to say something about the consumers of texts—the hearers and readers. They have tended to be regarded as pretty well passive in their relationship to texts. But if we are interested in the possibility of 'resistant readings', or in the construction of texts which can have the function of enabling 'resistant readings', then the role of readers has to be re-thought quite fundamentally, and their participation in texts treated as a much more active one.

Other questions are associated with these. For instance, how does any one reader come to read a particular text? Do readers come across texts 'out of the blue'? Clearly the answer is 'no'. The texts that I read are in the main entirely predictable from my place in social and institutional structures. An inventory of things that I read in the course of a day would give a pretty good indication to others about my social place. In other words, it seems that we occupy positions which already structure our access to texts, and structure our participation in them; that is, we occupy specific 'reading positions' which affect both what we read and how we read what we read. Similarly with my writing: a reasonably representative collection of texts written by me would give you a fairly accurate indication and description of my social place. So another set of questions to consider concerns that network of relationships in which any member of society is placed which determines the set of texts in which she or he participates as consumer and producer. These are fundamental and crucial questions in any attempt to intervene in ideological processes via the production and reproduction of texts.

In answering these questions it is necessary to have a theory which permits a discussion in which linguistic and social matters can be addressed at all times with ease. A usual—and in my view misleading—way of handling this talks about moving from social to linguistic matters, or vice versa. That mode of talking presupposes a distinction between language and society as discrete objects, an effect which is further reinforced by the use of the spatial metaphor contained in 'moving from . . . to'. The three cateogories which I propose to use in this paper emphasize the total connectedness and 'oneness' of linguistic and social processes, with perhaps more emphasis now on the one and now on the other. The categories are discourse, genre and text.

Not only has linguistic theory approached language very much from the point of view of the speaker/writer, the producer of language (indeed, linguistic theories are constructed in that way); it has had little to say about how texts are read or heard, reconstructed and understood.[3] Perhaps most importantly, linguistic theories are silent about the reasons for writing. Why speakers or writers should wish to speak and write, what they might want to speak and write about, and how, is not a question in linguistics. Indeed, it is barely a question in communication theory, where the notions of 'transmission of information', or of 'the mutual construction/sharing of meaning' predominate. As long as language is regarded as an autonomous system, perhaps as one which 'correlates with' certain social and cultural matters, just so long these questions cannot be posed within linguistics. Once language is seen as one aspect of social life, its structures and processes as specific kinds of social structures and processes, the questions can be asked. If we are then further prepared to consider these social structures and processes in time and history, the essential questions about the politics of texts can be asked, and answers attempted.

In debates around the issues of the nuclear arms race these formulations are central. Clearly, words alone will not interrupt the processes at work. However, an understanding of the ideological and political effects of texts, and an understanding of their function in all social, economic and political processes is just one, but a necessary, part of a strategy for intervening in the totality of these processes. It is important to know what texts come into being via whose agency; what readings are constructed in these texts, and how they might be resisted or subverted; what readers are envisaged for these texts and how these readers are positioned in these texts. Strategies designed to counter the weight of the dominant forces in this field are political strategies carried via linguistic/textual means.

4.2 INSTITUTIONS, MEANINGS AND DISCOURSES

The starting-point of my account is the listener/reader, speaker/writer, seen NOT as an isolated individual, but as a social being, located in a network of social relations, in specific places in a social structure. An explanation for differing modes and forms of speaking can be attempted when we look at the phenomenon from a linguistic AND social perspective. Then we find that these speakers share membership in particular social institutions, with their practices, values, meanings, demands, prohibitions, permissions. We also begin to get an explanation for the KIND of language that is being used, that is, the kinds and range of texts that have currency and prominence in that community, and the forms, contents and functions of those texts.

Institutions and social groupings have specific meanings and values which are articulated in language in systematic ways. Following the work particularly of the French philosopher Michel Foucault,[4] I refer to these systematically organized modes of talking as DISCOURSE. Discourses are systematically organized sets of statements which give expression to the meanings and values of an institution. Beyond that, they define, describe and delimit what it is possible to say and not possible to say (and by extension, what it is possible to do or not to do) with respect to the area of concern of that institution, whether marginally or centrally. A discourse provides a set of possible statements about a given area, and organizes and gives structure to the manner in which a particular topic, object, process is to be talked about, in that it provides descriptions, rules, permissions and prohibitions of social and individual actions.

Discourses tend towards exhaustiveness and inclusiveness; that is, they not only attempt to account for an area of immediate concern to an institution but also attempt to account for increasingly wider areas of concern. Take as an example one discourse which determines the manner in which the biological category of sex is taken into social life as gender—the discourse of sexism. It specifies what men and women may be, how they are to think of themselves, how they are to think of and to interrelate with the other gender. But beyond that the discourse of sexism specifies what families may be, and relations within the family—what it is to be a 'proper father' or 'a mother', the 'eldest son', 'our little girl'. It reaches into all major areas of social life, specifying what work is suitable, possible even, for men and for women; how pleasure is to be seen by either gender; what artistic possibilities, if any, there are for either gender. A discourse colonizes the social world imperialistically, from the point of view of one institution.

Discourses do not exist in isolation but within a larger system of sometimes opposing, contradictory, contending or merely different discourses. Given that each discourse tends towards the colonization of larger areas, there are dynamic relations between these which ensure continuous shifts and movement, progression or withdrawal in certain areas. To exemplify some of the points I have been making, here are some short segments from a larger text. In reading each extract, attempt to bear in mind these questions: (i) why is this topic being written about? (ii) how is the topic being written about? (iii) what other ways of writing about the topic are there? The first extract is from a pamphlet published by the Campaign for Defence and Multilateral Disarmament.

WHY BRITAIN NEEDS AN INDEPENDENT DETERRENT...
Deterrence works! We have the experience of 38 years of peace to prove it. An independent nuclear deterrent is Britain's guarantee that we will never be left naked and alone to face nuclear blackmail or attack.
Clement Atlee, the leader of the first post-war Labour government, started Britain's independent nuclear weapons porogramme. That policy has been

reinforced by every successive government—Labour and Conservative—since then.

History has shown that a situation could well arise in which Britain might have no choice but to stand alone in the face of the aggressor. We stood alone against Nazi Germany for two years. In the nuclear age, even a two-hour delay in an American declaration of its commitment would be too late.

The possession of an effective nuclear deterrent by a European member of NATO guarantees that the Kremlin will know that Soviet forces cannot occupy Western Europe without risking unacceptable consequences for the Russian homeland.

... TRIDENT

A deterrent has two requirements: it must be invulnerable and it must be able to reach its target.

An invulnerable system is one that allows time to ensure that there is no computer error or human misjudgement. The submarine is currently the safest platform for a deterrent; and the Trident is the most capable missile available.

Polaris submarines cannot continue beyond the mid-1990s when they will be almost 30 years old. Few people would expect their cars to last that long in top condition. A refurbished Polaris would be almost as expensive—and far less effective—than Trident.

The cost of the Trident system will be approximately 3p in each Pound budgeted for Defence. It allows for four submarines, with at least one guaranteed 'on-station' at any given moment.

It is a modest investment that will keep Britain safe well into the 21st century.

THE SOVIET THREAT TO EUROPE ...
The SS-20
—the replacement for the hundreds of Soviet SS-4 and SS-5 missiles targeted on Western Europe. Each has three warheads and a destructive power equal to 100 Hiroshima bombs. With a range of more than 3,000 miles, it can strike any point in Western Europe, even if withdrawn behind the Ural Mountains as the Kremlin has suggested in its proposals for a European Nuclear Free Zone.

The SS-20, on its tracked launcher, is mobile and can (unlike any current Western launcher) be reloaded. There are now over 300 launchers in position.

... AND NATO'S RESPONSE
Cruise
At the request of its European members, NATO decided in 1979 to modernise its nuclear forces in Europe by replacing ageing bomber aircraft with Cruise missiles.

These missiles fly subsonically at low altitudes (200 feet or less) to attack heavily defended enemy military targets such as airbases and weapons dumps. The fact that the Cruise is small and difficult to detect on radar gives it a greater chance of getting to its target than manned aircraft, which would suffer high losses.

In a period of tension, the Cruise missiles—which are transported on mobile launchers—would be moved away from their bases, making it impossible for the enemy to pinpoint and attack them.

The United States has maintained nuclear bases in Britain for more than 30 years under Labour and Conservative Governments. The use of these bases in an emergency would be a matter for the JOINT-DECISION of the British and American Governments.

Pershing 2

Designed as a fast retaliatory weapon, if the West were attacked, the Pershing 2 could reach Soviet bases, from West Germany, in 15 minutes. It has a range of just over 1,000 miles and could not reach Moscow.

(The text is accompanied by drawings; for instance, 'Why Britain needs an independent deterrent . . .' has a drawing of a huge bear standing on a map, looking menacingly from its Russian base at the rest of Europe and Britain. '. . . Trident' on the other hand has a picture of a submarine with the Union Jack flying and three salts on the conningtower.)

Each of the brief text segments works somewhat differently, so my answers to the three questions differ in detail. Broadly speaking, however, my answer to the first question is the same in all cases: 'To position the reader in a specific way in this debate, in response to the contesting accounts provided in different discourses'. In the case of the first text segment, the reader is drawn into an account structured by the discourses of 'popular memory', a common-sense and mythical account of history (and the clichés which are characteristic of it) and of a common-sense pragmatism. Clearly there are other ways of writing about the issue of an independent deterrent. The second segment is structured in different discourses, a homely bourgeois economic discourse ('Few people would expect their car . . . A refurbished Polaris would be almost as expensive . . . It is a modest investment . . .') and a discourse of honest tradesman/mechanic activity ('An invulnerable system is one that allows time . . . The submarine is currently the safest platform . . .')—much as a builder might talk to a prospective client about the merits of differing building techniques.

Each segment is constructed in different discourses, so that the text as a whole brings into play a significant sample of the range of discourses which construct everyday life and which constitute common sense. So, as a last example, the 'Cruise' segment talks about the issues in terms of the technical discourses that can be brought into play around 'modernising', 'saving lives' (saving the lives of air-crew who would otherwise suffer 'high losses'). In the text overall, a number of discourses are brought into effect; in the case of each segment, and of the text overall, the discourses are marshalled in particular ways, so that the text provides a plausible, coherent surface, which offers a single reading position to its readers. This seeming paradox of a multiplicity of discourses and the single overall reading position suggests further answers to my questions. The topic is being written about, firstly, because there is a challenge which has to be dealt with and, secondly, to effect the resolution of the challenge by bringing a range of familiar discourses into action, by integrating and assimilating the challenge within the known and the safe. While the challenging discourse is absent from the surface of the text, it does nevertheless construct the text in part, for instance, in defining the questions which have to be answered and the mode of the answer. That also provides a further answer as to HOW the topic is written about.

The task of marshalling the variety of discourses into a congruent structure is an ideological one. A differing ideological position would lead to a different arrangement of discourses and a different resultant text. Ideology can be seen therefore as the 'politics of discourse', marshalling discourses into certain alignments in the cause of larger political aims. Of course this is so whether the text is from the political right or the political left. As a contrasting example, here is an extract from a pamphlet handed out by the Socialist Workers' Party at the anti-nuclear rally in Sydney on Palm Sunday, 1984. The front page of the pamphlet says 'It's up to us to put a stop to war'; and underneath that text is a picture of a group of marchers holding a banner which reads 'Stop Nuclear Madness'. Here 'Nuclear Madness' is conjoined with all forms of war, in such a way that war of whatever kind is the dominant category, of which 'nuclear madness' is one example. The text on the inside (of a folded sheet of A4) reads:

> Scientists predict that if only 1% of the world's 55,000 nuclear weapons were used we could face changes in the climate so harsh that food could not be produced.
>
> As if that's not enough . . . Today, the potential exists to destroy the world 40 times over! The task of the antiwar movement in fighting the threat of war is unquestionably an urgent one.
>
> But while demanding NO NUCLEAR WAR, we must remember that war, conventional war, has already begun. Today, the US government is waging a more and more overt war against the peoples of Central America.
>
> In El Salvador, Reagan is supplying huge quantities of arms and US 'advisers' to the murderous junta in a desperate attempt to crush the popular insurrection there. In recent weeks, 2,000 US troops were rushed to the border between Honduras and El Salvador.
>
> In Central America, Reagan is gearing up to launch a new Vietnam-style war in which 1,000s upon 1,000s would be killed. Indeed, there is no guarantee that Reagan will not resort to the use of nuclear weapons to gain the victory he needs in the region. Australia is an absolutely integral part of the US war machine.
>
> The Labor government is supporting Reagan's policies in Central America. Hawke's foreign policy is in the same framework as the Liberals' policies of the 1950s and 1960s which led to Australian involvement in Vietnam. Hawke pledged to Reagan that Australia would be the United States' most constructive ally.
>
> Today, we pledge to be the strongest opponents of this sort of foreign policy! US OUT OF CENTRAL AMERICA!
>
> Australia is the host for 20 US bases. Six of these are essential to the US targeting and firing system. They contribute directly to the danger of nuclear war. No facilities of any sort should be provided to US military forces or military related activities. CLOSE ALL US BASES IMMEDIATELY. NO VISITING US WARSHIPS.

> The ANZUS treaty which links Australia militarily to the US is used as a justification for Australian involvement in US war-plans. It is a reactionary alliance aimed at stemming popular struggles for independence and justice in the Asia-Pacific region. The ANZUS alliance has been used to justify sending Australian troops to Vietnam, the establishment of the US bases and spy stations in Australia, and the right of nuclear armed US warships to use Australian ports. END ANZUS!
>
> Australia mines and exports uranium which goes (via reactors) to making more nuclear bombs. We've got more than 30% of the western world's uranium. STOP URANIUM MINING!
>
> In its August 1983 budget, the government allocated a massive $5,280 million to 'defence' spending. This contrasts drastically with the amount allocated to job creation: a mere £958 million—only 18% of the military budget. MONEY FOR JOBS NOT WAR!

Clearly enough the text is constructed by a variety of discourses (of war, politics, nationalism, economics, employment), in a specific ideological conjunction, which sees nuclear war as one part only of a larger social and political problem. The answers to my questions are as before. 'Why is this topic written about?' 'To position readers in specific ways in response to the different discursive contestations around this issue.' 'How is it written about?' 'By situating the problem in a particular conjunction of discourses, which gives the problem a particular place and definition, and which situates the reader in a particular way *vis-à-vis* the problem'.

In the colonization of areas of social life, discourses (in their operation in texts) attempt to reconcile contradictions, mismatches, disjunctions and discontinuities within that domain by making that which is social seem natural and the problematic seem obvious. The effect of this is that the areas accounted for within one discourse offer no spaces for analysis, everything is of one piece, a seamless fabric of tightly interwoven strands. The accounts provided within one discourse become not only unchallenged, but unchallengeable, as 'common sense'. If the domination of a particular area by a discourse is successful, it provides an integrated and plausible account of that area which allows no room for thought; the social will have been turned into the natural. At that stage it is impossible to conceive of alternative modes of thought, or else alternative modes of thought will seem bizarre, outlandish, unnatural.

Given this view of language, it can be seen how the speaking/writing and reading/listening of individuals is determined by their positions in institutions, by their place within certain discourses and by their place particularly in intersecting sets of discourses. It allows us to link speaking and writing, listening and reading to social place and to social/institutional meanings, without giving up a serious notion of the individual as social agent. Perhaps most significantly from the point of view of this discussion, it allows us to begin to think about the activity of reading in a serious fashion. If readers occupy the same discursive positions as those expressed in a text, they are likely to be compliant readers. That is, their habitual use of and exposure to a certain discourse or set of discourses will have made the world as constructed in that discourse seem natural, obvious, and inevitable. And, as in sexist discourse, the set of discourses may have constructed subject positions for the hearer–reader/consumers or writer-speaker/producers. The task is therefore one of interrupting these subject and reading positions via the construction of texts which offer differing, alternative subject and reading positions. On the other hand, readers who already occupy different discursive positions are less likely to adopt the reading positions constructed for them in a text. They are more likely to be resistant readers. One strategy therefore is to develop texts which encourage resistant readings of specific other texts, and which have the long-term effect of repositioning readers permanently.

4.3 TEXTS AND THE MOTIVATIONS OF TEXTS

Discourses strive towards total and encompassing accounts in which contradictions are resolved or at least suppressed. If problematic areas are resolved in this way and the social is made natural, when everything is both 'obviously natural' and 'naturally obvious', what then is there to talk about? What is the motivation for speech? There are two answers of a broadly similar kind. Within any social group there are a number of discourses, because a number of significant institutions operate within any one social group. Hence any group will be using a number of discourses offering alternative or contradictory accounts of reality. That is, even though any one discourse accounts for the area of its relevance, there are overlapping areas of interest where differing accounts are offered, which are contested by several discourses. Take a capitalist economic discourse on the one hand and a Christian religious one on the other. The one suggests that the 'natural' condition of 'man' is to be acquisitive, competitive and aggressive, and that society is founded on a dynamic where individuals acquire power by depriving others of their power. The other enjoins its adherents to divest themselves of wealth, to be meek, to offer the other cheek. In Western technological societies, capitalist economic discourses have coexisted for several centuries with Christian religious ones. Countless sermons have been preached in a constant attempt at an ideological reconciliation of these two discourses. More recently these two discourses have entered a new and antagonistic relationship, with the growth of liberation theology.

For any member of a social group discursive multiplicity, contestation, difference is both a description of their history and an account of their present social position at any given moment. The individual's history is composed of the experience of a range of discourses, passing through the intimate relations of the family and its discourses of authority, gender, morality, religion, politics; into school and its discourses of knowledge, science, authority, aesthetics; to work and adulthood. The discursive history of each individual therefore bears the traces of the discourses associated with the social places which that individual has occupied and experienced. These form, like sedimentary layers, the linguistic experience and potential of the speaker. It can be seen how individuals from similar social positions, with similar social histories, have significantly similar linguistic experiences and therefore have quite similar forms of language available to them. At the same time, to the extent that the discursive histories of individuals differ—a situation more likely than that of total congruence for many members of social groups—their experience of language, their positioning towards the linguistic system differ. Added to this is the present social position of an individual: depending on their place in social institutions—work/profession, leisure, family, political affiliations, sexual relations—their present experience of discourses will differ.

A theory of language based on this account explains two fundamental factors at one and the same time: the social determination of an individual's knowledge of language on the one hand, and individual difference and differing position *vis-à-vis* the linguistic system on the other. A theory which makes no allowance for the social determination of linguistic practice is obviously deficient; at the same time a theory which ignores individual difference in linguistic practice—a matter equally apparent to any observer—is also deficient. In a discourse-orientated theory of language both find a plausible and motivated account. (This account leaves aside factors whose importance is difficult to assess, differences which may be due, for instance, to biological variation or to intangibles such as imagination.)

4.4 DIFFERENCE AND TEXT

The social/discursive history of an individual, as well as their present social position, determines their access to the set of discourses in a society. The unresolved tensions among the discourses used by the one speaker, and those used in interaction, produce a need for discursive resolution. There are likely to be problems at any time, arising out of unresolved differences in the individual's discursive history, their present discursive location and the context of discourses in interactions. That difference is the motor that produces texts. Every text arises out of a particular problematic. Texts are therefore manifestations of discourses and the meanings of discourses, and texts are the sites of attempts to resolve particular problems.

Dialogues, whether conversations, interviews, debates, are the clearest examples. In their structure they display discursive differences at every point. However, it is my contention that all texts are dialogic in their construction. Given my account of discursive difference as a normal and permanent state for every individual (though in significantly differing degrees), even those times of seeming silence, spent in traffic-jams or weeding the garden, are occasions of discursive contention, leading to the construction of texts which never see the light of day. If every text is constructed in discursive difference then every text attempts to conceal—more or less successfully—the problematic which has given rise to its formation. Every text therefore offers the opportunity for intervention in quite precisely identifiable places, that is, in the spaces left by unresolved difference. These are the spaces which can be explored and exploited in the construction of alternative texts, with alternative discourses, and with alternative reading positions.

Here to illustrate my point is a text which displays its dialogic nature clearly, showing the attempted discursive resolution of an ideological and political problem area. The writer was the Bishop of Norwich, the occasion the impending CND Easter demonstrations in 1982 protesting against the then planned installation of cruise missiles in the United Kingdom. The genre is that of a diocesan news-sheet such as is pinned up in church porches, hence the title of the sheet, *Church Porch*.

FROM OUR BISHOP
Peace and its Defence
Some Christians take a full pacifist position, and although I respect them, I do not believe that in an imperfect world we can withdraw from our corporate and social responsibilities. These include loyalty to our Queen and Country and involvement in its defence.
But what of nuclear arms? Again, I respect those who take a stand against nuclear arms, and as a Diocese I hope we are all praying for the reduction of nuclear arms, as a result of the negotiations between Russia and our ally the United States, continuing at this time of writing.
I pray for a step by step balanced reduction of nuclear arms, with international U.N. inspection, but I believe that the demand for unilateral nuclear disarmament is a destabilising influence for world peace, and I believe that Christians with a good conscience can boldly resist the unilateralist call, even though they may receive hard criticism for so doing. 'There are no unilateralists in the Kremlin' is worth repeating.
What can Christians do for world peace? We can think the unthinkable and pray for heroic change. What if Poland was allowed free democratic elections and free Trade Unions? What if East Germany was allowed also a democratic option to choose its own government? What if Christianity was allowed the right to evangelise in Russia and in China? The Third Reich seemed set for a thousand years, and today has crumbled into past history, and however mighty are the forces of evil, God is omnipotent, and is planning 'New Heavens and a New Earth, where righteousness dwells'. The Christian has both the Advent Hope of Christ's return to judge the world and to receive His Church, and the Resurrection Hope of eternal life through the triumph of Christ's Cross and Resurrection, so we are called to lead, and to work for righteousness and justice as well as peace.
The eternal truths that unite us in Christ are immensely stronger than the human views, unilateralist or multi-lateralist, that could divide us, and I pray that this letter may help us to move forward together as both 'soldiers and servants of Christ' to save and serve the world which He loves, and for which Christ died.
May God be with you.

The opposing positions are neatly set up in the text: pacifism vs. militaristic nationalism, pro-nuclear vs. anti-nuclear, an anti-Soviet position vs. a non-anti-Soviet position, Christian vs. secular solutions. The text is constructed around these oppositions, by a series of overt and covert negations: 'ALTHOUGH I respect them . . .', 'I DO NOT believe . . .', 'in an IMperfect world', 'Again, I respect those . . . [with an unexpressed negative *but*]', 'I hope . . . [BUT I cannot be certain]' . . . 'the demand . . . is a DESTABILIZING influence . . .', etc. The negations are all associated with one segment of the diocesan audience, so that the conflict and opposition of groups within the diocese is acknowledged. The Bishop's ostensible task, however, is to unite, not to divide, so he must find strategies for constructing a reading position which can unify this group. He uses a number of features. One is the use of pronouns and collective nouns: the use of *we* ('I hope we are all praying . . .' and *our* ('our ally the United States'), and here the assumption of shared activity; the use of the collective noun *Christians* ('What can Christians do . . .') and *Christianity* ('What if Christianity was allowed . . .'). This feature is not entirely unproblematic, as in 'I believe that Christians with a good conscience can . . .', which clearly excluded unilateralist Christians. Another feature is the use of religious genre: '. . . and however mighty are the forces of evil, God is omnipotent . . .'; that is, the syntactic/textual forms characteristic of certain religious genres are employed in sections of this text. Lastly, the use of religious discourse, that is, the mode of talking which presents an organization of social life from the point of view of the institution of the church; the last third of the text is an example of this. It is within this discourse that the Bishop attempts to find the resolution to the contention.

The ideology which organizes the text is that of the State–Church: of necessity it uses the discourses of the State but gives them a place subordinate to the religious discourse. Sections of the text are clearly structured by the discourse of official, state bureaucracy, to the point of being a direct echo: '. . . a step by step balanced reduction of nuclear arms, with international U.N. inspection, . . . the demand for unilateral nuclear disarmament is a destabilising influence for world peace . . .'. These are both the terms of state bureaucracy and its syntax —e.g. the nominalizations, which each contain a number of full clauses. (I do not wish to analyse this language in detail here, as analyses can be found in a number of places.)[5]

The uneasiness of the Bishop's position is signalled by a number of other factors, such as the switch from the private mode of the singular pronoun *I* and the syntax of (relatively) casual speech to the public mode of the abstract or plural collective noun, and the syntax of formal writing: '. . . I respect all those who take a stand . . . and as a DIOCESE I hope WE are all . . .', The Bishop's private world, the world of his prayer, includes and incorporates the state's public language: 'I pray for a step by step balanced reduction . . .'.

In my view the problematic which gave rise to this text has not been adequately dealt with by the writer, the discontinuities are everywhere apparent, in quite different features of the text. Here the spaces that could be exploited are the disjunction of the public and private mode and of its languages (shown in a number of features), the unreconciled opposition of sections of the audience, the contrasting and conflicting discourses of the State and of the Church; and no doubt there are others. The Bishop's task is perhaps particularly difficult because there is no single, strongly defined institution which gives coherence to his audience. The Church of England is for this purpose a weakly framed coalition of quite disparate groups, none of which shares a clearly defined set of principles, beyond those to which the Bishop appeals. The point is significant because it highlights the difficulty of constructing coherent texts in the absence of a coherent and well-known audience.

What gives rise to this text? The contention of discourses arises outside the immediate institution of the Church, in the clash between the State's attitude towards nuclear armament and that of the CND. The Church is drawn in as it is the State Church; to give the debate legitimacy within the discourse of the Church it has to be reclassified as a debate around 'peace'.

While interviews perhaps display the structure of difference particularly clearly, all texts are in fact constructed around this dynamic. As I have just demonstrated, even texts constructed by one speaker or writer are no exception. Take the sentence I have just written and you have just read: 'even texts constructed by one speaker or writer are no exception'. It was motivated by a silent dialogue of myself with an imagined other interactant to whom I had attributed a view something like: 'Yes, but what about single-speaker texts? Surely they're not about difference; they're just someone telling you something, just giving you some information'. My 'even texts . . .' was a response to that imagined view. The Bishop's text is a clear example of some of the different voices, which contend around the meanings of and give rise to *peace* and *disarmament*, and give rise to this section of the larger text. Dialogue is for that reason the linguistic mode which is fundamental to an understanding of language and its uses. In dialogue the constitution of texts in and around difference is most apparent. Here it can be most readily discovered, analysed and described, and the processes of resolution of differences traced to their more or less satisfactory conclusions. Most speech genres are ostensibly about difference: argument (differences of an ideological kind), interview (differences around power and knowledge), 'gossip' (difference around informal knowledge), lecture (difference around formal knowledge), conversation. But as I pointed out above, single-speaker and writer texts are no less constituted in difference and constructed around its resolution than are dialogues. Indeed the task of the author/ writer is precisely this: to attempt to construct a text in which discrepancies, contradictions, disjunctions are bridged, covered over, eliminated.

4.5 LEADERS, DISCOURSES AND TEXTS

A particularly charged example is that of a (political) leader. The discursive task of the leader is constant; the detail of its execution differs, depending on the group of which she or he is leader. Where the group is well established, the leader's task is to produce texts which function as paradigm examples of the relevant discourse(s) and function continuously to reproduce, reconstitute the group around the discourse(s). The texts produced by leaders should provide reading positions which resolve all potential conflict, and which give a single plausible and congruent reading of the text. The task of the leader may also be one of recruiting new members, as in the speeches and manifestos of political leaders at election time. Here individuals with ideological and discursive allegiances other than those of the leader's group have to be addressed via a text which offers them the possibility of affiliation. Lastly, the leader's task may be to give definition and coherence to an entirely new group. In such a case it is the leader's task to construct texts which offer the possibility of assimilation of hitherto disparate discourses in a single text, or set of texts, and to hold out the promise of unification, coherence and plausibility of a new grouping constituted initially entirely by the manner in which discourses are brought together in texts. The formation of a new political party would be a good example. Note that this procedure reverses the usual social/linguistic process where discourses arise out of social institutions and give rise to specific texts. In this case there is no such institution: if the leader is successful an institution may be formed through and via the operation of texts.

Take as an example the anti-nuclear movement. A very disparate set of groups come together under this broad banner. In Australia (unlike in the United Kingdom, for instance) it includes groups opposed to the mining of uranium, the issue of land-rights, groups concerned with those opposed to the continued existence of US bases and facilities, groups opposed to nuclear weapons on various grounds and many others. No single institutional basis unites them. For instance, at the Palm Sunday Peace March in Sydney in 1984, just some of the groups distributing pamphlets connected with the issue were: The Socialist Workers' Party, the Outlook Media Group (a Christian group), the Disabled Gay Peace Workers, Church of Scientology, Northside Peace Group, PND (People for Nuclear Disarmament), NDCC (Nuclear Disarmament Co-ordinating Committee), Hare Krishna Centre, Dee Why Ministers' Fraternal, Wilderness Society, Release of Turkish Prisoners Committee. Other groups were handing out pamphlets there, seemingly in broad alignment with the anti-nuclear cause. Most groups participating in the march carried banners but did not distribute leaflets, for instance, Sydney Drinkers against Nuclear War, BUGAUP (Billboard User Graffitists Against Unhealthy Promotions), etc.

Any text constructed to address that large group faces the problem of bringing together discourses of a most disparate kind, and attempting to construct a text in which these are brought together in a coherent, plausible manner. It is a daunting task, perhaps an impossible one. Here are some brief extracts from a speech given by the main speaker of the rally, Dr Helen Caldicott.

. . . . Thank you, thank you fellow Australians. You're a great country. [Loud clapping and shouts.] This is the best country in the world. [Clapping.] And that's why we have an enormous responsibility because we have to lead the earth to survival, and it's Australia that started it fourteen years ago with the French tests. It was us who took the lead to take the French to the Court of Justice at the Hague, to discipline her. And now she tests underground, and it was marches like this that stopped the French blowing up bombs in the Pacific. When I tell the Americans what the Australians did about the French tests they all stand up and cheer. The Americans think the Australians are fantastic people. [Clapping, yells.] Then Australia took the stand against uranium mining.

. . . They haven't seen the last epidemic. How many leaders of the world, and mostly the leaders of the world are old men . . . that's true isn't it? . . . Reagan and Chernenko are old men . . . how many leaders of the world have watched the explosion of a single hydrogen bomb . . . felt the heat on their face two hundred miles away ... like an oven door opening ... watched the bomb explode through their hands and their closed eyes and the bones of their hand light up ... seen a battleship rise up in the water like a splinter and disappear? How many leaders of the world have helped a child to die? ... of leukemia ... and supported the parents before and forever after in their grief. You've all lost somebody you loved: a parent, a child, a relative or a friend. You know the grief it leaves and you never get over it. I suggest that the people of ... who are running the world, if they're not in touch with their feelings, they're not appropriate people to be running the world in this nuclear age ... and we should get rid of them.

... bomb's gonna come in, it's gonna come in at twenty times the speed of sound at tree top level and explode right here on us in the fraction of a millionth of a second with the heat of the sun ... and it will dig a hole right here three-quarters of a mile wide and eight hundred feet deep. And of all of us, and all of these buildings and all of the earth below will just go up in the mushroom cloud as radioactive molecules up there into the stratosphere. Six miles from ...

... is our planet. We are brothers and sisters with the Chinese and with the Russians and with the Americans, we are one human race, one humanity. [Applause.] One humanity, one spirit, one earth. And it's interesting, and one death ... that's right, we'll all go together when we go. And it's interesting that great psychiatrist Jesus who lived two thousand years ago said it's easy to love your friend, what it's hard to do is love your enemy, and the nuclear age has brought us full circle now to know that we have to actually love those Russians, because it's not up to us or Bob Hawke or Ronald Reagan whether or not we live or die, it's up to the Russians ... And they're paranoid, that's why they shot down that jet. When a paranoid patient comes into hospital you don't threaten them, you ...

... playing yet'. A little boy aged eight stood up before some doctors and said 'nobody wants to be given a broken present at Christmas, that's how I feel about my life'. What have we done to our children? And there aren't communist babies or capitalist babies. A baby is a baby is a baby. [Sedate applause.] And next time you see a baby, a tiny newborn baby, look into its eyes and see the incredible innocence in those eyes and the archetypal wisdom, and know it's the babies we're going to save. The babies and the planet now and forever more. We have to give up as it says ...

... of time. Will man evolve spiritually and emotionally enough ... and women, to know that we can't fight and we have to live together in peace. If we can't we'll blow up the world and you and I will know that in our lifetime. Before we die, we will know whether the human race can do it or not. If we die in a nuclear holocaust, we'll know we failed. If we die of natural causes in our lifetime, we'll definitely know that we succeeded. You can do nothing less with your life than this ... to give up everything for the planet. And even if you fail, as the bomb goes off, you can die with a clear conscience. But it makes the earth so precious and I really and truly believe that the people of the earth are rising up and the politicians will have to stand aside and give us what we want. We want the earth to continue and we want to live; and have children and life to go on for evermore. [Applause.]

A number of quite distinct discourses operate here: medical, Christian, populist (Jungian) psychiatric, patriotic, sentimental–parental, romantic, patriarchal, technological, prophetic, feminist. The traces of these different discourses are evident enough; they have not been closely integrated by the writer/speaker into anything like a seamless text: the discursive differences are not resolved. Consequently the text is unlikely to provide that definitional impulse which would act to give unity to the diverse groups which had assembled on that day to hear the speech. Although the text is that of a single writer, the different discourses are clearly evident, so much so that it has been beyond the writer's ability to control that difference. It would not be difficult to imagine this text as a dialogue among a number of speakers: the 'parts' would not be hard to assign. It would be a somewhat static wooden dialogue, a bit like an initial declaration of position, but a dialogue nonetheless.

The underlying dialogic nature of this text gives rise to the question about the function of author/writers generally. I mentioned above that in general it is an ideological and political function, that is, to control and if possible to eliminate difference, perhaps to establish the dominance of one discourse. If that is not possible, the author/writer might attempt to use the text to alter the manner in which particular readers will read and reconstruct this and other texts. If it is the case that we read certain texts because of our social institutional situation, and if it is also the case that we read texts in ways determined by our social place and discursive history, then a particular text might be used to alter the way in which we read other texts. If our readings are determined by a particular position which we 'have', or adopt, it might be possible to construct a new coherent reading position for future texts. Tony Bennett, in an article 'Texts in history: the determinations of readings and their texts', uses the term 'reading formation' to talk about the 'set of discursive and inter-textual determinations which organize and animate the practice of reading, connecting texts and readers in specific relations to one another in constituting readers as reading subjects of particular types and texts as objects-to-be-read in particular ways'. He continues: 'This entails arguing that texts have and can have no existence independently of such reading formations, that there is no place independent of, anterior to or above the varying reading formations through which historical life is variantly modulated within which texts can be constituted as objects of knowledge.' The function of the writer is to construct texts which confirm or alter the manner in which a particular text is read.

In this respect there is a possible distinction between the notion of 'writer' and of 'author'. Authors are writers whose social and cultural construction endows their writings with greater power and valuation, a power which transcends that of any writer and carries enormous ideological and political weight. A text written by an 'author' speaks in its own right and for all time—that is, its modality is that of the universal present. Helen Caldicott had been constructed as an author (and 'star') even before her arrival in Sydney, so that her speech was potentially endowed with that power.

4.6 KINDS OF TEXTS: GENRE

Language always happens as text, and not as isolated words and sentences. From an aesthetic, social or educational perspective it is the text which is the significant unit of language. Texts arise in specific social situations and they are constructed with specific purposes by one or more speakers or writers. Meanings find their expression in text—though the origins of meanings are outside the text—and are negotiated (about) in texts, in concrete situations of social exchange. Texts are the material form of language; in particular, texts give material realization to discourses. Hence the meanings of texts are in part the meanings of the discourses which are present in and have given rise to a specific text.

The social occasions of which texts are a part have a fundamentally important effect on texts. The characteristic features and structures of those situations, the purposes of the participants, the goals of the participants all have their effects on the form of the texts which are constructed in those situations. The situations are always conventional. That is, the occasions in which we interact, the social relations which we contract, are conventionalized and structured, more or less thoroughly, depending on the kind of situation it is. They range from entirely formulaic and ritualized occasions, such as royal weddings, sporting encounters, committee meetings, to family rituals such as breakfasts or barbecues or fights over who is to do the dishes. Other, probably fewer, occasions are less ritualized, less formulaic; casual conversation may be an example. The structures and forms of the conventionalized occasions themselves signify the functions, the purposes of the participants, and the desired goals of that occasion.

Take, as an example, a committee meeting. It is an occasion which is highly conventional and ritualized; its conventions and rituals have specific functions and goals. These might be characterized broadly as the intention to reach decisions in certain ways, to involve designated categories of people in decision-making, and to reach decisions which are seen as equitable, and politically sustainable. These functions and goals, conventions and rituals, have effects on the texts which arise in such occasions, and give rise to conventionalized forms of texts which are themselves expressions of the meanings of the social occasions in which they arose.

The conventionalized forms of the occasions lead to conventionalized forms of texts, to specific GENRES. Genres have specific forms and meanings, deriving from and encoding the functions, purposes and meanings of the social occasions. Genres therefore provide a precise index and catalogue of the relevant social occasions of a community at a given time. A few examples of genre are: interview, essay, conversation, sale, tutorial, sports commentary, seduction, office memo, novel, political speech, editorial, sermon, joke, instruction.

The meanings of texts are therefore derived not only from the meanings of the discourses which give rise and appear in particular texts, but also from the meanings of the genre of a particular text. Both discourse and genre carry specific and socially determined meanings. Discourse carries meanings about the nature of the institution from which it derives; genre carries meanings about the conventional social occasions in which texts arise.

Texts are therefore doubly determined: by the meanings of the discourses which appear in the text, and by the forms, meanings and constraints of a particular genre. Both discourse and genre arise out of the structures and processes of a society: discourses are derived from the larger social institutions within a society; genres are derived from the conventionalized social occasions in and through which social life is carried on. Clearly, these two kinds of meaning are not at all unrelated and consequently there can be matching and overlappings between certain discourses and certain genres. There are preferred conjunctions of discourses and genres, and prohibitions on other conjunctions. For example, the social institution of medicine has given rise to medical discourse. That institution (or subgroupings of it) also have conventionalized occasions such as lectures, (the writing of) scientific papers, meetings, research committees, experimentation, job interviews, conversations, formal dinner speeches, etc. Because there is a close link between the nature of the institution and the kinds of occasions that characterize it, at times it seems as though discourse and genre are identical. However, that is not so. It is easy to demonstrate that many of the occasions (and genres) of the institution of medicine occur in many quite other institutions while the generic features remain constant.

Little work has as yet been done on the study of genre. What there is has been carried out in a very different paradigm, that of literary criticism, and on literary texts. Clearly, however, generic forms are of great significance in the determination of the meanings of texts, and the construction of readings. The place, function, valuations of participants in social occasions are structured into the forms of genres, so that quite precisely circumscribed (reading) positions are constructed in a given genre. The kind of genre chosen for the expression of certain discourses therefore has significant effects not only on the meanings of the text, but on the possibilities of readings of the text. In relation to the topic of the nuclear debate, the significance of genre lies in knowing which genres are available to anti- and pro-nuclear groups, and what the effects of these genres are on the meanings of texts, and the possible modes of reading. The interrelation of genre and social occasion suggests that texts are severely limited in this respect: the social occasions in which groups and individuals opposed to nuclear arms operate tend to be those in which groups and individuals supportive of nuclear arms also operate, with the difference that the pro-nuclear establishment has institutionalized control of or access to a whole range of genres closed off to anti-nuclear groups.

To make this point somewhat more concretely, the facing page shows the text of the first side of a two-sided newsletter from a peace group. Without analysis it is obvious that the text is constructed entirely within the demands of this particular genre. The effect is that habitually established modes of reading (and of other social practices of which the text is one part) will be called into effect. That raises the serious problem of how one might construct texts which avoid, pre-empt or even subvert such habitual readings, or how to utilize the effects of such habitual readings for the ends of the anti-nuclear movement.

Dear Friend,
this is the first issue of what we hope will become a regular bi-monthly newsletter. The intention is to keep everyone informed about events happening locally and globally. At the last meeting it was agreed that there was an urgent need for a bulletin like this. It goes without saying that all contributions and suggestions will be gratefully accepted, please forward them to Bill Peisley via our PO Box 543, Artarmon 2064. Letters, poems, small cartoons, etc. are most welcome.

EVENTS—BEEN AND GONE
Northside Peace Group got off to a flying start for the year with our Disarmament Fair at North Sydney on March 3rd. We had the first sunny Saturday for weeks, a good attendance, and a healthy £1,300 in takings to back up our future work. Most importantly, the enlightenment process, the message that this group is all about, was canvassed in the true spirit of a village Fair.

Our thanks to all those who helped with donations of goods, working on stalls, and publicizing the Fair. Thanks also to other participants in the Fair —Manly-Warringah Peace Movement, Greenpeace, Action for World Development, Movement Against Uranium Mining, SNEPS, SANA, and others, and to North Sydney Council and the staff of the Leisure Centre who eased the way.

Particular thanks is owed to Paul Farrell, who carried much of the burden of organizing the Fair. Paul has now departed for eight months in Europe, and we all wish him well and hope that he returns before too long.

In other work: Sheila Morrison spoke to a seniors class at Monte St. Angelo school; stalls were held at North Sydney Market day in February and March; and several thousand notices about the April 15th Rally have been distributed. We have taken out an ad for April 15th in two editions of the North Shore Times; a most generous donation from an anonymous supporter has covered most of the cost—our thanks.

Epping Peace Group held a rally in Beecroft Park at the end of March— some 250-300 people attended.

EVENTS—COMING READY OR NOT.
* APRIL 15th—PALM SUNDAY RALLY
Where will you be on April 15th? What about being at Hyde Park South at 1.00 pm (march to Domain for music, stalls, speakers). This march will be occurring in cities and country towns around Australia—come yourself, bring family and friends, and we'll have a co-ordinated demonstration of our resolve to Stop the Drop.

Northside Peace Group will be marching—we will be at the local groups assembly point before the march, ie: the steps into Hyde Park from Liverpool St., halfway between College and Elizabeth Sts. (Note: *not* the point discusseed at our last meeting).

Just before the march, at 12.30pm, there will be an Ecumenical Service at the south-west corner of Hyde Park.

4.7 STRATEGIES

The force of my argument so far tends in two opposed directions. On the one hand, power seems to lie with the producers of texts: the power to marshal discourses into certain configurations, to act on the pre-existent subject positions of readers (as 'real men', 'patriotic citizens', 'concerned Christians'), to construct reading positions, to select genres and to control possibilities of reading. On the other hand, I have suggested that readers can resist, construct 'their own meanings', and make 'their own sense'. But this opposition does not remain paradoxical as long as we acknowledge that readers are active, and that the linguistic, textual/discursive and ideological system is not static, but exists in time, in history, and in contingent social situations, which are themselves full of contention. There are occasions where readings and reading positions are enforced, as in school textbooks which form the basis of examination and assessment, and in other similar situations, particularly at work. There are occasions where subject positions are enforced, as in the labour-force, where both men and women are subject to the constraints of sexist discourse and practice. There are many situations where readings cannot be enforced, where subject positions can be rejected. Given the varying discursive histories of individuals, their various locations in present social structures, their differential involvement in social processes, the concept of unproblematically compliant reading is a comforting myth for ideologues, but it does not match with actual practices. Readers are to a significant extent free to construct texts in a mode closer to their own discursive position. It is here where any thinking about strategies needs to begin: who are the intended readers for texts, what are their discursive positions, what kinds of texts can achieve certain kinds of shifts in discursive/ideological positioning.

The question of textual intervention in the nuclear debate is a political question, and therefore a question ultimately of the larger social/political institutions in which texts are produced as one aspect of social/political processes. It is important to see this clearly: linguistic action, autonomously conceived, misses the fundamental points. Once this is acknowledged, one can begin to focus on specific areas. Many of these I have already mentioned in the course of this chapter: an analysis of the processes of reading, of its constraints and possibilities; an examination of the social/discursive place of specific readers, and the effect of that on reading; the possibilities of longer term ideological/political realignments via the effects of strategic texts. There is the need for the continued production of texts which necessitate the response by the pro-nuclear establishment—for without that there will be silence. There is the continued need to analyse and expose both the meanings and forms of specific discourses, so that effective counter-texts may be constructed. And there is the need to analyse how the pro-nuclear argument is embedded in a wide variety of those discourses which constitute the social life of most individuals, obviously and naturally, discourses of work, the family, morality, nationalism, sexism and patriarchy.

Given the institutionally entrenched nature of ideology, of discourses and of texts, there is one final question I wish to pose. It is clear that there is no single pro-nuclear discourse, but rather that pro-nuclear arguments are totally embedded in a wide variety of other discourses. If pro-nuclear texts are therefore constituted in and by this plethora of other discourses, what is it that gives all these texts their remarkable coherence and force? My suggestion is that all the texts are constituted around a basic anti-Soviet attitude, which may be more or less present in the texts, or constructed by its absence. The Bishop's homily is one example. The disinformation pamphlets produced by various government-sponsored fronts such as the ones cited earlier here are clear examples. Perhaps less obvious, though in one sense clearer, examples are newspaper reports. For instance, the front-page article of *The Daily Telegraph*, Monday, 13 December 1982:

20,000 WOMEN IN MISSILE PROTEST
Proposed Cruise site encircled
About 20,000 unilateral nuclear disarmers, most of them women, yesterday encircled the base at Greenham Common, Berks., where 96 United States Cruise missiles are due to be based a year from now.
The women, many with toddlers in push-chairs, clasped hands to form a human chain around the nine-mile perimeter fence.
Men, including Mr Wedgwood Benn and Mgr Bruce Kent, general secretary of the Campaign for Nuclear Disarmament, were encouraged to keep a low profile and given a special area in which to protest.
Male reporters, including teams from Soviet television and *Pravda*, were told to keep their distance.

And the *Daily Express* of the same date:

WOMEN RING MISSILE BASE IN ANTI-NUCLEAR PROTEST
Express Staff Reporter
A Russian TV crew filmed the mass anti-nuclear protest by women at Greenham Common yesterday.
Reporters from the Kremlin mouthpiece newspaper *Pravda* were also at the besieged American air base in Berkshire.
As the Soviet cameras rolled, the 30,000 demonstrators milling in the mud appeared as unwitting dupes of a propaganda coup by Moscow.
The film of bedraggled mothers and children chanting against NATO's defence policy is sure to be screened in millions of homes in Russia and other Warsaw Pact countries this week.
The Soviet journalists had a field day after signing in at the Press tent to get their official passes.
Later the Moscow TV crew were huddled in earnest conversation with some of the organisers of the demo which was peaceful throughout. They also filmed women erecting slogan placards.
The protesters, many of them members of the Campaign for Nuclear Disarmament, held hands to form a human chain round the nine-mile perimeter of the base where 96 American nuclear Cruise missiles are to be sited as a deterrent to the Soviet military threat.

On this front page the main story is set off by a smaller piece at the bottom 'Send a card to a soldier', which contrasts the loyalty and patriotism of a housewife with the activity of the Greenham Common women, which is constructed as basically treasonous.

This strategy is also employed by the *Daily Mail*, whose main story again locates the Russian threat:

> It was a day of triumph for the women of protest. They forecast 20,000 would be at the Greenham Common RAF base in Berkshire yesterday.
> In fact, about 30,000 turned up to form a nine-mile human chain around the base in protest against the siting of American Cruise missiles there.
> They defied pouring rain and waded through ankle-deep mud to deliver their message. They sang songs, too, and pinned children's clothing and family photographs to the perimeter fence.
> But it was not only a triumph for the peace movement. It was also a coup for the Soviet propaganda machine.
> There to record the event were representatives from *Pravda*, the official Soviet newspaper, *Tass*, the Kremlin's news agency, and Soviet television. The Bulgarian news agency was also represented.
> But after signing in and picking up their official badges the Russians were shy about explaining who they were. Asked if they were from the BBC or ITN the cameramen just smiled and carried on filming. At one stage the Soviet TV crew were seen huddled in earnest conversation with some of the demo organisers.
> Certainly their film will make wonderful footage for the Kremlin in the propaganda war which surrounds the whole nuclear issue.
>
> DELEGATION
> But the organisers, who have been camped outside the gates of the camp for 14 months, insisted they were not being used.

If this assumption is correct, any strategies aimed at interrupting the effect of pro-nuclear texts will have to come to terms with that question; particularly so as many anti-nuclear texts take that same basic stance, in only a slightly modified form as 'a plague on both your houses'. Helen Caldicott's speech is a clear instance of this. In other words, the main focus of anti-nuclear texts may need to be shifted to deal with the real focus and motivating ideology of pro-nuclear texts.[6]

NOTES

1. See, for instance, Coward and Ellis (1977), Kress and Hodge (1979), Fowler, Hodge, Kress and Trew (1979), Kress (1985), Chilton (1982, 1983), Good (1985), Torode and Silverman (1977), Hall, Hobson, Lowe and Willis (1980), Spender (1980).
2. Here I am thinking of the effects of feminist critiques on social practices in a wide area, from ways of talking to changes in the legal code; or the beginning of effects on professional practices in medicine (e.g. doctor–patient relations), in education (e.g. the changing views of children's texts), and indeed in the peace movement (cf. Chilton's articles mentioned above).

3. Not all linguistic theories are alike in these respects. The work that has influenced my own thinking most is that of Michael Halliday, the theory of systemic linguistics. His view of language is a thoroughly socio-cultural one. Nevertheless, it (as indeed my own previous work) is a producer-centred approach to language.
4. See, for instance, Foucault (1971, 1972) and his 'Orders of Discourse' (1972).
5. For instance, in *Language as Ideology* and *Language and Control*, particularly Chapters 2, 5 and 10.
6. I wish to thank Ann Curthoys for comments particularly on the conclusions of this chapter.

Part II
The discourse of deterrence

5 The logic of deterrence: a semiotic and psychoanalytic approach

William Van Belle and Paul Claes
Katholieke Universiteit, Leuven, Belgium

5.1 THE DISCOURSE OF DETERRENCE

In official NATO defence policy, words play as big a part as arms. While the arms race continues, the leaders repeat magical formulas to ward off evil spirits. The key term in this exorcism is the word 'deterrence'. But this word does not stand on its own: it is part of a way of reasoning which has a more or less narrative character. In this study we shall try to analyse the logic of that way of thinking by means of the semiotic theory of A. J. Greimas and the psychoanalytic theory of J. Lacan. Before doing so, we shall give an account of the basic terms and the arguments used in deterrence discourse. As sources for our description we shall use some more or less official documents, propaganda material, articles and interviews diffused by NATO spokesmen, army officers and politicians in Belgium and The Netherlands.[1]

The official NATO defence policy is said to be based upon the doctrine of deterrence of the enemy, and it is also presumed that the Warsaw Pact follows the same policy: often the phrase 'mutual deterrence' is used. In the absence of source material we shall not speak here about the strategy of the Soviet Union, but it is likley that the logic of deterrence exists there as well.[2] It seems strange that two political systems that differ so much economically, socially and politically resemble each other so closely in the field of defence. One may put it even more strongly: this defence strategy can only be successful because it is the same for both opponents. In this symmetry we recognize the MIRROR RELATIONSHIP, which is the key to understanding this strange logic.[3]

NATO strategy is based on the triad *détente, deterrence* and *defence*. The triple alliteration suggests that even strategic systems are sensitive to wordplay. Since the onset of the nuclear arms race the second term of the triad has been emphasized. Thus the *NATO Handbook* for instance says: 'the primary purpose of the Alliance is to maintain the security of member nations by deterring aggression' (p. 19).

What does deterrence consist of? Since it would be impossible to defend one's own population against a nuclear attack, NATO tries to prevent such an attack by striving for a military balance of mutual terror or deterrence. The threat behind deterrence is mutually assured destruction. There is a kind of pact between the opponents that says: if you attack me, you will kill me, but before I die, I will kill you. In other words, your murder will be at the same time a suicide. Officially NATO maintains that 'the policy of deterrence is entirely consistent with the pursuit of *détente*. NATO must continue to maintain its defensive strength to provide a firm basis for negotiations and a guarantee of its own security until such security can be achieved through firm agreements which entail a reduction of military strengths on both sides' (*NATO Handbook*, p. 21). Also defended is the paradoxical thesis that the negotiations on arms reduction will be helped forward by increasing our military strength. In the newspaper *Het Volk* (18 February 1983) was the following headline: 'Reagan: refusal of the missiles in Europe will harm disarmament'. And the *Defensiekrant* (20 January 1983) summarized an interview with NATO Commander Bernard W. Rogers in the following title: 'Willingness to arm now leads to fewer arms later'.

According to this logic, opponents of further armament are not striving for 'real' peace, but for 'peace in subjection' (Pax Sovietica), because they are led, or misled, by the Soviet Union. They are also continually represented as supporters of UNILATERAL disarmament. As a result they are seen as neutralists who are undermining the unity and the security of the alliance. In the interview in the *Defensiekrant* mentioned above Rogers says:

> He who thinks that unilateral disarmament—or pacifism or neutralism— helps, misjudges history. Such statements do not lead to peace; and even if peace is maintained, its cost will be the loss of freedom and of the possibility of living as you like . . .

And in an interview in the weekly *Knack* (26 January 1983) he makes clear what 'real' pacifism means:

> 'Freeze' is a moratorium—it is pacifism. God, there is nobody more peaceful and nobody in this world who wants peace more than me . . . And it is the fate of a real pacifist, that he gets peace at any price, including his own freedom.

In 1983 Belgian politicians of the majority party tried to substitute the euphemism *ontrading* ('dissuasion') for the word *afschrikking* (deterrence).[4] Probably 'deterrence' has too many associations with the 'terror', widespread among a large part of the population, of a nuclear war or accident. But the strategy itself has not changed. To get a clear insight into it, we shall start with excerpts from an article published in *Militaire Spectator* (January 1983) by P. H. de Vries, a Dutch cavalry captain. We have chosen this article because it gives a virtually complete demonstration of a logic that in the discourse of other NATO spokesmen often appears only in fragmentary form. As we find in all NATO documents a common stock of phrases, sentences and arguments, we can use other texts to illustrate and eventually clarify de Vries's reasoning.

5.2 HOW TO DETER?

In his article de Vries says:

> In Western Europe we have had on the one hand the North Atlantic Treaty Organization (NATO) since 1949, and, on the other hand, the Warsaw Pact (WP) since 1955. Given the ideological contrast between these two power blocs, the mutual mistrust connected with it and the existence of a certain balance of power, one attempts to prevent war by means of deterrence. Deterrence is sometimes defined as the product of the *capability* to cause to the enemy unacceptable damage and the *intention* to use this capability if necessary. If one of these factors is nil, then the product is also nil. Since it is nearly impossible to establish the value of these factors objectively, much importance is given to the concept of *credibility*. The credibility of the product of deterrence stands or falls with the credibility of the factors 'capability' and 'intention'. [p. 28.]

The same elements, capability and intention, are found in the article 'Afschrikking en evenwicht' by the Belgian General Robert Close:

> I repeat what deterrence means. It consists in having the material means (and the intention to put them into operation) that enable one to inflict upon the enemy such severe losses that there is no proportionality between the hoped-for advantage and the sustained damage. [p. 78.]

We shall now investigate these two factors in more detail.

5.2.1 Capability

The capacity to deter consists in having sufficient armament, especially in the nuclear domain, to be able to respond to every attack. When does one have sufficient nuclear arms? The answer to this question is apparently not so simple. It is clear that the number of nuclear arms, deemed necessary for a credible deterrence, has been increasing 'deterrently' since the beginning of the 1950s.[5] The destructive power has even reached an 'overkill-capacity', but even that is apparently not sufficient, nor is a global balance between the two superpowers.[6]

Since the 1950s the answer to this question has been made dependent on the so-called flexible-response strategy. Three kinds of weapons are distinguished: conventional weapons, tactical nuclear weapons (for use on the battlefield), and strategic nuclear weapons (which have mainly a deterrent function, although NATO does not exclude an initial, limited use of them). Deterrence is only deemed effective if, of each of these three kinds of armament, one possesses a sufficient number to cope with the opponent's every aggression. An imbalance in one domain may be compensated for by an advantage in another domain. In the official pamphlet *Vrede in Vrijheid* one reads the following:

> A lack of parity in one of the three categories of the triad or even with respect to particular types of arms creates a partial imbalance. The opponent may attempt to take advantage of this. In so doing he can force us to give way or to start a dangerous escalation.

It is clear that by such reasoning the arms race can go on endlessly.

Meanwhile the triad mentioned above has been replaced by another one. The expression 'short- and intermediate-range nuclear missiles' (and, more often than not, 'intermediate' only) is now frequently substituted for 'tactical nuclear weapons'.[7] In that way NATO can insist on the superiority of the Soviet Union in land-based, intermediate-range missiles. In *Vrede in Vrijheid*, which was intended for secondary schools, pupils could see a graph in which the land-based, intermediate-range missiles were compared, whereas other types of missiles were not mentioned. In that way the superiority of the Soviet Union appears to be overwhelming: 1,300 warheads to nil.

James Bush of the American Center for Defense Information tells us how this reclassification of arms came about:

> He [President Reagan] approached the Soviet Union with the idea that if they would dismantle their SS 20s, the United States would not deploy the Pershing IIs or the Ground Launched Cruise Missiles; what became known as the zero-zero option. In order to justify our proposal for a zero–zero option, ... it was necessary to take the SS 20s out of the description of a Theatre Nuclear Force. Our own forces no longer became Theatre Nuclear Forces, they became Intermediate Nuclear Forces, INF Forces as it were. Now we also ... INF Forces didn't do the whole job ... we had to talk about Long Range INF Forces. And then in order to fully isolate the SS 20, we had to talk about Land-Based Long Range INF Forces. NATO had no Long Range Land-Based Intermediate Nuclear Force. And the only way that could be balanced was to put in the Pershing II missiles and the Ground Launched Cruise Missiles.[8]

This example illustrates how words seem to play an even more important part in the capability of deterring than real destructive power. There is nothing to prevent the United States from inventing a new category of arms to compensate for that part of the Soviet nuclear arsenal for which they say they have no equivalent.

5.2.2 Intention

The intention to deter means the willingness to use nuclear arms in case of aggression. Leo Tindemans, the Belgian Minister of Foreign Affairs, said in an interview with the weekly *Trends* (20 January 1983) that the best defence is to be found in the willingness of the population to defend itself in the firm belief of fighting for a just cause. And this implies that the population is united in supporting that cause. In such a line of reasoning the peace movement must be a negative factor: it impairs the unity of the alliance and hence the credibility of the factor 'intention'. De Vries stated in the same interview:

> By insisting on nuclear disarmament—or unilateral disarmament—one shows that one does not have the intention to use these arms. As a result the credibility of the factor 'intention' of the product 'deterrence' diminishes, and in that way the credibility of deterrence as a whole is impaired.

The credibility of the intention is also invoked as the reason why NATO is not to make a 'no-first-use' statement: 'Renouncing the first use of nuclear weapons would permit the Soviet Union to calculate its risks and eventually to engage in war in Europe'.[9] Our reaction against an attack must be 'unpredictable' so that the risks for the aggressor are incalculable.[10]

5.2.3 Credibility

The credibility of our deterrence depends on the credibility of the factors 'capability' and 'intention'. But, according to NATO spokesmen, there are shortcomings in both domains. Therefore we have to 'deploy' new missiles (Pershing II, cruise missiles, MX-missiles—named 'Peacekeepers' by President Reagan) on the one hand, and on the other hand we have to convince peace movements of the fact that they may bring about a disastrous nuclear war by undermining our credibility. Thus General Close writes: 'Whatever the motives of these demonstrations are (and sometimes they are noble), I think that they lead to suicide, because they are unilateral' (pp. 79-80). And NATO Secretary-General Luns goes further in the appraisal of the peace movements when he says that they 'undermine the basis of democracy when they take action against decisions that are democratically taken by democratic institutions'.[11]

5.3 WHY DETERRENCE?

What justifications appear in official discourse to explain why such a strategy of deterrence has been developed? The answer to this question is predictable if we remember the mirror situation in which both opponents find themselves. We deter because they deter (and vice versa). This logic can also be found in NATO sources. Again the factors 'capability' and 'intention' play a dominant role. According to these sources the Warsaw Pact has the 'capability' of frightening NATO. Comparative statistics are used to illustrate that thesis. By means of 'objective' figures there is a constant attempt to prove that the opponent has global or partial superiority. Such comparisons escalate the arms race, in spite of the existing overkill capacity of 50,000 warheads and the statistically increasing probability of an 'unintended' nuclear war.

In addition, the Soviet Union is assumed to have the 'intention' of conquering the world, with nuclear weapons if need be. That intention can be derived from their actions as well as their ideology. General Close points out that in sixty years the Soviet Union has appropriated a territory of 3,400,000 sq. km., which means 'on average a territory as great as that of France every ten years' (p. 74). And in *Soviet Military Power* it is stated that '. . . the Soviets continue to build far greater numbers of missiles and warheads than are necessary for a credible deterrent capability'.[12] The events in Afghanistan and Poland, and other Soviet military actions such as the shooting of the South Korean Boeing airliner, serve as proofs of bellicosity. (On the other hand, the Korean and Vietnamese wars, the destabilization of Chile, the political and military interventions in Central American countries would prove the imperialism of the United States.)

General Rogers says in an interview with *Knack* (26 January 1983) that he would like to talk with Marshal Victor Kulikov, Commander of the Warsaw Pact Military Forces, to persuade him of the fact that the Europe Allied Commando has no offensive plans (except 'counterattacks as part of the defence strategy, because counterattack is the basis of a credible defence'). On the other hand, he does not believe that the Soviets have only defensive plans, because Soviet ideology aims at the conquest of the world. The main argument for the supposed Soviet urge to conquer the world appears to be their totalitarian regime, the existence of which means a threat for Western democracies:

> The most important thing is to be convinced that one has to deal with two worlds that are diametrically opposed, one of which strives for world domination and uses every means to attain this goal. One of these worlds is the world of freedom, the other one is the world of the Gulag. [Close, p. 81.]

Such a totalitarian regime can also easily start a war, whereas in the West such a decision would have to be taken democratically:

> For parliamentary democracies it is psychologically, technically and politically impossible to begin a military attack. How could we proclaim mobilization without being attacked first? Only totalitarian regimes are able to plan and to carry out such an aggression. [Tindemans in *Trends* 20 January 1983.]

The description of the peace movement as a fifth column, allegedly used by the Soviet Union in their psychological warfare, fits completely in this climate of fundamental distrust. The Soviet proposals for arms reduction are also seen as part of that psychological warfare: their only aim is to sow dissent in the West.

Thus the great difference between NATO and the Warsaw Pact, in the discourse of NATO spokesmen, is that the former is purely defensive, the latter fundamentally aggressive. Yet we know—and this is the important point for our argument—that the Soviet doctrine, whatever other differences it might have, projects the mirror image of this position. In this sense, the logic into which both powers are locked is, as we shall suggest below, 'imaginary' in the sense of Lacan. Not surprisingly, therefore, paradox seems intrinsic to deterrence discourse; indeed, the fact is often vaunted by its practitioners. Capability and intention are components of credibility essential in practice to BOTH sides. The potential ambiguity of the terms is also in part responsible for potential paradox. One is 'capable' of inflicting damage on the other, yet not 'capable' of doing so in a slightly different sense, because of the knowledge that the other, too, is 'capable'. Intention, even more obviously, is liable to paradoxicality, for one must 'intend' yet not 'intend' to destroy the other. And it is not always a matter of speaking conditionally ('we (only) intend to do X, IF . . .'), as the texts cited in section 5.2.2 suggest. Further related paradoxes abound: one has to arm to disarm, the more probable the use of nuclear weapons, the less probable, and so forth. Not only in discourse but also in reality do attack and defence converge. The system of deterrence is such that defending oneself can only be an act of aggression, because it consists of a destructive attack. Conversely, an attack could also be a destructive defence out of fear. In this disastrous mirror relationship the boundaries between defence and attack have disappeared.

5.4 THE SEMIOTICS OF THE STRATEGY OF DETERRENCE

We will systematize now the strategy of deterrence by means of the theory of meaning of the French semiotician A. J. Greimas.[13] For Greimas, meanings are not 'references', but relations between language terms. As the basic structure of meaning he proposes a relational whole, the so-called SEMIOTIC SQUARE, the four terms of which exist by virtue of their mutual relations. Horizontally the terms are connected by contrariety (a qualitative opposition of the type white/black) and diagonally by contradiction (a binary oppositionof the type white/non-white). This gives the following semiotic square:

$$\begin{array}{ccc} \text{white (a)} & & \text{black (b)} \\ & \times & \\ \text{non-black}\ (\bar{b}) & & \text{non-white}\ (\bar{a}) \end{array}$$

To describe military antagonism we can form the following square:

$$\begin{array}{ccc} \text{friend (a)} & & \text{enemy (b)} \\ & \times & \\ \text{non-enemy}\ (\bar{b}) & & \text{non-friend}\ (\bar{a}) \end{array}$$

In the cold-war situation that we live in, you could put NATO in position (a), the Warsaw Pact in position (b), the opponents of the Warsaw Pact (e.g. dissidents) in position ($\bar{b}$) and in position ($\bar{a}$) the opponents of NATO (e.g. that part of the peace movement that favours the dissolution of NATO). People who want a dissolution of both alliances are in the (a) and (b) position.

On to the foregoing square we may then project the semiotic square of deterrence:

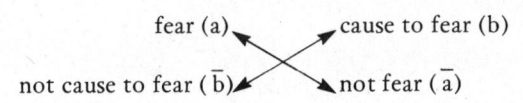

$$\begin{array}{ccc} \text{fear (a)} & & \text{cause to fear (b)} \\ & \times & \\ \text{not cause to fear}\ (\bar{b}) & & \text{not fear}\ (\bar{a}) \end{array}$$

Since the beginning of the cold war the general attitude of the West towards the Eastern bloc can best be described as one of 'fear'. One only has to think of the famous words 'Nous avons peur' of the Belgian Secretary-General of the UN, Paul-Henri Spaak. That fear (a) is caused by the frightfulness (b) of the Warsaw Pact. In ($\bar{a}$) we can place the attitude of those who do not want the peace strategy to be determined by fear, e.g. by trusting the Warsaw Pact instead of mistrusting it, as is generally the case. In ($\bar{b}$) we find the attitude of those who are against the strategy of deterrence and, for instance, aim at unilateral disarmament.

Official NATO policy is based both on 'fear' and 'cause to fear'. To the real or imagined threat of the Russians they oppose their own threat. In that way a completely symmetrical set of relations comes about, which gives a semiotic square of the following form:

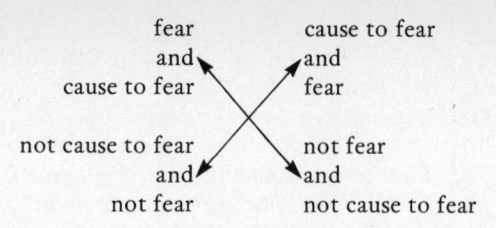

```
         fear              cause to fear
         and                    and
    cause to fear               fear

    not cause to fear         not fear
         and                    and
         not fear          not cause to fear
```

This is a paradoxical situation in which both opponents are at the same time frightened and frightening, are both perpetrators and victims of terror. In this square the peace movements are in the position $(\overline{a})$ and $(\overline{b})$. They believe that the strategy of deterrence is not efficient. The idea on which this strategy is based is that it is supposed to lead to a kind of paralysis of the opponents. Fear and deterrence are said to keep each other in balance, so that aggression can be averted. But this line of reasoning takes no account of the dynamics introduced into this static model by the arms race, nor of the dynamics of the mirror relationship. We will now turn to the discussion of these two points.

5.5 DETERRENCE AS NARRATIVE (WITHOUT A HAPPY ENDING)

In an expansion of his semantic theory Greimas has elaborated a narrative theory,[14] some elements of which we shall use here. One of the most simple types of narrative is the story of conflict, with two acting entities (called ACTANTS) opposing each other. These actants are the SUBJECT (the 'hero') and the ANTI-SUBJECT (the 'villain'), who try to eliminate each other by depriving each other of value objects. These objects take the form of modalities, such as ability, will and knowledge. The reader will recognize a correspondence with the terms of the logic of deterrence. We shall try to extent this parallelism now.

In order to be able to fight the anti-subject, the subject has to be competent: he has to possess the modalities that make him dominant. A more powerful actant, the DONOR, may give him these modalities. In the narrative of deterrence the role of the subject is played by the military command of NATO, the role of the anti-subject by the command of the Warsaw Pact. The donor of competence to the military commanders is the civil community, by which they are given the modalities of ability and will—'capability' and 'intention'.

The modality of ability consists in 'sufficient' armament. The public authorities procure (the credits for the purchase of) such armament. There is a permanent tension between the army asking for new resources and the government trying to cut expenses. But armament is not only a matter of defence but also of the business world. The military-industrial complex will persuade the army to exaggerate the necessary ability in order to get more credits. It is difficult to establish an objective picture of 'sufficient armament' because the armament of the adversary is hard to assess and because dissimilar arms are being compared. The modality of will consists in the intention to use, 'if necessary', a certain ability. In principle the military commanders are dependent on the public authorities and must receive their 'will' from them. In NATO propaganda roles are often reversed, the military officials wanting more resolution from the civilians. This seems to be a dangerous evolution: defence ought to remain an instrument of the civilian state.

In an ordinary story the fight will begin as soon as the subject has acquired the competences of ability and will. That is wholly impossible in our story, because it would mean self-destruction. The fight takes place on an 'imaginary' level: the level of belief. Most stories that are fought on the level of knowledge are based on the category of truth. The moment the subject has acquired the modalities of being-able-to-know and wanting-to-know, he may beat his adversary by unravelling his riddle. One may think of detective stories as well as folk tales. The narrative of deterrence is a little more subtle because it is based on the category of **PROBABILITY**.

The paradox of the politics of deterrence is that it combines the most spiritual power—belief—with the most material power—destruction by nuclear arms. But looking more carefully we see that the logic of deterrence rests on a confusion between both powers. In fact credibility is interpreted in two contradictory ways. On the one hand, it is defined as a kind of make-believe: your adversary must believe something you do not really believe yourself, namely, that you will use nuclear weapons at any price (even your own existence). So the threatening becomes a show—'an appearing'. On the other hand, credibility means that you increase the objective probability of the use of nuclear weapons in order to be as convincing as possible. So the threatening becomes real—'a being'. The contradiction between appearing and being, between subjective likelihood and objective probability is unsolvable and undermines the whole logic. Unable to recognize this fundamental error, its defenders continue to draw pathological conclusions from invalid premises.

The dynamics of that illogical logic arise from the idea that security is enhanced by enhancing insecurity, a mode of reasoning leading to the following spiral of pseudo-syllogisms:

Deterrence functions only if it is credible.
Credibility is something gradual.
Consequently, deterrence may be increased by gradually increasing the quantity and sophistication of nuclear weapons (smaller warheads, etc.).

Credibility is a matter of probability.
Consequently, deterrence may be increased by increasing the probability of the use of nuclear weapons (smaller and more accurate systems, launch on warning, etc.).

Credibility is greater if restraints are fewer.
Consequently, deterrence increases as we subject the use of nuclear weapons to less restrictions (e.g. if we do not promise not to use nuclear arms first).

The fundamental role of the concepts of deterrence and credibility in this schematized rationale for nuclear arms is apparent. Such terms and the premises in which they occur are assumed to be valid descriptions of facts. The most general, and unspoken, conclusion, however, is the following paradox: the more security, the more insecurity.

5.6 THE 'IMAGINARY' CHARACTER OF THE STRATEGY OF DETERRENCE

We have mentioned several times that the mirror relationship is at the basis of the strategy of deterrence. This mirror relationship is described in the psychoanalytic theory of Jacques Lacan. We cannot discuss here in full Lacan's theory of the constitution of the human subject and will therefore restrict ourselves to some basic notions in order to explain what Lacan means by the 'mirror relationship'.[15]

Lacan makes a distinction between three orders: the Real, the Imaginary and the Symbolic. These three orders co-exist in the subject and their mutual relationships determine the subject's desires and intersubjective behaviour. The Real is not to be understood here as external reality, but as what is psychically real for the subject: the events that one is not able to symbolize, for instance, psychical traumas. The Imaginary order is closely related to perception: images (e.g. the image one has of oneself and of other persons), representations, fantasies belong to it. The Symbolic is the order of language (discourse) and culture in general. It structures the other two orders. The Real and the Imaginary also need language to be represented—in so far, of course, as it is possible to represent the Real.

From the point of view of intersubjectivity the prototype of the Imaginary is the mirror relationship. This is a DUAL relationship, i.e. between two elements or subjects. The symbolic relationship, by contrast, is TRIANGULAR: it is structured and 'mediated' by language, the third element in the relationship. Within the dual relationship, because it is not structured by language (or by another element differentiating the two elements involved), it is impossible to recognize the other as different from oneself. It is a closed, completely symmetrical relationship of objectification and identification: one subject reduces the other to an object, which is the image he has of the other and with which he identifies himself. At the same time he himself is constituted as an object by the other. In this way, his conduct is determined by the fascination he has for the image of the other. According to Lacan, this relationship, because it is primarily narcissistic, leads to rivalry and aggressivity.

In its pure form the mirror relationship does not occur between subjects, because the Imaginary intersects with the Symbolic. But Lacan gives an example from the world of automata which may help us to understand the dynamic force of the arms race in the mirror relationship.[16] Imagine a robot, constructed in such a way that it has to go on modelling itself on an existing robot, which is of quite similar construction to the first one, the only difference being that the second one is a stage further in its self-construction. Such a situation brings about a vicious spiral of rivalry: the automatons have the same 'desire': self-construction, the fulfilment of which is to be found in the other. The other, as a different entity, is an obstacle to this fulfilment. For intance, each object that one of them desires to construct for itself will 'automatically' also be an object the other desires. This desire leads to aggression, according to Lacan, which can only result in the destruction of one robot, or in mutual destruction, unless the robots are able to stop the fatal race by talking about their mutual 'desire' to equal each other. In our fictitious example that is not possible, but it is possible in human relationships. Humans are able to talk and in that way to reflect upon and to distance themselves from their own actions.

In the logic of deterrence we recognize certain key elements of the mirror relationship described above. Both parties take the same position with regard to each other. And they have the same perception of each other: we arm because they do so; we will attack (defend ourselves offensively) if they attack us; we will stop armament if they disarm first, etc. The other party is not seen as a real 'other' (somebody who is different), but is always compared with an 'ideal image' of the self: 'democracy', 'freedom', etc. Therefore, it is not at all surprising that the mere existence of the other is seen as a threat. Talking, negotiating seems to be the only way of getting out of the fatal circle. And indeed that is also said in NATO discourse. But these negotiations are not seen as something exterior to the strategy of deterrence, but as part of it. The motto is: 'Talk with the Russians, but deter them at the same time'. For instance: 'This willingness to conduct a dialogue must not be explained in Moscow as a sign of weakness, because this would endanger peace, freedom and security' (*Vrede*, p. 12). To stop the spiral of armament, mutual trust is necessary, but we have seen that deterrence is precisely based upon a fundamental mistrust. A real dialogue should have as its subject the politics of deterrence itself. Any other alternative is 'deterrent'.

NOTES

1. Sources: *NAVO-zakboekje*, NAVO Voorlichtingsdienst, Brussel (1982); *Vrede in vrijheid* (Peace in freedom), Pamphlet of the Belgian Ministry of Foreign Affairs and the Ministry of Defence (1983); *Vrede* (Peace), Pamphlet of the 'Christelijke Volkspartij' (1983); P. H. de Vries, 'Afschrikking, kernwapens en de vredesbeweging' (Deterrence, nuclear arms and the peace movement), in *Militaire Spectator* (January 1983: 28–32); L. Tindemans, 'Vrede en internationale diplomatie' (Peace and international diplomacy), in *Hoe winnen wij de vrede?*, Leuven, Davidsfonds (1984: 11–25); L. Tindemans, interview in *Trends* (20 January 1983); R. Close, 'Afschrikking en evenwicht' (Deterrence and balance), in *Hoe winnen wij de vrede?*, Leuven, Davidsfonds (1984: 74–81); B. W. Rogers, interview in *Knack* (26 January 1983); B. W. Rogers, interview in *Defensiekrant* (20 January 1983). For the citations we have used the English edition of the *NAVO zakboekje: NATO Handbook*, NATO Information Service, Brussels (1979). All other citations are translated by us.
2. This is not to say that there are *no* differences in training, deployment and strategy, or in the way that such matters are discussed in Soviet manuals and propaganda.
3. This mirror relationship in the strategy of deterrence is also hinted at in S. Hilgartner et al. (1982: 209–215); and on the reciprocal rhetoric of the cold war, cf. Franck and Weisband (1971), and Chomsky (1982).
4. On euphemisms in Nukespeak, cf. Chilton (1982) and Hilgartner et al. (1982). It is perhaps also politically significant in this bilingual community that *ontrading* is a translation equivalent for French *dissuasion*, the standard equivalent for English *deterrence*, German *abschrecken*, etc. On possible semantic implications, see Chapter 6.
5. Cf. G. Prins (ed.) (1983: 86 ff.).
6. James Bush of the US Center for Defense Information has stated: 'In reality there was an essential equivalence existing before the SS 20s were deployed. There is an essential equivalence existing now, and there will be an equivalence existing after the Pershing

IIs and the Ground Launched Cruise Missiles are deployed, if they are deployed. What I am saying basically is that both sides have many more weapons than they need to do whatever job they might eventually want to do' (BRT television broadcast, Panorama, 26 May 1983).
7. For instance in *Vrede* it is said: 'To judge the equivalence or the unequivalence, we have to distinguish clearly between conventional weapons (non-nuclear armament), strategic weapons and intermediate range weapons' (p. 7).
8. BRT television broadcast, Panorama (26 May 1983).
9. V. Tornetta, 'The nuclear strategy of the Atlantic Alliance and the 'no-first-use' debate', in *NATO Review*, **30**, 5 (1982), p. 5.
10. Op. cit., p. 6.
11. Press Agency Belga (28 June 1983), our translation.
12. *Soviet Military Power*, US Department of Defense, (1983: 5).
13. A. J. Greimas (1970: 135 ff.). For an introduction to the theory of Greimas, see J. Culler (1975), Ch. 4.
14. Cf. J. Courtés (1976).
15. Cf. J. Lacan, 'Le stade du miroir' and 'L'agressivité en psychoanalyse', in *Écrits* (1966). An introduction of the problematic of the 'imaginary' is given in A. Wilden (1968: 159 ff.).
16. Cf. J. Lacan (1978: 67).

6 Words, discourse and metaphors: the meanings of *deter*, *deterrent* and *deterrence*

Paul Chilton
University of Warwick, Coventry, UK

6.1 DETERRENCE AS AN OBJECT OF LINGUISTIC INQUIRY

In a recent paper (1984) Pertti Joenniemi has pointed out the crucial importance of the term and concept *deterrent*. The term is indispensable in the discourse of the arms control community,[1] of the strategic planners and of government propaganda. Joenniemi notes that the concept is taken to be at once a factual description of the world as it is and a 'theory' of that world. However, there is no rational reason to think it is either. On the one hand, it is not a factual description, since (among other reasons) the concept is, Joenniemi claims, incomprehensible in some cultures. It is, one can add, well known that translation equivalents are problematic in many languages, the Russian lexical gap having been the best publicized and polemicized example.[2] On the other hand, it is scarcely a theory in any scientific sense: it is neither verifiable nor falsifiable. So what is it? In Joenniemi's view it can best be thought of as an '*ex post facto* explanation or guiding principle in the process of armaments' and thus 'not a result of political and analytical thinking in the first place but rather a socio-cultural product' (pp. 14, 15). As such it has its origins in intellectual traditions (individualism, *laissez-faire*, anti-collectivism) and in post-war reactions of power-politics to the nuclear revolution. In short, the function of the deterrence concept is to predefine, not describe, the domain of international politics. Joenniemi concludes that it might be fruitful to investigate the basis of the concept and its relations with other concepts in the culture.

This chapter makes a tentative start on such an investigation by examining the concepts associated with the words *deter*, *deterrent* and *deterrence*. There are many theoretical linguistic questions raised by such an attempt. It will have to suffice here to indicate briefly the kind of theoretical work that has influenced this chapter. I have assumed that the words we are concerned with are of a semantic type such that they specify at least part of their meaning analytically; that is, the words have a number of (one-way) entailments that seem to be necessarily true. However, we assume broadly the Quinean view of analyticity according to which analyticity is inextricable from some frame of beliefs (Quine 1960; cf. Pulman 1983, Downes 1984). This means that since beliefs are variable, some entailments seem less necessary or sure than others (cf. Downes 1983: 286 ff.). Semantic structure is taken to be identical (not necessarily co-terminous) with conceptual structure (cf. Jackendoff 1983; Johnson-Laird 1983). One useful way of talking about systems of belief underlying word-meanings is the theory of FRAMES or SCRIPTS (cf. Minsky 1975; Schank and Abelson 1975; Metszing 1980). Abelson's computer simulation of a cold-war 'ideology machine', used also by Downes (1978, 1984), shows the usefulness of the frame notion for our purposes (cf. also the discussion by Boden 1977: 69-75). In addition I shall examine the metaphor-like relationships between frames in pro-nuclear discourse (which is not of course their only habitat). It will be evident that the theoretical boundary between semantics and pragmatics is not at issue here, and indeed has no obvious relevance.

6.2 THE VERB *DETER*

6.2.1 It has been claimed that

> ... the basic essence of 'deterrence' as expressed in the verb 'deter' has no real equivalent in the Russian language ... This failure to express correctly in Russian the essential notion of the concept 'to deter' has naturally been reflected in a similar failure to express correctly in Russian either 'deterrent' or 'deterrence'. In other words, the Russian mind is singularly ill-equipped to apprehend the notion of 'the act of deterring' and not much better to apprehend that of the 'thing that deters'. [Vigor 1975: 476.]

This absurd and dangerous line of linguistic reasoning rests on obvious misconceptions: first, the idea that absence of a lexical item in a language implies the inability to grasp the corresponding concept; and second, the idea that the concept of deterrence is somehow an objectively given category waiting to be named in the several languages of the world, in which task English (and the English mind) has succeeded, Russian (and the Russian mind) failed. An alternative view of the situation is that different cultures have formed different stable concepts and lexical items in connection with military strategy. This is not only obvious for the difference between English *deter* and (for instance) Russian *otpugivat'* (literally 'to frighten off'), but also between the languages of Western alliance nations, for instance between English *deter*, German *abschrecken* ('frighten off') and French *dissuader* ('dissuade'). The semantics of these terms, however much they overlap and to that extent function as translation equivalents, are probably culture-specific. From that possibility, however, one cannot legitimately infer conceptual limitation. If we are concerned with international dialogue, such conceptual differences could be usefully investigated.

It is also apparent from Vigor's remarks that he sets great store by 'the essential notion of the concept of deterrence'. There is something fetishistic in the status accorded to the word *deter*. It would be as well to try to unravel its semantics in order to have some idea of the role of language in the conceptualising of the domain of strategy.

6.2.2 *Deter* seems to belong to a lexical field to which belong also the following verbs:

(a) stop, prevent, restrain, hinder, discourage, dissuade.
(b) forbid, prohibit.
(c) cause, make, have (someone do something), force, compel.
(d) let, allow, permit.

The conceptual distinctions between (a), (b), (c) and (d) have to do with whether some agent causes an event to occur or not to occur ((a) vs. (c)), and whether or not we are speaking of a causal state of affairs ((a) and (c)) or of what Miller and Johnson-Laird (1976: 510 ff) call a 'deontic state of affairs' ((b) and (d)). In the latter permissibility plays a role analogous to possibility in the strictly causal domain. There are some uncertainties: for instance, the classification of *discourage, dissuade, compel, coerce, let, allow*, in such a schema. We shall not attempt to characterize in detail the whole of this semantic field (for illuminating accounts, see Talmy 1976, Miller and Johnson-Laird 1976: section 6.3; Jackendoff 1983: 198–211). However, in theory it is possible to locate *deter* in such a field and thereby specify its meaning, both in terms of the concepts required to distinguish it and in terms of its relationship to other available terms in the taxonomy.

One further preliminary point concerning *deter* can be made. Just as permissibility can be seen as the counterpart of possibility, so obligation can be seen as the counterpart of necessity. Now as Miller and Johnson-Laird (1976: 510 ff.) point out, to grant permissions felicitously, you need authority, but obligations ('you ought', 'I promise', etc.) can be set up more or less freely under customs, traditions, conventions, perhaps supported by rewards and punishments. But this collection of situations shades off into those in which there are no conventions, or in which 'obedience is reinforced solely by inescapable punishment for disobedience' (ibid., p. 511), where one can no longer reasonably speak of obligation. It takes little political imagination to translate this into types of domestic and international relationship. If, to continue in general terms, obedience to an order issued from A to B is reinforced by inescapable punishment, and B appreciates 'that failure to carry out the order will result in punishment' (ibid.), then 'there is . . . an implicit threat of the form "Do that, or else . . ." hanging over the order'. This type of circumstance is formulated by Miller and Johnson-Laird in terms of basic concepts CAUSE, KNOW, ACT, PUNISHED, which would be involved in verbs like *force, compel, coerce*. A *coerces* B would assert at least that A's acting in a certain way caused B to know that B's not doing such and such will cause B to be punished. Causatives have implicit negative forms: to prevent someone doing something is to (at a minimum) cause someone not to do it. And if we ask what lexical items correspond to the conceptual structure associated with *coerce*, etc., one possible answer is *deter*: A *deters* B asserts minimally that A does something which causes B to know that B's performing some action will cause the punishment of B.

Enough has been said to indicate that *deter* is conceptually complex, with causation as a crucial element. The field of verbs we have glanced at represents causality in a reasonably obvious way. However, causality is not a designator of the field itself, but rather a basic psychological category that enters into the semantic specification of many verbs (cf. Miller and Johnson-Laird 1976; Johnson-Laird 1983, Jackendoff 1983; Pulman 1983: 169). This is not surprising given the human propensity to seek out relations *propter hoc* even when they are really *post hoc*. The category of causality we are postulating should expressly not be equated with philosophical or scientific concepts of causation. What we are up against is a linguistically encoded notion of causation which has psychological, probably cultural, currency but not necessarily empirical validity (cf. Talmy 1976: 89, note 31). In contemporary industrial society the 'conceptual core' of causality seems to be that ALL events have causes: 'on that basic hypothesis a person then seeks valid and socially acceptable criteria for asserting that events of particular types are the effects of such-and-such types of causes' (Miller and Johnson-Laird 1976: 490). Ideologies are characteristically preoccupied with causal explanation of events, and the ideology of deterrence is no exception. The causative element in the semantics of *deter* is crucial, since it may be mistaken for, and represented as, rational scientific explanation, the causality it postulates being supposed inherent in political reality.

Our task now is to consider the sentences in which *deter* can go under present predominant usage, and the entailments of such sentences—always assuming that there are degrees of firmness in entailments and that they depend on, and are interconnected with, present predominant belief systems.

6.2.3 *Deter* seems to be a basically transitive verb, normally *requiring* a syntactic subject or object. Consider:

(1) a Alf deterred Bert.
    b ?Alf deters.
    c ?NATO deters.

If it is indeed basically transitive, it may be said to reflect the importance of 'human action models' (Werner and Kaplan 1963: 57; cf. the 'transactive model' of Kress and Hodge 1979) very frequent in Indo-European languages and perhaps fundamental to the conceptualization of events. It means that events of empirically diverse types are neutralized linguistically to an agent–action–object schema, e.g. *Alf saw Bert, Alf hit Bert, Alf hates Bert, Alf horrified Bert*, etc., all of which may suggest that Alf is performing an action.

As far as *deter* is concerned (1)a is ambiguous: Alf may have done the same action (wielded a big stick, say) or just been terrifying[3] to behold. Intention will not of course be attributed to non-human subjects; but humans may or may not have intention attributed. If a six-foot ex-wrestler deters Mugsy, he may be just there or he may be shaking his fist. This ambiguity serves (nuclear) deterrence ideology, since one can claim that being 'strong' (well armed, etc.) is not in itself an action but a state. Thus (2)a would entail (2)b under a certain belief system:

(2) a Alf deterred Bert from mugging him.
    b Alf was a big bloke.

And 'Alf deterred Bert, though he did not intend to' is not contradictory. Some speakers may find that 1(c) is not anomalous; if so this may be because the object (presumably *Russia, Warpac*, etc.) is supplied unambiguously from the belief system, specifically a 'cold-war frame' discussed later in this chapter.

What subjects can occur with *deter*? There are some interesting restrictions:

(3) a The weather deterred Bert.
 b The stick deterred Bert.
 c Alf's wielding a stick deterred Bert.

In addition to human agents, collectivities of specific types (*America, armies,* etc.) can deter, as can natural phenomena and obstacles. In (3)b a *stick* will probably be interpreted not as a natural entity unassociated with human agency but an instrument, in particular one classified as a weapon or as an entity capable of inflicting injury. The slight awkwardness of (3)c (the paraphrase 'Alf's stick deterred Bert', 'Alf deterred Bert with a stick' or 'Alf deterred Bert by wielding a stick' seems better) has interesting explanations. Talmy (1976: 55) argues that in syntactic structures expressing a causal reaction between events, the caused event always appears in the main clause, whereas the causing event is always in the subordinate clause. If the causing event occurs in the main clause, it will, as in (3)c, be nominalized. A simple sentence like *Alf deterred Bert* expresses in its single (main) clause a final resulting event. And if an additional causing event is specified, it seems to be most naturally done with the causing event appearing in an embedded clause: Alf deterred Bert by [wielding a stick].

So what? One consequence is that it is difficult to assert directly the causing event, which is usually represented as a presupposition. If Alf deterred Bert by wielding a stick, then Alf wielded a stick. But if you make *Alf wielded a stick* the main clause, you are forced to specify what Bert did not do. *Deter*, then, permits you to let such things pass unsaid, and requires that you focus on the caused event. In 'NATO deters Russia' and 'nuclear arms deter Russia' a caused event is asserted, namely, that Russia does not do some unspecified actions; the causing event is left equally unspecified.

6.2.4 It seems that *deter* sentences express a particularly strong causal relationship between events. Among the sentences below, (4)a seems to strongly entail (4)b:

(4) a Alf deterred Bert from striking him.
 b Alf did not strike him.
 c ?Alf deterred Bert, but Bert (still) struck him.

On the other hand, (4)c seems contradictory. This is even clearer if we compare *deter* with other verbs[4] that can (intuitively) be placed in the same field:

    A hindered B from leaving, but B left.
    A prohibited B from leaving, but B left.
    A discouraged B from leaving, but B left.
?   A dissuaded B from leaving, but B left.
?? A prevented B from leaving, but B left.

As Talmy (1976: 106) notes, there are different situation types involved here. Suffice it here to compare *dissuade* with *prevent* and *deter*: *dissuade* (and other verbs like the positive series *persuade, talk into, determine*, etc.) does not entail the necessary acquisition of intent not to do X on the part of the person dissuaded, whereas *prevent* and *deter* do seem to. The latter involve what Talmy calls 'caused agency'. *Prevent* and *deter* seem identical, in so far as they both have an entailment X *did not do* Y. But *deter* and *prevent* are clearly not synonyms or even syntactically similar (cf. *nuclear weapons have deterred the Russians* vs. *nuclear weapons have prevented the Russians*). To approach some more specific semantic characteristics of *deter* we need to consider (amongst other things) what inferences can be drawn as to the typical actions of typical subjects.

6.2.5 Distinctions between verbs like *prevent, deter* and the non-negative verbs entailing performance (*get, make*, etc.) can be made, since such verbs incorporate a specification of the type of means used in causative agency (cf. Talmy 1976: 107). *Have*, for instance, specifies that the causing is done by means of giving instructions: *America had the British deploy cruise*. *Make* seems to specify that the causing is done by means of *threats*. *Threat(en)* requires separate analysis not possible here, but entails in some fashion at least the assurance of causing someone to suffer damage, loss, pain or death. A is involved in *make* and *deter* in the following type of sentence, where A is an animate agent:

(5) a ?A made B sign the treaty by promising more economic aid.
 b A made B sign the treaty by threatening to impose sanctions.
 c ?A deterred B by promising more economic aid.
 d A deterred B by threatening to impose sanctions.

With non-animate subjects we have instrument and natural category types:

(6) a The rain deterred John.
 b The jemmy deterred John.
 c ?The piano deterred John.

(6)a is interpretable because we know *John* designates a human and that humans in general don't like doing things in the rain, etc. (We know also from *deter* that John has an intention to do something.) (6)b is interpretable because *jemmy* is specified as capable of inflicting injury when used by a human agent and that a human will seek to avoid injury. Verbs like *make* and *deter* thus seem to inherently specify desire to avoid injury or unpleasantness on the part of the caused agents where a verb like *make* and *deter* is interpreted as intentional, *threat* seems inevitably entailed:

A deters B entails
A causes B not-to-do C by making threats

Verbs like *dissuade* and *discourage* differ crucially in this respect. (7)a and (7)b are suggestive, though the details require further careful research:

(7) a Alf dissuaded Bert from attacking Carl by ⎧ arguing with him.
⎪ promising to pay him off.
⎨ warning him of the con-
⎪   sequences.
⎩ ? threatening to beat up
      Bert if he did.

   b Alf deterred Bert from attacking Carl by ⎧ ? arguing with him.
⎪ ? promising to pay him off.
⎨ warning him of the con-
⎪   sequences.
⎩ threatening to beat up Bert if
      he did.

Whether one usually speaks of dissuading by threats is obviously discussable. It seems intuitively clearer that *deter* differs with respect to the speech acts entailed: *promise* is excluded, and *warning* and *threatening* included (ambiguously). The significance of this is that *threaten* like *promise* denotes a speech act, and that in real situations whether speech acts work or not (are felicitous or not) depends on conditions involving beliefs. Whether 'deterring' works in superpower relations depends on beliefs about beliefs about *intent* and *capability*.

6.2.6 It may be that one expects a sentence like 'The West deters Soviet aggression' to include something like 'by targeting nuclear weapons on them'. This raises the question of the entailment of specific instruments in *deter*, as for instance, *Joe stabbed Bill* entails (probably, though he could have used a hatpin, or any object falling within certain constraints) *Joe used a knife*. It is clear, however, that a nuclear instrument will be specified with high degree of probability if and only if the cold-war frame is triggered. This is not to rule out the possibility that certain people may believe, and seek to get others to believe, a necessary, bi-conditional entailment: NATO deters Warpac if and only if NATO deploys nuclear weapons.[5] Many meanings (entailments) come about by legal, quasi-legal and other modes of stipulation (cf. Johnson-Laird 1984: 196; Jackendoff 1983: 253, note 3 mentions the dangers).

6.2.7 Not only do the verbs in the *deter* field specify the kind of means of introducing an agent to act or not to act, they can also specify in addition what is induced and the kind of agent being induced. For example, *dissuade* sentences in which induced agents are rational seem more natural than ones in which they are not, though this is not the case for *deter*:

(8) a I dissuaded ⎧the intruder⎫ from attacking me.
                   ⎩? the tiger ⎭
    b I deterred ⎧the intruder⎫ from attacking me.
                   ⎩the tiger   ⎭

This, of course, follows from the means specified. If the means used is rational, then the induced agent must be capable of rational argument. The fact that *deter* does not have this requirement allows for disparaging inferences. In effect, strategic discourse in English has chosen between *dissuade* and *deter* and the choice makes possible (or results from) beliefs about the nature of enemies and conflict. If someone cannot be dissuaded, then they may be deterred; if so then they may not be rational; if they are not rational, they may not be human; and so on.[6]

The induced agent in a *deter* sentence acquires an intention, unlike the inducing agent who may be unintentionally deterring (by their physical strength, etc.). For the field of verbs in question the induced agent's relation to intention is criterial (cf. Talmy 1976: 106). One series of the verbs including, e.g. *order, prohibit* does not entail the acquiring of intent by the induced agent. A second series including *persuade, talk into, dissuade,* etc. entails the acquisition of intent but not (for many speakers, apparently) the execution of the intended action. A third series which includes *make, force, cause to, cause not to* and *deter*, seems in general to entail both the acquisition of intent and the execution of the action. Taking this with the specification of means, *deter* seems to entail that the inducing of fear is an effective method of inducing acquisition of intent. This portion of English vocabulary is concerned with causation of mental states, the conceptualization of control of others; the point here is that such conceptualizations need have no relationship to empirical reality.

6.2.8 The above discussion indicates that the semantics of the English verb *deter* is similar to that of *prevent*, with the addition of conceptual components having to do with intention and means: both verbs have causation as their fundamental concept. The 'conceptual core' is 'the layman's notion that some if not all events have causes' (Miller and Johnson-Laird 1976: 495). One can see why this might be so: the ability to predict consequences of behaviour, and the habit of doing so, would be an essential part of evolutionary adaptation. Following Miller and Johnson-Laird (1976), we might suppose that to make predictions one has to envisage possible (and impossible) states of affairs. Here, possibility and impossibility will be highly variable, subject to manipulation, and liable to overlap with what is permissible and impermissible. Whether a state of affairs is judged possible or not will depend on systems of belief.

Deter seems to represent a situation in which an event (e_1) causes an event (e_2) not to take place, which can be written: CAUSE (e_1, not-2). The latter will be accepted when a person is willing to accept either of the two following situations (a) and (b):

(a) (i) not possible (e_1 & e_2), (ii) possible (e_1 & not-e_2)
    (iii) possible (not-e_1 & e_2), (iv) possible (not-e_1 & not-e_2)
(b) (i) not possible (e_1 & e_2), (ii) possible (e_1 & not-e_2)
    (iii) possible (e_1 & e_2) which is equivalent to e_1 prevents e_2
    (iv) not possible (not-e_1 & not-e_2)

To make this concrete (a) and (b) might correspond to someone's saying

(9) America's deploying nuclear weapons deterred Russia from invading Europe.

where e_1, is, let us say, 'America deploys nuclear weapons' and e_2 'Russia invades Europe'. Condition (iv) in (a) allows for the possibility that the events e_1 and e_2 are independent. It is possible, logically speaking, that without nuclear weapons there would ALSO be/have been no invasion. Condition (iv) in (b), however, rules out the possibility that there could be no invasion and no nuclear deployment. Whether your starting schema for interpreting *deter* sentences is (a) or (b) depends on many factors, including exposure, one supposes, to propaganda. But there is an additional factor built into verb semantics and into *deter* in particular. Schema (a) can be regarded as specifying a *sufficient* preventive relation (there could be another event, say e_0, which was also preventive); schema (b) can be regarded as a *necessary* and *sufficient* prevention (e_1 is the only cause of e_2 not taking place). Now it has been said (Johnson-Laird 1976: 500) that English causative verbs express merely sufficient cause, and that anything stronger requires the speaker to say so explicitly. It is perhaps helpful in the present context to say that English causative verbs like *deter* and *prevent* are strictly ambiguous with respect to sufficient causes on the one hand and necessary and sufficient causes on the other. However, it would seem that there seems to be a discourse principle (cf. Grice's maxims of Quantity and Relevance (Grice 1975, 1978) and for an exposition, Levinson 1983: 101 ff.) to the effect that if alternative preventive events are not explicitly mentioned then they are not relevant. In other words, although (9) expresses a sufficient cause (there might have been other events preventing e_2) as far as logic is concerned, in actual discourse the interpretation, in default of further specification, is that the deployment of nuclear weapons is also a necessary preventive measure. If this is the case, then it is a problem inherent in communication as presently conducted.[7]

6.3 CAUSES AND CONDITIONS

The causal interpretation of *deter* is important for the production of many other utterances in the nuclear strategic domain. The association of causal sentences with counterfactual sentences has been much observed and discussed by philosophers, linguists and psychologists (Stalnaker 1968, Lewis 1973, amongst others). There are two possible counterfactual sentences associated with (9), depending on whether the speaker has in mind schema (a) or (b) above:

(9) America's deploying nuclear weapons deterred Russia from invading Europe.
(10) a If America had not deployed nuclear weapons, Russia might have invaded Europe.
    b If America had not deployed nuclear weapons, Russia would have invaded Europe.

It is (10)b that is normally asserted in pro-nuclear discourse, corresponding to a necessary as well as sufficient causal sense of *deter*. Even the modal *might* in (10)a does not capture the possibility that the event expressed in the antecedent clause could be causally unrelated. There are other complex aspects of conditions and the conceptualization and expression of possible scenarios that are central to this kind of discourse. The main point to make here, however, is that counterfactual and conditional sentences cannot easily make explicit the fact that, strictly, they express merely sufficient conditions or causes. There are many ways in which pro-nuclear discourse enables the inference to be drawn that the relationship between nuclear weapons deployment and absence of war in Europe is a necessary and sufficient causal one. For example, the frequent assertions, 'nuclear weapons have kept Europe at peace', 'nuclear weapons kept peace for forty years' and the like, involve the causal *keep* (cause-to-stay-at; cf. Jackendoff 1983: 198 ff.), and suggest an associated counterfactual like 'if it had not been for nuclear weapons, Europe would (?might) not have stayed at peace'.

Since counterfactuals causally relate observed events and non-events, they are involved in all apologetics arguing from historical facts. One frequently-heard counterfactual is:

(11) If Japan had had the atom bomb, America would not have atom-bombed Hiroshima.

There are several extraordinary moral and political aspects to (11) and its paraphrases, but we shall concentrate on linguistic aspects. The basic situation is that not-e_1 (Japan's not having atom bombs) is observed followed by e_2 (Japan being atom-bombed). The corresponding causal sentence is, interestingly, rarely if ever expressed, but if it is true that causals and counterfactuals are psychologically linked, then people are likely to infer it. The particular kind of causal relation that might be inferred for (11) depends on the background assumptions. Put schematically, speakers might believe either (a) or (b):

(a) (i) not possible (e_1 & e_2)   (b) (i) not possible (e_1 & e_2)
   (ii) possible (e_1 & not-e_2)   (ii) possible (not-e_1 & e_2)
   (iii) possible (not-e_1 & e_2)   (iii) possible (e_1 & not-e_2)
   (iv) possible (not-e_1 & not-e_2)   (iv) not possible (not-e_1 & not-e_2)

Schema (a) believes that without the atom bomb a country like Japan, may or may not be atom-bombed. This seems to be equivalent to the notion of 'letting' or 'allowing' something to happen: if e_1 is true then e_2 does not occur, but if you do not do e_1, then you do not prevent e_2, that is you *let* it happen, if it does. Under (a) then you can have, corresponding to (11): 'Japan's not having the atom bomb let America bomb Hiroshima'. However, as we saw above, the dominant assumption for (iv) is that it is impossible, as in (b), which is our earlier definition for necessary *cause*. Whence the extraordinary inference on (11) to the effect that Japan's not having atomic weapons caused the bombing of Hiroshima. Taken together, sentences (9) and (11) constitute a symmetrical model that it is the aim of deterrence discourse to establish and reinforce:

e_1 & not-e_2
not-e_1 & e_2

where e_1 is the possession of nuclear weapons, e_2 attack by an enemy. The causal and counterfactual sentences that can express them are (see Johnson-Laird 1976: 504):

e_1 prevented e_2
If e_1 had not happened, e_2 would (and must) have happened.

Some final observations will show the central productive role of this schema in deterrence discourse aimed at domestic opponents of nuclear arms. To oppose the deployment of nuclear arms can be represented as wanting not-e_1, which in turn can be represented in terms of either schema (a) or (b) above. So proponents of nuclear disarmament can be represented as *letting* (or *allowing*) or as *causing* e_2. Both representations are common. Under the *allow* interpretation, disarmers fail to take action (e_1) that would definitely prevent a possible event, if it occurred. A reflection of this is the notion of nuclear arms as an 'insurance' against possible events. Under the *cause* interpretation disarmers are represented as actually being the cause of (a future) nuclear war (cf. Japan in (11)). Humans, who are causes, can be so intentionally or unintentionally as we saw earlier, hence proponents of unilateral nuclear disarmament are represented as unwitting ('naive', etc.) or as deliberate supporters of Moscow ('communists', etc.).

6.4 DETER, DETERRENT, DETERRENCE AND DISCOURSE

6.4.1 The earliest occurrences of *deter* in English are non-particular. By the end of the seventeenth century (according to the OED), *deter* is frequently found in juridical contexts and, with the emergence of the criminological concept of deterrence, has remained there. An extension is to quasi-juridical contexts in institutions such as schools: canes deter delinquent pupils. After the Second World War there is a transfer from the domestic juridical frame to the international relations frame, specifically to the cold-war frame: atomic bombs deter communist aggression.[8] These changes reflect increased specialization that has such reflexes in use as the following:

(12) a Bad weather deters climbers.
      b ?Bad weather is a deterrent.
      b' ?deterrent weather.
      c ??The deterrence of climbers (by bad weather).
      d Deterrence is effective.
      e ??Deterrence.

(13) a Long sentences deter offenders.
      b Long sentences are a deterrent.
      b' deterrent sentences.
      d ?Deterrence is effective.
      e ?Deterrence.

(14) a Nuclear weapons deter the Russians.
      b Nuclear weapons are a deterrent.
      b' Deterrent weapons.
      c The deterrence of the Russians (by nuclear weapons).
      d Deterrence is effective.
      e Deterrence.

It is true that judgements of anomaly in cases such as the above are uncertain and clearly involve semantic factors other than only those we are interested in here, but the uncertainty itself is significant. We have something like the following situation. The meaning of *deter* will depend on the contribution of the rest of the sentence and context in which it occurs. Deterrence is less clear-cut. Any sentence *X deters Y*, where X is a potentially harmful or undesirable instrument or state of affairs, has a paraphrase *X is a deterrent to Y*. One cannot usually say *John was a deterrent to Bill*, in the same way one can say *the knife was a deterrent to Bill*, or the 'linguistic diversity in Germany was a deterrent to the unification of a fragmented empire'. *Deterrent* denotes a category of objects or states of affairs which may or may not be the instrument of human agency. What I want to suggest further, however, is that there are additional particularizations of *deterrent* as compared with *deter*. If this is so, the hypothesis is that when the semantic make-up of the participants in a sentence involving *deterrent* is not specified (left out or left ambiguous) in discourse, then a discourse processor will supply default interpretations deriving from the criminological (or nuclear and cold-war) frame of beliefs. (12)b seems unusual (humorous? metaphorical?), though not of course impossible, compared with (13)b and (14)b. (12)b' is very odd. (14)b' may be odd compared with (13)b' because *weapons*, unlike *sentences*, are not classed as deterrent or some other kind.

To see more clearly the differential effect of *deter* and *deterrent* in discourse consider:

(15) a Long sentences deter Jake. He's a slow reader.
      b Long sentences deter Jake. He's going straight.
      c Long sentences are a deterrent. Crimes are fewer than previously.
      d ?Long sentences are a deterrent. No one bothers to read them.

Deter permits ambiguity (a and b); *deterrent* has a preferred reading (though this could be tested empirically), d being less likely, or readable as humorous. These cases suggest that *deterrent* acts as a 'trigger' for a conceptual frame, here a criminological one. Precisely how such 'triggers' operate has not been researched, though obviously lexical collocation (which lexical items co-occur with *deter* in discourse) is a factor, as are grammatical and situational factors. Thus if someone (the actual identity or social role is not irrelevant, however) says, 'The deterrent has worked', a plausible follow-on is, 'Murder figures are down' or 'The Russians didn't invade'. But 'Our deterrent has worked' will most likely create an expectation only of the second, and other beliefs in the frame. That specific beliefs are present in a frame is apparent if one considers other discourse incoherences such as:

(16) a The bomb is a deterrent. The Russians do not attack Europe.
      b ?The bomb is a deterrent. The Americans do not attack Russia.

In such contexts, *deter* and *deterrence* behave similarly. Clearly there are many other statements, which happen to be empirically true in themselves that could still not 'naturally' follow the first sentences in 15a and b. But suppose we narrow that set down to a plausible subset involving appropriate actors, etc.; then we still might enquire why there is a further restriction specifying a further subset that alone can acceptably follow the first sentence. There are two possible approaches. One is to appeal to historical explanations, but these are another set of belief systems, whether or not they are held by expert historians, and may be thought of as equivalent to what we are calling frames—a coherent set of stereotypical expectations for a recurrent situation.[9] Another is to pin it on to the inherent semantic properties of *deterrent*, which might involve claiming that, as a matter of analytic entailment, if it is true that the Bomb is a deterrent then it is true that the Russians have not attacked Europe. But this is scarcely comparable to the cases (like 'if X is a bachelor X is an unmarried man', etc.), where we have some certainty about speaking of analytic entailment. Nevertheless, some people might well behave AS IF the first sentence of (15)a analytically entailed the second. If they do, we must explain that fact in terms of beliefs systems and frames. For the rest of us knowledge of their belief-system frames, even if we do not assent to them, will explain our sense of the anomaly of (16)b. At one end of the cline of analyticity we have the seemingly necessary entailments of *deter* (as discussed above) and at the other the, less necessary, revisable and socially variable belief frames associated with particularized *deterrent* and *deterrence*.

Such frames are social and political institutions requiring explanation in their own terms. Two points arise from this. First, from the point of view of sociology or political science, the linguistic contribution to the maintenance of such institutions cannot be neglected, and second, from the point of view of linguistics, any theory of meaning is likely to come adrift if it does not take account of historical factors of this order.

The word *deterrence* (c, d and e sentences in (12), (13) and (14)) needs careful discussion. (12)d is presumably odd because *effective* implies an intentional act—an intention to produce an effect on, and weather can't have an intention (except humorously). This would account also for the uncertainty of (12)c. And it is clear that you can't say *deterrence* and mean (12)a. But you can say (13)e and (14)e and mean either the deterrence of offenders or 'the deterrence of the Soviet Union'. I want to suggest however, that there is a tendency for *deterrence* to be even further particularized—to the nuclear/cold-war domain. In the absence of contextual prompting, how do speakers interpret d and e? Readers may test their own reactions. In this connection consider (17) a–d, where frame conceptions seem to introduce default interpretations for *deterrence*. What kind of sentence (what kind of actors and actions) does one expect to follow the first sentences of the following?

(17) a The deterrent was effective. Murders were fewer than previously.
 b The deterrent was effective. The Russians withdrew their missiles.
 c ?Deterrence was effective. Murders were fewer than previously.
 d Deterrence was effective. The Russians withdrew their missiles.

Deterrent seems versatile as between the legal and the nuclear frame, *deterrence* less so. If one encounters *deterrence* without contextual cues, default values will supply a cold-war, nuclear context. *Deterrence* in the absence of further specification has, it seems, specific default values. It is no doubt true that if you are reading the *Criminological Quarterly* and notice a headline 'Deterrence is effective', your expectations will be different from your expectations if you are reading (say) the *Journal of Strategic Studies*. Three points should be made. First, you are unlikely to encounter such a heading anywhere other than in the criminological or broadly strategic context. Secondly, I want to suggest that if the context is not determined (you are perhaps scanning headlines in the general news section of a newspaper), your expectations will most likely involve the cold-war belief frame, even if you are a crimologist, and even if you're not professionally interested in strategic policy. Thirdly, if this is the case, then we should not explain it in terms of inherent semantic properties of the word, but in terms of a preference order of frames—ideological frames at a historical moment.

What I have been attempting to indicate are certain broad, subtle and changeable semantic tendencies. The historical extension of the verb *deter* into other grammatical categories (i.e. the derivatives in *-ent* (adjectival and nominal) and in *-ence*) seems to involve increasing informational load. The derivatives and their associated concepts become particularized to specialist domains, and become indeed the object of discussion and definition by experts. What objects and practices count as a *deterrent* or as *deterrence* depends on a consensus of specialized professionals, though there will be variation, of course, within such groups. The process whereby *deterrence*, for instance, becomes quasi-analytically defined as *nuclear* deterrence can be explained in such a way. The semantics of this and other terms thus needs to be thought of as a product, not as naturally given in a neutral language independently of social, cultural and political forces. If one now considers the semantically more general term *deter*, its current semantics might be outlined in the following way. While it is usable in a general sense, without the particularized connotations of *deterrent* and *deterrence*, it is also the case that in one of the particular contexts triggered by (say) *deterrent*, *deter* will have an equivalently particularized meaning. This may affect whatever conceptual structure is stored in memory as the meaning of this term.

6.4.3 Let us consider the ways in which the conceptual frames I have suggested are associated with *deterrent* and *deterrence* might explain what is going on in discourse about the cold nuclear war. As Joenniemi points out, the metaphorical extension from the criminological to the nuclear-strategic frame is neither accidental nor without implications. One can conceive of a stage in the hypothesized semantic development of *deterrent* and *deterrence* where these terms are applied as metaphors in the strategic domain. The underlying rationale for such a transfer is partly a matter for historical, sociological and political explanation. But in order to explain social and political behaviour one also has to assume representations of the social and political world in minds. On this level one can propose that the mental model associated with the earlier use of *deterrent* is isomorphic to, or can be used to construct, an isomorphic model in the domain of superpower relations. The phrase 'can be used to construct' requires further investigation to establish the means by which particular meanings and metaphors get PROMOTED (as DIALECTS get PROMOTED to STANDARD languages) as standard meanings—an investigation that would require inquiry into the role of media and education and other communication networks. The general point here is that new and unfamiliar phenomena and states of affairs (the case of nuclear explosions and their implications for warfare is a prime case) can be given form and meaning; that is, it can be made possible for them to be understood, by mapping them on to existing cognitive models. Such a mapping in itself establishes cognition.

The situation may be even more complex, however, in particular discourse instances. Imagine the case of a schoolteacher, who, when asked how his school controls unruly pupils, replies (with a grin), 'We employ a variety of deterrents —up to nuclear weapons!'.[10] One way to explain what is taking place here would be as follows. The criminological context and the school discipline context are already conceptually analogous at a certain level of abstraction. They both involve the notions such as legitimate policy, legitimate agent, offenders, legitimate means of prevention, restraint and punishment. Using and understanding this conceptual frame would involve the term *deterrent* in its broad legal sense. If the same conceptual frame can be matched with a conceptualization of a school, which of course it can, then *deterrent* transfers easily and unsurprisingly, from state polity to school (or potentially to analogous polities), as sketched in Figure 6.1, where the arrows represent direction of metaphorical transfer. The transfer is easy presumably not only because the abstract frames are so close, but because the typical exemplifications of the *deterrent* concept for the two domains overlap—beating, detaining, admonishing, etc. To speak of the use of deterrents in school is to match two isomorphic frames, or to construct or adapt one (the school one) to match the existing one.

state polity ⟶ world polity
↓ ↙
school polity

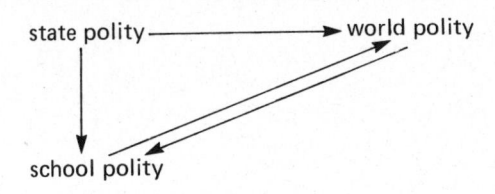

Figure 6.1

To explain the teacher's nuclear weapons joke, however, one has to assume also the nuclear particularization of *deterrent*. We are also assuming that that meaning has come about by a metaphorical transfer that involves seeing the relations between superpowers in terms of the legitimate polity frame hypothesized above. To use *deterrent* in the international politics domain results in (or is produced by) a set of correspondences that maps, e.g. legitimate agent on to e.g. NATO, and so on in an obvious fashion. If it is the case that this correspondence is fairly well established there should be other instances of the criminology-cold-war transfer, and given the closeness of the criminological and the educational frames (in the culture in question), we might expect school-cold-war transfers.

Readers may verify or falsify this from relevant discourse, but a number of corroboratory instances can be mentioned. The United States is frequently presented as having a 'policing' (legitimate agent) role. The Soviet Union is often presented as a delinquent with violent tendencies, and sometimes as a juvenile. The 'legitimate agent' concept is triggered in uses of *deterrent* in the following way. A gun used by a policemen can be a deterrent to (or deter) criminals; but there is something odd in saying that guns used by criminals are a deterrent to policemen (though, as we would expect, guns used by criminals can *deter* policemen). It seems that in these conceptual frameworks the term *threat* is reserved for offenders (criminals, delinquents and the Soviet Union). Accordingly, it is odd to speak of the Russian *deterrent*, but not of the Russian *threat*; and conversely for Americans, NATO, etc. We shall examine the way in which the state-polity, school-polity and world-polity schemes operate in the processing of discourse on nuclear arms shortly. But, for the case of the school-focused discourse of the teacher's deterrent joke, notice that the nuclear deterrent frame can be transferred metaphorically to the school frame. This seems to count as a 'fresh' metaphor. Not all metaphors or jokes are 'well formed' or acceptable, and in this case (possibly generally) that fact might be explained in terms of the conceptual isomorphism we have spoken of. Note, too, that metaphorical transfer in the opposite direction (e.g. 'the Soviet Union is an aggressive child in need of discipline') is also fresh but appropriate in the same sense.

6.4.4 Lest the examples above appear assembled *ad hoc*, let us examine the following piece of discourse, prepared and disseminated by the British Ministry of Defence.[11] Both sentences are headings printed in bold capitals: (18) and (19) are on the front of the folded pamphlet, (20) heads the small print text on the inside:

(18)

(19) How to deal with a bully.
(20) Peace through deterrence—the only answer to a bully's threat.

The question we are asking is: how are such stretches of discourse comprehended? And what we want to propose by way of answer is that institutionalized frames of belief are triggered which are then matched. At the bottom of the comprehension process must be some notion of relevance, in a modified Gricean sense. That is, the compulsive search for communication of meaning requires that relationships of relevance exist between utterances (and parts of utterances, too, though the question is not usually considered in those terms).

If a reader confronts (19) in isolation, it seems clear that a frame of beliefs (which are, perhaps, a subset of the school-system beliefs, discussed above) to do with school *bullies* is invoked. The pamphlet is in fact so set up that there are no VERBAL cues on the front to modify that default assumption. Is this, then, an educational psychologist's advice to playground monitors? Actually, there are pictorial cues (large snarling bear and small bulldog with a union flag on its back!), reproduced as (18). The interaction of pictorial cues in such communication is a question of psychological interest. One might speculate that on the principle of relevance the pictures, as well as the words, will be taken as 'utterances', and that, again on the relevance principle, verbal and pictorial utterances will be related. For this to happen, non-verbal and verbal representations must interact in the processing mind which is sorting out contextual implications. One might hypothesize that such processing will occur in non-verbal representation (on the assumption that it's easier to convert verbal propositions to concepts than it is to convert pictures into words), with possibly advantageous consequences for propagandists and advertisers.

This is a difficult matter to pin down, since we have no metalanguage for talking about pictorial representations. Note, however, that the two figures on the picture are 'read' conceptually (via the relevance principle, and bulldog and bear stereotypes with their associated sets of beliefs) as a 'sentence' with two participants and an action verb. In our pictorial metalanguage, if we had one, we might 'read' (18) as something like: BULLDOGS (SMALL, STRONG) FRIGHTEN OFF BEARS (BIG, STRONG, AGGRESSIVE). The cultural animal-stereotype belief system (plus the pictorial detail) also warrants: BRITAIN IS A BULLDOG and RUSSIA IS A BEAR. In other words, the picture expresses two conceptual structures. The relevance principle will encourage a search for contextual implications, which will presumably be something like: BRITAIN (SMALL, STRONG) FRIGHTENS OFF RUSSIA (BIG, STRONG, AGGRESSIVE). (On inferences drawn from conceptual models as opposed to propositions, see Johnson-Laird 1983, Chs 6 and 7.)

The problem for an understander is now to seek out the relevance between the pictorial utterance and the verbal utterance (19). The latter contains the argument *bully* and predicate *deal with*, each liable to give rise to stereotypical entailments and truth-judgements (ultimately dependent on beliefs, but likely to be perceived as analytic) enshrined in the schoolyard bully schema. For example:

(21) a If X is a bully, then X attacks those smaller than X.
     b X attacks those who are smaller than X.
(22) a If Y deal-with X, then Y stand-up-to X.
     b If Y stand up to X, then Y not-give-in-to X.
(23) c If Y deal-with X, then Y is strong.
     d If someone is strong, that someone is not weak.
(24) a If Y deal-with X, then X is afraid.
     b If Y deal-with X, then Y frightens X, etc.

These entailments, which as far as I can judge belong to the school-bully frame and the like, are prominent in public pro-nuclear arguments, and are often expressed directly, not of course AS entailments of a belief system, but as if they were empirically valid descriptions of the real world.

The point about the above-outlined set of *bully* propositions, and the set derived from the pictorial utterance is that they are (at least partially) isomorphic frames, i.e. they have similarities in terms of the attributes of the participant variables and the action predicates. This is sufficient for the relevance principle to conflate the two conceptual structures and to draw inferences.[12] For instance, the unspecified variables X and Y in the verbal utterance can be filled in as *bully, bear, Russia* and *(resister), bulldog, Britain*. It is interesting that the term corresponding to *bully* is lexically but not conceptually undetermined: one assumes that it is none the less potent.

The first two utterances, then, metaphorically relate three domains (i) bulldogs and bears, (ii) resisters and bullies, (iii) Great Britain and Russia. The first two are familiar schemata on to which a problematic, unfamiliar domain is being mapped. Inserting 'deal with' in (ii) corresponds to inserting FRIGHTEN OFF in (i). The next matter which a full account would have to deal with would be the nature of the process by which (20) is read as a relevant reply or solution, etc. to (18)/(19). One point worth noting is that, if as suggested, (18)/(19) leads to a non-propositional, non-verbal conceptual representation, then (20) functions to name this representation (as deterrence). We shall, however, focus on (20) istelf.

How are two noun phrases, related by the dash, understood? We have proposed that *deterrence* is particularized to a cold-war frame of beliefs. Suppose, however, you do not know the meaning of *deterrence* (you may be a foreigner, a child, or simply someone who doesn't read newspapers, etc.); then the second phrase, 'the only answer to a bully's threat', will help teach the meaning, given that you have a frame of beliefs for *bully*. We also have to assume at least the following:

(a) Comprehension of *peace through deterrence* in the same sense that if peace is through X, then X is some sort of instrumental object or action.
(b) Some conceptual model of peace and war (cf. Downes 1984: 298 ff.) evoked by the word *peace*, with attackers, defenders, goodies, baddies, winners and losers, etc., which has the stereotype cold-war participants as pictorially cued in (18).

If the potential understanders have to ask 'WHAT is the only answer to a bully's threat?', they are not likely to say 'peace' (syntactically possible), because of the properties of the bully frame, and are more likely to say, one assumes, 'deterrence is the only answer, etc.' than 'peace is the only answer to, etc.' This provides a kind of definition for *deterrence*, and may indeed illustrate one way in which people learn ideologically loaded particularizations of words.

Let us consider in a little more detail the role that might be played by stable frame beliefs (whether you understand *deterrence* or not) in the act of processing (20). Note first that (20) cannot be paraphrased as (25)a, which seems to have (25)b as a possible entailment but not (25)c:

(25) a   peace through deterrence is the only answer to a bully's threat.
     b   peace is the only answer to a bully's threat.
     c   ?deterrence is the only answer to a bully's threat.

The syntax permits (or excludes) the wrong entailments: as suggested above (25)b is meaningless under 'normal' prevailing beliefs; and (25)c is not automatically entailed. The syntax of (20), however, seems to give (20)c but not (20)b:

(20) a   peace through deterrence—the only answer to a bully's threat.
     b   ?peace—the only answer to a bully's threat.
     c   deterrence—the only answer to a bully's threat.

(20)b shares with (25)b the factors that makes then both ideologically implausible. It is not, however, ruled out by the construction, as (24)c is; there is still an ambiguity that the discourse processor has to resolve. The question is the familiar one in discourse linguistics of anaphora (cf., for instance, Brown and Yule 1983, Ch. 6). The second noun phrase of (20) picks out some element mentioned in the first—but which one? It is not just a question of syntax. Suppose someone wrote (26)a. It seems that the possible entailment would be (26)b rather than (25)c:

(26) a Peace through deterrence—the one desire of a war torn world.
   b Peace—the one desire of a war-torn world.
   c ?Deterrence—the one desire of a war-torn world.

Comparing (26)a, b and c with (20)a, b and c suggests that reference depends not just on syntax but on the meaning of the second phrase. The second phrase appears to refer more readily to the head noun of the first phrase, rather than to the noun of the modifying prepositional phrase. Note, however, that it is possible for the reference to be the WHOLE of the first phrase 'peace through deterrence', thus creating an ambiguity that does not apparently require resolution for basic interpretation. (26)a might be a powerful nukespeak slogan.

We are interested in asking what factors seem to make (20)c the preferred interpretation of (20)a. Given that readers reject (20)b, they still need to check the compatibility of *deterrence* and the 'only answer to the bully's threat'. If they are not compatible (or cannot be made compatible), (20)a as a whole will be judged incoherent. One way of explaining the ease with which reading (20)c is selected and interpreted is, as with (18) and (19), the particularization of *deterrence* to a cold-war frame, and some close similarity of structure between this and the *bully* frame. Both are presumably widely shared and stable models rapidly accessible in memory.

6.5 METAPHORS AND MORPHISMS

As in our analysis of (18) and (19) the assumption is that abstract conceptual representations are matched and conflated. This does not necessarily mean that the two structures are co-terminous: it may be possible to extend one in terms of the other—this is perhaps the main new point to be made about metaphor and analogy in the present context. It is now increasingly recognized that metaphor plays an important role in our conceptualizations, and that it is not to be dismissed as mere rhetorical ornament. Indeed, it is not to be classed solely as rhetorical ornament at all, since the most interestingly systematic cases are not novel, but so assimilated to our cognitive processes that they go unnoticed. Lakoff and Johnson (1980) argue that metaphor gives coherent structure to experience; Jackendoff (1983) uses similar notions to explain semantic structures in terms of metaphorical transfers of psychologically more basic structures, for example spatial concepts transferred to temporal ones. (For a general survey of the whole subject of metaphor see, for example, Ortony 1980.)

A pertinent example discussed by Lakoff and Johnson is the ARGUMENT IS WAR metaphor. 'This metaphor', they say (p. 61), 'allows us to conceptualize what a rational argument is in terms of something that we understand more readily, namely, physical conflict'. Further, they claim, 'not only our conception of an argument but the way we carry it out is grounded in our knowledge and experience of physical combat' (p. 63). The point here is not to pursue the content of this particular example, but to note that Lakoff and Johnson do not conceive of such metaphors as static structures, but as giving rise to inferences (Ch. 16). For example, the argument-is-war metaphor might yield loose syllogisms like the following:

an argument is a war
a war has victors
therefore an argument has a victor

It is the ability of metaphors to induce inferences in one domain on the basis of more complete or more familiar knowledge or belief in a more basic domain that is of interest.

A more explicit development of Lakoff and Johnson's ideas is to be found in Hobbs (1981). Hobbs's purpose was actually to formulate a discourse-processing system that could be implemented by computer. His approach is itself essentially metaphorical. It seeks to grasp the ill-understood process of metaphor in terms of another domain which is better understood. His model is in effect (though he does not present it in quite these terms) the mathematical notion of MORPHISM. We need not define morphism here, except to say that it is a function that maps an old domain into a new domain preserving the old domain's structure (see Figure 6.2). This is a highly useful concept to mathematicians who can prove theorems, for instance, in one domain by mapping its elements and relations on to a second domain, proving the theorem there and mapping back to the first. It is also the basis of the notion of mathematical modelling of physical processes.

Figure 6.2 represents what is termed a COMMUTATIVE diagram—commutative because there are different routes to the same result with the operations in different orders. Transferring this to language and discourse, we might suppose that metaphor is a morphism-like function. To reason about a new, unknown or uncertain domain (nuclear politics is a prime case) we map new terms into the old domain, do our inferencing in the old domain and map the results back into the new domain via the reverse or interpretative function.

Let us make this clear with Hobbs's own example, which as it happens is one that shows the utility of morphisms in the political sphere. His rather complex metaphor (taken from *Newsweek*, 7 July 1975) is

(27) we insist on serving up these veto pitches that come over the plate the size of a pumpkin.

Forgetting pumpkins for the present purposes, this metaphor matches and conflates, in our terms, a baseball-match frame with a House of Congress frame. 'We' are congressmen (pitchers) sending (pitching) bills (balls) to the President

NEW (UNKNOWN) DOMAIN

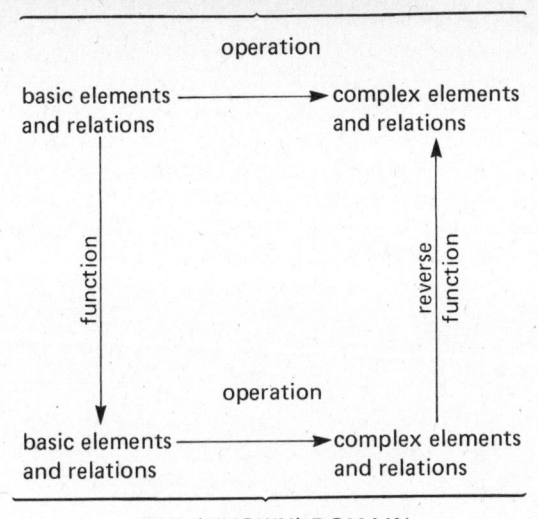

```
                    operation
basic elements ──────────────▶ complex elements
and relations                   and relations
      │                                ▲
      │ function          reverse     │
      │                   function    │
      ▼                                │
basic elements ──────────────▶ complex elements
and relations                   and relations
                    operation
```

OLD (KNOWN) DOMAIN

Figure 6.2

(batter) who vetoes (hits) or signs (misses) them. Apparently, baseball is better understood than the American political process. Hobbs's point is that to process (27) a discourse-understanding device must have access to the two frames and perform operations on them, which work roughly as follows. Congress is initially identified with a baseball-pitcher. Then:

> to interpret ... 'veto pitch', we must find the most salient, plausible relation between a veto and a pitch. From our knowledge about vetoes, we know that Congress must first *send* the bill to the President. From our knowledge about pitching, we know that for the Congress/pitcher to pitch, it must *send* a 'ball' to a 'batter'. We have a match on the predicate 'send' and on the agents of the sendings, Congress. We complete this match by assuming the bill is the ball and President is the batter ... [p. 90.]

An interesting consequence is that the structures on which (27) is based (or which, alternatively, it establishes) lead to a kind of prediction, which may or may not be erroneous. As with mathematical models of physical processes, so with linguistic models of political processes, the initial mapping into the known domain will represent selected features only, and the validity of the model as a model depends crucially on being able to reverse the right-hand vertical arrow validly. In Hobb's example one result is that *veto* is equated with *hit*, and President and Congress are set in an adversary relationship. (They may, of course, ACTUALLY be adversaries; metaphors and models cannot always of themselves establish the facts of the matter, though they may reflect or influence them to varying degrees.)

Figure 6.3 suggests how we might understand the relevant discourse processes, and at the same time modify Hobbs's account. It seems that two analogous frames are in fact known; they are assumed to be isomorphic, so that a reverse upward-pointing arrow can be inserted on the right. This perhaps corresponds to the situation discussed earlier in which the reader of the Ministry of Defence pamphlet already has well-established frames in both domains—i.e. he has sufficiently well-developed conceptual models for both *deterrence* and *bully*. The psychological—and political—function of the morphism is presumably to reinforce one, or indeed BOTH, frames. Of course the metaphor/morphism set-up may be invalid, misleading, deliberately deceptive, etc. Pursuing the mathematical analogy a little may help to show why, or at least how.

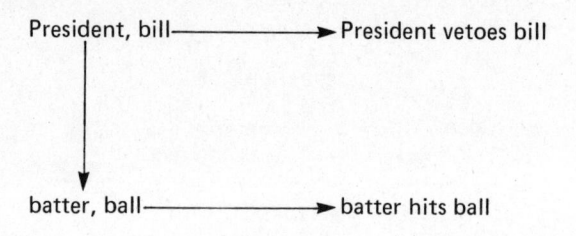

```
President, bill ─────────► President vetoes bill
    │
    │
    ▼
batter, ball ────────────► batter hits ball
```

Figure 6.3

Earlier we used the term 'isomorphism' to suggest match between structures. Now technically an 'isomorphism' is a one-one mapping from one domain to the other. If the example in Figure 6.3 were really isomorphic, then *President, ball*, etc. would be the ONLY elements to map on to *batter, ball*, etc. But clearly many other things could map on to—could be expressed metaphorically in terms of—baseballs; and presidents, bills, etc. could map on to quite other terms. Similarly, there is really no warrant for reversing the left-hand arrow—that would require isomorphism. However, it is as if there is something about discourse contexts of this type that makes speaker and hearer behave linguistically and conceptually, AS IF there were an isomorphism.

Turning now to the situation where *deterrence* (for example) is not understood or well understood by the processor, we can see how the assumption of isomorphism can lead to the learning of a meaning, an addition to the knowledge base. In the case of Figure 6.3 we are in a situation where the discourse processor happens to know *veto* and that the only plausible candidate to complete the picture is *hits*. But consider a situation in which the 'new' unknown domain really is uncertain, more so than Hobbs in fact assumes. We can't then easily speak of mapping new and unknown into old. The starting ('old') domain will be some widely shared belief—like the bully frame. It will contain, we suppose, (a) participants with attributes, e.g. oppressor (strong, aggressive, armed, etc.), victim (weak, peaceable, unarmed, etc.), defender (strong, peaceable, armed, etc.), and (b) typical frame-like story structures, with quasi-causal links, e.g.

victim is weak—oppressor attacks—defender stands up to oppressor—oppressor backs down

victim is weak—oppressor attacks—victim becomes own defender—oppressor backs down

The less sure ('new') domain includes the participants: US, GB, USSR, *weapons*, etc., but, let us assume, the relations between them are unclear. Is there a 'morphism'? The question is, can we construct a 'morphism' from *bully* to *cold-war*? In mathematical (we are speaking metaphorically, of course!) terms, this boils down to asking if we can map the *old* (known) domain into the *new* (less-known) one, and if we can find an operation or relation to complete the diagram (Figure 6.4), for example.

```
                BASIC                    COMPLEX
    OLD: defender, oppressor ──▶ defender stands up to oppressor
                │                           │
                │                           │
                ▼                           ▼
    NEW: GB, USSR ─────────────▶ GB arms against USSR
```

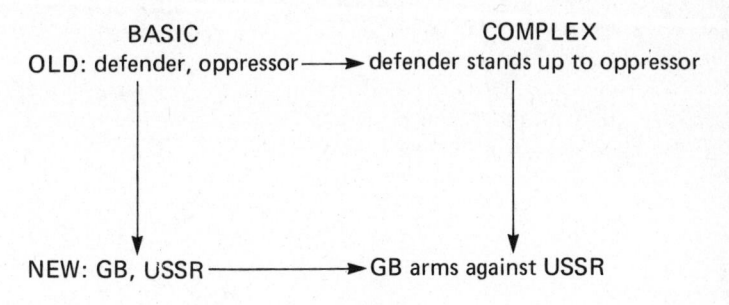

Figure 6.4

We 'know' that 'defender stands up to bully' can be derived, along with 'defenders must be strong', 'the weak are victims of oppressors', 'defenders must be armed', etc. from the *bully* belief system. We only know for sure that there are corresponding derivations in the new domain, if we assume the two are isomorphic. On that assumption, a term can be 'induced' to fill the question mark in Figure 6.4, whether it be the same ('stand up to') or *deter*. Once such an isomorphism is accepted all kinds of inferences may be drawn. For instance, if potential victims of bullies need to defend themselves, then smaller Western nations need to arm themselves; if defenders need to frighten off bullies with a convincing show of strength, then Western nations need nuclear weapons; moreover, if bully-scaring actually works (and the bully frame typically asserts that this is so), then deterrence actually works.

To illustrate further this approach to metaphor in discourse, and at the same time the role of metaphor in nuclear politics, we might consider the case of 'nuclear allergy in Japan', discussed in detail by Hook (1984). Hook carefully documents the development and legitimation of the metaphor in the 1960s and 1970s, and its use in public 'debate' against those who opposed the nuclearization of Japan. In our present terms this corresponds to the progressive construction of an 'isomorphism' with attendant inferences, which could be turned against opponents. That is, once the isomorphism was established by government media agencies in Japan, inferences could be drawn which contradicted dissident arguments. The known ('old') domain was the frame of beliefs surrounding the notion of *allergy*. The elements attributes and structures were something like the following:

(a) patient (abnormal, unhealthy, requiring cure, etc.).
 allergen (normally harmless to normal people, etc.).
 doctor (diagnoses, cures, etc.).
(b) allergen sensitizes patient.
 doctor cures patient by exposing patient to increasing doses of allergen.

The many inferences drawn from this frame can be mapped on to the nuclear political frame, in the fashion loosely pictured in Figure 6.5. What is induced here is a concept of pathological political behaviour. The productive capacity of the model gives rise to other legitimized conclusions, such as the notion that Japan could be progressively 'desensitized' by gradual increase of, for instance, visits by US nuclear-powered and armed naval vessels. Clearly, the establishment of a 'morphism' of this type depends on at least two factors: one is the existence of a relatively well-known and shared frame—in this case a current collection of authoritative medical lore; and the other is the use of political power to utilize information media. Hobbs makes these points in a general fashion: 'Any discourse is built on a shared knowledge base of possible inferences. By means of his utterances, the speaker plants inferences in the listener's head' (p. 90). Lakoff and Johnson, Jackendoff, and Hobbs himself, propose that metaphor structures the basic lexicon (by, for instance, mapping the perceptually well-understood spatial domain on to time expressions, in 'three hours long', etc.). Now if this is so, if we need metaphors to communicate at all, then this helps to explain why we may be so ready to assent to non-essential metaphors 'planted in the head'. Nevertheless, this bit of psycholinguistic speculation will not be the whole story: it remains an important task to examine the social and political processes by which 'planting' can be done in the first place.

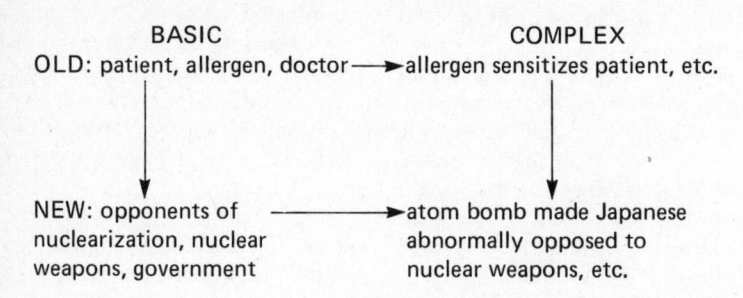

```
                BASIC                       COMPLEX
OLD: patient, allergen, doctor ——▶ allergen sensitizes patient, etc.
            │                              │
            │                              │
            ▼                              ▼
NEW: opponents of          ——▶ atom bomb made Japanese
     nuclearization, nuclear    abnormally opposed to
     weapons, government        nuclear weapons, etc.
```

Figure 6.5

NOTES

1. Cf. Barnaby and Windass (1983); also Walker (1980), Luckham (1984), Richter (1982) on the relevance of linguistic approaches in this area.
2. E.g. Vigor (1975).
3. It is an empirical psychological question perhaps whether (some) speakers decompose *deterrent* morphologically, or in any way relate it to *terror* and *terrify* on the basis of

a morpheme *terr*. If it turned out that the word *deter* actually obscures the connection with terror, that would be highly significant, but to be expected in view of the fact that 'The words "terror" and "terrorism" have become semantic tools of the powerful in the Western world . . .' (Chomsky and Herman 1979, Vol. I: 3.1, 'The Semantics of Terror and Violence: Retail Violence as "Terror"—Wholesale Violence as Maintaining "Order" and "Security" '). It is worth noting that in Chomsky and Herman the approach to word meaning contrasts a basic conceptual dictionary meaning with politically defined usage.

4. But not nouns: the noun *deterrent* has less strong entailment in some contexts: *Alf's stick was a deterrent, but Bert (still) hit him* seems less odd than (3)c (cf. also the criminological contexts considered below.) This may have something to do with (a) the fact that *deterrent* denotes a category containing prototypical and marginal cases (sticks are not such good deterrents as, say, machine guns), and (b) the association of *deterrent* with known situation types (e.g. the judicial) in which intended deterrents are successful in a statistical not a necessary sense. *Deter* is not particularized in this way. Something similar applies to *deterrence*, since it is evidently not redundant to say 'deterrence HAS deterred' (it has been said by Mrs Thatcher). Similarly, it is possible to state both 'the (nuclear) deterrent deters the Russians' and 'the (nuclear) deterrent does not deter the Russians', which is actually what is required for continuing arms production. For deterrence ideology there ideally has to be a concept *deter* with necessary causal entailments and there has to be at the same time the possibility that a particular *deterrent* does not *deter*. These semantic distinctions are not, of course, unique for the three words under consideration.

5. If *deter* does not entail nuclear weapons (except perhaps stipulatively in restricted contexts), nuclear weapons do not imply *deter*, as is often claimed, but *use*, as is often disclaimed. Tool and weapon categories probably inherently have a 'useable' semantic specification. The verb *nuke* does not mean *to deter with nuclear weapons* . . .

6. Vigor cited above, for instance, strongly suggests that the Russian mind is not rational, and that it cannot comprehend the concept *deter*; it is not clear whether he implies that they cannot therefore be *deterred*. In times of crisis (e.g. the shooting-down by Soviet planes of the Korean airliner in 1983) public rhetoric represents the Russians explicitly as not open to rational discourse; and this in spite (or conceivably because) of that other aspect of the stereotype that represents Russians as 'the most calculating, chess-playing people in the world'.

7. The Gricean maxims need not be regarded as immutable but as contingent on social and historical moments, as suggested, from a particular political perspective, by Sampson (1982: 209).

8. The *OED*'s earliest written occurrence of *deter* is 1579, its earliest occurrence in a legal sense 1594, its earliest occurrence of *deterrent* (adj. and noun) in a legal sense 1829, and of *deterrence* (also in a legal sense) 1861.

9. For the literature dealing with 'frames', see references mentioned in section 6.1, and in Chapter 12, pp. 221 ff.

10. This is an attested example: see 'The Front Line Against Youth Unemployment', *Daily Telegraph*, 19 July 1982. It is worth noticing that President Reagan's infamous 'off-the-record' joke of August 1984 merges the legal and the cold-war frames: 'Today your President signed legislation to outlaw Russia for ever. We start bombing in five minutes'. On anti-nuclear humour, see Chapter 11 below.

11. Designed and produced by Main Titles Ltd.

12. The design of the back of the pamphlet illustrates this point. The following are printed in a column: (i) [bold capitals] 'NATO's policy of deterrence has kept the peace in Europe for over 30 years'; (ii) three-quarters frontal drawing of bulldog; (iii) [lower case] 'That's a history lesson none of us can afford to ignore' [derived from school frame].

Part III
Aspects of media discourse

7 Getting the message across: a systemic analysis of media coverage of a CND march

Bob Hodge
Murdoch University, Western Australia

7.1 INTRODUCTION

The march, rally or public demonstration has traditionally been a major means whereby anti-nuclear campaigners have focused their message for a wider public. This chapter attempts to offer strategic maps of how such an event works as communication as it is appropriated by the mass media. In 1981, a group from the Birmingham Centre for Contemporary Cultural Studies studied the media coverage of the London CND Rally of 24 October 1981, a rally which was generally considered a highly successful one. They published an occasional paper on their findings, 'Fighting over peace'.[1] Their study is the source of the data analysed in the present chapter. Its conclusions probably apply fairly generally to anti-nuclear rallies in the English-speaking world. In May 1983, a group from Murdoch University studied a rally in Perth, Western Australia, another one that was rated 'successful'. Our group's procedures and conclusions were essentially the same as those of the Birmingham group. In this chapter, however, I want to go beyond report and interpretation, to suggest a general systemic model for thinking about rallies, one that might generate a whole range of possible strategies and tactics that organizers of such occasions may find useful to consider.

A rally considered as a piece of communication can in principle be seen as constituted by the primary kinds of structure recognized since Saussure as the syntagmatic and paradigmatic planes (Saussure 1973). The syntagmatic plane is the plane of text and action, the combinations, oppositions and transformations of meaning that occur in physical time and space, produced by specific agents, in specific kinds of social relationship, in relation to specific acts of interpretation. The paradigmatic is the plane which is the immediate source of the meanings assigned to significant elements, the site of the processes by which meanings are constituted, demarcated and transformed. Without the conjunction of both the syntagmatic and the paradigmatic planes, no meaning can occur (see Hodge and Kress 1983).

In describing paradigmatic relations, structural linguistics since Saussure has mainly represented them as binary, branching out in symmetrical, static, tree-like fashion. But Levi-Strauss, influenced by Jakobson, has proposed transformational processes operating on, constituting and eroding binary structures of this kind, producing parallels, analogies, and even nonce-structures. And Halliday's 'systemic' theory has introduced a subtle and precise notation for processes that occur in this plane. He takes seriously Jakobson's description of the paradigmatic plane as the plane of choice or selection. A system-network attempts to map the series of choices that unfold on the way to the final utterance or text. If meaning is derived from what is chosen AND what is deliberately not chosen, then a systemic analysis gives the fullest and most precise account we can give of meaning, at least in this sense of the term. Halliday's notation (cf. Kress 1976: 15), which I will use in this chapter, has the following conventions:

(i) Disjunction: [or] (either X or Y (or Z): oppositions, binary and others)
(ii) Conjunction: { or } (both X and Y (and Z): combination or fusion)
(iii) Realization: ↘

7.2 THE COVERAGE SYNTAGM AND NETWORK OF INFLUENCES

The Birmingham study is a useful starting-point for our enquiry, since in many ways it is an exemplary study of a classic instance. It begins with a number of methodological points. Firstly, though the primary data were a set of media texts, it insisted that the study of texts in isolation is not enough. The meaning of texts, and of events themselves, is a process of interpretation, carried out by readers who can operate with different frameworks of interpretation, or 'discourses' to produce different or unoppositional readings. The form of texts is also affected by the processes of media production, and these factors must all be taken into account. Finally, the group warn against a pessimistic, fatalistic account of the mass media, the kind of account which suggests that existing structures and forces can only be described, not changed or resisted. So they analyse the debate in terms of 'traps' and 'openings', possible points of danger and of interpretation.

Their analysis of media coverage of the rally is organized in terms of what we will call the syntagm of the rally story. They break it down into three phases: advance notices; reports; and commentary ('recuperatives'). These are, of course, ordered in time, transformationally related to each other, so the syntagm has the following form:[2]

preview ⇒ report ⇒ commentary

The transformations are not simply to be regarded as biases or distortions. They mark the presence of competing forces and the struggle for meaning. But syntagmatic forms on their own are without meaning. To carry out any analysis we need an account of systems and processes. The Birmingham study takes a useful step in this respect by isolating a number of key themes, issues which are sites and stakes of struggle. A theme is a topic, a category, which is 'inflected' differently by competing groups in a debate. That is, it is a set of abstract syntagms which have opposite tendencies and evaluations.

A study of a particular event naturally takes for granted the importance of that event, but such judgements are always open to contention. The Birmingham study showed the role that can be played by competing news stories: before the rally, stories about Sir Stewart Pringle, 'The Iron General', and IRA bombers were mobilized by the conservative press to combat the effects of reporting the rally. They also noted that the Falklands war overshadowed the rally of June 1982, with a decisive effect on how that event was perceived and reported. Of the many ways in which events can be categorized, one important one, in understanding a debate, is in terms of authorship and tendency. The anti-nuclear movement is the major author of an anti-nuclear rally. Other events can be produced and celebrated by hostile forces. Oppositional groups can also be authors of some parts of a rally—e.g. police activities, counter-demonstrations, or heckling.

The Birmingham study also devoted a lot of space to the structure of the media, seeing some of the differences and divisions within the media as potential 'openings'. Their account of the main types follows the commonly accepted format. They start from a division into electronic and print media. They then see electronic as, in general, more favourable than print media, commercial TV more favourable than BBC, tabloids more unfavourable than 'qualities', with the most favourable media being 'alternative' and left-wing print publications, and especially those aimed at the young. Cutting across the division by media, and more decisive in its effects, are divisions in terms of allegiance, the interests an organization supports and addresses.

At this stage I propose (see Figure 7.1) a systemic map of the constitutive networks involved in the 1981 rally, drawing on the Birmingham study data conclusions. In this map, the three primary categories correspond roughly to what Halliday calls the three major macro-functions of language, the ideational, the interpersonal and the textual (see Kress 1976). The first of these macro-categories, which we are calling 'content', consists of both themes and events, i.e. abstract schemata and specific occurrences, acting in conjunction to determine actual stories in the media. Both have the double inflection produced by the opposition between pro-nuclear and anti-nuclear protagonists, giving rise to pro- and anti-nuke thematic structures, pro- and anti-nuke events. Social relationships underlying a debate have a determining influence on every other category. In this network, I have only indicated the place of relationships in terms of class, gender, etc. This network will be explored in more detail later on in this chapter. At lower points in the system, several forces typically act together, so that a particular theme, event or text will be determined by a number of forces acting together, in complex ways that can only be unravelled by specific analysis. The whole system, in fact, is characterized by multiple determination.

In Figure 7.1 I use an asterisk to indicate my judgement—in the case of the October 1981 rally, as I read the reading of the Birmingham group—that that influence was the dominant one in any complex. Such judgements, of course, are contentious, relative, pragmatic—and essential for planning and tactical decisions. For instance, the asterisks included here indicate the judgement that the preview was dominated by thematic structures (though some may argue

BOB HODGE

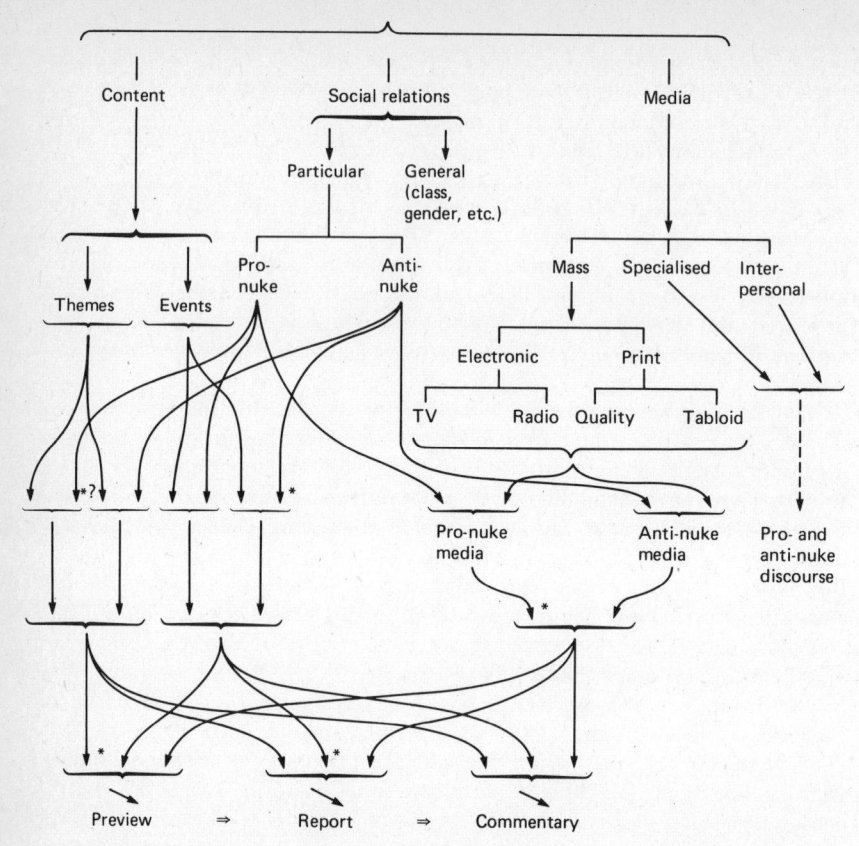

Figure 7.1 Network of media and other systems, October 1981 rally

that media structures are more decisive); reports, by the content of events; commentary, by media structures (though again, some might argue that thematic structures were more decisive here). Asterisks award dominance over event-structures to CND, with pro-nukes dominating the media, and perhaps also the thematic structures ('traps' loom larger than 'openings' in the Birmingham report, though this may not represent their overall judgement). Within the mass media, radio and television perhaps can be regarded as anti-nuke, but the mass media are overall pro-nuke.

Strategy suggests, then, that if there are no obvious means for overcoming the pro-nuclear bias of the mass media, especially the popular press, then specialized media should be exploited, as the Birmingham group suggest. But non-mass media, interpersonal networks of communication (of which a rally or demonstration is one example) may be an area where an anti-nuke asterisk may be affixed: perhaps via the institutionalized networks established by religious and education systems, for instance. In any case, we are not proposing any specific tactics that would be valid for all occasions: merely the general value of maps for planning purposes, to be used by the people close to the ground who have to make the actual decisions which will be realized in a new and, hopefully, successful anti-nuclear text.

7.3 WAR AND PEACE

The ideological battle, the search for 'traps' to avoid and 'openings' to exploit, is an important phase of the struggle. The Birmingham group's list of 'themes' and their inflections is a useful starting-point. But a list has only the simplest of structures. It is static, not dynamic. In order to make sense of the interrelations of possible meanings, and the myriad bewildering shifts that characterize debate, we need a structural and transformational account of the key themes.

We will start with 'peace', the most potent word of all in this debate. The Birmingham group lists five main 'meanings' of peace, but underlying these motifs we can posit a simpler, more powerful schema. Essentially, the supreme trap, the goal of pro-nuclear proponents, is a total transformation of peace into war: 'peace is war', as Orwell put it so graphically, in his description of the ideological underpinnings of Oceania in *Nineteen Eighty-Four*. Orwell is also useful on why this strategy is so effective. If war is peace (and peace is war), then these two categories, which function as polar opposites organizing a whole structure of relationships in between, become unusable. The result is what Orwell called 'doublethink', which is in fact the paralysis of thought, in the domain at issue. Both terms, and the area covered by them, become unavailable for effective thought. A paradigmatic transformation, establishing equivalence between two polar terms that constitute a paradigmatic structure, is a certain way of destroying that whole structure. In his work on aphasia Jakobson showed that where a distinction is lost (e.g. in the sound system) all dependent distinctions are automatically lost (Jakobson 1968). Loss of the distinction between vowels and consonants means the loss of the phonological system. A conflation-transformation, then, is a kind of aphasia—a far more practical and widespread way of eliminating thought, incidentally, than removing words from dictionaries, the crude method of the rulers in Orwell's fictional society.

The processes which lead in this direction can be illustrated by examples from the Birmingham report. Take, for instance, this from the *Sunday Mirror*:

> Police adopted a low-key, softly-softly approach and the protest passed off peacefully.[3]

The Birmingham group note the 'amazing causal link' whereby the police actions seem to be responsible for the peacefulness of the march—even more amazing, they suggest, if the actual numbers and behaviour of the police are taken into account. But there is a basis for this 'amazing causal link', which is far too common really to amaze. The crucial phrase to analyse is 'the protest passed off peacefully'. This derives from a deep structure

(X) protested against [Y] [about Z] peacefully.

In this deep structure, 'peace' is just one candidate among many to be Z, the subject of the protest. It is, however, an adverb, in both deep and surface forms, where it describes the mode of the action. The comprehensible processes, in this deep structure, are acts of antagonism, not peace. Peace, then, seems an almost accidental and contradictory property of this act of aggression—hence the ease of the *Sunday Mirror* operation of appropriating it on behalf of the police.

What a syntagm like this is doing—and examples could be multiplied endlessly—is to establish some kind of link between peace and its opposite, foregrounding potentially violent means and making the ends remote and barely accessible in deep structure. A passage[4] with a similar transformation is:

> European peace movements are not new. In the late 10th and early 11th centuries, anti-war protests, backed by the clergy, burst out across the continent. The militants forcibly occupied local castles chanting 'Peace, Peace'. [*Evening Standard*, 26 October 1981.]

Here words like 'burst out' and 'militants' connect violent, concrete actions in the surface of the text with the anti-war group (as though they had a monopoly on violence at the time, and the heavy fortifications on the local castles were designed purely with a future tourist trade in mind). 'Peace' is left as just a word, without a deep structure and therefore without meaning in the mouths of these chanters. A contradiction is set up between slogan and actions, and truth seems to lie, as always, with actions. War, fighting, and struggle seem like simple concrete facts: 'peace', in contrast, is almost empty of content.

The structure and history of the word *peace* make it especially vulnerable to emptying-out of meaning. It is relatively difficult to get from *peace* to a concrete state of affairs in the world. It is an abstract noun, and abstracts commonly do not refer directly to concrete referents. But a word like *truth* can be interpreted transformationally as derived from [*X says Y is*] *true*. The equivalent deep structure for *peace* would be *X is at peace with Y*, but this does not seem to advance explanation. Paradigmatically, the meaning of *peace* is fixed only by opposition to *war*, and it is *war* which is the unmarked term. It is peace which is the absence of war, not war which is the absence of peace. So the meaning of peace is always derived from that of war, which is thus the primary one of the two. As Marx noted in the *Grundrisse*, 'War developed earlier than peace' (Marx 1973: 109). A study of the etymology of the word comes up with the same conclusion. The Latin *pax, pacis* comes from *pactus*, the past participle of *pango*, what has been fixed, set in the ground, hence the treaty that resolves hostilities. *Pax* referred to the treaty that ended a war, not the absence of struggle that preceded it. Anti-nuclear campaigners might ponder the fact that *impact* comes from the same root as *peace*: this is part of the regrettable history trailed by this slippery but necessary word.

The other side of the contradiction is captured in the slogan 'Nato is THE peace movement' (Julian Critchley, *Daily Telegraph* 26 October 1981, p. 16),[5] where the guardians of peace are the war machine that is responsible for one half of the state of war that currently exists. But this claim expresses exactly the same contradiction as underlies the previous example: a naturalization of the transformation 'warlike means to peaceful ends' ⇒ 'war = peace'. As Saussure observed, in language habitual usage slowly and imperceptibly turns into law. Every use—by either side—of paradoxes which tend in this direction adds towards the pressures that will finally empty the term *peace* of any usable meaning.

This is why the same trope in anti-nuclear discourse is not innocent. The Birmingham pamphlet is entitled 'Fighting for peace', another example of the paradox. The 'Campaign' in 'CND' mirrors army language. So do 'march', and 'marshall', and other words used by campaigners themselves to describe their activity. There is even an insidious attraction in this transformational process: if war is peace, then war ceases to exist, since each term in the opposition is the privation of the other. The 'victory' occurs purely at the symbolic level. Its price is that peace, too, ceases to exist as a concept, but none the less there is a warm reassurance that comes from such transformational work. The irony is that any use of this aids the work of pro-nuclear propagandists, who gain more from the effective elimination of 'peace' from the debate. It is very important for anti-nuclear campaigners to insist that there are fundamental differences between war of different kinds and peace of different kinds.

7.4 CLASS, GENDER, AGE AND RACE NETWORK

Another useful aspect of the Birmingham analysis is its identification of the themes of class, gender, age, and race in the nuclear debate and the corresponding traps: the class trap, the gender trap, the youth trap, the race trap, and the Red trap. As their analysis shows, these issues cannot be put to one side by campaigners as irrelevant to the main issue, because they are mobilized by pro-nuke propagandists. Given the scope of the campaign, this wider framework is highly relevant. The campaign needs to unite a whole nation, ultimately a whole world, on this issue, an audience that in many other respects is fragmented.

Media theorists of the left have come late to the realization that the mass mind is itself an ideological construct, that in practice ideological content is refracted in a variety of ways by different audiences. Ideologues of the mass media, however, have shown their recognition of this premise in their increasingly skilful practice over many years, typically offering not simply a single monolithic ideological version of reality, but a contradictory set adapted to different purposes and different segments within audiences. Contemporary society can be seen in terms of the primary categories deployed by the Birmingham group: class, gender, age, race, and nationality. Everyone is socially defined in terms of every one of these features: they provide the basis for social identity, the hooks by which people are assigned to roles, or offered fantasy alternatives to those assigned roles. Ideological schemes have at least the two functions: to prescribe behaviours, and to make those prescriptions seem acceptable, even attractive. So ideologues can seek to reinforce the schema which legitimates the distribution of power in society, or can present the various roles and the social order itself as desirable in their own right. Propagandists in the nuclear debate can appeal to members of a dominant category by associating the conditions of that dominance with a nuclear theme. Or they can make a particular stance on nuclear arms seem a compensation for real conditions of existence.

We can extend the notion of a systemic network to represent the basic ideological repertoire in the terms as illustrated in Figure 7.2 (note that the binary terms used here represent a simplification, and more complex networks can incorporate non-binary divisions readily).

To illustrate some of the complex processes involved, we will start with one sentence, from the *Guardian*:

> A boy with purple hair trotted up to the Police Control van and asked for two choc ices ... [26 October 1981, p. 3][6]

'Boy' is marked for both age and sex. Purple hair is one of the many signifiers of rebellion against both adult control and gender identity (which we symbolize as m⇔f, the fusion of the two categories). 'Trot', and 'choc ices', however, signify extreme youthfulness and dependence, with the police control van a fusion of benign parent and friendly ice-cream van. The initial superiority of young over old is transformed (signified by ⇒) to restored superiority of the old. Expectations have undergone a dramatic change as we progress through the sentence. We can represent the network in Figure 7.3. The sentence is a token, partly determined (presumably) by events, though the full set of events that could have been reported is obviously very large. Other incidents could have realized the same ideological structure: the boy could have had spiked hair, tattoos, etc., and could have asked for any childish commodity, or even a cup of tea or water. The *Guardian* readership, white, middle-class, middle-aged, predominantly male, can then complete this ideological work in predictable ways. The text offers, attached to and defining the nature of the rally, a version of the world in which the initial threat to middle-aged dominance is swiftly transformed to reaffirmation, and the problematic mixing of genders is safely infantilized. The whole picture is clearly calculated to make the typical *Guardian* reader feel good, about him/herself and about the rally. It thus counts as pro-campaign, for that readership, though the price of that support is an essentially conservative ideological stance. But for a young, working-class readership, the ideological schema has nothing to offer. It is hard to imagine this being responded to positively by readers of an ideologically incompatible type—though they would be unlikely to read it, even if it came their way.

Another typical text which illustrates how ideological themes coincide to determine texts is the following passage from *The Daily Telegraph*:

> Would a neutral Europe retain its independence: it would not. The Soviet Union has long harboured the hope that the United States would be effectively removed from the European scene, leaving Soviet military supremacy as the backdrop of European politics. A neutral Europe would be the eunuch in the harem of the great powers. [26 October 1981, p. 26.][7]

The Birmingham group make the telling response to the last sentence: 'Just who our rampant, weapon-waving State is screwing at the moment remains unsaid!'.[8] But the whole passage is an interesting interplay and transformation of themes. This short text offers the two versions of political reality: a 'neutral [= neutered] Europe/England', and a strong NATO. 'Britain' is transformationally realized as 'Europe', with NATO as a higher-order realization of 'us', i.e. a surrogate

MEDIA COVERAGE OF A CND MARCH

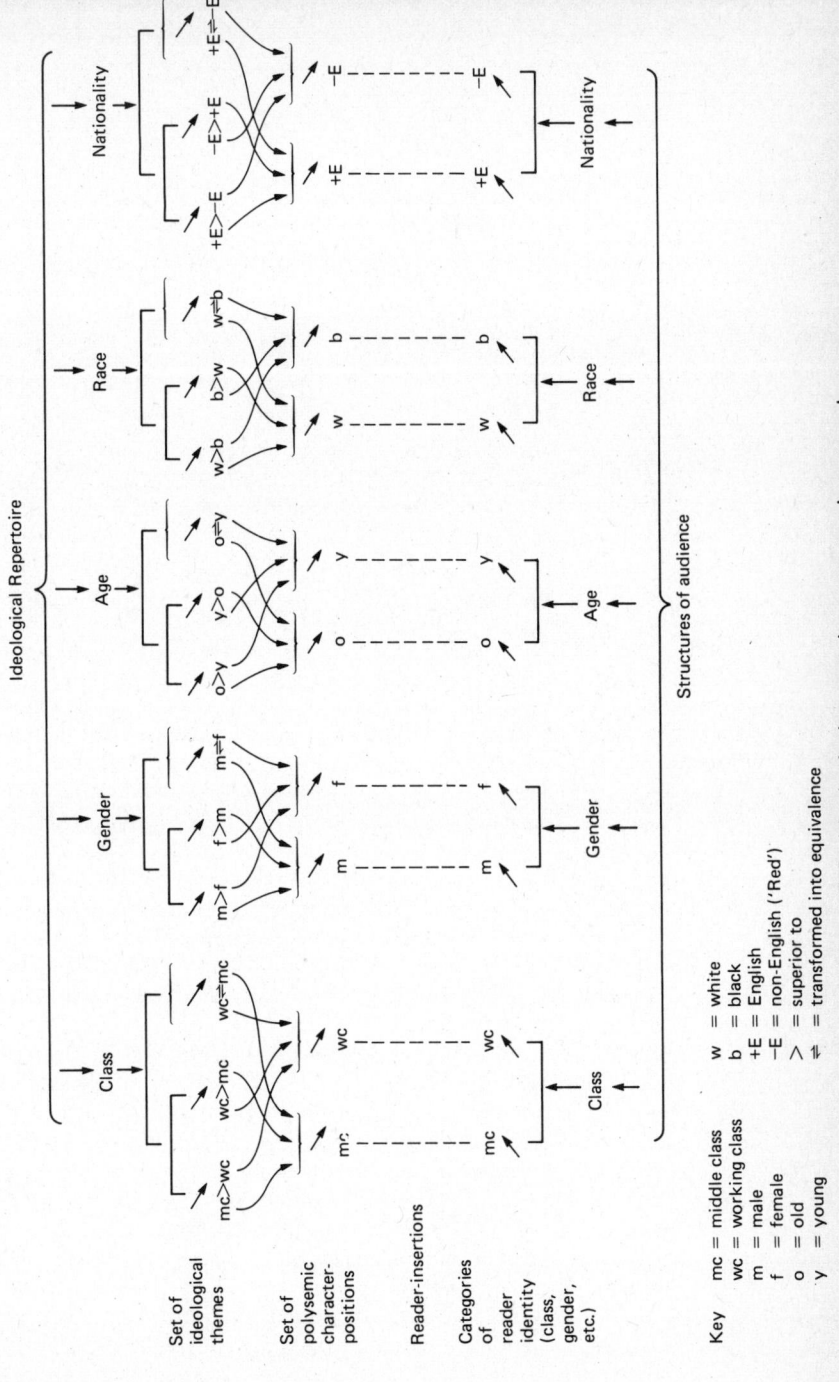

Figure 7.2 Ideological repertoire: a systemic network

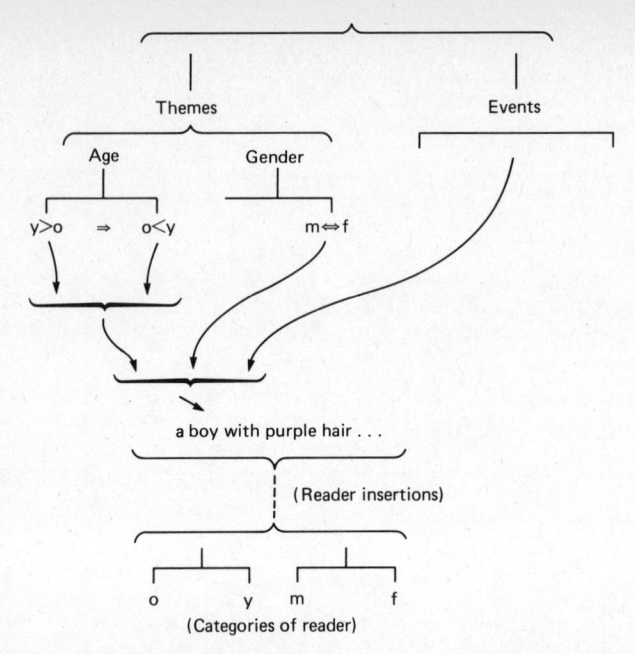

Figure 7.3 Events and themes in a sentence: a systemic network

Britain. The essential ideological operation performed is to establish an analogy between ideologies of nationality and ideologies of gender. The transformation has the effect of negation, reinforcing the surface 'it would not'. The eunuch analogy is in fact a confused one: Europe as eunuch is clearly emasculated, but what does 'the harem of the great powers' mean? Is it the harem, the collective wives of the collective males, who make up the Great Powers? Or is it the harem constituted by the Great Powers, who are, therefore, females, the lawful wives of someone—Europe or another—in a relationship which is the extreme image of male domination, in Western eyes. As the Birmingham group point out, the analogy isn't clearly worked out, but in fact its confusions concern the ideological form of masculine domination: $m \Rightarrow \phi$, or $m \Rightarrow f$, that is to say, the male is transformed to nothing, or to a female.

We can represent these relationships and oppositions in the systemic–transformational network illustrated in Figure 7.4. In its attempts to denigrate the concept of an independent Europe, this text promiscuously draws on all the gender-models available, in spite of the contradictions between them, but the model which is essentially affirmed is the patriarchal model, which is built on the dominance of powerful, older males. Again we can see a specific category of reader whose identity is especially confirmed by this transformation—adult, high-status, male. The frequent concern, especially in *The Times*, for maintaining Europe's 'will', which, the Birmingham group note, comes out of the same ideological structure. But this analysis points to one weakness of this strategy. Despite their disproportionate power, adult, high-status males in Britain are

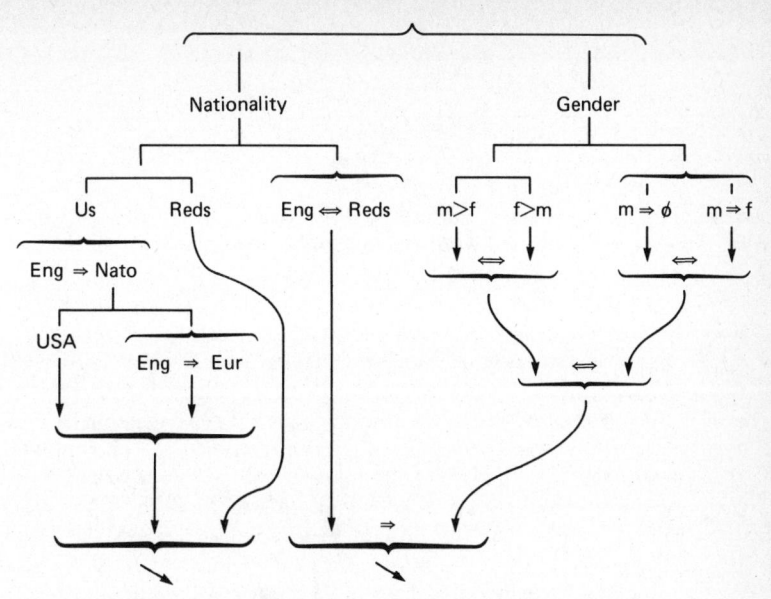

Figure 7.4 Gender and nationality: a systemic-transformational network

in a minority. The majority would feel alienated from this set of structures and transformations, although its very confusions would make it less easy to reject, or accept. One function of a systemic analysis of this kind is that it sets out clearly the vulnerability of certain ideological forms for various classes of reader: though for polemical purposes, of course, a systemic–transformational analysis will usually not be the most effective and compelling form for presenting the counter-arguments.

7.5 ANALYSIS FROM TEXT TO SYSTEMS

The preceding analysis has followed a top-down methodology, relying on the general frameworks being sufficiently part of our social knowledge for us to see the derivation of particular forms from them. But it is salutary to complement this by a bottom-up approach, attempting to work from specific texts to more general systems which seem implied, as the real choices which constitute the final text as a structure of meanings. Bottom-up analyses are typically tentative and inconclusive. But they show something of the complexity of the actual business of making meanings, and they can also suggest the presence and importance of systems that hadn't previously entered into the analysis.

As a text, I will take the following piece of polemic by Paul Johnson in the *Daily Mail*.

Many of those who surged to Hyde Park on Saturday were actual or potential SDP voters. Among such people, the same kind of well-meaning trendiness makes them want to ban the bomb and love Shirley Williams, although these emotions are, in theory, mutually exclusive. [*Daily Mail*, 26 October 1981, p. 6.][9]

Every word and every syntactic form here is, of course, the product of innumerable choices, though we do not know what the alternatives were, for the producer of the text. But in so far as systems are intersubjective, resting on shared knowledge, and the process of interpretation necessarily involves a reconstruction of this series of choices, I would claim a public status for my reading—even if some of our particular interpretations are contested.

A useful analytic procedure here can be termed the 'minimally contrasting pair principle'. In phonology, a minimally contrasting pair of sounds, e.g. /pin/ and /bin/, allows the isolation of the single feature [± voice] which distinguishes /p/ and /b/. Every choice is made in terms of a criterion or feature, so we can always in principle attempt to project the act of choice that immediately precedes the surface text, and every act of interpretation rests on innumerable such projections. Even if we can only produce a small set of alternatives rather than a single binary pair, we still derive important data, the elements that constitute the rationale of the system that we are deploying. With any systemic network, the number of features that constitute it must be considerably less than the number of items organized by it. The features determine the system. If you understand the features and their organization you understand the system as a dynamic process: why it does what it does, why it cannot produce what it cannot produce.

Given the massive redundancy of features, we do not need to be exhaustive. We will start, for illustrative purposes, with 'surged'. Two close alternatives here are *marched* and *went*, with *marched* closer. At this stage of the analysis we can't be sure that these are minimally contrasted, and we don't need to. A more appropriate term for what we are dealing with is 'marginally contrasting pairs' where one term marginalizes one or more other potential terms. *Went* is contrasted with the other two in at least two main ways. It is a more neutral term. *Marched* comes from the discourse of the marchers, while 'surged' has a negative force, from an oppositional discourse. Though neither word is from an elaborated register, 'surged' is also more emotive and more populist. To use Halliday's terms, these distinctions arise in an interpersonal system network. But 'surged' also contrasts with the other two words as a categorization of the kind of motion involved: i.e. in Hallidayan terms it realizes an ideational system as well. Two features distinguishing 'surge' and 'march' seem to be [+ energy] and [+ human]. We can represent the intersection of these systems as shown in Figure 7.5. That is, the choice of 'surged' involves selections in terms of all these criteria. Its meaning includes these criteria, and the acts of rejection involved: the dehumanization of the crowd, the populism, the anti-intellectuality, and the anti-nuclear allegiance.

Another piece of this text we will look at is 'actual or potential SDP voters'. This phrase contains a triad of smaller units, which we can see as the following marginally contrasting pairs: *voters/supporters*, *SDP/Social Democrat*, and *actual or potential/ϕ*. Ideationally, the crucial difference between *voters* and *supporters*

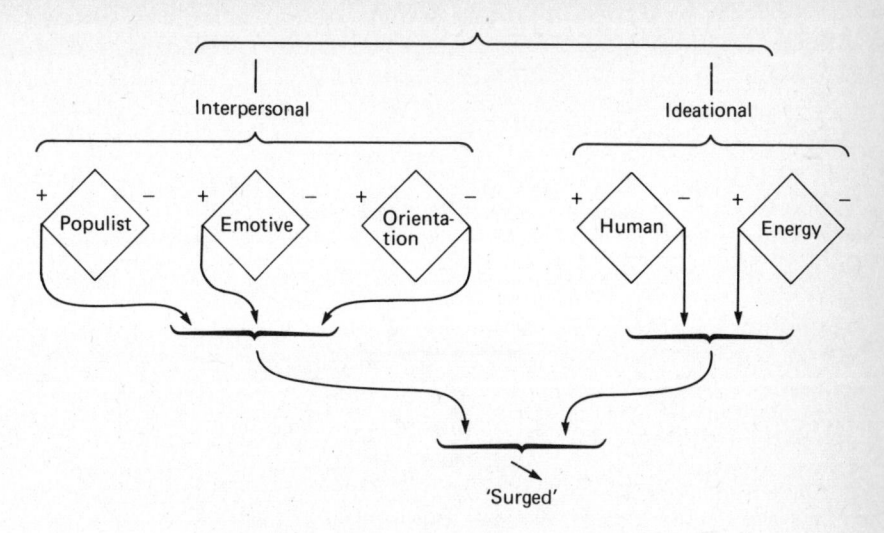

```
                Interpersonal                        Ideational
      +    -    +    -    +      -      +    -      +     -
    Populist  Emotive  Orienta-        Human        Energy
                        tion
                          ↓
                      'Surged'
```

Figure 7.5 A systemic network for word choice.

is that voting is an empirical act, as against the general allegiance signified by *support*. Interpersonally, *voters* is a precise, empirically verifiable term which comes from a scientistic discourse, the discourse of impersonal, objective, political scientists. *SDP*, semantically exactly equivalent to *Social Democrat Party*, differs only interpersonally. Acronyms signify the discourse of insiders, or experts, so familiar with the full term that only initials are needed. *Actual or potential*, redundant in more popular forms of discourse, interpersonally signifies a scientifically precise form of discourse, again the discourse of political science, reinforcing *voters*.

Similar structures of features occur frequently even in the short piece of text we have quoted. 'Well-meaning trendiness' ideationally contrasts feeling with tough rationality. Interpersonally it comes from conservative, non-scientific, middle-class discourse. At another level, the sentence has been transformed from 'Such people are middle-class trendies + they want to ban the bomb and love Shirley Williams'. One effect of the transformation is to shift the agents in deep structure, however confused it is claimed they are, into seeming merely the location and the object of the actions or feelings for which they are in fact responsible. This transformation (which we have not tried to map precisely here) is also determined interpersonally, since nominalization and reordering transformations of this kind signify middle-class, non-popular discourse. We can give a simplified systemic map of the syntax of this sentence as shown in Figure 7.6.

Another part of this sentence is worthy of attention: 'ban the bomb and love Shirley Williams'. The first phrase, 'ban the bomb', comes straight from anti-nuclear discourse. It is direct, untransformed, populist in level, but also precise. 'love Shirley Williams' is rather different. It is, in fact, semantically roughly equivalent to 'vote for the SDP, potentially or actually', but it deploys polar opposite features in the interpersonal system. It is highly emotive, not scientific

```
                    Ideational                    Interpersonal
                   (clause-type)
                        │                              │
            ┌───────────┴─────────┐         ┌──────────┴──────────┐
         Active  ⇒  Transformation       Middle class         Working class,
                    (nominalisation,     formal register      informal
                    etc.)
                             ╲             ╱
                              ╲           ╱
                               ╲         ╱
                                ╲       ╱
                                 ╲_____╱
                                    ↓
```

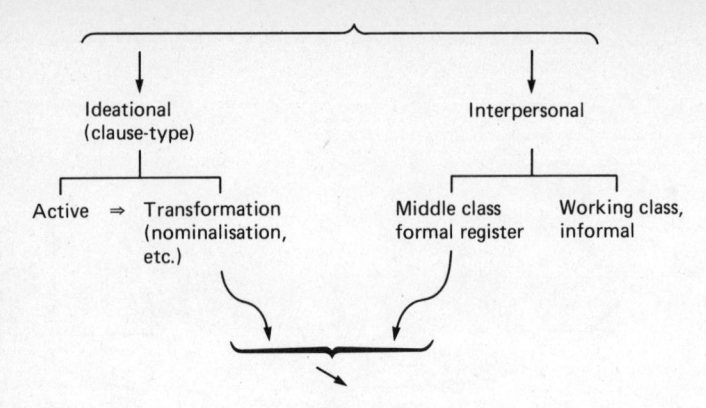

Figure 7.6 Ideological and class elements in the ideational and interpersonal components

in any sense, imprecise, populist, but probably middle-class, perhaps feminine as well. Both phrases are indirect quotations, and so they signify both their content and their typical speakers. In the case of the phrase about Shirley Williams, the speaker responsible, drawing on a campaign slogan 'I love Shirley Williams', is presented as awash with misguided emotion, unable to distinguish between an individual and a political party, incapable of political thought or scientific judgement. The comment by Johnson is interesting in itself. He calls these stances 'emotions', where the more precise word would be 'stances', especially for 'ban the bomb'; and he adds 'in theory', the phrase coming, now, from the discourse of political analysis, where it is presumed to be opposed, carefully and precisely, to an empirical analysis of practice. 'Mutually exclusive' similarly implies a logical analysis, and the discourse in which such analysis is normally reported, even though what we have in Johnson's text is his own polemical juxtaposition of different slogans, not a theoretical or logical exercise at all.

The analysis quickly became redundant, in terms of features specified, so we can begin to feel more confident about the relevance of these features. But equally interesting is the lack of consistency in Johnson's text. The suggestion of power and energy of 'surged' is contrasted to the feebleness imputed to the SDP; the discourse of anti-bomb marchers is juxtaposed to a range of other different kinds of discourse; Johnson's stance oscillates between emotive populism and scientific rationality, between affirmation and rejection of both intellect and feelings. The systemic confusion seems to point to confusions in the author, Johnson: about himself (whether feelings, his and others, are to be trusted or repudiated) and about the social relations establishing his discourse (whether he is distanced, impartial, above the crowd, or right down there amongst them). Some might claim that he shows a comprehensiveness, an ability to mobilize different discourses from a range of social positions, that his discourse strategies signify a transcendence of those divisions. To some degree that claim has substance, if we contrast this text with, for instance, the language of *The Times* or the *Guardian*. It is quite likely that that is how Johnson and his publishers would see his style. It is an example of a text that strives to create a larger consensus out of disparate groups, divided much as analysed by the Birmingham group. But we can use systemic-transformational analysis to show a sense of confusion rather than transcendence in the reader, attributed to the author, by noting the proliferation of either-or rather than both-and brackets, and the seemingly arbitrary choices Johnson makes in terms of basic features. The contradictions and confusions that emerge are symptomatic of sites of problems. At an early stage of analysis, all that we have explored are sites of disturbance of a particular individual, on a particular occasion, but the analysis is in a general form whose wider applicability is easy to test. Systemic analysis of this kind can help us in that search for 'traps' and 'openings' which the Birmingham study sees as the major aim of their study, and which is an aspect of the anti-nuclear struggle where kinds of linguistics should aspire to have something to offer.[10]

NOTES

1. Centre for Contemporary Cultural Studies (CCCS) (1982).
2. See Trew (1979). This extension of the term 'transformation' is argued for at length in Hodge (1982).
3. CCCS, p. 27.
4. CCCS, p. 31.
5. CCCS, p. 33.
6. CCCS, p. 53.
7. CCCS, p. 34.
8. CCCS, p. 31.
9. CCCS, p. 67.
10. This chapter has benefited greatly from discussion and comment from a number of people, particularly Alan Mansfield, Michael O'Toole, Bill Green and Peter Jeffery, and I gratefully acknowledge all their help.

8 Cultural silence: Nukespeak in radio discourse— a case study

Peter Moss
University of Adelaide, South Australia

8.1 BACKGROUND AND POLITICAL CONTEXT

For the purposes of this volume, South Australia and its industrial activity provides an ideal source of significant material. Since October 1979 two state governments—one Liberal, one Labour—have been involved in increasingly tortuous and deceptive public presentations of nuclear 'idealism'. In the process they have produced resounding silence as regards information about the nuclear industry. Media have played their parts in failing to represent the anti-nuclear case and radio has featured most prominently both in its coverage and in the more detailed background programmes which have been produced. The South Australian case is important because control of knowledge and the manipulations of opinion have been achieved without resort to gross tactics of legal intimidation or force. Rather, approved opinion made its case through selective radio presentations, releases and discussions abetted by 'main-stream' media's own accounts of the larger nuclear issue.

South Australia, the driest state in the driest country in the world, has massive, untapped mineral resources in its desert interior. From 1975, when the mineral deposit was first discovered, to 1981 the Western Mining Corporation (a 'joint-venturer', with 49 per cent ownership held by British Petroleum) had been locked in negotiations with the state government to gain agreements for a development project. An indenture agreement (a development contract between government and a private company) was signed in late 1981 with a Liberal government and confirmed in 1983 by a Labour government. The project, at Roxby Downs, some 300 miles north west of Adelaide, the state capital (and communications and media centre) has large copper, gold and silver deposits— but also the largest uranium ore deposit in the world. The reserves are estimated at 1,200,000 tonnes, which will produce some 3,000 tonnes of yellowcake per year.

The joint-venturers lobbied successive state governments to conclude an agreement during a period of large-scale unemployment and industrial stagnation. They were able to force an agreement with the governments on the most favourable terms, terms which give the South Australian community no obvious benefits but, potentially, many hazards. The indenture agreement guarantees that the state government provide and maintain services costing $A50 million (schools, a hospital, a major road and a large water-carrying pipeline), and electricity will be supplied to the mine and its processing plants at cost. In return, the taxpayers of the state 'receive' royalties at 2.5 per cent of the production value of the mine for five years and then 3.5 per cent in subsequent years. However, royalties are not payable by the corporation unless the mine has operated for sixty consecutive days at 85 per cent capacity! This indenture, whilst being a public document and therefore available for comment, has never been explained to the public by politicians and certainly not by the media.

Over a ten-day period (late August/early September) in 1983 the Campaign Against Nuclear Energy (CANE) organized a blockade of the Roxby Mine, aiming to stop work at the site in order to publicize the significance of the mine in the nuclear agenda.[1] Between 400 and 600 protesters from all over Australia were at the site at different times over the blockade period. It become a national media event.

8.2 MASS MEDIA AND KNOWLEDGE

Mass media obviously play significant roles in the presentation of the world to their audiences. In a broad cultural sense they select events out of the chaos of social life and integrate them into whatever prevailing ideology those media support. This media work entails the structuring and classification of events in order to make sense of the world. The significance of this is that the media are making sense of the world on behalf of their audiences and it is plausible, therefore, to think that they have an effect on the shape of a community's general beliefs. They are also significant brokers in the passage of knowledge between groups: for example, between those who 'make' news (politicians, entertainers, demonstrators) and those who receive and consume news (audiences). The ways in which media select and evaluate events is crucial in the production of cultural and political knowledge, therefore. The radio medium is particularly important because of the position it has come to hold in the dissemination of general knowledge for the mass audience. Over the past few years there has been a resurgence of popularity of this medium in Australia. This is partly because of a burgeoning of new AM and FM stations, both commercial and public. It is also a reflection of a shift in the medium's 'specialist' functions. More and more stations, and also larger proportions of time allocations within stations' programming, are being given over to talk formats, talkback segments, and news and current affairs. Radio is becoming the main filter of reality in its role of mediator of the world-out-there to isolated audiences.

Two recent pieces of industry-inspired research report some tantalizing information. For the past four consecutive years more time has been spent listening, by those people who tune in to commercial radio, than is spent watching commercial television. On average, radio is listened to for two hours a week more than TV is watched (22 hours, 25 minutes as opposed to 20 hours, 7 minutes). The greatest difference in time spent is with the 18-39 age groups. Adelaide radio listeners spend more time with the medium than listeners in any other Australian city.[2]

More interestingly, a recent report suggests that radio is not used merely for background noise (or as wallpaper, as the industry terms it), although it probably is on stations which concentrate on music output. But talk and news stations 'out-perform music stations in attention levels' of audiences. According to the report, over 50 per cent of the audience to two Sydney talk stations listen 'very carefully' to programmes[3] and news bulletins.

Given the above, there is considerable point in studying the ways in which this most ubiquitous of media deals with a nuclear issue. I shall analyse transcripts from the major commercial network (Macquarie) and from the national network (ABC).

8.3 THE DEFINITION OF EVENTS IN NEWS REPORTS

The blockade was a peaceful protest for the entire period except for minor scuffles and for several incidents which took place on one particular day. There were, however, many arrests; virtually all those arrested were charged with 'failing to cease loitering'—an accumulation of implicit negatives requiring a marked degree of semantic processing.

All this, of course, was of little media interest since there were few sensational events to play up and dramatize, and this was reflected in the radio reports. The following news segments are good samples of the kinds of reports offered to the nation:

ABC News Broadcast
Introduction
Reader: In the latest confrontation at Roxby Downs, 26 anti-nuclear protesters have been arrested in a non-violent demonstration at the Olympic Dam uranium mine. About 300 protesters marched on the mine shaft this afternoon and were accompanied by a large force of police and security men. The ABC's Peter Lewis was there.

Actualité
[Live recording of protesters chanting at police. Police superintendent requests them to leave otherwise they will be 'subject to arrest'.]

Report
Lewis: And with those words the arrests began outside the mineshaft at Roxby Downs. The anti-uranium demonstrators had marched about a kilometre from their forward base camp. Their object was to prevent the afternoon day shift reaching the mine. Police had formed an impressive cordon around the mine area which is completely barbed-wire-enclosed. At the main gate there were a number of the South Australian mounted police contingent. Behind the gate, heavy mine machinery and members of the Roxby management services private security force. There was no struggle from the demonstrators as the police led them away.

The gist of this report is that protesters were arrested for attempting to prevent work at the mine site and the incidents were peaceful. The broadcast, however, makes much more of it than this. The news introduction, which possesses a similar function to headlines in newspapers, highlights selected facts and prepares the audience for the more detailed report. But it is much more than a précis of the reported facts; rather it is the initial structure within which the listener's knowledge will be framed. In effect, the structuring of the actual report has determined the nature of the introduction, rather than the introduction presenting the main facts of the event. Although there was no violence in the blockade, the introduction nevertheless predefines the event for the listener by means of a lexical choice that assigns the event to the conceptual domain of conflict: 'In the latest confrontation . . .'. This prepositional phrase is placed in a marked theme (or 'topic') position: it is what the rest of the utterance is about. It is also old or given information—that is, it is the assumed basis for receivers of the message. Interestingly, there is also a prepositional phrase at the unmarked position in this sentence, which gives more specific information about the initial one, including the fact that the demonstration was 'non-violent'. This cancels the possible implication that the 'confrontation' WAS violent, but the cancellation is placed in a non-prominent position. The prominence of the 'confrontation' concept is somewhat reinforced by the lexical choices 'marched on' and 'large force'.

The general tone of the section is one of action in which the energy is supplied, implicitly, by the protesters. Conversely, the police appear to have little or no active role. In part this effect arises because the demonstrators (in the second sentence) are the theme or topic (rather than the police) in subject position. A consequence is the use of the passive construction (also in the first sentence), which allows the agents of the action expressed by the verb to be linguistically backgrounded or entirely deleted: 'protesters were accompanied by a large force of police', 'protesters have been arrested'.[4] A further step in such attenuations occurs in the report section with the nominalization of the verb *arrest*: 'arrests began'.

When the reporter-on-the-spot picks up the story, he uses the conventional radio technique of inserting an 'actualité' segment as introduction to his own composed and 'placed' comments. The 'actualité' item performs two functions in radio news-reporting. First, it brings the far near, and thereby imparts a sense of reality. Secondly, it conflates the past and the present, and in the sound of immediacy represents the tensions of experience as SHARED experience between reporter and audience.

The chanting of active protesters partially drowning out the measured requests of the police is selected to suggest the unruly nature of the event, with the police taking no active role, even in their own verbalizations: the protesters will be 'subject to arrest'. Lewis then continues his report in the vocabulary of control and containment. It is a clever linguistic structure because it does the next best thing to a report on violence—it presents the threat of violence. The key words seem to be:

Demonstrators	*Police, security forces and site*
marched	formed an impressive cordon
prevent	is completely barbed-wire-enclosed
forward base camp	were a number of the South Australian mounted police contingent

was no struggle from   heavy mine machinery
private security force
led away

The tension in this section of the report is between predominantly active demonstrators and the solidity of the police and their allies as agents of containment. The final sentence in Lewis's report encapsulates the 'ideological ambience' of the complete news segment. 'There was no struggle' is both declaration and surprise. What gives this remark point and makes a conclusion is precisely its frustration of an expectation—that demonstrators are normally violent, as indeed the linguistic choices used to describe their actions also suggest. In terms of general awareness of cultural and political realities, the news message implies that protesting is illegitimate.

The main commercial station in Adelaide broadcasts predominantly talk and news. Its reports from Roxby were not so tendentious as those of the national network but when there were off-days in news drama its reporter made a related, if slightly different, ideological frame for his audience.

Studio Reader
Twenty eight people are now appearing in court at the small South Australian opal mining town, Andamooka, after being arrested yesterday at the Olympic Dam uranium mine. Graham Warburton reports:

On-site Reporter
The Buffalo Lodge is the closest thing Andamooka has to a town hall. Last Saturday night, Buff's Hall, as the locals call it, was a wedding reception centre. Today, it's a court house. A magistrate has travelled 300 kms. from Port Augusta to hear the charges against 28 people of 40 arrested in yesterday's protest action at the mine. Most were charged with 'failing to cease loitering', the least serious charge on the Statute. One, however, is charged with assault. The 28 were released from custody last night in order to return for today's court appearances. For them, it's a little like being in the enemy's camp. Many of the people in Andamooka, who call themselves opal miners, are really unemployed. Some of the others have jobs at the uranium mine, their first full-time work, in many cases, for more than 2 years. Some, including those who are sitting watching outside Buff's Hall, today, hope to get jobs at Roxby Downs.

This report, presented as a local-colour item, is a juxtaposition of the familiar-normal and the disruptive-alien. It is done in four phases. The first phase is the three introductory sentences of the on-site report where the homely past is contrasted with the present—from wedding reception (shared feelings and celebration) to court house (accusation and retribution). The second phase extends the abnormality of the situation with the announcement of the magistrate having travelled a long distance to preside at the improvised courtroom, all brought about by the protesters' action at the mine. The third phase elaborates the news headline and provides the legal facts of the bulletin. The final phase reverts to the local setting and the abnormal, illegitimate nature of the blockaders' intrusion: the implication is that they are enemies who contribute to preventing willing workers from gaining employment.

In both of the above 'bad news days' the startling thing is that both reporters have chosen to create an ideological picture rather than to present listeners with an account of, say, the background to the dispute; or interviews with blockaders' leaders and mine representatives; or a review of the nuclear-fuel issue using overseas evidence and experience; or the 'local colour' of the American military communications base fifty miles away. In addition to these omissions, the protesters are placed in adversary roles at the immediate, local level rather than as representatives of a much wider movement expressing another assessment of the world.

On one day, the protesters drove a number of vehicles through the wire fence and 'bounced' a number of police cars in the only incidents during the whole protest that bordered on the violent. Predictably, the radio and television reports provided dramatic coverage of the events in which the central issues were buried in righteous outcry against violent means. More significant was the way both stations followed up the reporting of the incidents. In each case, the discussion format was used in studio interviews and the range of debate was unusually wide and varied considering the nature of the violence used in the blockade. I shall discuss three sections of radio talk, in some detail, because on the one hand they represent important methods for suggesting general cultural judgements, and on the other indicate how the nuclear protest movement grates on raw nerves in the communications establishment.

8.4 CONTROL OF TOPIC IN INTERVIEWS AND DISCUSSIONS

All the transcripts are from morning shows (9.00-12.00) and both programmes between them receive the largest proportion of the morning audience, age 18-50 years. The first segment is from the national network and represents a serious 'backgrounder' to the events mentioned above.

ABC Programme Hosts (H_1, H_2) and Roxby Spokesman (R)

R   The protesters represent many diverse groups and, unfortunately, despite what they say, some of them do espouse violence as a means of achieving their ends.

H_1 But many are very caring people, aren't they? And this, I imagine, is the problem for you—that whether or not we agree with their stance, they—you know—certainly feel very strongly about this and feel very sincerely for the future and for the future welfare of their children. It's a difficult thing for you to—it has to be handled with great delicacy, obviously.

R   Indeed. I'm sure there are many of them who do sincerely hold these views and indeed I'm sure there's a percentage of them who do sincerely believe in the non-violence concept. Unfortunately, one cannot be sure that all of them adhere to those sorts of conditions. But, yes, I would agree there are some who feel strongly about this—they're entitled to those views of course—but I believe they should respect the views of others and the rights of others, which is the norm in our community. [...]

But I think this protest will have its day and it will pass by and we'll get back to work—you know, that's the kind of work we want to do, to bring this tremendous development into operation.

H₁ How are you going to keep the lid on [the protest] though?

R Oh, I think it's a question of surviving it. I'm sure they will go away after a period of time.

H₂ Any idea about the period of time?

R Well. They have said that they will be up there for a period of seven or nine days and they'll seek to maintain a presence there, afterwards.

H₂ What's the point if they're only going to be there for seven to nine days?

R Indeed. I think that supports this issue that it's being done primarily as a political issue, to beat up some enthusiasm for their cause. I think they will indulge in these activities and perhaps escalate it on a daily basis—to maintain.

H₂ —to bring in fresh protesters.

R Maybe bring in fresh protesters or attempt some new activity which captures the media cameras. If they do this for the seven days they will have achieved the political attention which they aim to get. Now, whether they have any real influence on the electorate at large, whether they have any real influence on the significant political parties, is very much a moot question.

H₂ Being such a minority, it seems to me that it's a pointless exercise.

R I think it is. I think they are out of touch with what the majority of the Australian people feel.

H₂ —and how the [state] government feels.

R —and how the government feels. But, I think the majority of people will watch television coverage, for example, and they will make judgements about the kind of people they are and what their objectives are and the methods they will use. And I have a lot of confidence in the electorate at large. They'll judge these people for what they really are.

H₁ What do you think they really are?

R I think they represent a coalition of many minority groups. We see many faces up there that were at the Franklin river exercise.

H₁ But that's not a bad thing in itself, is it? To be concerned about major issues.

R Oh no. There's nothing wrong with being concerned. I would suggest that perhaps the silent majority became a bit more actively concerned rather than giving passive acceptance or passive support for some issues. You know, I have no argument about them being involved in these exercises, but it *is* often the same faces that one sees at one protest after another.

H$_2$ Are you suggesting, John, that maybe they're professional protesters?

R I've heard them called that. I think that there are people, by their political views etc., who find it appropriate and suitable to take part in these activities.

H$_2$ So, it doesn't matter what the issue is, so long as there's something to protest about.

R Well, some may be in that category—I'm not suggesting they're all in that category. I'm not suggesting that they don't sincerely hold those views but I think there are a number of people to whom the concept of protest is an interesting one and one that satisfies their views as opposed to the majority of people who are less active.

H$_2$ I'm intrigued to hear you say that some of the faces are familiar from the Franklin Dam issue and have now transferred their attention to Roxby. They would seem to be two separate issues.

R I think they are separate, too. And of course they might be people who feel strongly on both issues. But I make the point that they *are* the same faces.

H$_2$ Interesting.

Two general points are worth noting. It is the industry representative, not CANE's, who is accorded special treatment in having detailed opinion solicited; and he is provided with relaxed and supportive conditions of the studio discussion, not an *in situ* interview of the type chosen earlier in the day for one of the protesters (national AM news programme).

The discussion is an extraordinary piece of complicity on the part of the radio hosts. Although H$_1$ tries to act as the fair-minded spokesman for the serious-minded public, his brief is not to search out the issues but to indicate the many-layered complexity of the issue—for the Corporation! He provides the company with a human face—'[it is a] problem FOR YOU'; 'it's a difficult thing FOR YOU'; 'it has to be handled with great DELICACY' (emphasis added). His other questions gently probe the company man to explain what he stands for without in any way forcing the nuclear issue.

H$_2$ is obviously contemptuous of the protesters. He regards them as irrelevant ('a pointless exercise'), sinister ('bring in fresh protesters'), troublemakers ('professional protesters'), and as shallow activists ('it doesn't matter what the issue is, so long as there's something to protest about').

Apart from the opening comment in the sequence when R makes the strong link between protest and violence, the nuclear industry has no need to present a case because the hosts trivialize the issue through making the discussion an evaluation of motives of the protesters. Their questions give R wide scope for fully generalizing the protest movement as a coalition of psychological types ('the concept of protest . . . satisfies their views'), political agitators ('[it is] a political issue to beat up some enthusiasm for their cause'), a deluded minority ('they are out of touch with what the majority of the Australian people feel'), and violent activists. As presented, it is a bizarre mix and serves to justify the interspersed contempt of H_2.

R is allowed to make most of the text in this discussion and he dominates the proceedings largely by his oblique rhetorical style. In the absence of any hard pressure about the nature of his industry and the potential role which the uranium could play in weapons development, he is able to indulge his urbane method unhindered. The method depends in large part on subtle modalization, as exemplified in the following:

(i) Expressions of certainty, and predictions:
Oh, no. There's nothing wrong with being concerned.
They'll judge these people for what they really are.
I'm sure they will go away after a period of time.

(ii) The use of 'I think', which in general seems to imply authoritative rationality:
I think that supports the issue that it's being done primarily as a political issue.
I think they are out of touch with what the majority of the Australian people feel.
I think it is [a pointless exercise].

(iii) The ambiguous use of the expression of certainty in various contexts implying qualifications or doubt, or carrying negative presuppositions:
I'm sure that there are many of them who do sincerely hold these views.
Yes, I would agree there are some who feel strongly about this.
I have no argument about them being involved in these exercises.

Overall, he presents himself as judicious, fair-minded, tolerant; qualities which the radio hosts have 'allowed' in their refusal to draw on central issues of the blockade.

The second programme transcript is from the commercial morning programme.

Commercial Radio Breakfast Programme (Station hosts: H_1, H_2)

H_1 We've had a reporter up there covering the demonstrations for the past week. He says the demonstrations are a pretty widely varying bunch of people covering a wide spectrum of the community, ranging from professional people with university degrees to professional demonstrators with apparently nothing much else to do. There are a few of *them* up there, too. Some of them spend their whole lives travelling round the country going from protest to protest. . . . Don't smile. It's true.

H_2 I don't doubt it for a moment. I mean . . . eh . . . er, I feel for them because there they are, able to go from issue to issue. What will happen, what's going to happen—they're sort of victims of their own integrity, if you like. As long as there's something to protest about, there's a reason to live but what are they going to do in later years—what are they going to do with their lives? They're professional protesters.

H₁ I do like that. 'Victims of their own integrity.' That's a good way of putting it.

H₂ They're trapped in their own integrity.

H₁ But they'll never run out of causes, will they? There's always going to be some causes—there's always something around—nothing's ever perfect.

One of the demonstrators is a lady called Sophie Hoburn. She's spent most of the past ten years fighting for various causes—for Aboriginal land rights; against logging in rain forests; against dams in Tasmania and now against uranium mining. She's originally from Adelaide. She says she's one of about 200 people in Australia who spend all their time fighting for the environment. Now, these are the people that you and I would call professional protesters. That makes her very angry. She's there with her two sons, 16 and 17. Our reporter Graham Warburton asked her why they were all there.

On-site interview

Sophie Hoburn: Basically, to help save the world from destruction. That's the simplest answer anyone can give. It's a matter of commitment, and usually a lot of unity that goes with it. Er—when unity's not there it's usually not successful. It takes a lot of commitment to come to these things. Usually, they are isolated, the conditions are harsh. It's not a matter of being a professional demonstrator, of somebody coming to have a brawl with the police but rather somebody who's committed to trying to save the earth for our children's future.

R What else would you do if you were not involved in this? Would you be satisfied?

S No, definitely not. I have tried stopping, and saying, 'Well, let someone else do it'. We're copping the brunt of the abuse all the time. Sometimes, through the media; sometimes through the police and other groups of people. If I wasn't doing this I'd probably be doing the same as everybody else, closing off their consciousness, what they know is right and just living for the all mighty dollar in the suburbs.

R What do you feel when people yell things at you like 'Why don't you get a job?'.

S [Amused] The whole unemployment situation today just shows ignorance on the part of a lot of people. This *is* a job. I'd like to see support from people, moral support rather than the abuse because I think we are the front-liners in this type of thing and we are acting out the consciousness of a lot of people who can't be here. I'd like to see those people support us in other ways. That helps us a lot.

R Do you ever think there's much point in doing it when most of the people don't appreciate what you are doing?

S Well, in the history of humanity it seems it's always been that small groups of people have made the changes for the larger majority to follow on. I think that Gandhi proved that—it's just the way that it's gone.

Cut to studio

H₂ Well, I can identify with people protesting against the destruction of little baby seals and whales and rain forests and the wilderness in Tasmania but that barren, bleak awful part of the world, with all their integrity in protesting, I just can't identify with them. I look at them; I know they mean well; I know that in their heart of hearts they have a good deal of dedication to their particular passion, but, gee, I can't identify with them.

H₁ It's not the environment that they're up there to protect, is it? That's just where the uranium happens to be. What they're protesting about is the use of nuclear energy which they say is not only unnecessary but eventually is going to kill us all.

H₂ Yeh. Well, let me see some doctors; let me see some scientists instead of a whole pack of trendies, or hippies.

H₁ They're not trendies; they're not hippies either—that's a by-gone era—they're their own types of people. I don't think you can put a label on them. Conservationists they would call themselves and I think they'd accept the term 'Greenies', too.

H₂ I think there's a great element of politics in it and fewer and fewer professional politicians seem to want to align themselves with them.

H₁ Helen Caldicott doesn't mind.

H₂ She's not a politician.

H₁ No. She's a highly-qualified woman and she supports these people.

H₂ Yeh. Well, I'd feel happier if there were fewer people walking around waving red flags—quite frankly—we'll take a time check.

This segment is an example of an increasingly-used format on commercial radio—the studio discussion, not with guests (although this is a popular method), but with members of the station staff. It is an important method of channelling audience attention to issues which the medium wishes to have discussed. It is another way of producing and adding to audience knowledge.

This commercial station consciously sees itself as a lively rival to the ABC and will often take up aspects of issues which the national network will not touch. This has occurred, here, where the 'protesting voice' and the alternative voice (see next segment) are given air-time to put their views. It is an unusual discussion because it develops three points of view. Host₁ introduces the discussion with the familiar trivialization of the issues as regards 'professional demonstrators'. The reference has more-than-usual sharpness in this instance because of the contrasting of 'professional people with university degrees' with 'professional demonstrators with nothing much else to do'. The qualification at the end only partially deflects the strong implication that they have no social value.

H₂ takes up the lead offered in his usual blunt style. He is the most successful talk-back host in Adelaide with a radio persona fully appreciated and understood by his regular listeners. It is aggressive, individualist, centred in the 'virtues' of private enterprise and risk-taking. He reinforces the judgements already made about the protesters but shifts the focus to individual pathology ('victims of their own integrity'), circumstances with which his audience, mostly female in the 30–50 age group, can be expected to have sympathy. The phrase he uses is mannered but it is sufficiently startling, for his programme, for the co-host to repeat it with marked approval, a discourse move designed to elicit a repetition.

This long introductory segment, then, developed as a relaxed dialogue, has signalled to the audience the radio assessment of the blockade and has done it in the most potent way possible for a mass audience—through trivialization and by an explanation of the commitment in terms of abnormal social pathology. Again, the central issues of health, weaponry, international politics are ignored.

The second phase in the programme is the interview with one of the protesters. H_1, in the biographical introduction, keeps the audience focused on the professional protest theme, before playing the taped interview from Roxby. Sophie Hoborn changes the rhythm of the discussion drastically. She obviously is not anyone's victim and her direct but sophisticated answers to trite questions take the studio hosts by surprise (they clearly had not troubled to listen to the tape before the programme). H_2 sees the danger immediately and indulges in a strange, mildly hysterical outburst in an attempt to keep his audience from settling on the new perspective just offered. His repeated 'I can't identify with . . .', placed as opening and closing statements are not merely reflections of his own perplexity but are directives to his regular listeners not to make the effort to identify.

H_1 understands the technique but has obviously been impressed with the Hoborn tape and in his next two statements takes his colleague to task, especially for his gratuitous description of the protesters as 'trendies'. H_1 now takes on a mild advocacy role for the blockade. H_2 will not allow this and he deliberately collapses the whole discussion by invoking the authority of the establishment on his side—'doctors', 'scientists', 'politicians'. His final exploitation of the 'Red scare' trick effectively prevents any further possibility for the introduction of sympathetic alternative views.

This transcript is a good example of the potential strength of the radio medium. Once an alternative voice is allowed there is always the potential for it to reach beyond the conventional, predictable net of attitudes. Here, one of the medium's representatives was affected and began to make 'wrong' messages. The discussion also graphically exposes the power of the medium to obliterate persuasive alternative visions of society. And given the nature of this medium it is language whose power is recruited to ensure conformity. Skilful performers, and H_2 is certainly that, use words consciously to try to structure audience feelings and apprehensions. His language is not the Nukespeak of the military but, with other voices of power and authority, he floods the daily streams of issues with words which evoke cultural reflexes, reflexes which prevent a flexing of new muscles of thought.

The third radio interview on the Roxby issue is something of a rarity in media documents because it is an unscripted discussion of the general principles by which news media work and it is also related to the Roxby issue. It illustrates an interesting reflexivity, not to say professional incestuousness.

The same commercial station as discussed above runs a regular breakfast programme in which current issues are discussed. Roxby would obviously be a choice for the programme but the novelty of the segment lies in the station's choice to allow another ('opposition') journalist from a public subscription FM station.[5] The transcript follows.

AM$_1$ Helen, I'm interested in your claim that media reports have been misleading. How have they been misleading?

FM Firstly, I don't think it's specifically my radio station but from the protesters in general. Morale up there is fairly good except when they read and listen to the mainstream media and feel they are being misrepresented. It is a non-violent action and the only violence that has occurred has been directed *at* protesters by Western Mining Personnel.

AM$_1$ So, what are you saying? That it's not as violent as the press is saying it is?

FM I believe this is the case. For instance, in a lot of the news on television there's been coverage of where a policeman was hit by protesters' cars. The point is, Western Mining had blockaded *us* on a public access road and we wanted to get our vehicles through. We pushed our cars round the obstacles in the road itself and as we were pushing the cars around one of them got on to an embankment, police were standing in its path. No one was driving the car at this stage so a protester jumped in to try to stop it [moving down the embankment] but unfortunately one of the police was hit and bruised. That protester was arrested.

AM$_1$ Yeh. There's two sides to every story.

AM$_2$ Helen. Good morning. This is Murray Nichol, from the News-room. Were you at Roxby for 5MMM? [the FM station.]

FM No. I am opposed to uranium mining and am concerned about the situation arising around the world with the nuclear weapons build up.

AM$_1$ So you were up there as a protester yourself?

FM Yes. But I did some reporting for a number of alternative radio stations throughout the country.

AM$_2$ Yeh. I'm interested in that because I heard you say, 'The blockade *we* had . . .'. Now, how can you objectively report when you're personally involved and when that's your prime reason for being there? And, furthermore, from that vantage point, how can you criticize reporters who are up there doing nothing *but* reporting on it?

FM All angles of the action have to be looked at and one of the important aspects is that of the protesters themselves. Being a protester myself, I am more involved in the real reason why we're here, which is to stop uranuim mining.

AM₁ Yes, but you see that in itself is subjective news reporting. That's the argument I have with the whole criticism of what's being said up there. I can assure you that this radio station has no interest at all in giving biased reporting of the events. Why should we? We have no flags to fly.

AM₃ Can I interrupt? Paul Roberts in the News-room. It's an interesting question by Murray. The whole question of objectivity in reporting comes in because obviously everyone has their own biases at some stage or other. I don't believe anybody can be totally objective. You're influenced by your beliefs in the sorts of stories you follow; your approach; and who you approach even if it's unconscious. No one can be totally unbiased. Er. I'm just arguing whether you can be totally objective and I don't think you can.

AM₁ Well, I certainly can see that I could be totally objective and I'm sure that Graham Warburton, from our News-room, is being totally objective from Roxby Downs.

AM₃ Oh, I'm not saying that the reports are biased on our station. I don't think they are. I think we've been balanced.

AM₁ Good.

AM₃ But at the same time I don't think that anyone can say, totally truthfully, that they are totally objective about everything.

AM₁ I'll give a time-call, here. It's 16 past 7. Paul, go to your room!

FM Could I just interrupt? Our criticism is against mainstream media in general. The blockaders feel that a meal is being made out of what can be interpreted as violence whereas it is specifically a non-violent, civil disobedience protest.

AM₂ Well, what word do you use for shoving cars around and scuffling? You see, protesters always see that the violence is directed against them, but it's my experience and I've had considerable experience in demonstrations, that they frequently go out of their way to get it. And I'm sure you'll agree, as a demonstrator yourself, that there is an element involved in those demonstrations, and it's a minority, that go out of their way to seek trouble that will attract headlines and pictures on TV and radio reports. Now, I'm sure that you won't deny that.

FM The interesting point there is that, when we say non-violent we don't necessarily mean picking cars up and moving them out of the way.

AM₁ Oh, that's non-violent.

FM We mean, that nobody gets hurt. We don't want violence towards personnel.

AM$_1$ But do you agree with Murray that there are certain elements that go for violence because they know that it's going to get them on TV and in the paper?

FM This may well occur in a number of demonstrations but from what I've seen among the blockaders up there, I don't think there are any heroes up there.

AM$_1$ But are there people up there who are trying to get their name in the paper and on television by being violent?

FM I don't believe that's the case. I think that if there are people trying to get notice in the media then they tend to volunteer to be arrested and I think it's commendable that people are prepared to be arrested for a belief that they feel so strongly about.

The broad issue of journalistic objectivity is a complex one and cannot be discussed in this essay but the issue clearly is important in this transcript because it is another factor which creates ambiguity for the listening audience. An alternative version of some of the events is given and therefore offers the possibility for a widening of the Roxby blockade to issues of the roles of the police and security personnel, the possibilities of censorship (a word not even mentioned) and the other matters which FM raises. But all these are ignored in favour of professional protestations of integrity. Although dissension is allowed to develop between AM$_1$ and AM$_3$, the host (AM$_1$) has the power to control and cut off dissenting discourse, and it is he who attempts to catch the audience. His admonition to AM$_3$ is only semi-jocular (AM$_3$ in fact does not come back in this segment after being told to 'go to his room'), and however the members of the audience actually interpret the interchange, it still leaves the possibility for levels of doubt about the news. If AM$_3$ is correct, then the protesters' criticisms cannot be totally rejected; if AM$_1$ is correct then the station's reports must be accepted as accurate and therefore mainstream media can still be relied upon. Either way, the specific FM/protester viewpoints are side-stepped. The ensuing effort to negotiate the meaning of *violence* is in itself an interesting case of the political determination of word meaning. It is a significant ideological clash, but it is also a discourse move on the part of AM$_1$, who, together with his power to formulate the questions and terminate any exchange, is able to use it in order to continue the avoidance of anti-nuclear arguments.

The radio texts above strongly suggest that this increasingly important mass medium has taken on the role of cultural censor. CANE's explanations of the link between uranium and weaponry; the lack of foolproof safety procedures and the danger to workers' health; the historical relationship between peaceful uranium mining and nuclear weapons (the Canadian and Indian Governments' dispute in the mid-1970s is usually cited); the inevitability of some of the ore being used in weaponry; and the temptation to future Australian governments to use an industrial asset for its own defence industry: all these factors have been consistently ignored and have gone unreported.

The discussions and reports which I have examined in this essay illustrate how difficult it is for a non-establishment, alternative voice to get its views broadcast even when relatively generous air-time and general coverage is allotted to specific events. The energy which this mainstream medium devoted to trivializing the blockade, to questioning the credibility of protesters, and to personalizing the issue in narrow ways rather than extending the scope of the mine blockade into varied coverage aimed at community enlightenment, represents another disgraceful example of media's informal complicity in Nukespeak—in the Australian case, a muted, near-silent one.

But all this does not mean that each member of the listening audience would have interpreted or received the cultural messages in the ways that I have. In this sense, it is impossible to prove 'media-effect'; the variousness of experience in the different groups which compose the audience ensures this. However, since Current Affairs and News Radio are a language-medium above all else and given that much of the significant material in this case study has involved conversations, albeit in structured interview form, work in conversational analysis should provide a way of clarifying the nature of audience reception. Given talk radio's[6] affinity with the day-to-day conversational experience of listeners, an examination of the above radio texts in terms of discourse coherence should provide suggestive clues, at least, for the way audiences may have received the messages in the Roxby issue. I want now to give some informal indications of the peculiar features of radio discourse.

A basic element in conversational practice is in the initial 'move' and how this is received by the respondents. If the respondent does not accept the move, then the topic has to be reformulated or the topic must be changed altogether, so that a further initiating move has to be made. The opening of the ABC interview quoted above (p. 152) illustrates this:

R(a) The protesters represent many diverse groups and, unfortunately, despite what they say, some of them do espouse violence as a means of achieving their ends.

H$_1$ [But many are very caring people, aren't they?]$_1$; [And this, I imagine, is the problem for you—that whether or not we agree with their stance, they—you know—certainly feel very strongly about this and feel very sincerely for the future and for the future welfare of their children. It's a difficult thing for you to—it has to be handled with great delicacy, obviously]$_2$.

R(b) Indeed. I'm sure there are many of them who do sincerely hold these views and indeed I'm sure there's a percentage of them who do sincerely believe in the non-violent concept.
[Unfortunately, one cannot be sure that all of them adhere to those sorts of conditions. But, yes, I would agree there are some who feel strongly about this—they're entitled to those views of course—but I believe they should respect the views of others and the rights of others, which is the norm in our community.]$_3$
[But, I think this protest will have its day and it will pass by and we'll get back to work—you know, that's the kind of work we want to do, to bring this tremendous development into operation.]$_4$

H₂   [How are you going to keep the lid on, though?]₅

Diagramatically, the exchange can be represented by Figure 8.1. This is an interesting example because it confirms the tendency in Radio's reporting of Roxby. Conversationally, it shows the power of the host, since if he does not accept the initiating move, he can change the focus of the topic. This is done firstly by rejecting R(a)'s reference to violence, then his hedging (indicated by the lack of smoothness in his statement and by the changes of expression in formulating his point), and the implication that he is taking a sympathetic stand towards the protesters. His reformulation is inexplicit ('it's a difficult thing for you to do'), but not so much that R needs to jettison his argument: R(b) accepts [. . .]₂ with 'Indeed . . . indeed', etc. There is still room for him to make his point, and he extends the topic, having 'read' the early non-acceptance and ambiguity as a warning gambit. He does so in [. . .]₃, signalling his reformulation with 'Unfortunately' and 'But . . . but'. However, he later shifts to a new topic opened by 'But' in [. . .]₄, whereupon he is met with another non-accepting reply [. . .]₅, one which returns to the initial topic, a move here signalled by 'though'.

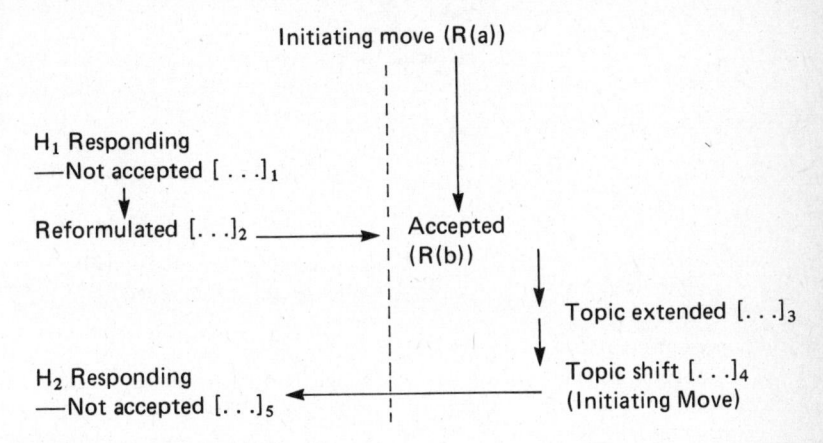

```
                     Initiating move (R(a))
                              │
                              │
                              ▼
H₁ Responding
  —Not accepted [. . .]₁
        │
        ▼
  Reformulated [. . .]₂ ─────────▶  Accepted
                                    (R(b))
                                       │
                                       ▼
                                   Topic extended [. . .]₃
                                       │
                                       ▼
H₂ Responding                      Topic shift [. . .]₄
  —Not accepted [. . .]₅  ◀────    (Initiating Move)
```

Figure 8.1

What we have is a dialogue marked by latent interpersonal conflict, to which the topic-switching is related, within a textually coherent framework. For the radio audience, the discourse represents low-level drama. This is perhaps typical for interview situations. However, given the regular audience for these kinds of programes, the fact of the host's implied support for the Roxby position (even if feigned for radio effect) has its own cultural force.

The above pattern is repeated very closely in other sections of that interview. It is likely that the conversational conflicts and topic-shifts sharpen listening attention. There is an important segment in the first commercial network conversation, quoted above, which follows the pattern just described and develops types of discourse acts in this type of exchange that are certainly facilitated by the medium and may be characteristic of it.

H_2a [Well, I can identify with people protesting against the destruction of little baby seals and whales and rain forests and the wilderness in Tasmania but that barren, bleak, awful part of the world, with all their integrity in protesting, I just can't identify with them. I look at them; I know they mean well; I know that in their heart of hearts they have a good deal of dedication to their particular passion but, gee, I can't identify with them.]$_1$

H_1a [It's not the environment that they're up there to protect, is it? That's just where the uranium happens to be.]$_2$ [What they're protesting about is the use of nuclear energy which they say is not only unnecessary but eventually is going to kill us all.]$_3$

H_2b [Yeh. Well, let me see some doctors; let me see some scientists instead of a whole pack of trendies or hippies.]$_4$

H_1b [They're not trendies. They're not hippies, either—that's a by-gone era.]$_5$ [They're their own types of people. I don't think that you can put a label on them. Conservationists they could call themselves and I think they'd accept the term 'Greenies', too.]$_6$

H_2c [I think there's a great element of politics in it and fewer and fewer professional politicians seem to want to align themselves with them.]$_7$

H_1c [Helen Caldicott doesn't mind.]$_8$

H_2d [She's not a politician.]$_9$

H_1d [No.]$_{10}$ [She's a highly qualified woman and she supports these people.]$_{11}$

H_2e [Yeh. Well I'd feel happier if there were fewer people walking around waving red flags—quite frankly]$_{12}$—[We'll take a time check.]$_{13}$

Broadly we can represent the moves made here as illustrated in Figure 8.2. There is a certain consciousness about this exchange, indicated by the sudden move from refusal to apparent acceptance which occurs (H_1c). Before that, H_1 had refused H_2's moves. Obviously, for the refusals to continue would endanger the whole exchange so he accepts the next two moves, even though one is a refusal of one of his own statements, presumably in order to keep the exchange going as required by the medium, which in this sense tends to encourage consensus. His expansions and reformulations make this possible. Unfortunately, for his argument, H_1, at point [. . .]$_6$, may appear to contradict his position at [. . .]$_2$. But H_2 does not pursue that possibility; instead he quickly shifts the topic at [. . .]$_7$ into areas which relate to his original thematic interpretations— the social and political marginalization of the protest. With time running out, H_1 has little option but to accept this, allowing H_2 to return (by means of his 'Yeh. Well . . .') to a particular theme, which then gains a final stressed position in the interview. That message in [. . .]$_{12}$ is then marked for the listening audience by radio's unique contribution to conversational practice—the ability to use the technology of the medium to force closure. H_2 invokes the time-check and terminates the segment. Again, the textual coherence and continuity is

H_1		H_2	
(H_1a)	Responding— Not accepted [. . .]$_2$ Expansion of original theme of interview [. . .]$_3$	(H_2a)	Initiating move [. . .]$_1$
		(H_2b)	Responding—Topic reformulated [. . .]$_4$
(H_1b)	Refusal— Loop to Expansion of (1a) [. . .]$_5$ Reformulation [. . .]$_6$	(H_2c)	Topic-shift [. . .]$_7$
(H_1c)	Accepts topic—Expands by counter example [. . .]$_8$	(H_2d)	Refuses example [. . .]$_9$
(H_1d)	Accepts refusal [. . .]$_{10}$ Reformulates [. . .]$_{11}$	(H_2e)	Topic-shift. Loop to expansion of original interview theme [. . .]$_{12}$
			Closure [. . .]$_{13}$

Figure 8.2

maintained as required by the medium (silence in the literal sense being unallowable). A minor drama is played out in an interpersonal conflict, which ends in resolution (of a kind) and in a final message provided for by the expectations within the programme genre. What is not probably perceived by audiences, however, is that the drama is essentially a struggle for topic in which the dominant speaker has peculiar power. It is in such ways that oppositional voices can be 'silenced'.

I have been able to use only a tiny proportion of the total number of radio documents devoted to the Roxby mine, but they are all of a piece and vividly illustrate the way a mass medium can culturally MANAGE dissent, without resorting to draconian measures. It is a subtle business because, whilst an alternative view of the world is suppressed, such information management also 'suppresses' Nukespeak. The result is a large part of a community held in thrall to ignorance.

NOTES

1. The mine's location is 50 miles away from the Joint Defence Space Communications Station at Nurrungai, operated by the United States Air Force. CANE constantly attempts to make this clear because of the potential link that Roxby could have in provision of material for nuclear arms. Nurrungai is a relay station for (i) Programme 647 satellites, which give early warning of Soviet missile launchings; (ii) 'Big Bird' satellites, which identify Soviet missile silos and other targets; and (iii) 'Rhyolite' satellites, which monitor Soviet and Chinese military telecommunications.
2. Radio Marketing Bureau, *The Time People Spend with Commercial Air Media*, FARB, Sydney (1983).

3. Radio 2GB, Sydney, *The Foreground Factor* (1983).
4. Obviously readers have the cultural knowledge to supply the agent when deleted; the point here is the degree of prominence in utterance. On similar cases, see Trew's 1978 and 1979 analysis.
5. This type of station is run on low budgets with mostly volunteer workers and is regarded as 'alternative radio'.
6. See Higgins and Moss (1982).

9 Disintegrating narrative: an analysis of the television film *The Day After*

Peter Jeffery and Michael O'Toole
Murdoch University, Western Australia

9.1 INTRODUCTION

We should make clear at the start that the puns carried by the participle in our title are deliberate. The film *The Day After* is both a narrative that itself disintegrates and that disintegrates the world it has represented. In studying the narrative structures of the film we shall ourselves be involved in deconstructing or disintegrating its narrative techniques and film language.

One of the most heated ideological debates in the 1970s and 1980s concerns the validity and role of such concepts as 'the individual' and 'society'. A prominent exponent of individualism as a national philosophy is, of course, the United States, where paradoxically it is maintained via such major SOCIAL institutions as church, university, hospital, boards of trade and attendant stock exchanges, railway and highway systems, television and radio networks, and, of course, military bases. As Foucault's work on the development of key social institutions so convincingly demonstrates,[1] the hegemony[2] of such institutions is established in both socialist and capitalist systems because of the emergence and advancement of nation states through industrial superstructuring. These then find expression in the representational systems of the culture. In the American context the pivot which allows the balancing of the contradiction of 'individual' and 'society', both in the system itself and in its cultural representations, is the nuclear family. Since each member of the nuclear family carries the couplet of the individual's prename and the family of patriarchal group surname, the person's identity and loyalties can be enlisted in either direction.

If we are to view *The Day After* as a disintegrating narrative, we are assuming integrated narrative as the norm. Indeed, the fundamental and ever-reassuring pattern of normal narrative moves from a disequilibrium, a period of threatened stability, back into a concluding return to equilibrium, a consolidation of integration of society, through the efforts of individual heroes at the point of crisis and seeming collapse. *The Day After* argues that the atomic holocaust will be apocalyptic and that society will not be able to reconstitute itself, because the individuals—if they survive—will have no capacity to reintegrate or reidentify. Hence, despite the normal priorities of TV networks and the culturally received patterns of narrativity, the film's makers risked experimenting with the unpopular mode of a disintegrating narrative. Indeed, the unpopularity of this unusual mode was clearly not lost on the sponsors who avoided all possible ad-spots in the last 80 minutes, whereas they had fully subscribed to the 'normal' pattern in the first half of the telemovie.

Many critics responded to the nation-wide presentation by deriding the narrative pattern as being embarrassingly simplistic and over-predictable because of the mundanity of family and individual representations, derived from the stereotypes of television soap opera. If, however, the normal practice of American politics is hegemonic, as we are claiming, then it is perhaps foolish or idealistic to assume that a text created by one of the top American networks will be radical in form or content, and perhaps the most that should be expected is a reformist progressive text. In its elementary deconstruction of the American way of life, *The Day After* asks 'Is anyone listening?' as the final credits roll over a windswept darkness—a reminder of the appeal to the consensual mode that brought about the end of American involvement in Vietnam and, earlier, the beginnings of racial integration in high schools by repeated exposure through news on the television networks. The film draws us into its crucial ideological shift not through a dramatic conversion, but rather by exploiting earlier common-sense, taken-for-granted conventions for representing the American way of life. This involves a gentler readjustment of the hegemony. Many more radical and extremist texts abound elsewhere, and these may have been formative in reshaping consciousness amongst community leaders and activist groups, but their general effectiveness is diminished by lack of access to the network, or by the severity of the demands they are making on relatively conservative audiences.

Further, normal critical practice in capitalist countries assumes an idealist aesthetic predominantly concerned with innovatory techniques, complexity or elegance of plot structure, psychological consistencies of characters or actors in the televisual narrative, and the like. If the practice were more concerned with contextual or socially conjunctural descriptions, then critics would adopt different criteria for evaluation and these would reflect the aesthetics of the general audience rather than that of an élite. By these new criteria, the effectiveness of *The Day After* would be measured by audience reception and resultant social action, especially in relation to an event in which one of the highest national television audiences participated. This in turn would have led to direct shifts in State Department public-relations statements and interactions. It could have affected, amongst other factors, the platforms of presidential candidates.

Commenting on the effectiveness of public manifestations such as antinuke marches, Hodge (cf. also the Birmingham Centre for Contemporary Cultural Studies) has argued (in Chapter 7) that it ultimately resides in their transformation into media events and attendant critical commentaries. *The Day After* was a national media event with progressive aims and brought into being by considerable resources normally jealously guarded by the Establishment, so its broadcast must be seen as a direct presentation of the nuclear debate in contrast to the modalization and transformation of other public anti-nuclear events, such as rallies or protest marches. This was made quite explicit in all the pre-announcements which invited extensive public discussion, even proposing that children be allowed to watch the film only if adults were there to discuss it with them.

In short, it is our contention that *The Day After* is usefully analysed as a progressive text grounded in normal television conventions, but that it denies the reaffirmative qualities of normal narrative conventions by exploiting a pattern in order to disintegrate it. This in turn requires a positive social action to deny such a realistic and culturally anxious message. Accordingly, the seemingly predictable patterns of the American way of life that *The Day After* assembles, in its early episodes, are best understood as deliberately commonplace structures and representations of countless televisual narratives, so that the ultimate disintegration begins to question the certitudes that producers and audiences conventionally utilize to understand America. The film's effectiveness, then, does not reside in the originality of its aesthetics (though, as we shall see, a case could be argued for the firestorm sequence), but rather in the resonances it has with the normal network audience and its ability to set these on edge, to make them friable and hence allow for ideological and social shift.

9.2 VISUAL SYNTAGMS AND COLLAPSING PARADIGMS

In line, then, with the epic quality of its theme—the destruction of America—the opening sequence of *The Day After* asserts a hegemonic and harmonious paradigm of institutions to make a seemingly unquestionable and complete 'syntagm' of American reality. From the 'omniscient' viewpoint of a fast, low-flying aircraft (silent helicopter or Pan Am Airlines), the audience moves across America in a sequence arranged according to a cultural logic: from a moment of wild forest concealing a large farm with proto-industrial layout of barns, sorting yards, dams, fields, tree lines and furrows, to nuclear weapons silos along a prairie rail-line matched by interstate highways that will ultimately lead to the city.

In a suspensory moment, that is none the less elided by the smoothness of the unfolding sequence, we are shown a corresponding paradigm of the elements of a small country township with its yellow church, its elementary suburbia and then a school bus that integrates the outlying farmsteads into some cohesive American whole—that of the American primary school system—so that we focus in on an internal shot of a primary school classroom with children sitting in a circular formation, for the informal but ideologically powerful grouping of story-telling and communal singing: a multicultural composition as behoves the greater America. In the disintegrating narrative, this cultural subset is recapitulated in the scene of 'skeletonization' (X-ray outlines of actors) before being vaporized in the ensuing fireblast sequence.

There is a tension here which seems to be relieved in the credits sequence by an apparently solitary cowboy riding down a single cattle-run on a lonely farm, but the pull-out of the zoom reveals that he is in a vast complex of such runs in a sales and marshalling yard, and the upward tilt of the camera finally indicates that the yards abut a fully developed megapolitan skyline—that of Kansas City. The interplay between fading pastoral and omnipresent industrial ushers in the next sequence: an assembly-line along which possibly natural juices or milk are pumped into plastic supermarket containers. Nature is being increasingly tamed for modern technological consumer society that is the real middle-America.

The camera continues its progress institutionally over a baseball diamond and university football stadium, showing the transformation of rural sports into nationally televised fixtures. When parklands follow, vouchsafed by the world of children, walking with their teacher in a comic crocodile line, or, more romantically, with young boys furiously pedalling cycles by ponds and through overhanging foliage, it all seems a nostalgic overlay of a memorialized past as with the plaques on seats and commemorative fountain systems. The truth emerges at the climax of this sequence with shots of the shift of commodities on the stock exchange boards at the Kansas City Board of Trade which range through the wheat, oats, soy-beans and soy-bean oil that had initially established the wild prairie or grasslands as prime agricultural land. The economic motor of America is perhaps already questioned by the counterpoint between the detached and untended phones of the stockbrokers and a small television screen with its unconsidered but omnipresent newscaster issuing moment-to-moment bulletins on this phenomenologically complex America from forestland through hamlet to major provincial cities.

However, what might read from a verbal description as a disjunct series of syntagms is actually rendered as a reassuringly sutured hegemony of expanding images of the Americas. The effect is achieved by the continuity of Virgil Thompson's musical score, by the cinematic device of dissolving between segments, and by the ever-present camera movement of onward progression through a continuous central zoom. Thus, even though we have indicated certain problematic subsets involving a tension between the stasis of country hamlet and the megalopolitan thrust of the industrial nation state, the sequentially unfolding nature of the cinematic medium belies those possible ruptures. Similarly, in the score from Virgil Thompson's 'The River' the individual moments of American provincial history are rendered as simple pastoral or folk melodies which yield to or are melded into the grandiose orchestral flourishes that bespeak the monolithic America.

The opening sequence, then, has been skilfully constructed, in line with a conventional consensus view of American hierarchy and unity in order to be deconstructed through parallel institutional chains, by a disintegrating narrative. That each following narrative segment is preceded by a recapitulatory excerpt of that opening sequence indicates an ironic sense in the film-makers, and makes what seemed an easily acceptable prologue a highly suspect and friable fictional construction, questioned by the diagnosis of the following sequential episodes.

If the prologue shows signs of careful construction in order to validate American institutions and Midwestern lifestyles, then the film proper sets out to construct with equal care the domains and institutions which create social and personal cohesion prior to the ultimate holocaust that disintegrates this America once and for all. The sites are predictable and range from family farms, military installations, university campuses, freeways, churches, hospitals, supermarkets and sports stadiums. The paradigmatic parallelism that will then obtain between sites already established and sites transformed into ongoing action-structures leads in turn to a conventionalized structuring of stability and collapse, easily read by a network audience. The correspondence of past and present views, however, is set on edge by the fact that all civilian sites are presented at an even narrative and camera pace against a much more rapid presentation of action in the military sphere, which carries to an ever-increasing degree a subcode of procedures that finally lead to civilian non-comprehension and the army's complete withdrawal from the action. Order is then represented as being kept—though deteriorating rapidly—by a rapidly constituted civilian guard reminiscent of the vigilantes of frontier America.

It is instructive, then, to contrast the first farm presented, which reveals the orderliness of a farmhouse, outbuildings and long lines of furrows cut by a tractor on a seeding run, with the slowly revealed army installation, a missile silo, helicopter and military trucks moving in and out of the security fences. Both farm and installation use fences for enclosure, but those of the farm are more generously and widely traced. And the ambiguous word *silo* implies an ironic pairing of the closed storage chamber, whose purpose is to conserve and nurture, with the open missile-housing, whose aim is destruction. A paradigmatic contrast is projected into the visual syntagm. Aboard the relief helicopter, which is flying in to exchange duty platoons, the soldiers are relaxed, still civilian and fresh from their suburban homes, chatting about domestic matters, reading the newspaper for its sports scores despite the alarmist headlines of impending East–West conflict. In the base a very different regime obtains: of code-books, of 'fail-safe' locks to be opened and closed, of clearly marked and numbered walkways and warning signals and notices. Thus, when the men in the helicopter land they adopt a 'scramble' pattern and run angularly, the camera using the cinematic register of 'hand-held' and unconventional placements to show their spasmodic and alienated behaviour pattern. The human-ness of the soldiers is only partially retrieved by the friendly but longing look of one black soldier pressed against the criss-cross wires of the base's perimeter, watching the farmer's wife and accompanying children patterned by the single strands of the clothes-line as they hang out the washing. Interestingly, the woman is rendered problematically as she awkwardly acknowledges the soldier's presence, as if she accepts the military presence with a reserve that prefers the autonomous harmony of a farming family and its peaceful agricultural pursuit.

Again the plenitude of the farm is illustrated by a cornucopia of food on the welcoming breakfast table for the hard-working farmer, and even emphasized by his forgoing the display to a domestically erotic response to his slip-clad wife and a good-humoured and musically footnoted escape to the upstairs bedroom, while the children ponder television and its own multi-channelled plenitude. The latter is, of course, technically rather than organically arranged, and provides a crucially premonitory and alienated sequence, which leads to the sterile plenitude of missile display when the final release buttons are pressed. As adult reviewers are mystified by the anti-language of military codes and behaviour, so, too, do the children fail to understand the contradictory discourse of the newscasters, interrupting whichever channel is summoned by their remote-control buttons to search for the normal domain of children's morning cartoon time. Hegemonically-minded, we as adult viewers note that the newscasters are multi-racial (some assurance of the pluralistic unity of the Americas), but we also cannot help noting the confusion on the networks which are normally the central and most reliable interpreters of events. Though the sequence ends with a climactic, frame-filling take-off of a huge Boeing, tilting upwards in a reassuring yet threatening dominance of the sky, and at that point of the narrative seemingly heralding a successful resolution of the crisis, that reassurance is completely cut away by the return to the farm several sequences later to see the impact of the detonated rockets.

Prior to the firestorms, then, we see the farmer on his tractor etched against his unending furrows and children in the fields reacting to the huge thrust of the rockets filling the silo and all its surrounds with billowing clouds of sterile vapour. The screen is again filled, but in an ever-diffuse way that collapses the remnants of formalized structure. It is rhetorically logical that from this point on in the narrative we do not return to the site of the first farm. The holocaust has erased it, and the military neighbours have gone underground, never to return to the audience's sight.

Interestingly, the domains of the military and the hospital (signalized as General Memorial with campus connections) are neither syntagmatically chained nor paradigmatically collapsed (except when a long line of male students undergo a medical inspection, which probably alludes to draft requirements in a state of national emergency). Indeed, television *habitués*, along with readers of romance novels and popular-science newspaper articles, still valorize the medical profession and its socially restorative functions. Though staffed by females, the hospital in *The Day After* is principally mediated by a patriarchal, didactic male WASP surgeon who is then flanked by a Japanese doctor (all American films on nuclear issues have a 'token Japanese', America's gesture of guilt for Hiroshima) and a glamorous white female nurse. The surgeon, Dr Oaks (strong and reliable as his name), functions as the central protagonist in the film and oscillates between solitary heroic individual, responsible citizen and teacher, and husband and father in a sophisticated bourgeois nuclear family. Though both the army and the hospital rely on rigorous patterns of discipline and esoteric language, it is only towards the end that the hospital codes itself into an inhuman scale for refusal of patients and finally acknowledges its ineffectuality in coping with, let alone curing, the social collapse.

Cinematically, the hospital is positively addressed with strong, uniform lighting that emphasizes white corridors, hygiene and efficiency; in tracking along with efficient medical practitioners, camera technique asserts purposeful, economic movement and procedures. Ironically, however, the sequence is introduced with a close-up of a medical X-ray photo and a didactic pointer by the hero doctor, who will later be rendered ineffectual and physically debilitated by radiation. The coldness of scientific explanation to a class of interns is immediately transformed into human response, when the chief doctors move through swinging doors—almost a fast, cutting editorial device—to examine the charts of a recovering patient to whom they speak in warm and encouraging terms. The *mise-en-scène* also carries the conventionalized, hence naturalized, artefacts of grateful social endowment, such as expensive indoor plants and donated paintings on the wall. Swift changes in costuming from casual jacket, formal suit, white hospital aprons and scrubbed hands into gloves show the easy confidence of the doctor and his sense of responsible and dignified social acceptance and initiative.

Following the blast, the hospital is presented in chiaroscuro, initially to simulate the fading power units with their abrupt moments of black-out, and to show an increasing smudging of textures in the anxious faces of the overworked nurses and doctors, haphazard patterns of bed-covering and arrangements, and a gradual but definite disordering of regularized behaviour and medical drills. The *mise-en-scène*, too, takes on a chaotic pattern of movements in the overcrowded corridors, contrasted with isolated moments, such as the scene in which a black orderly reassures a black woman patient as he wheels her on a trolley towards an operating theatre.

With the overwhelming flood of patients, the hospital's capacity is overstretched, so that the nearby campus with its basketball gym, hoops awry, becomes a staging camp and classification centre. These shots are strongly reminiscent of the celebrated sequence in *Gone with the Wind*, where wounded Civil War soldiers lie moaning as they are desultorily tended in a huge railway marshalling yard. The steady collapse is shown in altercations over access to hospital drugs and stores, so that the bureaucratic clerk is thrown against a wall and totally disregarded. Pessimistic images occur, such as the Japanese doctor finally admitting that his ministrations to a blast-blinded boy are cosmetic, and that the child might as well return to his family shelter as stay in the chaos. Such cameos humanize the final abdication of the control of health, when the hospital determines to admit only patients with radiation below a certain level; for all others medical help is pointless. As in modern military strategy, the hospital logistics are coded into an inhuman numerical scale.

With Dr Oaks himself, the text maintains a grudging continuity, for his loyal aides sustain him through the collapse of his domain, privileging him with scarce food, power for illumination, and even washing bowls, even though the water is dirty and cockroaches have emerged in the operating theatre. Despite these efforts, however, he is racked by spasmodic coughing, and finally collapses to be discharged himself from his site of social control and assurance. As he bounces on the back of a jeep to the ruins of his home, he witnesses the firing squads ministering death rather than the health of hospitals, an ironic reminder of the last self-defending instance of social control, even if its outcome is so totally sterile.

As Dr Oaks's institutionalized world in the hospital steadily disintegrates, the only continuity left in the hospital sequences is provided by a pregnant woman. In an interview perceived by the doctor as a routine prenatal she questions his every assumption, not from her own point of view, but from that of the unborn child. This offers an authentic moral touchstone for all Oaks's optimistic reassurances as well as for the act that has made all future births a genetic and environmental gamble. The irony is heavy:

Mother: If you were *in utero* and you had any choice about the matter, would you be dying to be born into a world like this?

Dr Oaks: D'you think that your baby's deciding whether or not to be born?

Mother: D'you think I'm holding back by force of will? Bad toilet training?

Dr Oaks: No, I think you've got to be willing to let your baby come whether you like it or not. You're holding back hope.

Mother: Hope for what? What d'you think's gonna happen out there? You think we're gonna sweep up the dead and fill up a coupla holes and build some supermarkets? You think all those people left alive out there are gonna say 'Oh, I'm sorry. It wasn't my fault. Let's kiss and make up'? We knew the score. We know all about bombs. We know all about fall-out. We knew this could happen for forty years. No one was interested.

Dr Oaks: I can't argue with you.

Mother: Argue with me! Please, give me a reason. Tell me about hope. Tell me why you work so hard in here.

Dr Oaks: I don't know.

In this crucial scene of the film it is not just the physical and organizational world—so strongly represented in the first half of the narrative—that has collapsed; it is the world of authoritarian morality, rational argument and officially sponsored hope. After this Dr Oaks himself, the public man *par excellence*, turns in upon himself and pursues the humble private goal of seeking out his home in Kansas City—site of all his bourgeois achievements and aspirations, haven of the once-nuclear family—before he dies. As he approaches the dusty, smoking ruins, his patriarchal authority makes one last bid for a hearing: 'Get outa my home!', he tells an old couple crouching by what may once have been the domestic hearth. The old man proffers an apple—last gesture of humanity, and they crouch together in a final *tableau mourant* as the camera recedes slowly, holding them at the centre of the ruined cityscape, petrified in a sterile image of redemption.

If the sites of military and health have been maintained as discrete elements, then the further sites of university, sport, economic and agricultural agency and church, while given relative autonomy when they are introduced, none the less are maintained also as sites of conjunction and intersection. This is illustrated by a seemingly transparent section devoted to the dialogue in a barber's shop just before the missile launch is announced. The American barber's shop, normally the site of confirmatory communal ideology, is usually filmed in a standard alternating-shot mode, but here it is formally undermined by a radical reverse-shot strategy, which carries the narrational function of pivot towards the holocaust and its consequences, but in a remarkably quiet, understated manner. The deconstruction occurs thematically as a consequence of the intruded discourse of the scientific expert, in what is normally a circuit of relayed, media-framed opinion delivered with amateurish but consensual force. In most films the barber's shop is seen as the traditional venue for village politics, opinion-sharing couched in reassuring gestures of masculinity. Normally the exchanges are carried by a modulated spectrum of small talk and arrant bull-dusting, and, with the barber as arbitrator, the protocol of the status quo is maintained at all costs.

Initially, then, the camera affirms this conventionality with an interplay between the barber and the young man about to get married, then uses a striking dolly to move on to a second client also having his hair cut and venturing well-worn opinions. At this level the scene could be taken as an enclosed sphere of discourse, with two displayers of easy-going masculinity and the two barbers as phatic respondents. The track, however, reveals a political marker among all the boxers, baseballers and sporting guernseys, and the conversation moves up an alarming peg until the clients appear to stabilize the conversation by enunciating folk wisdom in received normative stances regarding nuclear matters. However, the cutting and camera reveal a fifth person in the store, unnoticed until now, but marked as an intellectual by his national newspaper and spectacles. He breaks the self-affirmatory harmony by delivering further information in a superior and dominating voice that carries much more specialized knowledge. From this point the shot-reverse shots, which would normally be paralleled and paired, are presented disjunctively to carry five rather than four sources of speech. Further, the comments are delivered to the back of the groom's head rather than reassuringly face to face, and, not seeing his reaction, the audience is moved towards doubt. Thus, the last scene which would normally yield pleasant and affirmatory redundancy is left problematic by the lack of visually completed interactions.

Later in the film the intellectual appears in a sequence where the missiles create a 'firework display' above the cheerleaders and crowd-packed 'varsity' stadium. He marks his distinctive awareness of their significance by the conventionalized readjustment of his glasses. Finally, he is marked as 'University physicist', and is given a desperate set of scenes, in which he tries to remobilize a primitive valve radio after the complete power failure. It is his message ('Is anyone listening?') which marks the epitaph or epilogue of the film and which reappears as a headline in several reviews of the film. The discourse of science or specialization, then, appears in the communal site of the barber's shop, and is shown to emanate from the repository of such knowledge in the University, but is left as an apocalyptic witnessing rather than the basis of rational social mobilization or anti-nuclear counter-measures.

9.3 SEMIOTICS OF HOLOCAUST

The last moment of a unitary vision of America is manifested paradoxically through the holocaust itself. Because the iconography of the A-bomb is historically bound to its Japanese destruction or early tests, and is at the same time so awesome and so 'received' or accepted, the representation of the firestorms in *The Day After* has only gained grudging praise. It is certainly far fresher than the much-grained black-and-white archival footage, even if it could never match the requirements of the *Newsweek* correspondent, who wanted to go to Hiroshima to see the vestiges of a bomb victim vaporized into a permanent shadow upon a stone wall, because that image summarized for him the evanescence and power of the holocaust. Mere physical recording and replay of such holocaust, then, is not enough, for the event has a cultural resonance that requires symbolization through grotesque side-effects or semiotic structures developing psychological frames to equate with direct witness or involvement. *The Day After* does this at first with actual blast pictures that show permanent structures collapsing, colliding, exploding, transforming material into smoke and vapour marked by the semiotic overlay of a stridently red filter. In short, it uses much of its SFX resources on positioning cameras nearer the site of explosion than in earlier archival footage, and from more spectacular angles to allow for the implosion and expansion of the screen frame. This 'physicality', then, is used alternately with symbolically more ambitious X-ray figuration and striated film surfaces, to give a metonymic consolidation of earlier representations and filmic records.

The symbolization, of course, becomes more problematic. Which images resonate with whose imaginations? Thus *The Day After* is somewhat hurried and tentative with its interspersed X-ray scenes, and vaporizations, as if unsure —understandably—of the correct degree of exposure for fullest audience acceptance, as if the subliminal flicker would make for the most adequate representation. In those scenes retrievable more permanently through the stop-and-start mechanisms of the video recorder, the hegemonic scene of a central and 'natural' social institution echoes the film's prologue, key characters and narrative situations as both recapitulation and foreshadowing. We see the schoolchildren in a communal, ideological circle turn into stick figures and nothingness, as we do a woman in a wedding dress, and the ever-archetypal mother and child, while the firestorm engulfs and consumes a father in the open, a hitchhiker in the city, and animals in the fields, in a similar recurrent cinematic signifier of their physical transformation.

The atmosphere is initially positioned as some transcendental universal as if to reassure us that over all differing social conditions lies the sky, but because it then moves through contradictory colour ranges and is finally presented as striated screen surface to simulate atomic rain, its firmness of semiotic register is brought to the point of collapse. From this point on, the sky carries a darker hue; the ruins of the city will remain. There can no longer be the redemption of innocent and life-giving rain, nor the redemptive mood of reconstruction.

9.4 SEMIOTICS OF THE NUCLEAR FAMILY

The site of strongest institutional intersection is, perhaps, the nuclear family, an institution still dedicated to the contradictory ideology of discreteness and uniqueness. In so far as it is normative, the family reflects successful hegemony and it is accordingly coerced and persuaded by the strongest social means, even though the common-sense view is that the family is free to live its own lifestyle. As we stressed earlier, United States history has carried a hamlet/megapolis dichotomy, and, despite the Royalist colonialists of Virginia, the arrival of the Pilgrim Fathers established the Puritan texts in all their potent contradictoriness, with their stress on individual salvation, yet good works above good words; the sharing of God's abundance within the group and individual effort as the site of legitimated personal accumulation; fair wages and binding contracts for high interest as reward for risk. It is such a national grounding, that has allowed right-wing presidents to enlist liberal sentiments to oscillate against imperialist injunctions; and to set up the polarity between quietist or populist isolationism and capitalist economic expansionism as the motors of history, appealing at alternate moments to the people.

The Day After also carries an archetypal family, that of a successful, resolute and cautious prairie farmer, and it resonates to the political maxim that American elections are not won in the great metropolitan cities but in the small Midwest town, right down on the farm. We first see him in predictable checked shirt anxiously relaxing, for though his own daily physical work is over, he monitors the nation state through the increasingly gloomy world newscasts. From a seemingly mindless watcher the zoom transforms him into an intelligent, ever-concerned father. Outside his daughter is courted on the porch, and she is to awaken in him the conflict between his own conventionalized morality with its safeguard of prescriptive behaviour and the acceptance of his daughter's personal reactions and behaviour as the ultimate test of a developed individual morality. Such dichotomies provide neat theological points, even if they are also the staple of the melodrama or the 'soapie'.

To enhance the religious base further, *The Day After* presents the concerned farmer moving out on the porch to read the heavens of the evening sky. With its pantheistic undertones carefully arranged by a camera pan, the moment is reminiscent of similar strategies in *ET* and *Close Encounters of the Third Kind*, which used such transcendentality to great popular effect. Here the contract between man and God or the forces of nature is seen as individual, no matter how many other observers of the prairie skies there might be.

It is this individualized, atomized patterning which is reflected in one of *The Day After*'s earliest disjunctive moments. The local church as a small centre of community has yielded to nuclear anxiety by calling for a voluntary working roster to create a shelter along the lines of the World War II air-raid shelters and bunkers which were constructed with ever-increasing vigour and resources as that war progressed. Here in mid-America such activities seem quixotic, as is shown by the ineffectuality of digging with hand shovels rather than tractors from the farms. This, of course, contrasts strongly with the high technology of national military silos and bomb shelters. It is first introduced immediately after the screen has been filled with an eagle-like Boeing moving into tactical postion for 'attack/defense'.

The small church's gestures are futile, however. This sincerity and tranquillity of common purpose is shattered by the appearance of our farmer-hero's pick-up, which lurches into the frame's composition, so that the father can take his son back to the farm. Once out of earshot the farmer outlines a whole host of actions to be carried out in an equally defensive manner at the individual farmstead. Obviously, the farmer has a predetermined plan—he has outguessed his 'fellows'—but it pinpoints the paralysing dichotomy of where the individual ultimately owes his loyalty: to his personal nuclear family or to the commonality of society.

Back at the farm, the *mise-en-scène* asserts again and again the rigidity of the patriarchal order, and, in recasting the farmer as frontier woodsman in a beleaguered homstead, provides the normative and reassuring icon of the America which so resolutely stands against gun regulation on constitutional grounds laid by the early settlers. Replicating the orderliness of military sites, the farmer has already constructed a family fall-out shelter and set of defensive apparatuses, whose contradictorily male domestic is set against the feminine domestic—the hearth/kitchen. By positioning the 'father' in the doorway between kitchen and stairs leading to the basement, the film asserts him as the pivot of social meaning, as he ruthlessly renders his hysterical wife's discourse ineffectual. He commands her to leave HER kitchen and all her talk of the personal emergency of wedding arrangements, to enter HIS cellar, because of the 'national' emergency. It is no accident that his youngest daughter vacillates between the two parents and their conflicting priorities, to be finally convinced by the father.

In a parallel editing, the farmer clears the breech of his rifle in the same manner as the platoon sergeant primes his rifle to hold a dissenting black soldier at bay, before pulling down the bunker's hatch cover for final withdrawal. In the farmer's case the defensive stance is disarmed by his acceptance of the hitch-hiker survivor, scrabbling along with the family dog for food in the now-abandoned kitchen. The motivation here may be seen as mixed. It is partly moral in raising the question of the nuclear family's relationship to outsiders in an emergency, the tension between sheer survival and the remnants of compassion; but it has a crucial practical function in the plot structure in providing necessary information about the state of the outside world and the end of the social continuity previously taken for granted.

Though the patriarchal order has been asserted in the form of meaningful chores (the farmer's son filling canisters with water to be stored, as against the meaningless bed-tidying of the anxious mother), the holocaust drains all meaning from these social acts. The mother is then dragged downstairs more as a manikin than an individual, and even the rebellious teenage daughter passively takes hold of a teddy bear and resumes a little girl voice, showing how the orderly family structure is now at peril. In the atomic dust that pollutes the animal carcasses, the notion of property as the substantive social meaning and the creator of vocational identity is rendered as naught. Even the elder daughter argues on the irony of an unconsummated marriage as a barrier to femininity as the site of reproduction, as patriarchal ideology would have it, when she holds her now meaningless wedding dress to her.

Try as he might to make 'the day after' sempiternal, part of the external round, by moving out towards the social institutions of pre-holocaust America, the farmer is doomed. The church provides no spiritual ease or sustenance and indeed is the site of his daughter's collapse. His son's sight cannot be cured at the hospital, and his daughter loses her 'femininity' as she loses her hair while under care. Even the assertions of post-holocaust governmental agencies that the Government still holds the centre, that an omniscient paternal President still cares, that there are meaningful agricultural procedures, are dismissed as unproductive bulldust, with topsoil as material significance so sterile and wasted. All this contrasts with the purposeful anchoring offered at the beginning of the film by computers and stock exchange which cemented the prologue to a fundamental economic base. Finally, when the farmer surprises a group of refugees eating a polluted carcass on his farm, his own spiritual awareness following the renunciation of his initial proprietorial stance is literally shot down from under him, as he lowers his own defensive rifle in a gesture of peace and compassion. Ironically, the viewer is reminded of the Western movie maxim, 'Those who live by the gun, die by the gun', as the film lurches into total social disorder.

If the audience, then, is encouraged to position itself along with this prairie farmer, whose resolute philosophy and practice is insufficient to withstand the collapse of the holocaust, the film conventionally provides a transcending resolution—though some might ironically call it a spiritual escapism, whereby heavenly salvation is provided through the discourse of the church. In an uncompromising agnostic moment the church is revealed as a hollow sepulchre, all walls blasted away, a crazily swinging cross among the ruins. Instead of using this elemental simplicity as the site of a loving fundamentalism, the discourse, along with the hand-rung bell, becomes medieval and the sermon is one of hellfire, apocalypse and pessimistic lack of direction. The emergent theology rings true with the anachronistic imagery of sulkies and waggons, now that the carbonized fuel has vanished and modern transport is immobilized, suggesting a return to frontier days and harsher fundamental and individualistic prescription.

If by now the audience has learned to distrust institutional theologies, it could be drawn to the hope of transcendental release through the metaphysical theme of love. Here the film narrative explodes from the centre. Tension has been building up on the political front as TV and radio news-flashes report closer confrontations between NATO and the communist bloc over Germany, while on the home front family life has never seemed so peaceful and normal. The young wife settles the kids by the TV and greets her farmer husband with a lunch table of healthy country food and a whispered invitation to slip up to bed. While their private harmony is thus consolidated through direct physical contact, their two small boys grapple with the TV remote control to recapture the comic aggression of cartoon films. The previously smooth visual rhythm of *The Day After* suddenly disintegrates as rapid cutting alternates between grave TV announcers, shots of B-52 bombers taking off and two mystified small boys: the tragic significance of remote control has begun to be realized and direct human contact will be tainted with fear. The turning-point between 'the day before' and 'the day after' is the simplest act of love.

Framing this sequence is the more complex love story of Denise, the daughter of the older, more well-to-do farmer. Her fiancé has his hair cut, for their wedding on the following day, in the barber's shop sequence we have already analysed. He then gets caught up in the panic-buying in the supermarket before riding off on his motorbike. But he is one of four men who are caught out on the road by the impact of an ICBM—Dr Oaks, Billy, Stephen and he, all of them are important vehicles for this important metatheme of love. Denise and her family take refuge in their domestic fall-out shelter during the firestorm and eventually admit a young man who has survived; this is not the young blond fiancé (who has disappeared, a unit in a 'megadeath'), but Stephen, a fellow-student who hitch-hikes to the farm in time to survive. He becomes a surrogate fiancé to Denise.

While the surrogate lover is a favoured narrative device of soap opera—as of the classic novel and, indeed, the Shakespearean comedy—here it is given a grotesque and tragic twist. In the integrated narrative of the first half of the film Denise's sexuality becomes a focus of conflict with those closest to her. The fiancé wants to make love to her before the wedding, and after some hesitation she agrees, provided she can take the precaution of wearing a Dutch cap (prophylaxis ironically becoming part of the metatheme). But her younger sister has stolen the contraceptive device and in a family row that parallels the political row being reported on the TV (and intercut with it on the sound track), the warring sisters have to be restrained by first the mother and then the father. But the father has his own conflict with his daughter's sexuality, sitting up all night on the porch to catch her creeping back home. But if he cannot restrain her on the eve of her wedding, he is even less successful from his new patriarchal power base in the shelter; in a surge of hysteria, Denise bursts out of the cellar, seizes her once-symbolic wedding dress and, pursued by Stephen, dances around the radioactive farmyard (the negation, in negative, of earlier positive scenes). Her punishment, too, is sexually focused: during the tatty charade of a church service, near the end of the film, she has a haemorrhage which spells the end of all women's normal childbearing, as well as her own. Once again, the film has taken the elements of the soap opera—premarital sex, parental control, conflict with siblings, risk of pregnancy—and disintegrated them systematically.

If Denise and her fiancé and the young farming couple are anchored in a private domestic world, Billy (the black soldier) and Dr Oaks oscillate between their private and public spheres. But the metatheme of love is still important. Billy, recalled to his base for a nuclear alert (which might, early in the film, be only an exercise) has to reassure his loving wife. When they are furthest apart emotionally, he is shown in mid-shot—the hero's place—while a long-shot frames her distantly in a doorway. Suddenly, however, he moves to her and the camera moves to a reassuring and intimate zoom, barrelling up from floor level to a squarely composed shot of their embrace, rounding off the encounter. Maureen, the black wife, is another early victim of the holocaust and in his search for her Billy encounters a poor substitute for his love. The little man with whom he shares his blanket is deformed and inarticulate, perhaps mentally defective, but Billy protects him with all the fierce love he had had for his wife: in a disintegrating world, love for any least one of one's fellow men reveals a last token of integration and humanity.

This theme is played in a minor key in the two halves of Billy's plot-line. With Dr Oaks it is in a major key, opening and closing the film. Oaks represents success, both as official public man (his professional sphere) and as domestic man. His love for his wife, for his safely independent daughter and for his son is securely cradled in a luxurious neo-Georgian home in Kansas

City. But Kansas is the first target for the Soviet ICBMs, and all that safe bourgeois world disintegrates in a moment. When his professional world disintegrates, his moral authority challenged by the mother-to-be in the dialogue we reproduced earlier, Oaks resorts to 'going home'. But his wife and children are obliterated and the family home is a hearth among the smoking rubble. As we have seen, Oaks has to make do, in the closing scene, with the only love that is left—the common humanity he learns to recognize in the grotesque old man who has taken over his 'home'.

9.5 CONCLUSION

We count it as a considerable achievement of *The Day After* that it has faced the challenge of adopting the conventional themes, narrative devices and camera play of the Hollywood or TV network 'soapie' and making them all disintegrate before our eyes. Medicine, commerce, farming, religion, the military machine itself—all lose their hegemonic structures and integrating role. Domesticity, family love and sexual love rise above the institutions of society, but cannot survive the instantaneous death of the beloved. In a quiet, understated way quite alien to the soap opera, the film reasserts the one surviving reality— common humanity—but the price, as it courageously makes clear, is every social institution, including narrative.

NOTES

1. Michel Foucault's most accessible account of this is his *Discipline and Punish* (1979).
2. 'Hegemony' is a concept developed by Gramsci in his *Prison Notebooks* (1971) and widely used in cultural studies. It refers principally to the ability of the dominant classes in certain historical periods to exercise social and cultural leadership, and by these means—rather than by direct coercion of subordinate classes—to maintain their power over the economic, political and cultural direction of the nation.
    Here, as in other cultural studies, the term is used as a shorthand for the way everyday meanings, representations and activities are organized and made sense of in such a way as to render the class interests of the dominant 'bloc' into an apparently natural, inevitable, eternal, and hence unarguable, general interest with a claim on everybody (adapted from O'Sullivan, T., Hartley, J., Saunders, D. and Fiske, J., *Key Concepts in Communication*, London, Methuen (1983: 102-3).

10 Disarming criticism

Michael O'Toole
Murdoch University, Western Australia

10.1 THE RHETORIC OF BALANCE

There is a recurrent type of criticism of films about nuclear policy (whether civil or military) and disarmament. It is a type of criticism that never attacks its object directly, in the name of deterrence strategy; rather, it adopts a 'balanced', disarming rhetoric that seeks to render the film's critical message impotent, deterring, if one may borrow that metaphor, potential counter-argument and counter-criticism. The nuclear debate concerns events so disturbing to the Establishment, apparently, that they cannot just be left to editorials, but infect even film and television criticism.

Reviews of such films as *The China Syndrome*, *Silkwood*, *Testament* and *The Day After* have all adopted a rhetoric based on some recurring textual features, the main characteristics of which are:

1. *Structures of negation*: in the name of 'balance' every assertion of the film's positive qualities is offset by a nagging negation (e.g. 'but', 'all the same', 'yet, still').
2. *Modalized assertions*: every positive assertion is undercut (sabotaged and 'disarmed' from inside the clause itself, as it were) by a modal adverb or auxiliary ('entirely', 'somehow', 'really', 'certainly', 'a certain', 'not quite').
3. *Impersonal stance*: the source of authority judgements is specifically removed so as to be unavailable for contradiction or criticism; the authority for both positive and negative assertions is made vague, general or impersonal in the surface structure so that its ultimate negation is camouflaged. Evaluation is not anchored in any personalized point of view of authorship: 'is a worthy film' (who says?), 'somehow fails' (for whom?), 'It engages without really stirring' (whom?), 'One still feels' (who is 'one'?), etc.
4. *Cliché*: an advantage of clichés is that they allow people to go on speaking or writing without actually thinking. As George Orwell showed in *Nineteen Eighty-Four* in his discussion of 'Duckspeak', the set phrase has its own momentum and is presumed to need no further evidence or argument. The mode is 'monologic', as with proverbs or the Word of God in religious discourse, and it brooks no intervention by an 'alien voice' or alternative view of dialogic modes: 'it somehow falls at the final hurdle'; 'the effect of which does not quite add up to the sum of its parts'.

All of these examples, in fact, are taken from one brief final paragraph of a recent review of *Silkwood*, not by a hack reviewer in the right-wing popular press, but by Derek Malcolm, the senior film critic of the *Guardian*, widely considered the most liberal, and occasionally even radical, British mass circulation, 'intelligentsia' newspaper. The paragraph in full reads:

> On these terms *Silkwood* is an entirely worthy film. But all the same it somehow fails at the final hurdle. It engages without really stirring. It is intelligent, reasonably forthright and certainly well made. Yet one still feels it lacks a certain passion. It's a damning indictment, the cumulative effect of which does not quite add up to the sum of its parts.[1]

However much the liberal intellectual cinema-goer may be encouraged to see the film as 'entirely worthy . . . intelligent . . . forthright . . . well made . . . a damning indictment', their enthusiasm will be considerably dampened by the rhetorical devices which qualify or negate these positive aspects of the film at every turn of the syntax. We should point out that the four rhetorical devices exemplified here are not entirely discrete categories, but links in a chain of modalization. Structures of overt negation are partly realized by modalizing adverbs; these tend to make the stance still more impersonal; and all tend to coagulate into easily dismissive clichés.

The tendency to 'damn with faint praise' is largely confined to the final (though surely crucial) paragraph of the *Silkwood* review. In a *Newsweek* review of *The Day After* it is pervasive. Nor is this kind of rhetoric confined to film reviews on politically controversial issues. A line of criticism adopted by the newspapers for one or two films would be a trivial target. Unfortunately, the line adopted by *Newsweek* and much of the popular press in Australia and the United States typifies the rhetoric of a great deal of editorial writing and reportage in relation to nuclear issues. In our view, this 'balanced', apparently open-minded, yet systematically hostile rhetoric is insidiously destructive of rational debate. Linguistics and rhetorical analysis can unmask it as hollow and disreputable and, we hope, help to disarm it in the most critical debate of our times. Parallel with our own cinematic analysis of *The Day After*, then, we shall analyse some pervasive linguistic and rhetorical structures, first in *Newsweek*'s review of the film and secondly in an editorial in *The Australian* following the anti-nuclear rally of 15 April 1984.[2] The similarities are frightening. (The full text of both these articles follows in Appendices A and B to this chapter. Quotations are numbered for ease of reference.)

10.2 *THE DAY AFTER* ACCORDING TO *NEWSWEEK*

(1) 'The film's makers', wrote C. W. Gusewelle, a columnist for the *Kansas City Star*, 'had managed to make Armageddon dull'.

The reference to Armageddon in this sentence from the middle of the *Newsweek* review of *The Day After* is not, of course, accidental. The review carries the title 'Armageddon on the Screen' beneath a shot from the film of the black mushroom cloud rearing above a landscape with highway and the lone figure of a man, all about to be devastated. But Armageddon is also the media cliché for disaster; it is invoked to associate the film, by means of another 'authoritative' quotation, with the popular genre of disaster and horror movies:

(2) 'For most kids', said Rick Collett, an Oakland psychology teacher, 'the movie was mild compared to "Halloween II" '.

How better to emasculate this depiction of a disaster that is only the press of a button away than to compare it to a hobgoblin horror? These are two amongst several quotations offered to demonstrate the supposed failure of the film's makers' intentions—at least as interpreted by the reviewer:

(3) 'The Day After' was to have been a seismic event . . . It would scare viewers out of their apathy and into a heated debate over nuclear policy, even if it had a searing, traumatic influence on the imaginations of young children.

The film's failure is already, in the opening sentences, presupposed; and doubt is cast on its makers' care for the young. How better to evade the responsibility of offering a reasoned opinion than to load the syntax thus, to follow it up with supposedly cogent views from a local newspaper (Kansas City being the city devastated in the film) and to call upon the supposedly expert views of a psychologist and teacher? Here we find epitomized again three recurrent devices in the review for cushioning the reader from the full impact of the film: negation through spurious balance, invocation of bogus authority and reduction to cliché. Let us try to account for these devices in a more systematic way, while illustrating how totally they pervade this review.

1. *'Balance'*. (Pseudo-balance, of course, because of its automatic negation of the nuclear category.) Antithesis, paradox and the balanced period are rhetorical devices as old as speech-making. Several of the quotations given below, notably (9), exploit these devices: 'neither as X as Y, nor as A as B' (implying X : Y : : A : B; no further thought required). The pattern is not spasmodic, however; it is pervasive. Thus, within the nominal group, the depiction of nuclear holocaust is 'shockingly/realistic'; the 'special effect/ visions of destruction' were 'troubling/but not troubling enough'; to make 'Armageddon/dull' (paragraph three). Apposition is useful for equating 'a seismic event' and 'a made-for-television movie' (opening sentence of the text), while an extended balanced period (in paragraph two) juxtaposes 'to quieten the expected tumult' with 'probably tactical overkill' (note the low modality of 'probability'):

(4) The Reagan administration sent Secretary of State George Shultz on television 'to quieten the expected tumult'; later, 'government officials sheepishly admitted' that Shultz's appearance was 'probably tactical overkill'.

Perhaps our viewer really takes Reagan and Shultz themselves as rhetorical models. In the interview with the Secretary of State in ABC's 'Viewpoint' following the showing of *The Day After*, Shultz twice refers to 'balance' and twice uses an apocalyptic metaphor that makes Gelber's 'tactical overkill' sound mild (emphasis added):

> The point that I'm trying to make here is that in addition to having this policy of balance and deterrence, we have a policy of reduction. And in President Reagan's efforts to deal with this problem, reduction of nuclear weapons has been at the top of his list. REDUCTION ALL THE WAY DOWN TO THE POINT OF ZERO.
>
> ... what we should be doing is rallying around and supporting—as I think people by and large more and more are—the idea that we should be trying to reduce the numbers of these weapons. Of course, to do so means that we have to persuade the Soviet Union TO COME DOWN ALONG WITH US. And, hopefully, er, WHAT WE WOULD SHOOT FOR, as the President again said in Tokyo, HIS DREAM IS TO REDUCE DOWN TO ZERO.[3]

We are not denigrating antithesis, paradox and the balanced period as such: orators from Cicero to Martin Luther King have used them all to build persuasive arguments, historians from Edward Gibbon to E. P. Thompson have used them to convey a positive interpretation of past events. Alexis Gelber, the writer of this film review, uses them, however, to avoid conveying a real opinion, to disappear behind the smoke of others' conflicting intentions, opinions and reactions.

2. *Modality*. It all really has to do with his modal stance, the second and most linguistically describable of the devices we have pinpointed. Where does Alex Gelber stand? Is he with the film's makers?

> (5) 'The Day After' was to have been a seismic event, a made-for-television movie that WOULD GIVE the American public ... It WOULD SCARE viewers out of their apathy ... EVEN IF IT HAD a searing, traumatic influence on the imagination of young children. IN THE EVENT, after all the controversy ... 100 million Americans watched ... and THEY FOUND IT both more and less than they expected.

The distanced indirect discourse of 'was to have been', 'would give', 'would scare' and 'even if it had' allows the writer insight into their intentions, but he clearly does not share them and wants to underscore their failure to achieve these intentions in order to lead up to his climactic, if borrowed, line: the patronizing 'had managed to make Armageddon dull' (no mean failure, that!). So, does the reviewer identify with the film's audience? His omniscience about how 100 million Americans 'found it both more and less than they expected' appears to be based on audience research statistics of the most general kind and a handful of interviews and reports culled from provincial newspapers.

Gelber seems to volunteer an honest, unmodalized, opinion in his second paragraph (our quote (9)). But the film was not 'anticlimactic' to any climax he had experienced, nor did it provoke either shock or thought in him: again, he resorts to generalizing the expectations of 'its backers and foes'. Do his sympathies then lie with the United States Government? Apparently not, because (our quote (4) above) the Reagan administration had over-reacted and government officials 'sheepishly admitted . . . [probable] tactical overkill'. Again he reverts to authoritative generalization.

(6) The special effect visions of destruction were troubling, but not troubling enough; most viewers seemed to grasp that the real thing would be much more gruesome than anything television could create.

Well, it goes without saying that 'special effects' seen from the comfort of one's armchair are going to fall some way short of 'the real thing'. And he need not have been so condescending about the viewers' powers of imagination ('most viewers seemed to grasp', another shift in modality).

3. *Cliché*. As we saw at the beginning of this section, the dominant clichés are subjected to magnification (hyperbole) and reduction (litotes), and often these rhetorical devices are used to interact with each other. The opening paragraph takes the hyperbole of *The Day After* for granted ('Armageddon', 'Halloween II'), but then undercuts it with litotes ('managed to make dull', 'mild compared to'). Similarly, the sentence concerning the possible 'searing', 'traumatic influence' on its audience is followed by the derisive

(7) 'In the event', after all the controversy, breathless promotion and simple curiosity, 100 million Americans watched the ABC film last week, and 'they found it both more and less than they expected'.

'In the event' is a nice, and typical, phrase for cutting controversial media events down to size; no doubt *Newsweek* had access to audience research estimates of the audience size, but on what authority could the reviewer decide how all those millions 'found it'? Does that matter when the finding is a meaningless cliché ('both more and less than they expected')? The article opens with '*The Day After* was to have been a seismic event'; as we have seen, the event is killed off by 'In the event', but 'seismic', too, is extinguished by the bathos of a cliché that opens the second paragraph:

(8) By some standards, the response to *The Day After* was indeed seismic—the film drew an audience second only to the final episode of 'M*A*S*H', shown earlier this year.

The earthquake, it turns out, has exceeded, on the only scale the reviewer can conceive, the level reached by one episode of television's tame army soap opera.

After dismissing, by making cliché-figures out of them, ABC's carefully chosen panel of experts who discussed *The Day After* following the showing as 'the likes of Henry Kissinger, Carl Sagan and Robert McNamara', the review sums up reactions with a further pair of meaningless, but balanced, clichés:

(9) But the film was also anticlimactic. It was neither as shocking as it had been hyped nor as thought-provoking as its backers and foes alike expected.

The reviewer continues to subvert the seriousness of the film's aims and its viewers' responses with ready-made phrases, culminating in a quotation from a French daily paper and his own cliché-based observation:

(10) And in France, the daily *Libération* editorialized that 'the most

insignificant document on Hiroshima is 100 times more poignant than this Walt Disney-style production'. While that assessment may seem unfair, it does underscore an important point: that unpredictable, real events are almost always more shocking than any contrived dramas.

Then what price all fictionalized discourse: drama, film, TV, the novel? What should we do, await the raising of the curtain on the REAL denouement? And why keep this facile comment until the culmination of the review itself, if not to leave readers in no doubt about the doubtfulness of the film as significant political discourse? Not that the reviewer risks committing himself to a purely negative line: the French paper's assessment only 'may seem unfair' and real events are 'almost always' more shocking. As we have seen, the modalities of this kind of writing always offer an escape route for real opinions.

Gelber's position, it would appear (if we may parody his modal), is the awesome stance of one who is qualified to judge between the power of televisual representation and of 'the real thing'. This theme, signalled in (6), rehearsed in several carefully selected interviews and placed as climax in the resounding cliché we quoted in (10), is a sub-text to the whole review. Now if a reviewer commits himself to 'awe' over the prospect of a nuclear holocaust, he is representing that death-wish that Nicholas Humphrey (1981) has so convincingly diagnosed as a major factor in preventing people doing anything about the arms race our political leaders have led us into. He (the reviewer) is adding—in a mass-circulation and public-opinion-forming magazine—to the 'incomprehension', 'denial' and 'helplessness' (Humphrey's other factors) which have paralysed most of us. What we question here is not Alexis Gelber's right to share these natural human responses to the incomprehensible, but the irresponsibility of his stance in the article, the ease with which he exploits a few rhetorical tricks to blur issues, abuse our intelligence and denigrate a serious contribution to public awareness of the real issues that make 'the real thing' possible.

Possibly Alexis Gelber would deny authorial responsibility for the stance he has adopted; the by-line attributes the review to 'Alexis Gelber with bureau reports'. Derek Malcolm in the *Guardian* has no such alibi. In neither case is it clear whether the editors or proprietors of the magazine or newspaper have a direct influence on this kind of reviewing. This kind of rhetoric would have a relatively simple explanation under a totalitarian regime where state censorship induces self-censorship in media writers and editors. But *Newsweek* and the *Guardian* are published in democratic open societies where 'freedom of expression' and 'freedom to publish' are among the most treasured civil rights. So do the owners of these media have some stake in silencing genuine debate on nuclear issues, or do they merely have a temperamental preference for the status quo (a status quo which is daily being more destabilized by the accelerating arms race than by any proliferation of politically critical film reviews)? It may be too easy to assign responsibility for devious rhetoric to devious political manipulation by international capital. I fear that our reviewers are victims of a rhetorical virus that infects all their thought and has infected most of us on an epidemic scale with an incapacity to engage with nuclear politics.

This 'enemy within', the 'seventh enemy' as Ronald Higgins (1980) has called it, is far more insidious than direct political or economic control.

10.3 EDITORIAL RHETORIC: *THE AUSTRALIAN*

Direct political comment is, however, something to be expected in a newspaper editorial. *The Australian* is one of the Murdoch-owned chain, so an underlying economic motive is not far to seek. What game is the editorial writer of *The Australian* playing, then, in adopting the same non-committal rhetorical devices as the critics of *Silkwood* and *The Day After*? His or her commentary on the peace rallies that took place all over Australia on 15 April 1984 (see Appendix B) uses balanced sentence and argument structures, modalized assertions, impersonal stance and cliché almost to the point of parody. Indeed, they add a further pair of related devices—double negative and thematized conditional or negative —which defuse (and diffuse) the political debate even more. Let us start with the many examples of these two devices.

1. *Multiple negative.* 'it would be foolish to ignore'; 'it is difficult to refute the proposition'; 'it is impossible to reject the argument'; 'the Federal Government would be rash to disregard the fear'; 'None of these standpoints is deserving of ridicule'; 'It does not follow from this that they should succumb to calls for self-defeating unilateralism'. The typical pattern here, throughout the second half of the article, is to combine a negative assertion of mental process in the main clause with an implied negative of another mental process in the dependent clause, leaving the writer's opinions hanging unspecified somewhere in between; this clearly saves him from exercising his own mental processes.
2. *Thematized conditional, concession or negative.* As Michael Halliday[4] and others have shown, what writers choose to put first in their clauses or clause-complexes in English—the Theme element—tells us a good deal about their stance. *The Australian* editorial's stance is to cover its tracks even before it has made any: 'Australians are not celebrated for . . . nor are they prone to . . . The fact that . . . is a forceful indication . . .', 'Whatever the ulterior motives . . . it is obvious that . . .'; 'While it is perfectly true that . . . It would be foolish to ignore . . .'; 'Although the most rigid unilateralists . . . It is difficult to refute'; 'But, if they let it appear . . . they will have to meet'. This pattern of thematizing all the qualifying clauses clearly has much to do with the first of the rhetorical devices we highlighted in the *Silkwood* text —balance. The balancing act is not just performed at sentence level, however. The whole editorial is built around this principle.
3. *Balance.* The first two paragraphs thematize negatives and concessional clauses, but from paragraph 4 onwards whole paragraphs are juxtaposed:

P4 At one extreme [opposition to nuclear energy policy]

P5 Others confine their use of nuclear arms . . .

P7 But there is a strong, if not overwhelming case to be made for the advantages of the peaceful use of nuclear energy . . .

P8 And although the most rigid unilateralists may not be convinced . . .

This carefully balanced presentation of opposing arguments is rounded off with a masterpiece of negative non-alignment:

P6 None of these standpoints is deserving of ridicule.

In the last paragraphs the balancing propositions illustrate the dilemma facing the politicians:

P10 Government by demonstration is no way to run a democracy.

> But the Federal Government, and the Opposition, would be rash to disregard the fear of so many decent and responsible Australians.

The sustaining of such a careful balance of opposing points of view might seem the very essence of democratic discourse if the viewpoint opposed by the editorial writer did not always come first, to be neutralized in the next clause, sentence or paragraph, and if the writer's modalities did not so clearly reveal his real sympathies.

4. *Modalized assertions.* 'WHATEVER the ulterior motives of a small minority . . . IT IS OBVIOUS THAT . . .'; 'While it IS PERFECTLY TRUE . . . it WOULD BE foolish to ignore . . .'; 'It IS PERHAPS a major weakness . . . opinions APPEAR TO HAVE BEEN represented'; 'But THERE IS a strong, IF NOT overwhelming case TO BE MADE . . . safeguards are more stringent than they APPEAR TO BE at present', etc.

Modals, expressing uncertainty, doubt, possibility, probability, tip the balance towards what we may call an 'Establishment' view of the marchers' sympathies and demands: they rock the boat and some response from Government will be necessary to restore that highest value, the status quo.

5. *Impersonal stance* is the stock-in-trade of editorial writing, as of much other journalism. It makes possible the distancing of genuine processes through passivization and nominalization and the grammatical downgrading or disappearance of responsible agents: 'if only one side in the two major systems of alliances WERE WITHOUT nuclear arms [here not only the agency of such disarmament has disappeared, but so has the process, replaced by a preposition, WITHOUT], the danger of nuclear war WOULD BE INCREASED rather than REDUCED'. The increase or reduction are too general and vague even to resemble real processes and the possible agents who might increase or reduce the danger have vanished.

6. *Cliché.* As with the review of *The Day After*, it is the clichés that reveal where the 'balance' of the writer's sympathies lies. The element subversive of the status quo, and therefore to be feared, is stereotyped as 'political passions . . . mass demonstrations . . . ulterior motives . . . small minority . . . a strong display of dissent of this kind within a Western nation'. All the better, if, through a metonymic shift in P2, this insidious element can be associated stereotypically with plotting by the Soviet Government!

The editorial ends with an apparent concern for the views of 'so many decent and responsible Australians' and 'a large, determined and highly articulate section of our population'. Note how these real human beings (not to to be confused with the 'small minority' with 'ulterior motives') emerge as subordinate elements in complex nominal groups, qualifying 'fear' and 'resentment' (much less easy to come to terms with).

10.4 WHY?

Why do these writers do it? Is it economic pressure or political malice that prevents them from engaging with such significant contributions to the nuclear debate as *Silkwood, The Day After* and the anti-nuclear rallies? Is it an excessively formal literary training or a prescriptive set of journalistic rules too easily followed that makes them all resort to the same rhetorical tricks that erect straw adversaries (Disney, Mr Chernenko) and evade the issues? I believe they do it in part because of the normal pressures of journalism: deadlines and copy-length. As numerous studies of journalism have shown, both share and intensify through their writing the general public's responses to events. In the nuclear debate they are proliferating the psychological responses to the Bomb that tend to paralyse us all: incomprehension, denial, helplessness and awe. However, it is not the function of journalism merely to share the views of the highest common factor of their readers (as revealed by market research and sales figures), nor to protect at all costs the Establishment view of what constitutes the status quo (which, as we have said, is daily being further destabilized in the name of 'balance'). Surely journalists, together with academics, teachers and film-makers, should be leading and promoting active political debate in the clearest, least compromised rhetoric they can manage.

NOTES

1. *Guardian Weekly* (22 April 1984, p. 19).
2. *Newsweek* (5 December 1983) and *The Australian* (17 April 1984). See Appendices to this chapter for full texts.
3. 'Viewpoint' (20 November 1983) from a transcription of the broadcast discussion.
4. Halliday, 'Theme and information in the English clause' in Kress (ed.) (1976), and Trew (1978, 1979).

APPENDIX A

ARMAGEDDON ON THE SCREEN

'The Day After' was to have been a seismic event, a made-for-television movie that would give the American public a shockingly realistic depiction of nuclear holocaust. It would scare viewers out of their apathy and into a heated debate over nuclear policy, even if it had a searing, traumatic influence on the imaginations of young children. In the event, after all the controversy, breathless promotion and simple curiosity, 100 million Americans watched the ABC film last week, and they found it both more and less than they expected. The movie is scheduled for distribution to 40 countries, and this month people in Europe will be able to judge for themselves what sorts of fallout 'The Day After' will bring.

By some standards, the response to 'The Day After' was indeed seismic— the film drew an audience second only to the final episode of 'M*A*S*H,' shown earlier this year. Moreover, the vast bulk of the audience stayed with the grim film to the very end, and many viewers stayed tuned for a panel discussion with the likes of Henry Kissinger, Carl Sagan and Robert McNamara. But the film was also anticlimactic. It was neither as shocking as as it had been hyped nor as thought-provoking as its backers and foes alike expected. Afterward, there were few calls to the White House or to the several special centers that had been set up around the country to field panicky responses. The Reagan administration sent Secretary of State George Shultz on television to quiet the expected tumult; later, government officials sheepishly admitted that Shultz's appearance was probably tactical overkill.

The film itself was somehow bloodless—a collection of cardboard caricatures in a sketchy, melodramatic script. The special-effect visions of destruction were troubling, but not troubling enough; most viewers seemed to grasp that the real thing would be much more gruesome than anything television could create. The film's makers, wrote C. W. Gusewell, a columnist for the Kansas City Star, 'had managed to make Armageddon dull.' The film's shallowness seemed to leave people unmoved and apathetic. 'If anything, the movie just confirmed the feelings of people on both sides,' said Wally Sherwin, programming director for Los Angeles radio station KABC.

'Aftermath': Some people were moved to action. Janet Michaud, director of the Washington-based Campaign Against Nuclear War, said that by Wednesday 35,000 people had called for information on how to avoid nuclear war. Robert Bull, owner of a Detroit survival-goods store called 'Aftermath,' said that sales of such items as military clothes, blankets and freeze-dried foods doubled on the day after the movie. Still, most people seemed to forget about the film as the week went by, and most children who had watched the show seemed untroubled. Michael McGean, 13, of Salt Lake City, said he thought John Hersey's book 'Hiroshima' was much more alarming than the movie; Traci Killingworth, 17, of Oakland, Calif., said 'the issue was scarier than the movie.' 'For most kids,' said Rick Collett, an Oakland psychology teacher, 'the movie was mild compared to "Halloween II".'

The film begins with a series of vignettes about average middle-Americans —a farm family preparing for a daughter's wedding, college students registering for class, a heart surgeon talking at night with his wife. Intermittently, news bulletins crackle through the air with ominous messages about a vaguely defined conflict on the border between East and West Germany. Suddenly the bombs begin to fall, and in a four-minute holocaust sequence, the camera follows a horrifying series of images: the blinding light of a mushroom cloud, the rapid-fire vaporization of human beings into skeletons that dissolve into nothing, and raging fires that engulf buildings and bodies. When the actual bombing is over, the survivors try to get on with living, such as it is. Blinded, scarred and hairless from radiation sickness, the remaining inhabitants of Lawrence, Kans., wait to die in a cavernous gym. Others, turned into desperate savages by a crumbling social order, loot, pillage and kill.

Squatters: In the last scene, the surgeon (Jason Robards) leaves the inferno of the hospital where he has been working to make his way home for the last time. There, in the ashes of what was once his house, he sees a family of squatters. 'Get out of my house,' he yells in a feeble rage. An old man walks toward him and sadly places a hand on the surgeon's shoulder. As the two embrace, the camera moves back to show the decimated landscape. In a silent coda to the film, a printed message gives viewers a last instructive word: 'The catastrophic events you have just witnessed are in all likelihood less severe than what would actually occur in the event of a full nuclear strike against the United States . . .'

After the movie, ABC ran a panel discussion about the film and the issues it raised. Several of the guests were deterrence advocates: Lt. Gen. Brent Scowcroft, head of the president's MX-basing commission, spoke of a need 'to integrate our weapons-systems programs and our arms control' to reduce the chances of nuclear war; McNamara, the former secretary of defense, said he doubted whether nuclear weapons could be eliminated in the coming decades and maintained that 'we've got to be more daring' in putting forth arms-control proposals. Former Secretary of State Kissinger criticized the film: 'Are we supposed to make policy by scaring ourselves to death?'

During the early swirl of political controversy, ABC had planned the panel as a public-relations effort to balance the film's implicit disarmament message—and the effect it might have. Antinuclear activists had been hoping to use the film as a rallying point for the flagging nuclear-freeze movement, while conservatives argued that the film would lull the public into pacifism. In fact, none of that seemed to happen. Early polls showed that the film had prompted few viewers to change their minds about how to avoid nuclear war.

Whatever the film's merits or flaws, the fact that it was made for American television may be the most notable thing about it. (In many countries, 'The Day After' will be presented in movie theaters.) It was the brainchild of Brandon Stoddard, ABC's Motion Pictures president, whose earlier efforts included 'Roots' and 'Friendly Fire.' His proposal for the film stunned his colleagues; says Stoddard, 'Most ABC officials felt that if you put on anything terrifying, no one would watch and no one would make any money.'

Formula: Problems began the moment the filmmakers began discussing how to visualize ground zero. ABC's standards and practices department was so concerned about the film's potential for gore that it held director Nicholas Meyer to an odd formula: for every three people annihilated, seven inanimate objects would have to be destroyed. ABC had another problem to contend with: how to attract sponsors to what would undoubtedly be a controversial, depressing movie. The network eventually sold commercials at relatively bargain rates. Even so, few major advertisers bought spots on the show. And there were no commercials at all during the last 80 minutes of the movie— the period after the bombs fall.

How European viewers will respond to 'The Day After' is problematic. Reactions to previews have been decidedly mixed. In West Germany, Christian Democrat Dieter Wierich called the film 'impressive' but said he thought 'the peace movement will try to misuse the film as propaganda for their cause.' In Britain, David Watt of the Royal Institute of Foreign Affairs criticized the film for underestimating 'the probable devastation.' And in France, the daily Libération editorialized that 'the most insignificant document on Hiroshima is 100 times more poignant than this Walt Disney-style production.' While that assessment may seem unfair, it does underscore an important point: that unpredictable, real events are almost always more shocking than any contrived dramas. Still, for 2½ hours 'The Day After' creates its own kind of reality, and it is one that its viewers will hope never to meet.

Alexis Gelber with bureau reports
[*Newsweek*, 5 December 1983.]

APPENDIX B

BROAD HOPES OF PEACE

P1 Australians are not celebrated for their political passions, nor are they prone to show their feelings with mass demonstrations. The fact that some quarter of a million of our fellow citizens took to the streets on Sunday as a sign of their concern over the dangers of nuclear war is a forceful indication of how many people in our community are anxious about this issue.

P2 Whatever the ulterior motives of a small minority of the participants in the weekend's marches it is obvious that the demonstrators represented a broad spectrum of the Australian public. While it is perfectly true that such gatherings would be prohibited in the Soviet bloc and that Mr Chernenko and his assistants may be able to draw some comfort from a strong display of dissent of this kind within a Western nation, it would be foolish to ignore the breadth and depth of sincere feelings held by Australians of differing political persuasions.

P3 It is perhaps a major weakness of Sunday's meetings that a broad range of opinions appear to have been represented.

P4 At one extreme many of those who took part are opposed to the development of nuclear energy in any circumstances, even if its purposes are peaceful. It is because they hold this view that a significant minority of Australians, although probably most of the marchers, remain convinced that this country should refuse to allow its uranium to be exported.

P5 Others confine their opposition to the use of nuclear arms in military strategy. This group includes unilateralists, who believe that Australia should have no part in the siting or production of these weapons, whether or not other nations have them in their possession. Other opponents of nuclear warfare do not advocate unilateral nuclear disarmament but are insistent that the achievement of a universal and enforceable treaty banning nuclear weapons is one of the most pressing necessities facing the human race.

P6 None of these standpoints is deserving of ridicule.

P7 But there is a strong, if not overwhelming, case to be made for the advantages of the peaceful use of nuclear energy under adequate safeguards and for Australia to use its bargaining power as a uranium supplier to try to ensure that those safeguards are more stringent than they appear to be at present.

P8 And, although the most rigid unilateralists may not be convinced, it is difficult to refute the proposition that, if only one side in the two major systems of alliances were without nuclear arms, the danger of war would be increased rather than reduced.

P9 However, it is impossible to reject the argument that general nuclear disarmament is among the highest priorities of statesmanship. It may be true that neither of the super-powers and none of the other nations who admit to having a nuclear arsenal are likely to take the risks involved in its use. But this does not answer the problem raised by the acquisition of these weapons by more reckless governments. Nor does it take account of the growing apprehension that one or another of the many flourishing terrorist organisations throughout the world may obtain them.

P10 Government by demonstration is no way to run a democracy. But the Federal Government, and the Opposition, would be rash to disregard the fear of so many decent and responsible Australians.

P11 It does not follow from this that they should succumb to calls for self-defeating unilateralism or to cries that our uranium should be left in the ground. But, if they let it appear that they do not share the concern about humanity's survival shown on Sunday, they will have to meet the resentment of a large, determined and highly articulate section of our population.

[*The Australian*, 17 April 1984.]

11 'Nothing left to laugh at...': humour as a tactic of resistance

Bob Hodge and Alan Mansfield
Murdoch University, Western Australia

11.1 THE ROLE OF HUMOUR AND CARNIVAL

Outside official discourse, humour is a pervasive mode of communication. It is also one of the least researched; perhaps because of what Chapman and Foot (1976) call the 'tenderness taboo', perhaps because of what Eagleton (1981: 143) (among others) sees as the pessimism and melancholia of Western Marxism. But a glance at the discourse of nuclear campaigners, in a variety of contexts, shows that humour is a widespread phenomenon. Using a variety of data sources (CND rallies, newspaper cartoons, pamphlets) this chapter will suggest that we ignore the analysis of humour at our peril. Propagandists and proselytizers and salesmen have long recognized its tactical value. Satirists have shown for millennia that the antilanguage of comedy can carry an effective and feared critique. (The notion of antilanguage is discussed in Halliday 1978: 164–83.) On the one hand, the possibility of a nuclear holocaust or the insanity of a superpower arms race is not funny. But people who want to challenge this hegemonic madness need to consider the tactical role of humour in spreading the word.

There are three main claims commonly made on behalf of humour as a weapon. One is summed up by Lina Wertmuller's[1] comment that laughter is 'the vaseline which makes ideas penetrate better'. A second is that laughter is a shield which protects critics from being punished for their truths: 'humour is the only form of revolt left in this country' (Klein).[2] A third is that it creates solidarity among laughers: 'laughter is the shortest distance between two people' (Victor Borge).[3] There is truth in all three claims, as we will show, but the separate claims do not cohere, and we need to understand the contradictory ways humour works, the contradictions which in fact constitute the basis of the humorous. Much anti-nuke humour, for instance, is 'in-group' stuff. It is here that some of our most fundamental questions must be asked. Does the carnival atmosphere of many anti-nuclear rallies simply make us feel good, or, even more sinisterly, allow pro-nuke critics of the media to dismiss the critique because of the form? Is joking behaviour a displacement mechanism for fears too gross to imagine? Does it encourage complacency by neutralizing the issues? Is a vaseline-coated revolt not worth having?

Klein's comment refers, of course, to 'legitimate' revolt. As the old nursery rhyme illustrates, calling people names does not fit into the category of violence.

Whilst we disagree that 'names can never harm me', they certainly are not 'sticks and stones'. Experiences all over the globe do show that 'legitimate' revolt is not the only form of struggle. The British and European press have even suggested that some anti-nuclear campaigners in their frustration are looking in these directions. Even in situations of more militant protest, however, the battle and struggle through language and humour must still have a prominent place. In a situation like that in Northern Ireland, humour is by no means absent from the discourse of militant republicanism.[4] It is a distinguishing feature of CND rallies, however, that, for various reasons, they have a tradition of non-violence. Indeed, anti-nuke marchers often make use of explicitly anti-war symbolism such as flowers, balloons, linking hands and so forth. In some cases this gives the marches a carnivalesque atmosphere. Paradoxically, then, the macabre possibility of holocaust is dramatized through the use of the anti-war images, most notably the figure of the clown. Following the historical precedent set by figures such as the 'Fool' of Shakespeare's *Lear*, the paradoxical role of the clown (truth-teller and entertainer) is used to get the message across.

We can note here that the notion of carnival and the myths of the 'clown' have a particular significance for the anti-nuke movement. The 'paradox of the clown' becomes significantly a metaphor for the anti-nuke protest. Nuclear rallies appear as types of carnival. The appearance of protesters dressed as clowns is perhaps a focal point of this paradox. A theorization of carnival by Bakhtin allows one to deconstruct this paradox. Bakhtin's notion refers to a 'riot of semiosis'. Bakhtin (1968: 11) states:

> We find here [in the symbols of the carnival idiom] a characteristic logic, the peculiar logic of the 'inside out', of the 'turnabout', a continual shifting from top to bottom, from front to rear, of numerous parodies and travesties, humiliations, profanations, comic crownings and uncrownings.

Eagleton stresses this aspect of carnival:

> Absolutely nothing escapes this great spasm of satire, no signifier is too solemn to be blasphemously invaded, dismantled and turned against itself. The grotesque is intrinsically double-faced, an immense semiotic switchboard through which codes are read backwards and messages scrambled into their antithesis. (Eagleton 1981: 145.)

One problem with this apparent celebration of carnival—apart from the gap many would feel between this idea of fecund, exhilarating absurdity and the typical experience of a CND rally—is the basic ambiguity at its centre. Eagleton asks the pertinent question: 'Can their intoxicating liberation be politically directed? Are they successful in welding this experience of freedom to . . . other revolutionary experiences?'. He notes his own doubts: 'Carnival laughter is incorporative as well as liberating, the lifting of inhibitors politically enervating as well as disruptive' (Eagleton 1981: 148-9). There are strategic consequences of the ambiguity (of meaning and intent) of carnival, and humour generally. Humour is characteristically at one and the same time a revolt and a non-revolt. Satirists since the genre began have been protected (though not totally) by the ambiguity of their message and by social conventions that shield them. Those active in the CND debate are not exceptions. The protection, now, is not from the noose or sword of some despot, but from libel and defamation laws, and perhaps more significantly, from certain kinds of political and ideological response. It is difficult for a government or institution to respond in any official way to a humorous attack.

One consequence of this asymmetry is that there is far more anti-nuke than pro-nuke humour. This asymmetry is, of course, not solely due to the strategic features of humour. We can note the fact that one doesn't get many pro-nuclear rallies either, although one might analyse the military march-past, for example, in this light. The work of Chaney (1983) on mass communication as public ritual or the writings of Burton and Carlen (1979) on 'official discourse' would obviously be relevant here. Our point is that pro- and anti-nuke discursive strategies are quite different and significantly separated by the use or non-use of humour. This difference between pro- and anti-nuke discourse is reflected in a number of other issues where an oppositional or minority group opposes an entrenched establishment. The leftist press in Britain and Australia have two basic styles: satirical humour and declamatory denunciation. If you are in a minority, you have to shout. A similar situation applies in Northern Ireland.[5] The central issue this raises is: why should minority or oppositional discourse choose (or be forced) to use humour to such a degree? Is this one way in which these discourses are ultimately controlled, delimited by the official discourse? Or does it show a consistent grassroots sense that humour, for all its limitations, does serve a valuable function in any resistance movement? Learning a lesson from the discourse of the pro-nuke, whose defining characteristic could be said to be a hankering after a single ultimate weapon, we could perhaps suggest that humour has a positive part to play in a struggle that must be fought by many means on many fronts.

11.2 SEMIOTICS OF HUMOUR

The topic of humour raises some important methodological issues, prompting questions about where to go to in current theory for guidance or illumination. We will start with some general principles. Much humour is visual, or involves an interplay between visual and verbal texts, so the appropriate analysis must be semiotic, aware of the functioning of a multiplicity of codes. Jokes normally are allusive, constituted by processes of intertextuality, highly dependent on context for their effect. Every text or occasion of discourse (e.g. a cartoon or a rally) makes its meaning against a background of other texts, discourses and practices in a community, and these processes and contexts must be theorized. Finally, our analysis is concerned with actions, results: people doing or not doing things that may advance the campaign. It must address the functions as well as the forms of language. It must also have a subtle and an adequate account of power and pleasure, the dynamic principles underlying social action. Green and Mort (1982) have argued for many of the radical themes and activities of the 1970s and 1980s (CND, conservation, gender, race, ethnicity) that there is a need to reassess the ways in which power operates, and strategies of resistance. Generally they are critical of both pluralist and Marxist perspectives for '. . . failing both to provide an adequate account of the multiple relations of power and domination, and to formulate a politics which is aware of the specificity of particular struggles, without operating with a tokenism or a strategy of incorporation' (p. 60).

But for the analysis of humour and effects, the classic text is still Freud's *Jokes*, a work whose strengths only become more evident in the light of contemporary theories. Freud himself was perhaps only dimly aware of working towards a 'political-somatics' and an account of mastery and desire. Central to Freud's achievement was an account of the form and structure of jokes which opened the way to their interpretation and a theory of reading them. The key was his analysis of the technique of jokes, 'joke-work', processes which constitute both the creation and interpretation of jokes. These processes he found elsewhere in psychic life: in dreams, in symptoms, in literature, art and religion. They are characterized by a riot of transformations akin to the effects of carnival in Eagleton's description. Freud's theory of transformations sees them as simple in their basic properties but in practice blind, anarchic, polyvalent, multi-semiotic. In linguistic theory Chomsky's name is associated with a theory of transformations, but it is to Freud we must go to see how Chomsky's theory might be made into something useful, not vice versa (see Hodge 1977).

Underlying the unlimited semiosis of jokes is a duality of form. A public level of meaning is yoked to and opposed or subverted by another set of meanings that are excluded from the surface of the text, repressed. The structure of meanings corresponds to the organization of the psyche of joker and laugher, from which it derives. Freud often sees the under-meanings of humour as coming straight from the body's libidinal depths, from infantile modes of thought and feeling, but in many of the jokes he analyses (as is the case with dreams) the counter-meanings are typically sharper, more valid than the official meanings that they puncture or oppose. The distinction we are making, then, is between Freud as a theorist of desire and mastery, and the more traditional account of him as a theorist of egocentric personality development through psycho-sexual growth. Humorists, anti-nuclear or others, can't be simply dismissed as reverting to the infantile.

Another feature of joking discourse, noted by others as well as Freud, is its curious relationship to reality. In linguistics, this is the area covered by theories of modality (see Halliday 1970; Kress and Hodge 1979: Ch. 7). Modality —the degree to which an utterance is believed to be true, in some sense—is decisive for language to have effects. If people are persuaded that a version of the world is true, they will act accordingly. So to attack the modality of a statement is to weaken its possible effects. In general, the aim of propagandists is to win the highest possible modality for their vision of the world, and the lowest modality for their opponents'. Initially, jokes seem to have a negative modality. Freud pointed out the origins of jokes in childish play; 'as-if' modality frees the world of representations to be available for transformational activity. In dreams and jokes, modality is reconstructed so that everyday criteria of reality no longer apply in a straightforward way. Desires are presented as reality, present, past and future merge, things become their opposite, and the whole system of negation ceases to apply, revealing the intrinsic connection that exists between modality and negation. So laughter, the marker of humour and jokes, signifies a negative ('I was only joking: I didn't mean it') or a form of modality ('I didn't really mean it'). However, at the same time it carries the affirmative ('At some level I mean it—I'd like it to be true; maybe it is'). The strength of the affirmative which emerges—a strength that depends on many factors, many signals—is, however, still decisive on the effects of humour, even if it is harder to pin down. The humorist as polemicist still aims at high modality for his own meanings. The slipperiness of humour, its capacity simultaneously to say and not say its truths, is something it shares with all heavily modalized utterances, with all forms and degrees of negation. Irony, similarly, must be understood as a species of negation. Modality and negation derive from and reflect situations of conflict. So does humour, in its way.

Freud contrasted jokes with other forms of discourse—dreams, slips of the tongue, literature—in terms of the degree to which the underlying meaning was conscious and public. Schutz (1967) developed a more comprehensive theory, essentially based on the principle of modality. He envisaged the sense of reality of an individual as being divided into different 'provinces of meaning', each with a different 'accent of reality'. Such provinces are dreams, jokes, literature, science and religion, with everyday reality itself only one province of meaning, but a decisive one. Schutz sees each province as consistent in its own terms, but self-contained, existing behind boundaries which 'bracket off' reality in a distinctive way. For Schutz, there is no smooth regulated transition from one province to another, only a 'leap', a sense of 'shock' at the transition from one to another. This claim, open to dispute in relation to the other provinces of meaning, is especially dubious with the discourse of humour, where this leap, this sense of shock, typically occurs WITHIN the domain of humour as a defining quality. Modality-shocks, however, are precisely what we would expect if humour is a play of inconsistent modalities, arising out of a juxtaposition of discourses.

Schutz's notion of 'provinces of meaning' can be supplemented by reference to Halliday's (1978) concept of REGISTER. A register includes kinds of subject matter, kinds of social relationship and context, and specific modes of communicating, all cohering in a socially recognized form. Foucault's (1971) concept of 'discourse' can be seen as analogous, with Foucault more concerned with the overall structures and effects of a set of discourses at any one time. The value of the concept of 'register' is that it allows us, as part of our social knowledge, to read off contexts and kinds of participants from qualities of a discourse. Juxtapositions of discourse, then, involve not simply competing modalities, but also complex social meanings. Humour is a social phenomenon, resting on specific and sophisticated pieces of social knowledge: it is not simply the irruption of the infantile into social discourse that some readings of Freud would suggest.

In fact Freud's account of jokes as a social process still repays study. According to Freud, jokes with a purpose (as all anti-nuke jokes are) always have a butt, a person who is subjected to ridicule. But jokes, he insists, require a third person, an 'other' who will laugh and be won over by laughter. Jokes typically are texts, visual, verbal, behavioural or whatever. We can rephrase Freud's central point about jokes by drawing on terms from a later stage in linguistic theory. Benveniste (1971) has distinguished between the structures of *énonciation* (the act of discourse which constitutes the joke-text) and the structure of the *énoncé* (in this case, the joke itself). In this scheme, the butt is the subject of the *énoncé*, while the joker is the subject of the *énonciation*. In most jokes, the joke contains a number of texts, or utterances (not necessarily verbal), produced by the butt or by others in the world of the joke. The dynamics of a joke, then, rest on a transaction between the participants in the domains of *énonciation* and *énoncé*. Freud explains the transaction of the *énonciation*, whose outward manifestations are laughter (by the audience rather than the joker), a sense of pleasure and a feeling of solidarity, as an overcoming of a resistance, an inhibition, by the joker on behalf of the audience. The joke, then, is a kind of self-display by the joker, vicariously enjoyed by a similarly divided self (symbolized by the half-shaded circle in Figure 11.1a and b). But the figures in the world of the *énoncé* are themselves constituted in similar terms. The butt of a joke often reveals thoughts and motives of which he or she is, or ought to be, unaware.

Freud distinguishes between the comic and jokes on the grounds that in the comic, the joker is not necessary. But that is because the butt of the comic is also the producer of the joke: either a naïf who would be unaware of a level of meaning of his or her text, or someone who by a slip of the tongue (or of something else) reveals a subversive meaning. So both forms are constituted by the same component elements, differently related, which can then be combined into a general model (Figure 11.1b).

From this model we can see the social dynamics of a joke that works. It has a double action: shared hostility to the butt, and solidarity between jokers and audience. We can see why humour is so useful a weapon in the language of conflict. The final step in understanding jokes as a social process is to reinsert them into a larger scheme. The butt in the text must be a representation or transformation of something in the world common to joker and audience. The split psyche of butt, audience and joker must also be seen as social in origin and meaning. The structure of repressions in the individual was constructed, not born. The voice of authority originally came from outside and was introjected to form part of the individual psyche. Jokes and humour, then, have the effect of reversing this process of internalization. In a joke, the two voices, the two forms of discourse, separate out and stand irreconcilably opposed to each other, and the struggle is situated outside the laughter, in the butt: hence the sense of self-clarification that comes from a joke. In spite of the ambiguity, the polyvalence that is so characteristic of humour, or because of it, the ultimate effect of humour is a demystifying recognition of conflict, disparity, contradiction. The solidarity it also achieves between laughers is the solidarity of a common recognition of common situation and carnival truth. That is not a bad basis for solidarity, if it can be achieved. The anti-nuclear movement can be reasonably content that humour does have the prominence it has in anti-nuclear discourse.

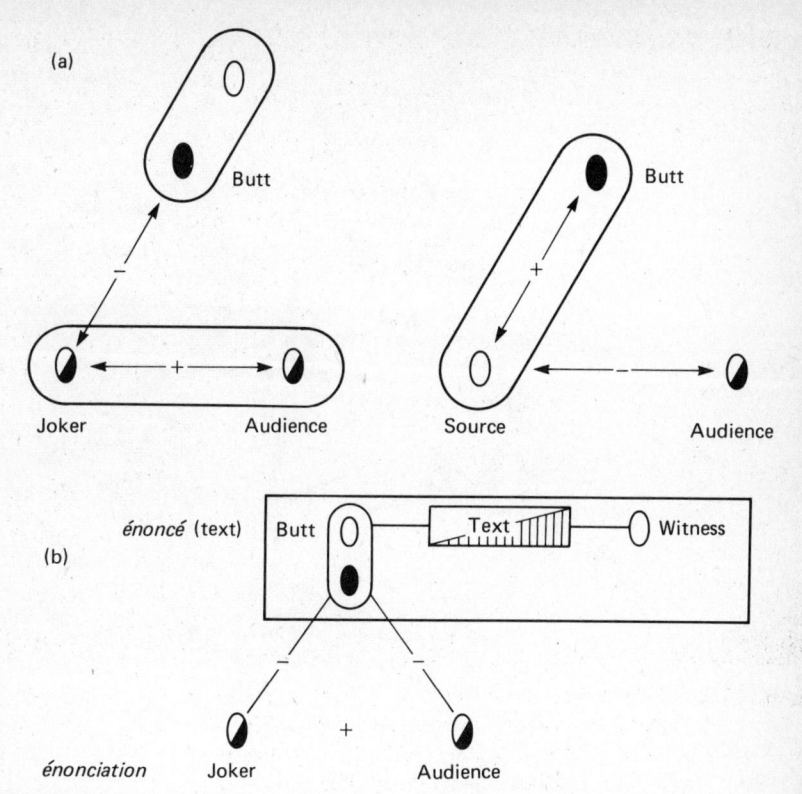

Figure 11.1

11.3 ANALYSIS OF ANTI-NUCLEAR HUMOUR

Humorous texts, like any others, do not have an invariant meaning and effect. Our discussion of humour has been intended as the framework for an analysis of specific types of texts and their different qualities. We propose now to analyse a number of typical samples of anti-nuclear humour, to try to suggest what they are saying and what they might be doing.

We will commence with a typology of anti-nuclear humour. Humour is constituted by opposing discourses, anti-nuclear and pro-nuclear, and opposing levels, surface and deep. We can then distinguish anti-nuclear humour in terms of the dominant surface discourse: anti-nuclear or pro-nuclear. As we shall see, by far the most common type is the second, where pro-nuclear discourse dominates the surface text, but we shall commence our analysis with anti-nuclear humour of the first type. For illustration we will take the following, the cover of a book of anti-nuclear cartoons, itself a cartoon (see Figure 11.2).[6] Literally at the centre of this text is a verbal text, 'No fission'. This, of course, is a pun, a conflation of 'No fishin' ' and 'No (nuclear) fission'. Such puns are common in placards carried on marches, which are then seen in newspaper photographs

Figure 11.2 Cartoon by Rolf Heinmann, reproduced with permission of the artist, from *No Fission: A Collection of Cartoons by Australian Artists*, Rolf Heimann (ed.), Access Magazines in association with Melbourne Bookmakers Press (1983).

or TV coverage of those marches. Television cameras are often alert to what are seen as the wittiest slogans. They are undoubtedly effective in terms of penetration of the audience/market. But what are they saying, and how do they work?

A first stage of analysis is to reverse the transformations which constituted the final text, with its fusion of 'fission' and 'fishin'' in the common sound. 'No fishin'' is the colloquial form of 'No fishing', a phrase from the register or discourse of public notices. The shortened form is a drastic erosion of the status of the original. This text emanates from an authority figure, a proprietor, a shire council or other public body which exercises power to ban a form of pleasure, a natural licence to hunt which still exists for urban dwellers, except where such notices stand guard. Behind the base 'No fishing' is a fuller form: '[I the duly authorized body order you that you will] not fish [in this place]'. This content, plus the social relations involved, are all implied as the deep structure or latent content of this utterance, for anyone who knows the relevant discourse. 'No fission' comes from a different discourse (protest slogans) and has a different derivation: '[We, citizens of this democracy, demand to you our rulers, that you do] not [allow nuclear] fission'. The surface form is a command, but the basis of the authority claimed is different. This text, too, carries its structure of enunciation, its version of society. These two histories and structures are then yoked together in the single notice. The relationship is one both of identity and difference. The identity is established by the pun, which achieves the transformation of 'No fishin(g)' into 'No fission', suggesting an equivalence. The differences which remain are themselves transformed into hypothetical equivalences: an order from an institution to its citizens into a demand from citizens to the government, a natural sport into an unnatural and lethal enterprise. This is the kind of inversion of the public order that characterizes the Bakhtinian Carnival.[7]

But the two notices are not equally present in the final text. The surface text says 'No fission'. 'No fishin'' is only implied by the picture and the pun. It has no objective existence. It functions as the subversive, intrusive counter-meaning. It is the surface meaning, 'No fission', which has high modal value for an anti-nuclear campaigner. It carries implicit in it the role and serious purposes of the campaigner. The joke, then, tends to undermine that seriousness, relativize its truth, weaken its modality. It is also the joke-meaning which carries the latent content of a killjoy, impersonal authority forbidding an 'innocent' pleasure, suggesting that that kind of authority has affinities with protesters. One effect of such a transformation is magically to turn a restrictive local authority into a supporter of a ban on nuclear fission, but at the same time nuclear protesters are seen as complicit in a restrictive power structure. These underlying meanings are contradictory both with themselves and with the explicit aims of a nuclear campaigner. But even that whole structure of contradictions is 'bracketed out', to use Schutz's term. The phrase is the title of a book of anti-nuclear cartoons, so we can assume that it is felt by its editors and readers to have retained its proper force. What it expresses is a kind of doubt, a withholding of total commitment from the CND campaign, a recognition of the pleasures of living (including fishing) that still exist outside a protest campaign. At one level, however, the oppositions are compatible with beliefs of the anti-nuclear movement: if there is fission, there will be 'no fishin''; instead polluted waters and a decimated populace. So the problem is not insoluble, but it remains a problem.

The rest of the cartoon also implies a certain negativity. For instance, to the right of the lone tree are three mushrooms—transformations of the mushroom cloud which is the symbol of a nuclear blast. Mushrooms are natural and benign (unless they are toadstools). These mushrooms, planted near the centre of Australia, are ambiguously either threat or neutralization of threat. In the sky around Australia we have to the left a sun, symbolizing warmth, power from nature, the alternative to nuclear energy. This alternative is made explicit in many of the cartoons we examined and is encapsulated in the simple opposition 'Solar not Nuclear'. To the right, set in a mathematically precise circle, as cool as the moon and surrounded by darkness and night, is the symbol of the Australia's Arts Action for Peace program. Again, the relation between the two symbols is one simultaneously of opposition and identity: the coldness, darkness and mathematical rationality of the peace movement, in contrast to the qualities of the sun, or the implication that in these dark times, the anti-nuclear movement is, like the moon, the only source of light. These implications are not pro-nuclear, but they are not consistently anti-nuclear. They seem more to be giving covert expression to doubts, anxieties, hesitations of nuclear campaigners. The expression of such doubts, alongside a strong commitment to the cause, is not, however, necessarily counter-productive, nor far from the conscious minds of the compilers of this book. Near the end of the collection, alongside another version of the 'No fission' notice, there is a verse which carries this sentiment explicitly:

> We are all of us afraid
>   Someone must take a stand,
> Here coward,
>   take my coward's hand.[8]

Although in some versions of the movement it might be thought that campaigners should have no inner doubts and that expression of such feelings should be disguised or suppressed, campaigners know that they are human, with many a hidden doubt and fear. The function of humour such as this cartoon's is to allow a common recognition of these feelings which is shared but not made vulnerable to attack. 'Humanity' and the saving of the human race from the destructive capacity of inhuman machines/politicians/soldiers is the level at which much of the movement's discourse is operating. With this cartoon the anti-nuclear message still has its existence, on the surface: it has been said, publicly, and the rest of the joke serves to give it emotional three-dimensionality, an appeal to readers who would feel threatened by an unqualified commitment.

But most anti-nuclear humour falls into the second category, with a surface discourse that is pro-nuclear. There are two major sub-types. In the first sub-type the subject of the *énoncé* is an archetypal proponent of the nuclear viewpoint, revealing the madness or absurdity of that position. A typical example is illustrated by another cartoon (Figure 11.3).[9] Again, a verbal text is at the centre of the joke, an utterance emanating from and defining the butt, the senior militarist. The immediate point of the joke is the transformational inversion of the well-known cliché, 'the destruction of civilization as we know it'. What is being transformed here is also a discourse genre, patriotic popular literature, in which this motive is always ascribed to the indescribably evil (and foreign) enemies of 'democracy'. 'On the other hand' claims quite different motives for the speaker. But the sentence itself is bristling with ambiguities. 'Civilization of destruction' is either 'to civilize destruction, i.e. to domesticate, to tame, or to appropriate it to civilization' (leaving further mind-boggling depths in which we speculate what might really be meant by this) or 'a civilization, i.e. a whole culture, built on or dedicated to destruction'. The 'it' of 'as we know it', in the cliché is taken to refer to 'civilization'. In the reworking, it seems to refer to 'destruction, as we know it', suggesting that 'we' are authorities on destruction, not civilization. Even if 'it' refers to 'civilization' the modal quality of 'we know' comes into play, casting doubt on how valid 'our' concept of civilization is in any case. Overall, we have the butt claiming a grand and initially impressive defence of his civilized motives, distinguishing himself from two kinds of imaginary opponent, writers of melodramatic fiction, and the villains of such fiction, but his real motives and meanings escape and betray him, and his whole edifice of justification collapses. The sequence of responses

HUMOUR AS A TACTIC OF RESISTANCE 207

Figure 11.3 Cartoon reproduced with permission from *No Fission: A Collection of Cartoons by Australian Artists*, Rolf Heimann (ed.), Access Magazine in association with Melbourne Bookmakers Press.

in the exemplary reader is given by the pictured audience: the first scientist amazed but impressed while the second frowns dubiously.

The scene portrayed warrants analysis, too, to make the point that humorous texts can make a multiplicity of points with great economy and considerable redundancy. The scene represented is some communications centre or ops room, with innumerable telescreens and computer terminals, all of them signifying high technology. Above is a map of the world which this technology will save. The words the general is speaking blank out part of Russia, China, India and South East Asia, like the labels which remove those countries from the category of 'civilization', in minds like that of the general. America also is significantly absent, for a different reason: it is outside the scene of potential conflict, nowhere but everywhere. In Peirce's terms, the picture is an iconic sign, a representation of a type of setting, but its distortions and gaps are also signifiers of the blindspots and limitations of the military-technological mind, indexical signs. This set of signifiers can be subsumed by the concept of a discourse or register which combines a theme (high technology and militarist efficiency) and modes of talking about it. In this case, the picture is related to innumerable authoritative, technically slick documentaries or films of NASA or the Pentagon, authoritative presentations of authority in action. But the artist has transformed this discourse in two ways, in order to undercut it: first by his style—childlike line drawings instead of the high-gloss cinematic images of the genre; second by his strategic replacement of the whirling discs of computers with the standard symbol for a nuclear danger area. The first transformation affects the modality of the original discourse, the second establishes, within it, an equation between dependence on computers (and high technology in general), and complicity with nuclear technology itself.

Underlying the proliferating meanings carried by both visual and verbal text is a common strategy. The thought processes, the meanings, assumptions and discourse of the enemy are presented with naïve fullness, so that the confusions, contradictions, illogicalities or blindnesses are exposed as though by the perpetrators themselves. In anti-nuke cartoons this self-exposure can be more or less subtle, more or less credible. The more credible they are, that is the higher their modality, the more effective they are. So an actual quotation which is a slip of the tongue, or more revealing than the speaker intended, is the most effective target for this kind of humour. The former Prime Minister of Australia, Malcolm Fraser, once said 'Life wasn't meant to be easy' and the phrase, taken as symptomatic of his puritan, patrician attitude, did more damage to his standing than any policy decision he made. The same can be said of a phrase like 'expletive deleted' with the Nixon tapes. In the cartoon we are analysing, Lofo (the cartoonist) has not used an actual quotation, but the verbal and visual discourse are eminently recognizable, and sufficiently authentic, to carry conviction. An effective joke carries a relatively high modality; though modality judgements depend on general assumptions and beliefs, so that what is credible to one person may be incredible to another.

Another version of this basic strategy can be seen in a pamphlet entitled *Meet Mr Bomb*, which is a complex parody of the simplistic kind of pamphlet used by government agencies to 'inform' the general public. Such pamphlets translate official discourse into a visual somatic and occasionally populist mode of discourse. The parody begins:[10]

> *I light up your life: a brief autobiography.*
> Hi! And welcome to the tale of my amazing life! It all begins—well, back at the beginning, nearly 50 years ago when ardent scientists around the world were competing for the honor of becoming proud parents. Unfortunately, all had problems: inability to maintain reaction: failure to reach cataclysm: in the case of laboratory accidents, premature evacuation—in short, they couldn't 'get it up'. Then came World War II.

The humour here works mainly through puns, which bring together not simply two opposite concepts, but opposing forms of discourse. 'I light up your life', for instance, re-uses the discourse of popular song, where the phrase would refer to the effects of love and beauty. Here 'light' is literal as well as metaphoric, and the 'lighting up' of a life is the lethal, blinding flash of a blast, not love and life. With the series of puns on 'reaction'/'erection', etc., nuclear discourse is converted to the discourse of psychotherapy. The scientists' initial failure is equated with sexual inadequacies, in the deep structure of the jokes, with sexual potency, 'getting it up', being the production of a nuclear blast. The early atomic scientists are implicitly criticized, but from the point of view of a macho and morbid form of sexuality. The problem with this form of humour is that the surface butt (early, pioneering physicists) and the deep butt (a male obsessed with his own potency) are not always tactically well-chosen antagonists for CND purposes.

The intricacy of the discourse of gender and sexuality with the nuclear debate is far too complex to be discussed in this chapter. It is crucial, however, in at least two senses. Firstly, because as Greenham Common, Pine Gap and so forth have shown, women are occupying in many instances literally the front-line in the anti-nuke struggle. The Greenham slogan 'Take the toys from the boys' shows at least one way in which the two struggles are articulated. Secondly, as is suggested in our foregrounding of Freud and Bakhtin, an analysis of power in contemporary society must be both 'positive' and 'negative'. Following Foucault (1980), this entails the development of a political somatics which must of necessity, in foregrounding desire, consider (and deconstruct) the discourse of sexuality. This, as emphasized in current feminist writing, is intricately bound up with gender identity and a patriarchal structuring of the social formation. In considering the above example, then, we must be aware of the way in which different struggles are related. This is not to be done in the traditional Marxist sense which often had the consequences of relegating such issues to the status of epiphenomena of a real struggle, that of class, but in a way whereby, as the Birmingham analysis[11] shows, class, gender and race struggles are all connected and bound up in the struggle of the anti-nuke.

Similar problems arise with the 'gallows humour' which is a feature of anti-nuke humour. Anti-nuclear campaigners want the general public to be aware of the horrific consequences of a nuclear holocaust: the horror, fully appreciated, will mobilize resistance. But a frontal attack on this topic can be counter-productive. People, faced with a horror they cannot endure, switch off. 'Gallows humour' gets around this problem by offering a vision of cataclysm, essentially the vision of an anti-nuke, but with the surface modality of a pro-nuke, a sense of its unreality, an emotional neutrality. In the *Meet Mr Bomb* pamphlet, for instance, there is a section on coping with the aftermath of the Bomb. The problem of 'intruders' into a private bomb shelter is dealt with by giving a series of recipes for cooking them: 'Intruder à la maison', 'Intruder Gumbo', 'Southern Fried Intruder', etc.[12] The homely discourse of recipes, with its factual modality and neutral tone, seems to negate acts of selfishness, murder and cannibalism in the breakdown of 'civilization as we know it', in the aftermath of the Bomb. Jokes on the theme of mutations are a common form of anti-nuclear humour. The *Meet Mr Bomb* pamphlet has a series of 'tips for post-nuclear teens', which includes:

> 8. Going out with a mutant? Don't be disturbed if, while feeling around under his or her clothing, you discover unfamiliar parts. That's the *fun* of mutant dating. Blurting a remark such as 'Yuck, that's disgusting' is insensitive.

or

Genitally speaking
Now occasionally, you may notice an organ falling off during sex. Do not be alarmed. This is a normal mishap following an all-out nuclear exchange, and will disappear after a decade or two. Simply say to your partner, 'I'm sorry, I believe your - - has fallen off.' Or alternately: 'Oops, there goes my - -'.[13]

Here the deep structure contains a projection of the consequences of nuclear war that is even more horrific, in some respects, than the worst CND fears. The mixture of matter of fact modality and nightmare content is a contradiction, which may be resolved by different people in different ways. Paradoxically, if the nightmare vision has too high a modality—as for a committed and knowledgeable anti-nuke—then such jokes will not be experienced as funny. Someone who finds such jokes funny assigns the images a relatively low modality value, and enjoys the sado-masochism that underlies them. That might sound like a negative judgement on their likely effectiveness. In practice, modality is an ambiguous phenomenon. 'Gallows humour' presents its target as both real and unreal, as a way of distancing the unthinkable so that it can be turned on its head, and subjected to a sense of control. If that is necessary, at some times, for many people in coming to terms with nuclear truths, then this type of humour has its role to play. The licensed revolt of carnival truth, then, may be capable of real political advance. Nicholas Humphrey (1981: 494) has given two reasons why people fail to act on their stated belief that a nuclear war is a horrendous possibility. One is our inability to comprehend the 'facts' of megatonnes and megadeaths:

> We close off from such nonsense. Try as we may we will not get the message. Our minds are minds finely tuned by culture and by evolution to respond to the frequencies of the real world. And when a message comes through on an alien wavelength, it sets up no vibrations.

Another reason is a deliberate blindness, a denial or censorship of truths that are 'too painful or inconvenient'. Carnival truth and gallows humour resolve both these problems by declaring these 'facts' as nonsense, as absurd, thereby allowing them access via a non-alien familiar channel in our minds. The price, of course, is that the original problem still remains, of presenting these truths with a high modality, as truths to be acted on, by people who previously couldn't and wouldn't understand or act. The crucial question to ask here, as elsewhere on the topic of humour, is: when the laughter stops, will belief be stronger, and action on behalf of the anti-nuclear cause be more likely?

NOTES

1. Lina Wertmuller, cited in *The Book of Quotes*, New York, Sunrise (1979: 225).
2. Larry Klein (comedy writer for the 'Tonight Show'), ibid., p. 207.
3. Victor Borge, ibid., p. 207.
4. A. Mansfield, work undertaken for Ph.D. thesis, University of Wales (1984).
5. Mansfield, ibid.

6. *No Fission: A Collection of Cartoons by Australian Artists*, Rolf Heimann (ed.), Access Magazine in association with Melbourne Bookworkers Press (1983).
7. For many people we have shown this cartoon to, the phrase 'Gone fishin' ' seems irresistibly suggested. By whatever means these readers get to that meaning from the surface, it seems a sufficiently common reading to count as a public meaning of the text. It reinforces the subversive affirmation of hedonism, the carefree enjoyment of life, the siding with nature over culture, that we can derive more systematically from 'No fishin' '.
8. *No Fission*, op. cit., p. 62.
9. Ibid., p. 45.
10. *Meet Mr Bomb: A Practical Guide to Nuclear Extinction*, New London, New Hampshire, High Meadow Publishing Co. Inc. (1982).
11. Centre for Contemporary and Cultural Studies (1982) and on gender and nculear technology see Easlea (1983).
12. *Meet Mr Bomb*, op. cit., p. 19.
13. Ibid., p. 23.

Part IV
Towards a critical linguistics

12 The concept of context and the theory of action

Erich Steiner
Universität des Saarlandes, Saarbrücken, W. Germany

12.1 'CRITICAL LINGUISTICS'

'Critical Linguistics' is a term taken from Roger Fowler and Gunther Kress (Fowler *et al.* 1979: 185 ff.; Kress and Hodge 1979; Steiner and Schmitz 1982), who use it to refer to the application of linguistic methods in the investigation of the ideology (i.e. system of beliefs and meanings) underlying a text and reinforced by it.[1] Once the underlying system of beliefs has been characterized, a given text may be shown to serve and/or reflect the interests of a class or group of people—not necessarily the group of people producing or reproducing the text. The notion of 'critical linguistics', therefore, has particular interest at a time of acute ideological conflicts between people, social classes, and nations. There have, of course, always been linguists who have expressed themselves against political oppression, aggressive wars, and other phenomena occurring at times of political crises. The connection, between such views and the linguistic methodology of people holding them, is in some cases only a very weak one. 'Critical linguistics', however, claims a more direct connection between the analytical work and the political context of the analysis of the texts. In a sense, 'critical linguistics' is a way back to rhetoric, but not just to rhetoric as we have inherited it from antiquity. What we require is a rhetoric enriched by, and not separated from, the methodology of linguistics, where both logic and grammar have played an important role.

12.2 RHETORIC

The concept of situation has always been present in rhetoric in a natural way. In classical democratic Athens, there were three institutionalized 'contexts of situation' in which it was important for citizens to have knowledge in rhetoric —namely, the different kinds of public gatherings where political (or deliberative), forensic (or judicial), and ceremonial (or epideictic) speeches had to be made. The structure and content of a particular speech would be dependent on these situations and their components (cf. Aristotle, *Rhetorica*, 1.3), though beyond these basic types we find little generalization to a more comprehensive typology of 'situations'. The concept of activity is also implicitly present. With the institutionalization of certain forms of social behaviour (jurisdiction, political decision-making, etc.), the corresponding forms of activity of individuals engaged in it were regularized, too, i.e. goals were set in advance, and possible means of achieving these established. Of these activities, making a speech was only one type, but a very important one, and as such the focus of attention of rhetoric. Four out of five phases of making a speech (*inventio, dispositio, elocutio, memoria, pronuntiatio*) were thought of as mental actions and operations, in which the physical 'situation' was thought of as being reflected rather straightforwardly (the best-known codification is Cicero, *de Inventione*, I.vii.9). There was clearly no way of getting at these processes in any other way than introspection. Dialectics dealt with concepts and inferences (arguments, predicates, syllogisms), but did so without connecting them in a direct way to 'situation'.

There was none the less a clear social and political motivation behind the early flourishing of rhetoric: the making and understanding of clear and persuasive speeches in assemblies where serious matters in the life of the community were under discussion. Rhetoric had grown in a natural climate of democracy for the free citizens (i.e. those who were not slaves) and it had a clear function. There was at first no question of separating it mechanically from dialectics and grammar. Classical rhetoric, dialectics, and grammar had an overall unity which is often lacking in modern conceptions, but which the 'critical linguist' might seek to recover.

The forms and functions of codified rhetoric underwent many mutations with the changing political circumstances of the Roman Empire, the Christian Middle Ages, the Renaissance and the spread of literacy. In our own period codified rhetoric has re-emerged in the province of the technocratic expert rather than in general education. Atkinson (1984), for instance, has rediscovered through empirical study of political speeches the effectiveness of methods taken for granted by rhetoricians ancient and modern. Most politicians at some stage undergo rhetorical training; courses in rhetoric are sold by publicity agents to management in industry. In these contexts, rhetoric is subordinated to the maximization of profit and the exercise of power. One role for 'critical linguistics' would be to extend knowledge of such techniques.

12.3 LINGUISTICS

The advantage of modern linguistic methods over traditional approaches seems to be that the criteria used for identifying units of analysis are relatively explicit and orientated towards formal features. This advantage, however, seems to be bought at the cost of a serious weakness of linguistic methods in the case of some of the dominating schools. Modern linguistics, at least in its structuralist orientations, for a long time neglected meaning. There was an almost complete restriction to questions of form, which, though understandable within the context of the development of scientific attitudes towards objective criteria, is a serious obstacle for many kinds of application. Until well into the 1960s, few procedures had been developed for the description of meaning (notable exceptions are French functionalism, British functionalism, the Prague School, and some Marxist conceptions of language). When meaning re-entered linguistics, it was again in a Cartesian, mentalist, idealist perspective (the work of Katz, Fodor, Postal, for example)—the scientific tradition which had been criticized by, at least, American structuralism. Since then, linguists have again become used to talking about such interesting, but hardly accessible, concepts as 'innate ideas', 'features', 'relations', 'intuitions', etc., with their modern roots in cognitive anthropology, formal logic, and cognitive psychology.

In view of all this we have to admit that the situation for anyone using linguistic methods to find out more about the meaning(s) of texts is somewhat problematic. Procedures for analysing the forms of language seem to be overdeveloped in relation to what they can show us about the meanings of texts. As far as the analysis of meaning is concerned, however, the critical linguist still has to rely on intuitive categories (topic, concept, truth, falsehood, contradiction, conclusion, etc.), which can be related to a good traditional grammar almost as well (or as badly) as to the most advanced linguistic frameworks.

Is there any way out of the dilemma, if on the one hand we insist on the centrality of meaning in any critical analysis, and if on the other hand we reject an idealistic conception of meaning—that is, one relying too heavily on the postulation of inaccessible, unobservable, and innate cognitive categories? In other words, is there a productive solution to the contradiction between a narrow behaviourism and a narrowly idealistic mentalism? Our approach to this problem will be to take as a starting-point neither mere mechanical sequences of physical events, nor abstract relations between hypothesized cognitive categories and structures. Instead, we shall take HUMAN ACTIVITY. In the present perspective, we assume that human activity has two complementary aspects. There is on the one hand an external aspect, describable as physical events, ranging from things, persons, and the linguistic output, etc. And on the other hand there is an internal aspect, describable as psychological processes like motivation, planning, hypothesis-building, creation of mental models, comparison of the mental model with sensory input, etc.

Both aspects can be transformed into each other, the internal into the external with the help of language (for example, co-operation within working groups), and the external into the internal (for example, the ontogenesis of language, where external interactions are internalized, cf. Vygotsky 1962; Weir 1962; Gopnik 1982; McNeill 1980). In the rest of this chapter we shall look at attempts to describe (part of) human activity without isolating these two aspects from each other. In particular, we shall consider concepts such as CONTEXT, SITUATION, ACTIVITY, ACTION as interconnected categories.

12.4 CONTEXT AND ACTION: SOCIOLOGICAL MODELS

If we wish to work towards a synthesis of theories of context and activity in order to go beyond the mentalist–empiricist controversy, we have to build up a set of categories which can be used for the explanation of human interactive activity and which can be linked to linguistic analyses. It is relevant not only to consider work in linguistics, but also the theory and data to be found in sociology, psychology and political economy. This is an ambitious programme, but the reasons for making a start are obvious: the concern of critical linguistics is to relate language to its users, and to seek some principled way of bringing out the ideologies inherent in their communications.

The concepts of situation/context or activity/action in their external aspects, i.e. referring to things, persons, processes in a particular constellation, are present in several disciplines. The object of study of sociology is, almost by definition, the social situation in which people live and act. Definitions of 'actions' or 'situations' are frequent in the works of leading sociologists of our century (cf. Weber 1922). In particular, Talcott Parson's ideas on this area are worth describing briefly (cf. Parsons 1937: Ch.II) because they link up easily with the conceptions of models of 'action' and 'situation', which we shall discuss later. Parson's 'act unit' has the following components:

1. one or several actors;
2. and END, towards which the action is directed;
3. the SITUATION, consisting of
   (a) CONDITIONS, not under the actor's control;
   (b) MEANS, under the actor's control;
4. orientation of these elements towards the end.

Note that one element in particular is not present in this framework, namely the PROCESS, event, or activity itself. It is partly this lack of the dynamic element of activity which gives some sociological conceptions the static character of a 'scenery' of elements, instead of that of an ongoing and ever-changing process. It is particularly where a rather deterministic concept of role is introduced to cover the potentialities of human behaviour in a 'situation' that there is the danger of a rigid determinism from conventions to human activity (cf. Mead 1934).

The concept of role has been very influential in sociology and neighbouring areas, but it has also been controversial (cf. Bernstein 1980; Haug 1972). For our purposes the concept of role is at best unnecessary, and at worst misleading. It is misleading if taken as the basic category to explain activity, in that it tends to obscure the influence of basically economic class interests, filtered through the ideological and political spheres of society—the influence, in particular, on the determining of human cognition and 'activity'. If, on the other hand, the label of 'role' is only attached to concepts referring to 'potential of action in a certain situation, given such and such interests, intentions, plans of the actor', then, of course, it does not obscure our view. But in that case it would receive a very general interpretation, referring to a concept that is already fully covered by other terms, as we shall see below. What we have just said about certain sociological conceptions seems to apply to some more recent approaches as well (cf. Edwards 1976). The theories of 'activity', which we shall concentrate on, are centred around the individual, and we must be careful not to lose sight of the essentially social character of 'activity' and of the 'situation'.

In attempts to come to grips with the concept of situation, it has always been difficult to decide how to generalize from the multitude of individual situations in such a way as to be able to make statements which are not either trivial, or else powerful and interesting, but in no way supported by their concept of 'situation'. Developments in sociology, psychology, anthropology, and linguistics illustrate this difficulty all too well. One solution is to take one particular type of 'situation' as a model for all relevant 'situations'. Another conceivable approach is that of first making an empirical sample of (or descriptions of) many situations, and then trying to generalize, i.e. abstract the recurring patterns from these (cf. Cantor *et al.* 1982).

An example of the first type of approach is Marx's analysis of the 'working process', an analysis on which he built his account of the foundations of capitalist society (cf. Marx, *Capital*, Vol. 1, Part III, Ch.X). Marx's analysis unites within its perspective the dynamic activity aspect with the static situation aspect, and can easily be made to link up with contemporary ideas about goal-directed action. Of course, this model is not without predecessors: classical economists like Ricardo and Smith had, up to a certain point, followed a similar process. Approaching Marx's model from our perspective, we note first a distinction between 'work' and 'activity'. 'Activity' is human behaviour which is not viewed with respect to a certain product. As such, it is the more general category in the sense that 'work' presupposes 'activities' (like running, thinking, resting, eating, etc.), but 'activities' may or may not be realized as 'work' (building a house, opening a door, hammering a nail in, etc.). This distinction is also to be found in frameworks by von Wright (1963, 1971, 1972) or by the Russian School of psychology which we shall discuss later. The working process, then, is seen as consisting of the following stages and entities:

1. the materials on which one works;
2. instruments;
3. worker/agent;
4. working operations;
5. the end for which one works;
6. the product.

Several characteristics of this system of categories should be noted. It is a 'system' in the sense that the meaning of any of its elements is determined not by its physical appearance but by its place in the network of relations in the system. A human being, for example, is not necessarily an agent, but may equally be any of the above terms, 1, 2, 5 or 6. The objection to a capitalist mode of production, for example, is that the worker is the instrument of capital rather than the agent or subject of his/her work. Equally, a material object, like a hammer, can be 6, 1, 2, 5. Note, however, that in a large-scale analysis, i.e. one not restricted to minimal working processes, the only unit that can realize 3 is humans, beings with the potential of consciousness. Machines cannot be 'workers' in a Marxian analysis.

Another characteristic of this system is that it unites external and internal factors to some extent. At least 5 is to be seen as a mental entity, but 4 also is meant to include external activity and internal cognitive activity. It is this feature of the whole system which, among other things, has prevented a 'mentalist–empiricist controversy' in Marxian psychology. Marx himself used this framework to analyse the fundamental mechanism of production in capitalist society, questions of central importance being those concerning who determines 5, and who has control over 6—clearly, decisive questions for the whole process of social interaction, as well as for individual psychology.

Marxian thinking has a long tradition in critical analyses of texts, but attempts to use his categories of 'activity/work' for constructing models of action and cognition have been rare (cf., however, Rossi-Landi 1974; Steiner forthcoming). Marx's choice of the working process as the model of a 'situation' is certainly not arbitrary, and it seems to me to be an interesting development when models of 'goal-directed action' from cognitive psychology and related areas are brought in contact with the world of productive work in modern industry (cf. Leplat 1971-2; Leplat and Pailhous 1971-2; Weill-Fassima 1971-2; Hacker 1982, 1978; Singleton 1972; Hoc 1972).

This is as far as we shall take our considerations of models of the external aspects of 'activity' and 'situation'. Certain major approaches that we cannot discuss here should be mentioned. Anthropology, for example, has produced models of 'situation'. Behaviourist psychology, too, has always had a concept of 'situation', a concept, however, that appears to be a collection of entities only connected by the relations of stimulus, response, and reinforcement. The systems that we are looking at there are richer in the sense that they include external and internal factors, as well as a whole variety of relations between terms (means–end, cause, purpose, etc.) which could be reformulated only clumsily, if at all, in behaviourist terminology.

12.5 CONTEXT AND ACTION: PSYCHOLOGICAL MODELS

From the days of Thorndike, Watson, and Weiss onwards, the investigation of human behaviour was methodologically orientated towards what was describable as chains of stimuli and response. This excluded the development of scientific hypotheses about cognition, in so far as it was not describable in such terms. Despite counter-currents like Gestalt psychology, Piaget's or Bruner's theories of cognitive development, behaviourism dominated the scene. Behaviourism did in fact have a concept of 'activity' and 'situation'; but behaviourist concepts did not seem to go very far beyond common sense, couched in stimulus–response terminology, and this would include treatments of language such as Skinner's *Verbal Behavior* (1957). The turning-point came with the development of frameworks which demonstrated, on the one hand, that certain important areas of human activity were in principle not accessible to behaviouristic methods, and, on the other hand, that there had come into existence a new way of lending empirical credibility to non-behaviourist frameworks in the form of the computer and its programs (cf. Chomsky 1959; Miller, Galanter, Pribram 1960). Since then, theorizing in psychology and related fields has shifted towards processes and units of cognition and perception. In some cases, this has led to the assumption of certain processes in the brain which can easily be regarded as inner reflections of external activity. Take, for example, Miller, Galanter and Pribram's influential notion that external and internal activity can be regarded as consisting of a hierarchy of units which may in turn consist of units assembled from the same basic building blocks, the so-called

TOTE-units ('test-operate-test-exit'), a mechanism which was supposed to be a universal of human activity (cf. also Pribram 1971). Another example is McNeill's attempt (1979, 1980) to explain the structure of linguistic and cognitive activity partly through an assumed iconic relationship between motor action and language early in ontogeny. Further, the general structure of human activity, it has been argued recently, defines the context (the situation) as interiorized in stable cognitive representations, without which understanding and meaning are impossible (cf. Weimer and Palermo (eds) 1982; Parret and Bouveresse (eds) 1981; Mandler and Johnson 1977; Stein 1982; Denis and Dubois 1976; Garnham, Oakhill, Johnson-Laird 1982).

Conceptions of human activity have received further impulses from the modelling of intelligent human activity, especially problem-solving tasks, in artificial intelligence (cf. Newell and Simon 1972; see also *Journal of Pragmatics*, 6, 3/4). A good example of this general approach can be found in Schank and Abelson's *Scripts, Plans, Goals, and Understanding* (1977). The authors define a set of semantic primitives which can be linked in various chains of causality (pp. 22 ff.), and are assumed to stand for states and processes in the real world. An important notion is that of 'script' (pp. 36 ff.), which has its origins in Minsky's work on the representation of background knowledge in what he termed 'frames' (Minsky 1975; cf. Metzing 1980). A script is a 'standard event sequence' and exists only for certain stereotyped and recurrent 'situations', such as 'visit to a restaurant', 'birthday party', etc. It is essentially a sequence of steps in an action, seen from the angle of one particular agent. Scripts can interact, and can be embedded within each other. The generalized version of a script, i.e. a projected way of acting not tied to recurring 'situations', is defined as a plan (pp. 69 ff.). Plans describe the set of choices a person evaluates when he/she sets out to accomplish a goal. A plan is thus a series of projected actions for the realization of a goal, where the 'projection' may take the form of a program or mental picture. Goals, plans, and actions can be embedded within each other. Goals require a motivation (p. 123), and plans and realized actions will, in order to be successful, have to fulfil the ncessary and sufficient conditions for the state(s) of affairs given in the goals.

Abelson's (1973) application of the script concept gives a concrete example that is of direct relevance to the concerns of this book. His aim is to construct a computer model for the representation of ideological systems and their relation to political discourse. Using conceptual primitives to represent stereotype action sequences along the lines sketched above, he proposes an 'Ideology Machine' that models cold-war beliefs and is capable of simulating responses to foreign-policy questions by a right-wing American ideologue. The system depends on a 'master script' which defines answers such as 'When Free World uses power, then there are Commie defeats. When Free World doesn't use power, then Commie schemes will yield Commie victories', and so on (Abelson 1973: 291; see also Boden 1977: 69 ff.). This approach has been neglected in studies of political discourse, with the exception of Downes (1978, 1984). It might be objected that the kind of discourse behaviour modelled by such programs is severely restricted as far as the potentiality of human behaviour is concerned. However, the very 'boundedness' of Abelson's master script may be regarded as an accurate model of the way people may behave in certain kinds of situation. As Abelson himself points out,

> Members of the peace movement find it abhorrent and indeed impossible to indulge in Hermann Kahnian conjectures as to what might lie beyond nuclear war, whereas rabid anti-communist hawks do not mind that exercise in the slightest, but have no stomach whatsoever for imagining the future following a communist victory. [p. 292.]

Whatever one thinks of Abelson's assumptions here, there is a suggestive framework for comparing variations and conflicts between ideological systems.

For our purposes, two points are worth noting. First, concepts that have for a long time been regarded as unscientific ('thinking, planning, visualizing a situation', and the like) are operationalized by writing programs which will lead to observable external behaviour based on these concepts. Secondly, the ancient notion of a 'reflection of external reality in cognition' is operationalized, the external behaviour of program and machines in this case being that of producing text. Seen in this perspective, the work of Schank and Abelson, and others in AI and cognitive science, is clearly important for any attempt to make our key concepts explicit. It was developments within AI, computer science, psychology, and, to some extent, linguistics and philosophy, which towards the end of the 1970s led to the development of the new interdisciplinary field of 'cognitive science' concerned with 'internal activity', i.e. cognition. It can be seen as a response to developments which we have indicated here. The old distinctions of 'mind–matter' and 'mentalism–empiricism' are breaking down due to advances in the neurosciences, the modelling of goal-directed action, linguistics, cognitive psychology, and philosophy. The basic method involves the forming of hypotheses and constructing of models of mental representations, the writing of programs that simulate the postulated activity, and empirical verification in the neurosciences, psychological experiments, linguistic data (cf. Johnson-Laird 1980).[2]

If we are looking for a theory of activity that bridges the gap between the internal and the external, another place we might look is the Russian School of Psychology and Neurophysiology connected with the names of Vygotsky, Luria, and Leont'ev (but also Anokhin, Bernstein, Gal'perin). The basic way of thinking in this group is Marxian, i.e. dialectical–materialist, and 'activity' has been conceived from the outset as productive, that is as goal-directed activity in the widest sense. Further, internal and external activity are regarded as mutually transformable, though primacy is given at least phylogenetically and in a broad sense causally, to external activity. Explanation of cognitive processes is related to neurophysiological data, an approach that has been connected to extensive research in aphasia. 'Activity', in this view, can be described on a hierarchy of levels: neurophysical, psychological, sociological. But, while phenomena on each of these levels of description can often be used in correlation with each other, it would be wrong to explain one level in terms of the other—the fallacy of reductionism. The correlation that has been sought most often in this school is that between data from the level of 'activity' with data from the level of neurophysiology. A clear focus of interest is the functional organization of the higher cortical functions (language, perception, planning, cognition). Among other things, the Russian School proposes a solution to the old localist vs. non-localist controversy in hypotheses about the functional structure of the brain. The general drift is to seek to overcome both of the extreme views by employing the notion of a 'functional system' which is built up in the brain and the whole nervous system, according to task, goal, and objective of the activities going on at a given time. These functional systems are regarded as coded reflections of functional systems in working processes. The correlation with the level 'above', i.e. the organization of activity in groups and larger units of social organization, is established within a Marxist sociology.

Let us now look at the theory of 'activity' and its relationship to linguistic activity in particular. In giving this brief account, I am drawing on material that is to be found in various places in the publications of members of the Russian School, though nowhere in the condensed form I am casting it in here. The aim is to give a useful integration of their ideas.

The theory operates with three ranks of structures within the overall structure of activity. These are ACTIVITY, ACTION, and OPERATION. ACTIVITIES are human behavioural units in their most general form, answering to needs (cultural and/or physiological). That is to say, they are aroused by those needs and have objectives that will satisfy those needs. The activity ceases with the reaching of the objective, the satisfaction of the need. Examples of activity are eating, moving, working, thinking. Looking more closely at the whole phenomenon of activity, we find that an activity can be realized by one or more ACTIONS. An action is defined by its conscious purpose or goal, designed to fulfil (partly) the need, reach the objective of the activity which it realizes. Actions, in this framework, are composed of four phases:

(i) MOTIVATION, where a course of action is invoked in relation to the need of the general activity;
(ii) PLANNING, where a program for the action is developed, alternative hypotheses evaluated and related to their probable outcomes;
(iii) EXECUTION, where the action is actually carried through.
(iv) EVALUATION, where the outcome is checked against the original plan, its execution checked, and, in case of failure, the whole action re-entered. Each of these four elements or phases of action is realised or filled by units of activity (used here in the general sense) from one rank below operations (cf. Searle 1980 for a discussion of what seems to me to be a similar distinction).

Operations are units of activity defined by a task orientated towards the reaching of the purpose and goal of the action which they realize. In the case of an individual, operations realizing motivation, planning, and evaluation will take place mostly inside the organism, whereas operations realizing execution will be external in the case of bodily actions. Operations are thus the lowest unit within this framework, and do not have a structure in terms of the sensor-motor components of behaviour as analysed in detail by neurophysiology.

Recent years have seen the laying of the foundations of theories of 'activity', of which the Russian theory is an early variant (cf. von Cranach and Harré (eds) 1982; von Cranach, Kalbermatten, Indermühle, Gugler 1980; Rehbein, 1979). Theories of goal-directed action try to integrate the concepts we have been considering, combining insights from all the areas mentioned in this article. The picture that emerges is, in a very broad outline, the following.

Goal-directed action is organized in two dimensions. It is organized sequentially, i.e. it exhibits a temporal–spatial structure with the possibility of segmentation of units. And it is organized hierarchically, i.e. goal-directed action is analysable on several levels which realize or instantiate each other (bottoms-up), or predetermine each other (top-down). The terminology for levels or ranks varies between 'activity-action-operation', 'act-action-operation', and 'act level, strategic level, operational level'. These differences in terminology reflect genuine differences between the approaches, but there is none the less an emerging area of consensus. We can characterize 'action' in the following fashion (cf. von Cranach 1982: 35 ff.). It is

— goal-directed, i.e. a mental model of goals determines the action;
— planned, i.e. alternative paths of solution are run through mentally before the execution;
— intended, i.e. there is a definite quality of volition leading to the execution;
— conscious, i.e. the actor is subjectively aware of the action and its parts;
— socially directed (or controlled), i.e. society exerts a hierarchy of control mechanisms by influencing the actors' cognition and/or circumstances of execution.

The general sequence is something like the one we have already found in the Russian School: motivation-planning-execution-evaluation. While in the assumption of a hierarchy of units the levels are separated, they are within the same framework linked to each other by feedback-loops; that is, monitoring processes on one level can induce changes on other levels. Situation, then, in this perspective, is defined as the spatio-temporal frame within which 'acts' are embedded. Its primary constituents are objects, processes, and participants relevant to the act. It is through these 'situations', as well as through states of consciousness, planning strategies, etc., that a society or classes in a society control the activities of the individual actor. Components of 'situations' have already been discussed from a different angle, and have been specified for working processes on several levels of generality (cf. Hacker 1978). The crucial point is that 'context' and 'situation' on the one hand, and 'activity' and 'action' on the other, are really aspects of the same phenomenon, namely goal-directed action. In the case of the former, goal-directed action is looked at in a static light, in the latter it is looked at in a dynamic light. It is of great importance for 'critical linguistics' that the question of social control is an integral part of the model. Our actors no longer act as isolated individuals who are only dependent on their abilities of strategic planning and effective execution, but their activities are controlled, i.e. choices between different paths of solution as well as influence on higher levels of activity are restricted or enhanced by the society they act in. This is especially important in the case of class societies, where activities in the political field in particular often have to be seen as deriving from class interests (for an interesting notion of 'freedom' on choice on different levels cf. Hacker 1982).

12.6 A LINGUISTICS OF CONTEXT AND ACTION

The theory of goal-directed action which we have outlined above goes some way towards an integration of the internal and external aspects of 'activity'. We now ask whether there has been a significant line of development of the concepts of 'activity and action' and 'context and situation' in linguistics. This question is not an easy one to answer, because, while these terms seem to be ubiquitous in current linguistic literature, quite often they seem to be lacking any organic relationship with the rest of linguistic analysis. The methods used for linguistic analysis on the language-internal levels and those used for the analysis of 'situation' appear to have too little in common to lead to a convincing overall analysis of language and context as closely related, even inseparable, phenomena. Some aspects of this difficulty within the dominant traditions in linguistics were discussed in section 12.3 above. There are, however, promising exceptions and I propose now to look at one school of linguistics in particular, Firthian and neo-Firthian linguistics. This school was, with the possible exception of tagmemics, the only influential school of thought to take the connection between linguistic and situational analysis to be a necessary part of its work (cf. Steiner 1983; Monaghan 1979).

There was no question of seeing language as an autonomous abstract system:

> From the functional point of view you see your whole man in action with his fellows, and his language as various modes of action in contexts of situation. Language is not a sort of intellectualized general will—but part of the man himself and his continuing activity, dynamic, purposive, creative.

When J. R. Firth wrote these lines (Firth 1934: 18–24) it was a statement which was regarded by many linguists as either a statement of the obvious without any clear consequences for linguistic methodology, or else as an utterly unjustified widening of the borders of linguistics proper that implied an unscientific methodology.

And yet Firth already had a certain tradition behind him. The German psychologist Wegener had already insisted on the importance of developing a concept of 'situation' for psychological and linguistic analyses, which he applied to, among other things, theme-rheme analyses of clause (Wegener 1885). Karl Bühler was to develop this line of thought further from the point of view of the psychology of language (Bühler 1934). In Britain, it was Alan Gardiner who tried to integrate the analysis of linguistic form into the analysis of situation, following ideas of Wegener and developing them further (Gardiner 1932). Still more important for Firth's ideas was the emphasis which the anthropologist Malinowski placed on the 'context of situation' and the 'context of culture' (cf. Hasan forthcoming; Malinowski 1935). However, the concepts of 'situation' developed in this environment lacked both generality and a set of descriptive concepts permitting the analysis of linguistic and situational items in such a way as to relate them to each other explicitly. Firth tried to solve this problem by proposing the analysis of both types of items in terms of 'system' and 'structure' (choice and chain, or paradigm and syntagm). A set of categories was needed in terms of which every situation could be described and which could enter into systems and structures. Firth suggested the following framework for a situational analysis:

> A context of situation for linguistic work brings into relation the following categories:
> A. The relevant features of participants: persons, personalities:
>   (i) The verbal action of the participants
>   (ii) The non-verbal action of the participants
> B. The relevant objects.
> C. The effect of the verbal action. [Firth 1950: 181 ff.]

Items A, B, and C give us the slots that have to be filled in any description of a 'situation', which yields its STRUCTURE. The SYSTEMS, however, from which choices are made at each given point were never more than hinted at and remained underdeveloped for a considerable time (but cf. Mitchell 1957).

It was not until well into the 1960s and 1970s that work on the concept of register by Halliday and others began to fill this gap. Halliday developed the notions of FIELD, TENOR, and MODE, which together, he claimed determine the register of any piece of speaking or writing, linking texts more explicitly to 'situations'. Those features of the situation which determine the medium in which any linguistic activity goes on, will determine the 'mode of discourse', i.e. all those features of the particular text dependent on the medium, such as physical realization (sound-waves, marks on paper, impulses on a magnetic tape, etc.), ways of emphasis (underlining, stress), some patterns of cohesion (paragraphing, pauses, etc.), mean utterance length, ways of indicating information distribution, and so forth. Those features of the situation which determine the interpersonal relationships of interacting participants, determine the 'tenor' of discourse; for example, whether the text expresses solidarity between interactants, or whether it expresses an inequality of power, as in patterns of turn-taking, patterns of question–answer or order–compliance patterning. 'Tenor' of discourse is also determined by other features of the 'situation', such as degree of formality, degree of mutual acquaintance, etc., as expressed in the choice of lexical items, utterance length, ways of expressing modality. Those features of the 'situation' which determine the remaining aspects of text structure collectively make up the 'field' of discourse. Subject-matter certainly belongs here. As in the case of tenor and mode, choices in all of the functional components of language ('ideational', 'interpersonal', 'textual' in Halliday's terminology) will be affected. For example, field of discourse will determine choice of lexical items (which will also be determined by level of formality and needs of thematic progression), as well as expresssions of modality (which will also be influenced by power relationships).

The notion of 'register' has never been an easy one to understand because the relationships to the categories of the 'context of situation' on the one hand, and to the functional components in the semantics of the language on the other, have, to my knowledge, hardly ever been formulated in an entirely clear-cut way. However, the concept of register is being applied extensively in empirical work on all sorts of texts, and more clearly defined patterns are beginning to emerge (cf. Lemke forthcoming; Young forthcoming; Ellis and Ure (eds) 1982).

Within 'tagmemics', the linguistic analysis has always been part of a wider analysis of behaviour (cf. Pike 1967). This is achieved by extending the basic grammatical unit of 'tagmeme' into the analysis of 'behaviouremes' in human activity. While it seems clear that a tagmemic analysis opens the way to relating language and behaviour, I am not so sure that it permits the consideration of those important internal characteristics of activity, namely, planning and evaluation of hypotheses and models which are emphasized in the theories of action discussed above. Furthermore, as 'tagmemics' has never so far been used in anything like a critical analysis of political texts, it is hard to form a judgement on other than purely theoretical grounds.

Other schools, too, have at various points emphasized the importance of viewing linguistic structures only in a close connection with structures of 'situation' and 'activity'. This is certainly as true of the work of the Prague School, of French functional linguistics around A. Martinet, of the sociolinguistic work around W. Labov, as it is of the important contributions by Dell Hymes and co-workers, and of functional grammar as practised in East Germany. Pragmatics, as represented in West Germany by Wunderlich, and, from a more philosophical angle, by Habermas, and as represented in East Germany by Klaus and others, has developed models which try to integrate non-linguistic and linguistic activity into one framework. Developments in linguistic pragmatics will certainly have to be followed closely by anyone working on a critical analysis of texts. Finally, modern text linguistics, particularly in the work done by van Dijk and de Beaugrande, has produced models of text comprehension and production that are inseparably linked to some of the developments we have been discussing here. However, of all the schools and directions within linguistics which we have been discussing, it is Firthian and neo-Firthian systemic linguistics that seem to have undergone the most continuous theoretical and practical development in the area we are interested in.

12.7 THE ROLE OF THEORY

There are two obvious questions that we might consider at this point. First, do we really need all this knowledge from such a variety of fields in order to carry through an insightful critical analysis of texts? And secondly, if we do, how do we use it in the practical task of analysing texts without falling into the trap of an unguided eclecticism?

The critical analysis of political texts is by no means an invention of the twentieth century, or people have engaged in such analysis throughout history and in all kinds of situations without any deep knowledge of the kind of fields we have been looking at. This is only true, however, in a trivial sense. Of course, people from past centuries did not have knowledge of the modern developments we have sketched. But successful analysts and producers of political oratory of the past have in general had very comprehensive knowledge of all aspects of human life, as then conceived, and of the motivations, planning and execution of human actions. Theories of textual analysis restricted to the text in a narrow sense seem to be largely a product of our century—art for art's sake has hardly ever been the ideology of the critical analyst. How are we to talk about such matters as underlying interest, contradiction, means and ends, justification, untenable conclusion, etc., if we disregard developments within the fields mentioned which try to define these concepts in such a way as to make them applicable? How are we to convince anybody of our statements about texts, if we disregard findings from, say, linguistics and the psychology of perception and information storage, which show us how messages can be structured in order to achieve maximum effects? How are we to know what the meaning of a certain text is in the context of political actions and constellations, when somebody else may maintain that no reliable statements can be made because 'human activity is too complicated anyway to know where it comes from and where it leads to'?

These considerations apart, it is not by chance that human activity has recently shifted again to the centre of interest. On the one hand, many powerful institutions have an active interest in being able to control people, whether because of the needs of automation, or because of the problems of enforcing legislation; and the means and resources at the disposal of those institutions are growing at an alarming rate. On the other hand, however, many people concerned about exactly these developments need to develop their own models of how the world could be, models which could in many cases profit from a deeper knowledge of the motivations and mechanisms of human activity. If we do not use all the available knowledge in the interest of liberty, oppressive institutions are likely to use it in the interest of restriction: psychological warfare, advertising campaigns, the use of AI programs in warfare against external and 'internal enemies', declaring political opponents mentally ill, etc.

Assuming the desirability of the critical analyst's knowledge of theories and models such as we have been discussing, how do we manage to integrate these into one coherent model and into analytical procedures? Clearly, it would be wrong to pick bits and pieces from a whole variety of models without regard for theoretical consistency. One reasonable procedure would be to start from ONE framework, that of the Russian School, and to test and elaborate it in the light of competing models.

There are several reasons for this particular choice. The Russian theories of activity sketched above have a comparatively long history. They have grown out of work orientated towards neurophysiology, which gives them an interesting testing-ground for their hypotheses, while not at all implying that 'activity' is reduced to neurological patterns and systems. Between a neurological description of activity and a description in terms of 'activity', there is a clear distinction of levels. The Russian theory has developed in close contact with linguistic studies, especially in child language development and psycholinguistics. What is more, the Russian theories have a remarkable history of application, in two fields at least: aphasia and the organization of work processes (cf. Corson and Corson (eds) 1976; *Psychological Research*, **41**, 1979/80; Hacker 1978), which, again, provide important testing grounds for theoretical developments. But what does this framework link up with as far as more large-scale frameworks of human activity are concerned? The dominating socioeconomic view is quite clearly Marxist, the dominating philosophy that of 'dialectical materialism', and some characteristics of the approach, such as the lack of a sharp mind–body dualism, or the general inclination towards application of theories to experience, are directly derivable from this philosophy. Moreover, as Marxian thinking has a strong tradition in, and was born from, critical analyses (one thinks, for instance, of the *German Ideology* of Marx), it looks like a promising candidate for a large-scale framework. It is worth emphasizing that this thinking, if applied, should be applied rigorously, thoroughly and in equal measure to the discourse and practices of East and West. The whole theoretical field from macro-structures (sociology, economy), to individual structures ('activity' and 'actions' of the individual), to micro-structures (the sensory-motor events) is thus unified by one general methodological approach and one general philosophy of science. Furthermore, the idea of the 'system' has been incorporated into the approach at all levels from a very early stage onwards (cf. Pawelzig 1970), and the theory can be brought together in interesting ways with linguistic frameworks based on the notions of 'system' and 'structure' (cf. Steiner forthcoming).

In making a critical analysis within the type of framework suggested here, I hope that we can contribute towards the achievement of several aims. We can provide a further clarification of the question of how and what kinds of ideologies are created and maintained through language. At the same time, such work should reflect back on the theoretical development of text linguistics and discourse analysis. In particular, questions concerning the form and content of text structure, the segmentation and classification of units of that structure on all levels, but on the semantic level in particular, may receive interesting answers in the analytical work. But there will also be, one hopes, wider effects of such work. One of the most pressing problems of our time, and one of the reasons for this book, is the threat of war. To be able to justify a strategy such as atomic war, the agencies interested in it have to be able to produce very powerful ideologies, i.e. systems of meanings and beliefs. It is part of the essence of the approach advocated here that ideologies are not only described as systems in isolation, but that their function in serving certain interests (profit, dominance, expansion, etc.) is also brought to light. Through this type of analysis, we are destroying a myth, another ideology, and one highly relevant for and influential among scientists and academics—namely, the myth that scientific insight can be gained by supposedly detached observation, from an impartial point of view in an ivory tower. I am suggesting rather that insight and knowledge are derived from actively taking sides: by unveiling an ideology, such as that of deterrence, we are making it vulnerable, we are, at least to that extent, opposing it. We are not 'neutral observers'; we are taking sides against forces of destruction. This view of rational enquiry does not take the doctrine of detachment for granted; rather it assumes that knowledge can be sought out of concern, out of a feeling of involvement and responsibility.

NOTES

1. See Trevor Pateman (1981) for a critique of certain elements (especially Whorfianism and semantically-based transformational grammar) in their approach, and for an interpretation of it in terms of Frankfurt School Critical Theory.
2. It should be borne in mind, however, that funding and motivation for much of this type of work comes from the increasing demand by industry and the military for expert knowledge systems of all kinds (cf. Bobrow and Collins (eds) 1975). The military and police support for, and application of, cognitive science, with its overlap with linguistics, should be noted. For an account of the use of cognitive science for military and political ends, see Weizenbaum (1976).

Bibliography

This bibliography includes all references mentioned but not detailed in the body of the text, and, in addition, bibliographical references of general relevance to the subject of this book. References to documents—newspapers, pamphlets, radio, television and film texts, etc.—are not included here.

Abelson, R. P. (1973), 'The structure of belief systems' in Schank, R. C. and Colby, K. M. (eds), *Computer Models of Thought and Language*, San Francisco, W. H. Freeman.

Atkinson, M. (1984), *Our Masters' Voices: The Language and Body Language of Politics*, London, Methuen.

Aubrey, C. (ed.) (1982), *Nukespeak: The Media and the Bomb*, London, Comedia.

Bakhtin, M. (1968), *Rabelais and His World*, trans. H. Iswolsky, Cambridge, Mass., MIT Press.

Bakhtin, M. (1973), *Problems of Dostoevsky's Poetics*, trans. R. W. Rotsel, Ann Arbor, Mich., Ardis.

Barnaby, F. and Windass, S. (1983), 'A new language of defence', Briefing Paper No. 1, *Just Defence* (April).

Beedham, C. (1983), 'Language, indoctrination and nuclear arms', *UEA Papers in Linguistics* (June): 15-29.

Benson, J. and Greaves, W. S. (eds) (forthcoming), *Systemic Perspectives on Discourse*, 2 vols., Norwood, NJ, Ablex.

Benveniste, E. (1971), *Problems in General Linguistics*, trans. E. Meek, Miami, University of Miami Press.

Bernstein, B. (1980), *Codes, Modalities and the Process of Cultural Reproduction*, Department of Education, University of Lund.

Bobrow, D. G. and Collins, A. (eds) (1975), *Representation and Understanding. Studies in Cognitive Science*, New York, Academic Press.

Boden, M. (1977), *Artificial Intelligence and Natural Man*, Brighton, Harvester.

Brown, G. and Yule, G. (1983), *Discourse Analysis*, Cambridge, Cambridge University Press.

Bühler, K. (1934), *Sprachtheorie*, Stuttgart, Gustav Fischer.

Burton, T. and Carlen, P. (1979), *Official Discourse*, London, Routledge and Kegan Paul.

Cantor, N., Mischel, W. and Schwarz, J. (1982), 'A prototype analysis of psychological situations', *Cognitive Psychology*, 14, 1: 45-77.

Centre for Contemporary Cultural Studies, Media Group (1982), *Fighting Over Peace*, Stencilled Paper 72, Centre for Contemporary Cultural Studies, Birmingham University.

Chafe, W. (1970), *Meaning and the Structure of Language*, Chicago, University of Chicago Press.

Chaney, D. (1983), 'A symbolic mirror of ourselves: civic ritual in mass society', *Media Culture and Society*, **5**: 119-35.
Chapman, D. and Foot, R. (1976), *Humour and Laughter. Theory and Research Applications*, London, Wiley.
Chilton, P. (1981), 'Nukespeak', *Sanity*, **5** (Oct/Nov).
Chilton, P. (1982a), 'Nuclear language, culture and propaganda', in Aubrey, C. (ed.), *Nukespeak. The Media and the Bomb*, London, Comedia.
Chilton, P. (1982b), 'Nukespeak', *Undercurrents*, **48**: 12-14.
Chilton, P. (1983), 'War, work and Falktalk', *Category B*, No. 4: 17-26.
Chomsky, N. (1959). Review of B. F. Skinner, *Verbal Behavior*, in *Language*, **35**: 26-58.
Chomsky, N. (1971), 'Deep structures, surface structures and semantic interpretation', in Jakobovitz and Steinberg (eds), *Semantics: An Interdisciplinary Reader in Philosophy, Psychology, Linguistics and Anthropology*, Cambridge, Cambridge University Press.
Chomsky, N. (1982), *Towards a New Cold War. Essays on the Current Crisis and How We Got There*, London, Sinclair Brown.
Chomsky, N. and Herman, E. S. (1979), *The Political Economy of Human Rights*, 2 vols., Nottingham, Spokesman.
Clark, H. and Haviland, S. E. (1977), 'Comprehension and the given-new contract', in Freedle, R. O. (ed.), *Discourse Production and Comprehension*, New Jersey, Ablex Publishing: 1-40.
Corson, S. A. and Corson, E. (eds) (1976), *Psychology and Psychiatry in the USSR*, New York, Plenum Press.
Courtés, J. (1976), *Introduction à la sémiotique narrative et discursive*, Paris, Hachette.
Coward, R. and Ellis, J. (1977), *Language and Materialism*, London, Routledge and Kegan Paul.
Cranach, M. von (1982), 'The psychological study of goal-directed action', in Cranach and Harré (eds) (1982).
Cranach, M. von and Harré, R. (eds) (1982), *The Analysis of Action*, Cambridge, Cambridge University Press.
Cranach, M. von, Kalbermatten, U., Indermühle, K. and Gugler, B. (1980), *Zielgerichtetes Handeln*, Bern, Huber.
Culler, J. (1975), *Structuralist Poetics. Structuralism, Linguistics and the Study of Literature*, London, Routledge and Kegan Paul.
Davis, H. and Walton, P. (eds) (1983), *Language, Image, Media*, Oxford, Blackwell.
Denis, M. and Dubois, D. (1976), 'La représentation cognitive: quelques modèles récents', *L'année psychologique*, **76**: 541-62.
Downes, W. (1978). 'Language, belief and verbal action in a historical process', *UEA Papers in Linguistics*, **8**: 1-43.
Downes, W. (1984), *Language and Society*, London, Fontana.
Eagleton, T. (1981). *Walter Benjamin. Or towards a Revolutionary Criticism*, Verso, New Left Books.
Easlea, B. (1983), *Fathering the Unthinkable*, London, Pluto.
Edwards, A. D. (1976), *Language in Culture and Class*, London, Heinemann.

Ellis, J. and Ure, J. (eds) (1982), *International Journal of the Sociology of Language*, **35** (special issue on register and change).
Fawcett, R. P. (1980), *Cognitive Linguistics and Social Interaction*, Heidelberg, Groos.
Firth, J. R. (1934), 'Linguistics and the functional point of view', *English Studies*, **16**: 18-24.
Firth, J. R. (1950), 'Personality and language in society', in Firth (1957).
Firth, J. R. (1957), *Papers in Linguistics 1934-1951*, London, Oxford University Press.
Foucault, M. (1970), *The Order of Things*, London, Tavistock.
Foucault, M. (1971), 'Orders of Discourse', inaugural lecture delivered at the Collège de France, *Social Science Information*, **10**, 2: 7-30.
Foucault, M. (1972), *The Archaeology of Knowledge*, London, Tavistock.
Foucault, M. (1979), *Discipline and Punish*, Harmondsworth, Penguin.
Foucault, M. (1980), 'Body/Power', in Gordon, C. (ed.), *Power/Knowledge*, Brighton, Harvester Press.
Fowler, R., Hodge, R., Kress, G. and Trew, T. (1979), *Language and Control*, London, Routledge and Kegan Paul.
Franck, T. M. and Weisband, E. (1971), *Word Politics: Verbal Strategy among the Superpowers*, New York, Oxford University Press.
Freud, S. (1960), *Jokes and their Relation to the Unconscious*, trans. J. Strachey, London, Routledge and Kegan Paul.
Gardiner, A. (1932), *The Theory of Speech and Language*, Oxford, Clarendon Press.
Garnham, A., Oakhill, J. and Johnson-Laird, P. N. (1982), 'Referential continuity and the coherence of discourse', *Cognition*, **11**: 29-46.
Gazdar, G. (1979), *Pragmatics: Implicature, Presupposition and Logical Form*, New York, Academic Press.
Goffman, E. (1981), *Forms of Talk*, London, Routledge and Kegan Paul.
Good, C. (1985), *Die Vermittlung sozialer Wirklichkeit in der Presse: ein Beitrag zur 'kritischen Sprachwissenschaft'*, Mannheim, Institut für deutsche Sprache.
Gopnik, A. (1982), 'Words and plans: early language and the development of intelligent action', *Journal of Child Language*, **9**: 303-18.
Gramsci, A. (1971), *Prison Notebooks*, ed. and trans. Hoare, Q. and Nowell Smith, G., London, Lawrence and Wishart.
Gray, Colin S. and Payne, Keith (1980), 'Victory is possible', *Foreign Policy*, **39** (Summer): 16-21.
Green, N. and Mort, F. (1982), 'Visual representation and cultural politics', *Block*, **7**.
Greimas, A. J. (1970), *Du Sens*, Paris, Seuil.
Grice, H. P. (1975), 'Logic and conversation', in Cole, P. and Morgan, J. L. (eds), *Syntax and Semantics 3: Speech Acts*, New York, Academic Press: 41-58.
Grice, H. P. (1978), 'Further notes on logic and conversation', in Cole, P. (ed.), *Syntax and Semantics 9: Pragmatics*, New York, Academic Press: 113-28.
Hacker, W. (1978), *Allgemeine Arbeits- und Ingenieurpsychologie*, 2nd ed., Bern, Huber.

Hacker, W. (1982), 'Objective and subjective organization of work activities', in von Cranach and Harré (eds) (1982): 81–98.
Hall, S., Hobson, D., Lowe, A. and Willis, P. (1980), *Culture, Media, Language*, London, Hutchinson.
Halliday, M. A. K. (1967), 'Notes on transitivity and theme in English II', *Journal of Linguistics*, **3**: 199–244.
Halliday, M. A. K. (1970), 'Functional diversity in language, as seen from a consideration of modality and mood in English', *Foundations of Language*, 6, 3: 322–61.
Halliday, M. A. K. (1978), *Language as Social Semiotic*, London, Edward Arnold.
Halliday, M. A. K. (1983), *Short Introduction to Functional Grammar*, Linguistic Department, University of Sydney.
Halliday, M. A. K. and Hasan, R. (1976), *Cohesion in English*, London, Longman.
Halpern, B. (1961), 'Myth and ideology in modern usage', *History and Theory*, **1**, 1.
Hasan, R. (forthcoming), 'Meaning, context and text: fifty years after Malinowski', in Benson and Greaves (eds) (forthcoming).
Haug, F. (1972), *Kritik der Rollentheorie*, Frankfurt, Fischer.
Higgins, R. (1980), *The Seventh Enemy*, London, Pan Books.
Higgins, C. S. and Moss, P. D. (1982), *Sounds Real*, St. Lucia, University of Queensland Press.
Hilgartner, S., Bell, R. C. and O'Connor, R. (1982), *Nukespeak. Nuclear Language, Visions and Mindset*, San Francisco, Sierra Club Books. Reissued as *Nukespeak. The Selling of Nuclear Technology in America*, Penguin Books, Harmondsworth, 1983.
Hobbs, J. R. (1981), 'Metaphor interpretation as selective inferencing', *Proceedings of the Seventh Joint International Conference on Artificial Intelligence*: 85–91.
Hoc, J. M. (1972), 'Représentation mentale et modèles cognitifs de traitement et de l'information', *Le travail humain*, **35**, 1: 17–36.
Hodge, R. (1977), 'Freud, Chomsky and depth analysis', *UEA Papers in Linguistics*, **1**.
Hodge, R. (1982), 'Transformational analysis and the visual media', *Australian Journal of Screen Theory*, **7**.
Hodge, B. and Kress, G. (1983), 'Functional semiotics', *Australian Journal of Cultural Studies*, **1**.
Hofstadter, R. (1970), *Anti-intellectualism in American life*, New York, Alfred A. Knopf.
Hook, G. (1984), 'The nuclearization of language: nuclear allergy as political metaphor', *Journal of Peace Research*, **21**, 3: 259–75.
Hook, G. (1985), 'Making nuclear weapons easier to live with. The political role of language in nuclearization', *Bulletin of Peace Proposals*, **16**, 1: 67–77.
Humphrey, N. (1981), 'Four minutes to midnight', *The Listener* (29 October): 493–9.
Hymes, D. (1971), 'On communicative competence', in Pride, J. B. and Holmes, J. (eds), *Sociolinguistics*, London, Penguin: 269–93.

BIBLIOGRAPHY

Jackendoff, R. S. (1972), *Semantic Interpretation in Generative Grammar*, Cambridge, Mass., MIT Press.
Jackendoff, R. S. (1983), *Semantics and Cognition*, Cambridge, Mass., MIT Press.
Jakobson, R. (1968), *Child Language, Aphasia and Phonological Universals*, The Hague, Mouton.
Joenniemi, P. (1984), 'Arms and language—in the beginning there was the word', *GDI* [Gottlieb Duttweiler Institut] *Papers*, 34: 21-44.
Johnson-Laird, P. N. (1980), 'Mental models in cognitive science', *Cognitive Science*, 4: 71-115.
Johnson-Laird, P. N. (1983), *Mental Models: Towards a Cognitive Science of Language, Inference and Consciousness*, Cambridge, Cambridge University Press.
Kempson, R. (1975), *Presupposition and the Delimitation of Semantics*, Cambridge, Cambridge University Press.
Kress, G. (1976), *Halliday: System and Function in Language*, Oxford University Press.
Kress, G. (1985), 'Ideological structures in discourse', in T. van Dijk (ed.), *Handbook of Discourse Analysis*, Vol. 4, New York, Academic Press.
Kress, G. and Hodge, R. (1979), *Language as Ideology*, London, Routledge and Kegan Paul.
Lacan, J. (1966), *Écrits*, Paris, Seuil.
Lacan, J. (1978), *Le moi dans la théorie de Freud et dans la technique de la psychoanalyse*, Paris, Seuil.
Lakoff, G. and Johnson, M. (1980), *Metaphors We Live By*, Chicago, University of Chicago Press.
Lee, D. (1977), 'Language and perspective: a textual analysis', *UEA Papers in Linguistics*, 5: 1-17.
Leech, G. (1980), *Explorations in Semantics and Pragmatics*, Amsterdam, John Benjamins B.V.
Leech, G. (1983), *Principles of Pragmatics*, London, Longman.
Lemke, J. L. (forthcoming), 'Ideology, intertextuality and the notion of register', in Benson and Greaves (eds) (forthcoming).
Leplat, J. (1971-2), 'Planification de l'action et régulation d'un système complexe', *Bulletin de psychologie*, 25, 10/11: 533-8.
Leplat, J. and Pailhous, J. (1971-2), 'La taxonomie des tâches en psychologie de travail', *Bulletin de psychologie*, 25, 10/11: 539-45.
Lerman, C. L. (1983), 'Dominant discourse: the institutional voice and control of topic', in Davis, H. and Walton, P. (eds) (1983).
Levinson, S. (1983), *Pragmatics*, Cambridge, Cambridge University Press.
Lewis, D. K. (1973), *Counterfactuals*, Oxford, Blackwell.
Luckham, R. (1984), 'Armaments and culture', *Current Research on Peace and Violence*, 1: 1-64.
Malinowski, B. (1935), *Coral Gardens and their Magic*, New York, American Book Company.
Mandler, J. M. and Johnson, N. S. (1977), 'Remembrance of things past: story structure and recall', *Cognitive Psychology*, 9: 111-51.

Marx, K. (1970), *Capital*, London, Lawrence and Wishart.
Marx, K. (1973), *Grundrisse*, Harmondsworth, Penguin.
Marx, K. and Engels, F. (1970), *The German Ideology*, London, Lawrence and Wishart.
Mawrence, M. and Kimball, J. Clark (1961), *You Can Survive the Bomb*, Chicago, Quadrangle Books.
McNeill, D. (1979), *The Conceptual Basis of Language*, Hillsdale, Erlbaum.
McNeill, D. (1980), 'Iconic relationships between language and motor action', in Rauch, I. and Carr, G. F. (eds) (1980), *The Signifying Animal. The Grammar of Language and Experience*, Bloomington, Indiana University Press.
Mead, G. H. (1934), *Mind, Self and Society*, Chicago, University of Chicago Press.
Metzing, D. (ed.) (1980), *Frame Conceptions and Text Understanding*, Berlin, De Gruyter.
Miller, G., Galanter, E. and Pribram, K. (1960), *Plans and the Structure of Behavior*, New York, Holt.
Miller, G. and Johnson-Laird, P. N. (1976), *Language and Perception*, Cambridge, Cambridge University Press.
Minsky, M. L. (1975), 'A framework for representing knowledge', in Winston, P. H. (ed.), *The Psychology of Computer Vision*, New York, McGraw Hill, 1975.
Mitchell, T. F. (1957), 'The language of buying and selling in Cyrenaica', *Hesperis*, 44: 31-71; reprinted in Mitchell, T. F. (ed.) (1975).
Mitchell, T. F. (1975), *Principles of Firthian Linguistics*, London, Longman.
Monaghan, J. (1979), *The Neo-Firthian Tradition and its Contribution to General Linguistics*, Tübingen, Niemeyer.
Newell, A. and Simon, H. (1972), *Human Problem Solving*, Englewood Cliffs, Prentice Hall.
Ortony, M. (ed.) (1980), *Metaphor and Thought*, Cambridge, Cambridge University Press.
Orwell, George (1949), *Nineteen Eighty-Four*, London, Martin Secker and Warburg.
Osgood, C. E. (1979), 'Conservative words and radical sentences in the semantics of international politics', *Studies in the Linguistic Sciences* (Department of Linguistics, University of Illinois), 8.
O'Sullivan, T., Hartley, J., Saunders, D. and Fiske, J. (1983), *Key Concepts in Communication*, London, Methuen.
Parret, H. and Bouveresse, H. (eds) (1981), *Meaning and Understanding*, Berlin, de Gruyter.
Parsons, Talcott (1937), *The Structure of Social Action*, New York, Free Press.
Pateman, T. (1981), 'Linguistics as a branch of critical theory', *UEA Papers in Linguistics*, 14/15: 1-29.
Pawelzeig, G. (1970), *Dialektik der Entwicklung objektiver Systeme*, Berlin, VEB Deutscher Verlag der Wissenschaften.
Pike, K. (1967), *Language in Relation to a Unified Theory of the Structure of Human Behavior*, The Hague, Mouton.
Pribam, K. (1971), *Languages of the Brain*, Englewood Cliffs, Prentice Hall.

Prins, G. (ed.) (1983), *Defended to Death. A Study of the Nuclear Arms Race from the Cambridge University Disarmament Seminar*, Harmondsworth, Penguin.
Pulman, S. (1983), *Word Meaning and Belief*, London, Croom Helm.
Quine, W. (1960), *Word and Object*, Cambridge, Mass., MIT Press.
Radio Marketing Bureau (1983), *The Time People Spend with Commercial Air Media*, Sydney, FARB.
Radio 2GB (1983), *The Foreground Factor*, Sydney.
Rehbein, J. (1979), 'Handlungstheorien', *Studium Linguistik*, 7: 1–25.
Richter, H. E. (1982), *Zur Psychologie des Friedens*, Hamburg, Rowohlt.
Rossi-Landi, F. (1974), 'Linguistics and economics', in Sebeok, T. A. (ed.) (1974), *Current Trends in Linguistics*, Vol. 12 (3 books), The Hague, Mouton.
Sampson, G. (1982), 'The economics of conversation' in Smith, N. V. (ed.), *Mutual Knowledge*, New York, Academic Press.
Saussure, F. de (1973), *Cours de linguistique générale*, T. de Mauro (ed.), Paris, Payot.
Schank, R. and Abelson, R. (1977), *Scripts, Plans, Goals and Understanding*, Hillsdale, Erlbaum.
Schegloff, E. (1971), 'Notes on a conversational practice', in Giglioli, P. (ed.), *Language and Social Context*, London, Penguin.
Schutz, A. (1967), *Collected Papers I: The Problem of Social Reality*, The Hague, Martinus Nijhoff.
Searle, J. R. (1980), 'The intentionality of intention and action', *Cognitive Science*, 4: 47–70.
Singleton, W. T. (1972), 'Total activity analysis: a different approach to work study', *Le travail humain*, 35, 2: 241–50.
Skinner, B. F. (1957), *Verbal Behavior*, Englewood Cliffs, Prentice Hall.
Spender, D. (1980), *Manmade Language*, London, Routledge and Kegan Paul.
Stalnaker, R. C. (1968), 'A theory of conditionals', in Rescher, N. (ed.), *Studies in Logical Theory*, Oxford, Oxford University Press.
Stein, N. L. (1982), 'The definition of a story', *Journal of Pragmatics*, 6, 5/6: 487–508.
Steiner, E. (1983), *Die Entwicklung des britischen Kontextualismus*, Heidelberg, Groos.
Steiner, E. (forthcoming), 'Working with transitivity: system networks in semantic-grammatical description', in Benson and Greaves (eds).
Steiner, E. and Schmitz, W. (1982), Review of Fowler *et al.* (1979) and Kress and Hodge (1977), *Network*, 3: 28–35.
Talmy, L. (1976), 'Semantic causative types', in Shibatani, M. (ed.), *The Grammar of Causative Constructions, Syntax and Semantics*, Vol. 6, New York, Academic Press.
Thompson, E. P. (1980), 'Protest and survive', in Thompson, E. P. and Smith, D. (eds), *Protest and Survive*, Harmondsworth, Penguin.
Torode, B. and Silverman, R. (1977), *The Material Word*, London, Routledge and Kegan Paul.
Trew, T. (1978), 'Theory at work', *UEA Papers in Linguistics*, 6: 39–60.

Trew, T. (1979), 'Theory and ideology at work', in Fowler, R. *et al.* (1979).
Vigor, P. H. (1975), 'The semantics of deterrence and defense', in McGwire, M., Booth, K. and McDonnell, J. (eds) (1975), *Soviet Naval Policy. Objectives and Constraints*, New York, Praeger.
Vygotsky, L. S. (1962), *Thought and Language*, Cambridge, Mass., Harvard University Press.
Walker, R. B. J. (1980), 'Political theory and the transformation of world politics', *World Order Studies Paper*, No. 9, Center of International Studies, Princeton, 1980.
Walker, R. B. J. (forthcoming), 'Contempoary militarism and the discourse of defence', *Alternatives*.
Weber, H. (1922), *Wissenschaft und Gesellschaft*, Tübingen, Mohr.
Wegener, P. (1885), *Untersuchung über die Grundfragen des Sprachlebens*, Halle, Niemeyer.
Weill-Fassima, A. (1971-2), 'La notion de la régulation en psychologie du travail', *Bulletin de psychologie*, 25, 10/11: 546-51.
Weimer, W. E. and Palermo, D. S. (eds) (1982), *Cognition and the Symbolic Processes*, Hillsdale, Erlbaum.
Weir, R. H. (1962), *Language in the Crib*, The Hague, Mouton.
Weizenbaum, J. (1976), *Computer Power and Human Reason. From Judgement to Calculation*, London, W. H. Freeman and Co.
Werner, H. and Kaplan, S. (1963), *Symbol Formation: An Organismic–Developmental Approach to Language and the Expression of Thought*, New York, Wiley.
Wilden, A. (1968), *The Language of the Self*, Baltimore, Johns Hopkins University Press.
Wilson, D. (1975), *Presupposition and Truth-conditional Semantics*, London, Academic Press.
Wright, G. H. von (1963), *Norm and Action*, Routledge and Kegan Paul.
Wright, G. H. von (1971), *Explanation and Understanding*, London, Routledge and Kegan Paul.
Wright, G. H. von (1972), *An Essay in Deontic Logic and the General Theory of Action*, Amsterdam, North Holland.
Young, D. J. (forthcoming), 'Some applications of systemic grammar to TEFL, or whatever became of register analysis', in Benson and Greaves (eds) (forthcoming).

Index

Abelson, R., 104, 221, 222
abstract nouns, 76, 136
acronyms, 3, 143
activity, theory of, xx, 217–27, 228–9
age, 137–40
agent, 51, 106, 108, 109, 110, 143, 150, 190
ambiguity, xxvi, 39, 62, 106, 114, 121, 155, 161, 171, 198, 202, 206
America, United States of, 34, 45–63, 76, 94, 95, 117, 167–81, 206
analogy, 49, 53, 121, 140
analyticity, 103
anaphora, 121
Anokhin, P. K., 222
anti-language, 171, 197
antithesis, 185–6
aphasia, 135
Aristotle, 216
article, 43
Atkinson, M., 216

Bakhtin, M., xxvii, 22n, 198, 205, 209
balance (military), 91, 93
balance (rhetorical), xxvi, 11, 13, 183, 185, 189–90
Barnaby, F., 126n
Beaugrande, R. de, 227
behaviourism, 217, 220
beliefs (belief systems), xxiv, 4, 21, 104, 106, 109, 110, 114–15, 118, 125, 148, 209, 215
Bennett, T., 80
Benveniste, E., 202
Bernstein, B., 218
Bernstein, N. A., 222
Boden, M., 104, 221
Bobrow, D. G. 230n
Bouveresse, H., 221
Briggs, R., 6
Brown, G., 121
Brown, H., 63n
Bruner, J. S., 220
Bühler, K., 225
Burton, T., 199
Bush, J., 94, 101n

Caldicott, H., 78, 80, 86
Campaign Against Nuclear Energy (CANE), 148, 154, 161
Campaign for Defence and Multilateral Disarmament (CDMD), xxii, 11, 15, 19, 27, 68–70
Campaign for Nuclear Disarmament (CND), xxv, 5–15, 19, 23, 27, 28, 29, 30, 34, 38, 42, 75, 77, 85, 131, 134, 137, 197, 198, 199, 205, 209, 210
Cantor, N., 219
capability, 3, 93–4, 98, 109
Carlen, P., 199
carnival, xxvii, 20, 22n, 197–9, 202
Carter, J., 61, 63n
cartoons, 11, 202–8
causality, 106–8, 110, 111–13
causatives, 105, 111
censorship, xxv–vi, 15, 161, 188
Chafe, W., 36
Chaney, D., 199
Chapman, D., 197
Chesterton, G. K., 51
Chilton, P., xiii–xiv, 21n, 63n, 87n, 101n
Chomsky, N., xviii–xix, 36, 63n, 101n, 127n, 200, 220
Church of England, 29, 35, 40, 76–7
Churchill, W., 7
Cicero, 186, 216
Clark, H., 25, 36
class, 137–40, 143–4, 209, 224–5
clause, 57, 107, 189
cliché, 70, 183, 185, 187–8, 189, 190, 206
Close, R., 93, 95, 101n
cognitive anthropology, 217
cognitive psychology, xxvii, 217, 220–2, 230n
collective nouns, 76
Collins, A., 230n
collocation, 114
cold war, xvii, xxii, xxiii, 97, 106, 113, 114–21, 221–2
commitment of speaker, 24
communication theory, 67
communicative competence, 25
communist links, 8–14, 27
comprehension, 118

INDEX

concessional, 189
conditional, 111–13, 189
Conservative, 5, 8, 13, 15, 21, 25, 27, 32, 34, 35, 36, 38, 44
context (*see also* situation), 5, 24, 116, 217–27
conversation, 25, 162–5
conversational maxims, 24, 233, 127n
    Quantify maxim, 31, 37, 111
    Relevance maxim, 31, 111, 119
co-operative principle, 24, 32
Corson, E., 228
Corson, S. A., 228
counterfactuals, 111–12
Courtés, J., 102n
Coward, R., 87n
Cranach, M. von, 224
credibility, 95
Crosland, S., 41
cruise missiles, xviii, 4, 5, 13, 16, 17, 21, 40, 69, 70, 86, 94, 95, 101–2n
Culler, J., 102n

denial (psychological), 188, 191, 210
denial (rhetorical), 30, 32–9, 40, 41, 43
Denis, M., 221
deterrence, deterrent, xxiii, 4, 10, 12, 28, 70, 91–101, 102–21
dialects, 116
Dijk, T. von, 227
directives, 46
discourse, xiv, xx–xxi, xxiv–xxv, xxvii, 4, 5, 11, 16, 23, 51, 60, 65–85, 91, 111–13, 122–6, 142–4, 161, 175, 188, 190, 199, 201, 202, 203, 204, 206, 208, 209
discursive difference, 74–7, 80
doublethink, 13, 14, 47, 135
Downes, W., 103, 104, 221
Dubois, D., 221
Duckspeak, 3, 183
Dutch, 92, 101n

Eagleton, T., 190, 197, 200
Edinburgh, Duke of, 10–11
Edwards, A. D., 218
Einstein, A., xviii
Ellis, J., 87n, 227
énoncé, 202, 206
énonciation, 202
entailment, xxiii, 24, 103–4, 106–10, 115, 119, 120, 127n
ethnography, 24, 25–6
euphemism, xiv, 3, 4, 31, 92, 101n
event, 57–61, 107, 133–4

Falkland Islands, xviii, 4, 5, 10

family, 16, 19, 20, 68, 167–81
film, 52, 167–81, 183
film technique
    close-up, 172
    dissolve, 170
    dolly, 175
    filter, 176
    hand-held, 171
    mid-shot, 180
    pan, 177
    reverse shot, 174, 175
    tracking, 172, 175
    zoom, 169, 170, 177, 180
Firth, J. R., 225–6, 227
Fiske, J., 181n
Fodor, J. A., 217
Foot, R., 197
Ford, A., 18, 21n
Foucault, M., xxii, 68, 87n, 167, 181n, 209
Fowler, R., 21n, 215
frame, 44, 49, 53, 104, 113–26, 221–2
    allergy frame, 125
    baseball, 123–4
    bully, 117–18, 121, 124–5
    cold war, 104, 116–18
    criminological, 114–16
    school, 117–18, 127n
France, 5
Franck, T. M., 101n
Fraser, M., 208
French, 101n
Freud, S., xxvii, 200–2, 209
functionalism, 216

Galanter, E., 220
Gardiner, A., 225
Garnham, A., 221
Gazdar, G., 44
Gelber, A., 186, 188
gender (sex), 68, 73, 137–41, 144, 199, 209
genre, xx, xxii, 67, 81–4, 206
German, 101n, 104
gesture, 26
Gibbon, E., 186
Goffman, E., xxi, 25
Good, C., 87n
Gopnik, A., 217
Gramsci, A., 181n
Green, B., 145n
Green, N., 199
Greenham Common, 5, 13, 15, 16, 18, 19, 23, 85–6, 209
Greimas, A. J., xxiii, 91, 97, 102n
Grice, P., xxi, 24, 25, 31, 32, 111, 118, 127
Gugler, B., 224
Gundry, D. W., 9, 10

INDEX

Habermas, J., 227
Hacker, W., 220, 224, 228
Haig, A., 63n
Hall, S., 87n
Halliday, M. A. K., xx, xxii, 21n, 25, 36, 57, 58, 60, 87n, 131 ff., 133, 142, 189, 191n, 197, 200, 226
Halpern, B., 63n
Hamilton, L., 7
Hartley, J., 181n
Hasan, R., 25, 225
Hastings, M., 6
Haug, F., 218
Haviland, S. E., 25, 36
hegemony, 181n, 167-8, 176, 181n
Heimann, R., 204, 207, 211n
Herman, E. S., 127n
Heseltine, M., 7, 8, 12-13, 15, 21n, 24, 39-42, 43, 44
Higgins, C. S., 166n
Higgins, R., 189
Hilgartner, S. et al., xiii, 21n, 101n
Hiroshima, 112
Hobbs, J. R., 122, 123, 124, 126
Hobson, D., 87n
Hoc, J. M. 220
Hodge, R., 21n, 87, 106, 131, 145n, 168, 200, 215
Hofstadter, R., 63n
Hook, G., 125
Hume, B., Cardinal, 7, 8
Humphrey, N., xxvi, 188, 210
Hurd, D., 9
Hymes, D., 25, 227
hyperbole, 187

ideology, xiv, xv, xvi, 4, 13, 16, 21, 26, 44, 47, 54, 59, 65-87, 93, 96, 104, 106, 114, 120, 127n, 135, 137-41, 168-9, 174, 176, 178, 215, 218, 221-2, 229
illocutionary force, 31
imaginary, 99, 100
impersonal stance, 183, 189, 190
implicature, 24, 31, 35, 37, 38
Indermühle, K., 224
Indo-European languages, 106
information, 38
instrument, 107, 109
intention, 62, 94-6, 98, 108, 110
intertextuality, 199
irony, 33, 34, 201

Jackendoff, R. S., 36, 103, 106, 109, 112, 121, 126
Jakobson, R., 131-2, 135
Jeffery, P., 145n

Joenniemi, P., 103, 116
Johnson, M., 121, 122, 126
Johnson, N. S., 221
Johnson, P., 141, 144-5
Johnson-Laird, P. N., 103, 105, 106, 109, 110, 111, 221, 222
jokes, xiv, xxvi, xxvii, 114, 117-18, 127n, 197-211
journalism, 20, 161, 191

Kalbermatten, U., 224
Kaplan, S., 106
Katz, 217
Kempson, R., 37, 44
Kent, B., 7-11, 15, 17, 85
Kimball, J. C., 63
King, Martin Luther, 186
Klaus, G., 227
Kress, G., 21n, 60, 87n, 106, 131, 132, 133, 191n, 200, 215
Kulikov, V., 96

Labour Party, 5, 13, 30, 40, 41
Labov, W., 227
Lacan, J., xxiii, 91, 100, 102n
Lakoff, G., 121, 122, 126
Latin, 136
Latinate, 11
Lawrence, D. H., 45
Leech, G., 24, 44
Lemke, J. L., 227
Leont'ev, A. N., 222
Leplat, J., 220
Levinson, S., 44, 111
Lévi-Strauss, C., 131
Lewis, D., 111
Lewis, P., 149, 150, 151
lexicon, xxiv
  lexical choice, 10, 17, 61-2, 143, 150
  lexical field, xxiv, 62, 107-8, 110
  lexical gap, 103-4
linguistics, xviii-xix, xxiii, 24-5, 65-7, 145, 215, 216-17, 225
  critical, xiii, xxvii, 215-17, 224, 225, 227-9
  functional, 57, 216
  sociolinguistics, 4
  structuralist, 216-17
  systemic xxv, 131-2, 145, 226
  tagmemics, 225, 227
  transformationalist, 200
litotes, 187
logic, xxiii, xxvii, 91, 92, 99, 111, 217
Lowe, A., 87n
Luckham, R., 126n
Luns, J., 95
Luria, A. R., 222

INDEX

macro-functions (components), 133, 226
  ideational, 133, 142, 144, 226
  interpersonal, 133, 142, 143, 144, 226
  textual, 133, 226
Maitland, O., 7, 19
Malcolm, D., 184, 188
Malinowski, B., 225
Mandler, J. M., 221
Mansfield, A., 145n, 210n
Martinet, A., 227
Marx, K., 136, 219–20, 222, 229
Marxism, 197, 200, 216, 223
masculinity, 14–20, 138, 172, 174–5, 178, 208-9
Mawrence, M., 63
Mayhew, P., 6
McNeill, D., 217, 221
meaning, xx, xxii, 24, 57, 65–8, 80, 82, 103–4, 109, 124, 135, 141, 161, 201, 202, 203, 205, 208, 215, 217
media, xxi, xxiv–xxvi, 26, 116, 132–5, 137, 147-9, 164-5, 168, 188
mentalism, 217
metaphor, xxiv, 11, 18, 51, 104, 118, 120, 121–6, 186, 198
Metzing, D., 104, 221
Miller, G., 105, 106, 110, 220
minimal pair, 142
Ministry of Defence, 8, 44, 118
Minsky, M. L., 104, 221
mirror relationship, 100
Mitchell, T. F., 226
modality, modals, xiii, 36–7, 60, 98, 111, 155, 183–4, 186–7, 188, 189, 190, 200-1, 205, 206, 208, 209, 226
modulation, 60
Monaghan, J., 225
morality (ethics), 8–14, 19, 22–4, 34, 42–4
morphism, 121–6
morphology, 127n
Mort, F., 199
Moss, P., 166n
MX missile, xviii, 3, 5
myth, xxi–xxii, xxvi, 29, 40, 45, 54, 56, 62, 70

naming, 54–7
narrative, 98–9, 166–81
NATO, xviii, xxiii, 11, 13, 32, 34, 35, 69, 91–4, 97, 98, 101, 138
negation, negatives, 9–10, 75–6, 140, 149, 183–4, 189, 201
neologism, 13
Newell, A., 221
Nixon, R., 208
nominalization, 107, 143, 150, 190

Norwich, Bishop of, 75–6, 85
Nott, J., 12, 24, 42–4
nuclear freeze, 49–50, 93
Nukespeak, xxi, 34, 101n, 147, 158, 162, 165

Oakhill, J., 221
Oestreicher, P., 9
Ortony, M., 121
Orwell, G., xiii, 3, 4, 135, 183
O'Sullivan, T., 181n
O'Toole, M., 145n
oxymoron, 12

pacifism, 11, 75, 92
Pailhous, J., 220
Palermo, D. S., 221
paradigm (beliefs), xxiv, 4, 5, 8, 10–12, 14, 16, 21
paradigm (linguistic), 131-2, 135–6, 169, 170, 172, 226
paradox, 12, 13, 15, 20, 70, 92, 96–9, 185–6, 198
Parkinson, C., 7
Parret, H., 221
Parsons, T., 218
passive, 150, 190
Pateman, T., 230n
Pawelzeig, G., 229
Peacekeeper (missile), xviii, 3, 95
Peirce, C. S., 207
period (rhetorical), 185–6
Pershing II missiles, xviii, 94, 95, 101–2n
phatic communion, 37
phonology, 135, 142
Piaget, J., 220
pictorial cues (visual text), 118–21, 208
Pike, K., 227
Pilger, J., xxvi
Pine Gap, 209
polar opposites, 135–6, 143
Polaris, 69, 70
popular culture, 61-7, cf. also 166–81
popular song, 208
Postal, P. M., 217
pragmatics, xxi, xxiv, 23, 24–5, 104
press, 5–20, 133, 135–44, 197, 203
presupposition, 12, 24, 155
Pribram, K., 220, 221
priests, 8–14
Prins, G., 101n
process, 57–62
pronouns (personal), 46–9, 50, 51, 59, 76
propaganda, 11, 20–1, 91, 98–9, 119, 137, 197, 200
psychoanalysis, xxvii, 91, 100, 200
psychotherapy, 208

INDEX

Pulman, S., 103, 106
pun, 167, 203–5, 208–9

quantification, 50
Quine, W., 103

race, 137–8, 199, 209
radio, 148–65
readers, reading, 66–7, 70, 72, 80, 84, 138–41, 145
Reagan, R., xxvi, 5, 45–51, 63n, 95, 127n
register, xx, 3–4, 142, 171, 201, 204, 226–7
Rehbein, J., 224
religious discourse, 51, 73, 76, 177–9, 183
repression, 200, 202
rhetoric, xvii–xviii, xxvii, 10, 24, 39, 42, 44–5, 62, 101n, 183–4, 215–16, 127n
rhetorical questions, 30–2, 40, 41, 42–3
Richter, E., 126n
Rogers, B. W., 92, 96, 101n
Roman Catholic Church, 9–10, 14
Rossi-Landi, F., 220
Roxby Downs, 147–9, 151–2, 159, 161–2, 163, 165
Ruddock, J., 8, 13, 19
Russell, B., xxiv
Russian, 103, 104
Russian School (of psychology), 222–5, 228

Sampson, G., 127n
Saunders, D., 181n
Saussure, F. de, 131, 136–7
Schank, R., 104, 221
Schegloff, E., 25
schema (see frame)
Schlesinger, J., 21
Schmitz, W., 215
Schutz, A., 201, 205
script (see frame)
semantics, xiv, xxiii, 24, 57, 103–4, 110
semiotic square, 97
Shakespeare, W., 198
Simon, H., 221
Silverman, R., 87n
Singleton, W. T., 220
situation, xx, 81, 108, 215–16, 217–27
Sizewell, 7, 19
Skinner, B. F., 220
soap opera, xxvi, 177, 180, 181
Socialist Workers Party, xxii, 71, 78
Social Democratic Party (SDP), 141
Soviet Union (Russia), xv, xviii, 8–14, 27, 29, 30, 32, 34, 39–41, 43, 47, 49, 50, 58, 60, 69, 85, 86, 91–3, 96–7, 101, 117–18, 127n, 206

Spaak, P.-H., 97
speech act, 109
speeches, 23–44, 185, 215–16
Spender, D., 87n
SS20 missiles, xviii, 69, 94
Stalnaker, R. C., 111
'Star Wars', xviii, xxi, 52–4
Stein, N. L., 221
Steiner, E., 215, 220, 225
syllogism, 99, 122, 216
syntagm, 55, 131–2, 136, 169–72, 226
system, 226
system network, 132, 133, 138, 140, 141–3
systemic-transformational, 140–1, 145

Talmy, L., 105, 106, 108, 109
television, 26, 167–81, 204
terror, 10–11, 92, 127n
text, 25, 65–85, 141–4, 199, 202, 203, 206, 207, 215, 217
Thatcher, Margaret, 23, 27–39, 42, 44, 127n
theme (of clause), 150, 189, 226
Thompson, E. P., xxvi, 6, 7, 34, 186
Thorndike, E. L., 220
Tindemans, L., 94, 96, 101n
topic (or theme, of discourse) 138–40, 152, 163–5
Tornetta, V., 102n
Torode, B., 87n
transformation, 132, 135–45, 168, 200, 202, 204–5, 206, 208
transitivity, 106
traps and openings, 132, 134, 135, 137, 145
Trew, T., 21n, 87n, 145n, 191
Trident, xviii, 19, 21n, 43, 55, 56, 69

unilateralists, 11, 13, 27–9, 39–42, 92, 94–5, 189, 190
Ure, J., 227

Vaughan, G., 6, 7, 8, 19
verbs, 57, 59, 61–2, 104–11, 150
Vigor, P. H., 104, 127n
Virgil, 4
Vries, P. H. de, 92–3, 94, 101n
vulnerable audience, 28, 39
Vygotsky, L. S., 217, 222

Walker, R. B. J., 126n
Warsaw Pact, 13, 93, 95, 96
Watkins, P., xxvi
Watson, J. B., 220
Weber, H., 218
Weill-Fassima, A., 220
Weimer, W. E., 221
Weinberger, C., 6
Weir, R. H., 217

Weisband, E., 101n
Weiss, A. P., 220
Weizenbaum, J., 230n
Werner, H., 106
Whorf, B. L., xiii, 230
Wilden, A., 102n
Williams, S., 142, 143, 144

Willis, P., 87n
Wilson, P., 44
Windass, S., 126n
women, 14–20, 178, 180
Wunderlich, D., 227

Yule, G., 121